Interventions

with Children and Youth in Canada

Interventions

with Children and Youth in Canada

Maureen Cech

OXFORD
UNIVERSITY PRESS

OXFORD
UNIVERSITY PRESS

8 Sampson Mews, Suite 204, Don Mills, Ontario M3C 0H5
www.oupcanada.com

Oxford University Press is a department of the University of Oxford.
It furthers the University's objective of excellence in research, scholarship,
and education by publishing worldwide in

Oxford   New York

Auckland Cape Town Dar es Salaam Hong Kong Karachi
Kuala Lumpur Madrid Melbourne Mexico City Nairobi
New Delhi Shanghai Taipei Toronto

With offices in

Argentina Austria Brazil Chile Czech Republic France Greece
Guatemala Hungary Italy Japan Poland Portugal Singapore
South Korea Switzerland Thailand Turkey Ukraine Vietnam
Oxford is a trade mark of Oxford University Press
in the UK and in certain other countries

Published in Canada
by Oxford University Press

Library and Archives Canada Cataloguing in Publication

Cech, Maureen, 1951–
Interventions with children and youth / Maureen Cech.

Includes bibliographical references and index.
ISBN 978-0-19-543024-0

1. Social work with children—Canada—Textbooks.   2. Social work
with youth—Canada—Textbooks.   3. Problem children—Canada—Textbooks.
4. Problem youth—Canada—Textbooks.   I. Title.

HV745.A6C414 2010   362.70971   C2009-906135-X

Cover image: Mimi Haddon/Getty Images

Printed and bound in Canada.

2 3 4 – 16 15 14

Contents

Review Questions and Discussion Questions are included at the end of each chapter.

Afterword: Setting Structural and Strengths-Based Targets   286

List of Figures

List of Tables

Acknowledgements

The list of references at the end of this book indicates the hundreds of researchers and theorists to whom I am grateful. The stories reflect the many children and families who have taught me so much over the last 30 years. Then, there are those students and front-line workers whose questions have challenged my own practice: Kenna McCall, Xiaoxue Xiang, Ken Barter, Anthony Adema, and Monica Byrne, in particular. Thanks to my family—Jeremy Cech, Alexandra Prestera, and Carl Toole—for patiently reading and re-reading the manuscript as it was in development. To these generous folks, and especially to Ella for her inspiration and love, I offer my heartfelt gratitude.

Preface

There was an old woman who lived in a shoe;
She had so many children, she didn't know what to do.
She gave them some broth without any bread;
She spanked them all soundly, and sent them to bed.

—(Anonymous)

The old woman in the shoe spanked them all soundly and sent them to bed. The next morning the children awoke, played, misbehaved, and the routine was repeated. She again spanked them all soundly and put them to bed. Like the old woman in the shoe who has no bread we repeat traditional interventions: spanking, restraints, incarceration, foster care. They work for a while, at least until the next day when there still is no bread.

Wisdom resides in traditional folk tales and stories for children. I teach through the medium of children's stories, and have sprinkled some of my favourite passages throughout this book to entice the reader into further exploration of children's literature. A wealth of information on children's behaviour, language, and life experience is revealed within the pages of these books. Some children's stories provide the wisdom that so often is lacking in adult reports. Truths are revealed by the old woman in the shoe—the futility of punishment rather than such structural interventions as fixing the shoe, supplying the bread, and providing adequate education for both parent and child.

This book interweaves the wisdom of children's stories with current Canadian medical, psychological, sociological, and educational information. No single science provides the requisite background for working with children. This tapestry of ideas, plus a few of my own, challenges us to work with children, rather than on them, and engage with children as persons with rights. Like all new ways of working, this requires adjustment on the reader's part and even further change on the part of the practitioner. In Gerry Fewster's words (2002: 17): 'Any real change in our way of being with our children calls for nothing short of a revolution.'

This necessary revolution is grounded in tradition, however, through our Canadian respect for the child as a member of the community and our respect for Mother Earth. The structural approach that positions a child in the centre of a structure reflects the Medicine Wheel of interconnectedness in which the child is the hub of the wheel. This

Medicine Wheel reminds us how our lives connect to the land, to one another, and to the values that we share. Unlike the bio-medical model this wheel does not crush the child under a label or medicate the child to run faster and faster around the wheel. The structural and strengths-based approach is a revolutionary response to the child as a person, a citizen of Canada today (not a future citizen) with rights and responsibilities.

In recognizing the child as a person and as a citizen we move from the privileged position of experts with universal wisdom who label behaviour as 'right' or 'wrong'; such experts diagnose misbehaving children as individuals who have gone 'wrong' in a society based on what is 'right'. We move also from the privileged sector of adulthood with its generalized air of universal wisdom that convinces many in society that children need rough handling and punishment. Rather than assessing, labelling, and punishing children we assess the structural determinants of children's behaviour and development. Perhaps society is not always 'right', particularly when it reflects multiple layers of oppression in which children try to live productive lives. We assess and label these structural determinants and advocate for change. That is our role in the revolution. We don't change behaviour—that is the child's role.

But, back to the bread. The old woman in the shoe did the best she could within her shoe, but she always came back to that empty cupboard. There was no bread. She knew it and the children did, too. What to do? Traditional interventions (spanking) work in the short term. But the long term begs for a full cupboard and a bigger shoe, the structural and strengths-based approach taken in this book.

This is not a do-it-yourself book or instructional manual for parents as stressed as the old woman in the shoe who didn't know what to do; nor is it a cookbook full of intervention recipes that can be pulled out and followed to make children better. There are already many such books available for sale and resale because they offer panaceas, those short-term repair jobs on children, always on the assumption that the children need repairs, rather than the shoe. This book suggests another way of working with the child as a person with rights and a child of Mother Earth.

Organization

There are 11 chapters in this book, each one presenting a theoretical basis for the next. Within each chapter are additional kinds of information: Points to Consider with thought-provoking questions; Notes from the Field, with case studies and examples; and Group Exercises that offer group experiences related to the chapter topic. Each chapter ends with a summary, review questions, and discussion questions. The review questions prompt the reader's understanding and recall of the material within that chapter, and provide a review of the key points. The discussion questions invite the reader to further explore the topic, either internally as part of self-reflection and personal development, or externally as a part of applications in work practice in the community.

Chapter 1 is the foundation for the ensuing chapters. It describes the structural and strengths-based approach of the book, mainly by contrasting this approach with more traditional approaches to children. Three key structural determinants for children in Canada are examined: poverty, the DSM-IV, and the Convention on the Rights of the Child. Each one of these structural determinants affects the daily life of children, particularly at moments of high risk when children may need adult intervention and support.

Chapter 2 examines our changing social construction of the child. In pioneering Canada the child was seen as valuable; in a more industrialized and urbanized twentieth century, the child was seen as vulnerable. Today the child is seen as social capital. On the margins throughout this evolution of social construction are children who are developmentally delayed, children with different abilities, children who live in poverty, First Nations and Inuit children, and children of new Canadians. Their marginalized location, always subject to adult control, determines the services available to them, as well as the structural determinants impacting their daily lives. Their location is determined, also, by their age, which is a socio-political determination. The shifting age limits of 'childhood' continue to create problems, placing responsibilities in some areas, and removing freedoms in others, depending on where children live in Canada. These age and social limits frame the social construction of the child.

How social location and structural determinants affect children's development is explored in Chapter 3. Children have specific developmental needs that may or may not be met. As children grow and develop they form a more stable picture of their own gender and sexual orientation, and this picture may or may not meet adult approval. Their needs in these critical learning periods call for both a caregiver and a structural response.

The importance of this response is the focus of Chapter 4. When this response is synchronous and nurturing, the child usually thrives. When this response is neglectful and dismissive, the child may be injured to the core and may suffer cognitive, emotional, and physical delays. These attachment injuries and delays in turn affect behaviour, and interventions that address the behaviour rather than the attachment injuries rarely work. That is why an understanding of attachment and attachment injuries is so important. This understanding is the foundation for developing a healthy working relationship with the child.

What that relationship looks like is explained in Chapter 5. The relationship theories of Carl Rogers infuse this chapter because they demand an equality that is vital to affirming the child's personhood. The Rogerian relationship based upon congruence, respect, and empathy equalizes the power construct between child and worker so that both are engaged in exploring behaviours and managing change. The worker learns about the child's culture, and the child explores the meaning of behaviour with the worker. This relationship does not happen in isolation but is framed by a structure that is empowering, as exemplified in community capacity-building. Responsibility for change shared by the community, worker, and child positions the child as a participant in the community and a problem-solver rather than a problem.

Having gained this positioning we are ready for the first meeting. Chapter 6 introduces guidelines for this meeting that reflect Rogers' congruence, empathy, and respect.

The worker is congruent, sharing case notes and co-creating a genogram with the child and family. The worker listens while the child informs. The worker is empathic, and tries to understand the presenting problem from multiple perspectives within the family and community. The worker is respectful and focused on the child, while recognizing and respecting parental authority and investment.

Listening to the child is not as simple as leaning forward and paying attention. Listening is a learned skill that demands authenticity, affirmation, and presence, all of which culminate in the AHA! Moment described in Chapter 7. Listening prompts telling, which then demands more attentive listening as the child combines memories, emotions, and reactions into a life narrative. This weaving, or autobiographical reasoning, happens naturally as the child tries to make sense of the world and the people within it. When the child's story becomes problem-saturated and the child turns to the worker for help, the worker can support the child to externalize then contextualize these problems so that they become part of a more hopeful, re-authored life narrative.

Most often the telling of these stories is through play. The words become toys, and the grammar is the play action. Children tell stories naturally through play as they try to make sense of their world and the world of the adults with whom they interact. Children choose specific materials to act out emotions, memories, abuse, and neglect, and the worker listens and observes. When there is a theoretical framework for this observation, the play is seen through the lens of psychoanalysis, family relations, object relations, or cognitive behaviourism. The play acquires new meanings and in Chapter 8 these meanings are webbed and mapped so that the meanings beneath and within the play become clearer.

Understanding play and play behaviour is challenging because of the social constructions around this behaviour. We have been conditioned to believe that certain behaviours are negative, while others are positive. This understanding does not always match the understanding of the player: the child who behaves. The child may understand a play episode or particular behaviour quite differently from the adult observer. Behaviour that appears to be negative may be viewed as a gateway to communicate or to feel powerful or to learn new skills.

The traditional and common behavioural controls—spanking, restraints, incarceration—produce only short-term effects on this 'negative' behaviour. Significant behavioural change happens when the child decides to change and the child manages the change. In Chapter 9 we examine ways to understand the role and meaning of behaviour, and to engage with the child in behavioural change.

Chapter 10 alerts us to situations of high risk in which the child may be injured or worse. We find out about these situations through listening and observing closely the play of children, and by responding appropriately to disclosures of risk. Our response may be crucial to the child's safety. Our response is framed by law and by 'best practice', as well as by our own respect for the personhood of the child. Traditional interventions such as apprehension and placement of children do not always work, as the 'no-home' placements of some children indicate. However, structural interventions that focus on moving and altering structural supports rather than moving and altering children have proved to be successful.

We conclude by examining an increasingly popular intervention with children—group work. We compare groups and gangs, and examine why children voluntarily join neighbourhood gangs but are often involuntary members of groups. The dynamics, leadership, communication styles, and membership are factors that determine how effective this intervention is for children. Gangs and groups once again affirm the interconnectedness of the Medicine Wheel. The child is a person and is also a social being. The child wants that interconnectedness with peers, with the community, and with the family. How to make that connection affirming and hopeful is the challenge for workers who are asked to facilitate groups for children.

The Children

'Children and youth' is the current Canadian phrase describing a full range of persons up to the age of 24. However, the contradictory meanings, boundaries, and dimensions of the word 'youth' are described in Chapter 2. These contradictions, and the central role of the Convention on the Rights of the Child, have led this author to favour the word 'children', and to often use that word alone. This category is clear and defined by the Convention as including persons up to the age of 18.

This category of children includes those whom the Youth Criminal Justice Act (YCJA) calls 'youth', the 12- to 17-year-olds who fall under this legislation. This category of children excludes the 18- to 24 -year-olds who also are called 'youth' by the National Youth In Care Network (NYIC). This category also excludes the 18- to 26-year-olds who are called 'youth' by the Royal Canadian Mounted Police (RCMP) when referring to youth gangs.

The word 'children' reminds us that the 15-year-old living on the street is a child with a right to shelter, and that the 14-year-old expelled from school is also a child with a right to education. The Convention defines these rights, and it is our responsibility as adults to ensure that Canadian children are accorded these rights in their daily life. Naming persons up to the age of 18 'children' is a first step to acting on this responsibility.

Chapter 1

The Structural and Strengths-Based Approach

We have to be more than just observers of children's suffering; we have to be partners in their struggles.

—Senator Landon Pearson

The line at the checkout is long. People wait, looking at their carts and the food they want to buy, glancing at their watches as the dinner hour approaches. At the front of the line, a woman's bank card is rejected causing a further delay. At the back, one of the latecomers abandons his cart with a growl and heads for the exit doors. A child begins to cry—first quietly, then louder—while the parent tries unsuccessfully to get her to sit still in the shopping cart.

When a child misbehaves in public, all eyes focus on two persons. The first is the child. The second is the parent. The customers look at the child, then the parent, and wonder why that child doesn't stop crying and why that parent doesn't get his or her child to 'behave'. These two questions also form the dominant discourse of countless books on children's behaviour that offer behaviour modification advice to parents, workers, and teachers. This reaction to children's behaviour is repeated in the classroom, the emergency ward, the courtroom, the community centre program, and the child welfare meeting room. Professionals and members of the public look at the child, then, at the parent to decipher the origin of the child's behaviour. Rarely do they use a wide-angle lens to focus on the structure of the overall environment and to refocus on the strengths within the child, the parent, and the family. Yet within this environmental structure, which includes social assistance, education, health, child welfare, and youth justice, lie many of the answers both to where the behaviour originates and how to change it.

In this chapter, we examine what it means to take a structural and strengths-based approach to behaviour, and how this kind of approach may be applied specifically to children. We consider two projects that identify current structural determinants of health in Canadian children: the National Longitudinal Survey of Children and Youth (NLSCY) and Health Canada's Population Health. We give particular attention to three structural determinants of behaviour, the most important of these being poverty. The second structural determinant of behaviour—the *Diagnostic and Statistical Manual of Mental Disorders* (DSM-IV)—appears to be an innocuous assessment and categorization tool for children's disorders, but, in fact, is a structural determinant that categorizes children only by their deficits, rather than by their strengths. The third determinant we will focus on is the United Nations Convention on the Rights of the Child (UNCRC). Few children know about or understand this international legislation, a lack of knowledge which in itself, as we will see, is the result of deliberate socio-political action by adults. Katherine Covell (2007: 241) calls children's rights outlined in the UNCRC 'Canada's best-kept secret'.

The structural and strengths-based approach to behaviour has been applied to adults and to families, but workers rarely apply this approach to children. This omission is intentional and reflects a pervasive cultural belief that children are relatively untouched by the larger system of structural determinants, or macrosystem, because they belong to their parents and not to society as a whole. In this chapter, we will see how this cultural belief can harm children and how the structural and strengths-based approach can benefit them. This approach also may influence our own behaviour in such community contexts as the grocery store line-up. Rather than focusing only on the child or the parent (or even on both individuals), the structural and strengths-based approach widens our focus to include such determinants as accessibility to food, nutritional norms, and patterns of consumerism, all of which impact children's behaviour. When these determinants change, so does the child's behaviour. Knowing how these determinants can change allows us to refocus on the child's strengths and readiness for change and empowers us to facilitate change so that the child stops crying, the parent relaxes, and the line-up slowly moves forward.

Objectives

By the end of this chapter, you will:

- Understand the structural and strengths-based approach to children's behaviour.
- Identify the key structural determinants of health in children's lives.
- Demonstrate how to take the structural and strengths-based approach to a child's behaviour.

What Do We Mean by 'Structure'?

The child is located within a social **group** that is larger than the immediate family. This structure includes the legal framework for children's rights, the social assistance that provides housing and economic stability for the child's family, and the child protection system that determines whether or not the child will remain with the family or be moved into foster care. The structure also includes the education system, health care, child care, and the culture, traditions, and mores of the greater community. This complex structure affects every aspect of the child's life, and the child, in turn, affects the structure through continuous, dynamic interaction. This structure is not always obvious to the child because, like a fish in a bowl, the child is inside the structure and rarely sees the constricting glass, even when colliding with it. It is unlikely that the very young child can identify homophobia, for example, even as the child's parents are experiencing it during a preschool interview with the child's teacher.

Bronfenbrenner (1979) calls this outer structure the **macrosystem**, and identifies several systems or structures nested or embedded within this larger structure. The smallest one is the **microsystem**, the child's immediate setting. The child's microsystem is the environment in which he or she lives together with caregivers, parents, or guardians. The most obvious microsystem is the home in which the child lives. The daily life of the newborn is experienced very much at the microsystem level.

The microsystem nests within a **mesosystem** that includes the child's surrounding community. At the mesosystem level are the connections among the settings in which the child lives and operates. The mesosystem may include the school and daycare, for example—settings in which parents meet with teachers with or without the child. The mesosystem may also include community centres and drop-in clinics, arenas and skating rinks, all of the settings in which the child lives and plays.

The largest structure is the macrosystem. At the macrosystem level are the socio-political constructs and structural determinants that affect the child. These include concepts and circumstances that affect another person's attitudes towards children at a given time, as well as such social inequalities as poverty, lack of affordable housing, unemployment, racism, sexism, and gender inequality. These systems interact with one another in a dynamic way, and each system impacts the child.

An ecological model includes these spheres of influence on the child and demonstrates how the child interacts and develops in multiple settings and multiple relationships. The child may develop social skills with siblings that do not work the same way with school friends, so the child adapts social skills from the microsystem and reformulates them to fit the mesosystem. Dishion and Stormshak (2007: 18) describe how this interaction among systems happens as older children become involved with deviant peers: 'Each level of influence is potentially powerful in shaping the developmental trajectory of the child. Moreover, interactions across relationships can define a system that is uniquely powerful. . . . For example, there is a dynamic interplay between parents' reduced monitoring in adolescence and the youth's association with deviant peers.'

Challenging Traditional Models

Bronfenbrenner's (1979) ecological model is fundamental to the structural and strengths-based approach. His ecological model centres on the child's **social location**, a cultural position that influences how a person sees herself/himself as well as how others view that person. The child's social location is continuously impacted by structural or macrosystem factors that determine access to resources. The structure can have a positive or negative effect on the child's social identity and sense of self. The structure determines whether or not the child will be born in a hospital, and whether or not the child will receive requisite care after birth. And it continues to affect every aspect of the child's life—from education, to health, to socialization, to recreation—even though the child cannot necessarily identify or name each particular structural determinant. The child may know only that he or she feels depressed and lonely, but may not be able to identify those structural determinants that cause this depression and loneliness.

The structural and strengths-based approach challenges traditional models that locate the origin of a child's behaviour, difficulty, or problem within that child or the child's family. Such models suggest that the 'real' obstacles or problems are the lack of knowledge, motivation, and self-efficacy on the part of the child, or the child and the family. Traditionally, the worker examines and assesses the child in order to locate problems. The structural and strengths-based approach challenges this model by suggesting that it is not necessarily qualities inherent in the child that are problematic, but the lack of knowledge, willingness to change, and respect for children in aspects of the *structure*—such as the legal, educational, and political systems—that pose the larger problems. The child has *strengths* that need to be examined because these strengths are the basis for behavioural change.

Commenting on a series of reports leading to the massive restructuring of child welfare in British Columbia in 1996, Wharf and McKenzie (2004: 87) stress the importance of investigating the structure instead of the child: 'The welfare of children should be seen in a societal and community context that recognizes that poverty, inadequate housing, and the lack of supports to families severely impacts the ability of parents to care for their children.' They note further that 'the reports criticized the "social cop" approach to practice that restricted the role of child welfare staff to intrusive investigations.'

Traditional models position the child within nesting, interrelated systems; however, the child at the centre of these systems has become the focus of investigation and diagnosis. The structural and strengths-based approach also positions the child centrally, but the focus of investigation is the structure (macrosystem). The emphasis is on the child's strengths within the structure or macrosystem that impacts the child's life context and behaviour. This change in emphasis is illustrated below in Figure 1.1.

The nested systems of structures can be described as a constellation of interrelated elements that affect the child's achievement of potential. Carl Rogers (1951: 41) described these interrelated elements as 'obstacles' half a century ago, when he insisted on healthy working relationships with clients: 'Therapy is not a matter of doing

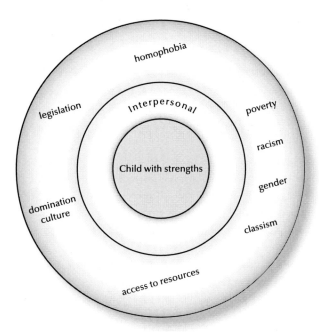

Figure 1.1 The Structural and Strengths-Based Approach

something to the individual, or of inducing him to do something about himself. It is instead a matter of freeing him for normal growth and development, of removing obstacles so that he can again move forward.' Removing these structural obstacles or determinants involves advocating for children's rights as well as for those resources that are necessary for the child's optimal development.

Anne-Marie Ambert (2007: 23) describes the macrosystem in Canada as one in which the nurturance of children, and children themselves, are devalued. The macrosystem puts Canadian children in a powerless position. She makes this assessment not to blame or accuse or to hunt for a source of oppression, but to identify which specific structural changes are necessary for children to become successful in their lives. The goal of the structural and strengths-based approach is not to change the child but to change the structure. This is an encompassing and positive approach that widens the consideration of behavioural influences beyond the child and the family and into the structure itself.

The structural and strengths-based approach also has been described as the **upstream approach** because it seeks first to identify structural determinants, acting like toxins or pollutants upstream, so that the health professionals downstream can then use the traditional biomedical model to cure the few 'fish' that really are sick. The upstream approach combines the structural and the biomedical approaches, and is more adaptable to workers grounded in the biomedical approach who are unlikely to want to change their approach. It still gives them the chance to fish downstream, looking for deficits, toxins, and pollutants, and to apply their biomedical approach to these deficits.

Group Exercise   1.1

Structural Determinants

This group exercise demonstrates how the structural and strengths-based approach changes the dynamic of the intervention. The work of each small group is captured on posters affixed to the wall so that other groups can add their ideas to the poster when they come to it.

The exercise begins with a review of the structural approach by the group leader. Each small group is then given a poster board on which a child's challenge is printed; for example, obesity, low birth weight, eating disorders, poor literacy rates in elementary school, or homelessness. The small group then identifies the structural determinants that create or maintain this challenge and prints them on its poster board.

When the groups have completed their poster boards, the leader signals each group to move to the poster board of the group nearby. Each group adds ideas to this poster board and then moves on, until all of the small groups have had a chance to add their ideas to all of the poster boards. Then, the full lists of structural determinants are read aloud and discussed as a whole by the larger group. The leader assigns a final task: to identify or to recommend structural supports that would counter the structural determinants so that these challenges for children can be met and overcome.

Many of the current government programs for children follow the upstream approach. In Health Canada's smoking cessation program, for example, tobacco companies' advertising, media advertising, and workplace culture are targeted ahead of the individuals who are addicted to tobacco. According to Health Canada's Population Health approach, three of the 11 determinants of health are biomedical deficits, but the remaining eight are structural and upstream: income and social status, social support networks, education and literacy, employment and working conditions, social and physical environments, health services, gender, and culture.

Similar determinants of health for children are used in the National Longitudinal Survey of Children and Youth (NLSCY), and in Human Resources and Skills Development Canada's (HRSDC's) 'plan of action' document, *A Canada Fit for Children* (2004). The latter describes children as, 'powerful agents of social and cultural change,' and goes on to state that 'We in Canada recognize the importance of participation of children to their own healthy development' (HRSDC, 2004: 54). This federal affirmation of children as 'powerful agents' recognizes that the child can decide to change and has the ability to change, an affirmation that is strengths-based and fully in line with the intent of the Convention on the Rights of the Child.

This affirmation has not been accompanied by the necessary structural changes to support the child's decision to change. The eight structural determinants identified in the Population Health approach remain problematic in the lives of children. A child living in poverty simply does not have regular, consistent access to nutritious food, adequate clothing, standard housing, or recreational facilities. The child may *want* to become healthy through exercise and eating well, but without the prerequisite structural changes, the child's achievement of health is unlikely. More often, the child still is considered to be both the problem and the nexus of the solution: if only the child ate properly and exercised more, the obesity problem would be solved. According to this approach, rather than Canadian society being refitted to support the child, it is up to the child to fit into '*A Canada Fit for Children*' (ibid.).

Poverty

Poverty has been identified as the most significant structural determinant or risk factor in a child's life (Conway, 2001; Health Canada, 1999; Statistics Canada (NLSCY, 2006). According to the government of Canada (2003) report *The Well-being of Canada's Young Children*, children living in poor families have twice as many negative outcomes as other children—outcomes including chronic health problems, hyperactivity, school problems, and emotional disorders. Children living in poor families also have three times the rate of conduct disorders found in children whose families are not poor.

This does not mean that parents living in poverty are necessarily inadequate parents, or that children raised in poverty have no chance of reaching their potential or their optimal developmental level. What it does mean is that poverty is the greatest structural determinant affecting a child's present and future life. Poverty makes childhood harder—much harder. Because of the connection between poverty and negative outcomes for children, Willms (2002: 8) suggests that 'the term "children at risk" has almost become synonymous with "children living in poverty"'.

Poverty is not caused by children's laziness or disobedience; it is something that happens to them. Poverty is *done to* children. Although they need to eat and be clothed and housed, they are not legally allowed to work to buy this food, clothing, and shelter; nor are they allowed to apply for social assistance until they are 16 years of age.[1] Child labour is confined by legislation, and Canadians as a whole do not support child labour. Children are victims of poverty and cannot do anything to change their own condition. Their powerlessness adds to the feelings of inadequacy and failure they have about being poor. They are marginalized and, despite needing social services—if, indeed, such services are available—most children actually use such services far less than adults do.

Children living in persistent poverty report going straight outside to the schoolyard at lunchtime because they do not have a lunch at school; skipping school on field trip days because they do not have the money to participate; feeling embarrassed about living in a shelter or about having a parent who is unemployed. A child who lacks adequate nutrition does not have the stamina to participate actively in sport and,

On the United Nations scale of poverty, Canada ranks ahead of the United States and the United Kingdom, but remains in the bottom half among 20 OECD[4] countries, many of which have a lower gross domestic product (GDP)[5] than Canada's (UNICEF, 2007). The ongoing debate over the definition and measurement of poverty helps to distract the public's attention from the numbers of children who suffer as a result of living in poverty in Canada, and from considering what action can be taken to alleviate their poverty. The consensus of economists in 2008 was that one in nine children in Canada live in poverty, one in four children in First Nations communities, and that these numbers are concerning (Campaign 2000, 2008).

Poverty can be described as persistent or transitory. **Persistent poverty** is a chronic condition in which families struggle throughout their entire lives, or even through successive generations, to make ends meet. Poverty becomes a lifestyle; as certain kinds of doors remain closed, it feels to the impoverished that there is no way out of such grinding and deep deprivation. Persistent poverty in the family is said to be the most difficult and damaging kind of poverty for children (Covell and Howe, 2001: 43).

Short-term or **transitory poverty** occurs when families face immediate challenges such as death, illness, or unemployment. Families who normally have adequate means can suddenly drop below the LICO because a parent has been made redundant in the workplace or a child in the family requires expensive medication for a severe or chronic illness. The family turns to government support for short-term help but, as noted by the Canadian Council on Social Development (2006), the inconsistent nature of this support makes it detrimental to the child's healthy development. In most situations of chronic disability or illness, the government's supplements are minimal, at best.

In 2006, for example, over half of all Canadians who turned to the government for short-term support (social assistance) also had to rely on food banks to get enough nutrients to survive (Novick, 2007). When the food banks run out of supplies, or do not have appropriate food for a child with special dietary needs, then the child goes without food. In the film *Poverty Makes Me Sick*[6] (Children's Hospital of Eastern Ontario, Ottawa, 2002), an Ottawa mother whose child has a peanut allergy is given only white bread and peanut butter at the food bank, so her son eats plain white bread at every meal. This is neither appropriate nor healthy, but the mother lives in transitory poverty and has no other options.

The problem of poverty has been addressed by governments at every level. However, most of the actual work accomplished with children living in poverty is done by non-governmental organizations, volunteers, and religious groups who operate within the charity model. In 1989, the federal government launched Campaign 2000, a structural model with the stated goal of eliminating child poverty in Canada by the year 2000. The story of Campaign 2000 is of a well-intentioned structural intervention that has proven woefully inadequate. The first step in the campaign was to identify, assess, and evaluate the depth of poverty in Canada. 'Measurement' was the overriding goal. The next step was to apply a series of financial income transfers via their parents or guardians to poor children, then to tear off these 'band-aids' and reapply them under new names. Thus, in

1993, the family allowance, a universal benefit of $33 per child per month, was discontinued along with child tax credits. The allowance and the tax credits were replaced by a Child Tax Benefit (CTB), an income-indexed payment per child per month. In 1998, the name of this monthly payment was changed to Canada Child Tax Benefit (CCTB) and, nine years later (2007) the previous child tax credit was re-introduced. In the interim, the old family allowance benefit was resurrected, but only for children up to the age of six. This was renamed the Universal Child Care Benefit (UCCB), a monthly non-indexed (but taxable) benefit. This period also witnessed the establishment of subsidies, such as the National Child Benefit Supplement, for children with special needs and for children of parents with low income. Parents had to apply for each of these benefits on separate forms, either at the child's birth or at tax time (assuming the parents filed an annual income tax return). Is the child still bleeding despite these financial bandages? Parents who cannot work because they do not have childcare would say, yes, and a community watchdog organization, the Canadian Council on Social Development (2006), suggests that the children most in need of financial supports benefit only minimally from any of these payments: 'Government transfers . . . do make a difference. The child poverty rate in 2003 was 18%; without government transfers, it would have been 27%.'

From 1989 to 1999 the Canadian GDP increased by 50 per cent. This increase widened the gap between rich and poor as user fees, school fees, and the cost of living increased. The number of Canadian children living in poverty increased by 42 per cent and nearly doubled in Ontario (McCarthy, 2000). The number of people using food banks more than doubled, and half of these users were children (Covell and Howe, 2001). By 2004, one in eight Canadian children had no dental care; one in six children was born to a mother who did not receive prenatal care in her first trimester; and 40 per cent of the homeless population were children (Ruane and Cerulo, 2004: 32). While some families lived on half a million dollars or more per year, others struggled along on less than a living wage as part-time, contract, and seasonal workers without extended health benefits and without government support. Their children experienced relative poverty, which means, for example, that they never see a dentist throughout their childhood years. Most at risk of poverty are children of lone mothers and children whose parents are disabled, First Nations, or new immigrants. By 2005, 11.7 per cent of all Canadian children, and 33.4 per cent of the Canadian children of lone mothers, lived below the LICO. This compares to 7.4 per cent of Canadian families living below LICO in the same year (Collin, 2007).

Children in poor neighbourhoods are said to suffer 'poverty by postal code,' as there is no consistent municipal planning for the equal provision of services in rich and poor neighbourhoods. The geographical ghettoization of the poor continues and is reinforced by the NIMBY ('not in my backyard') attitude prevalent in manicured and gated neighbourhoods. This attitude encourages the location of social housing, group homes, Head Start programs, and food banks in urban neighbourhoods, while gyms, arenas, and pools are located in affluent, suburban neighbourhoods (Novick, 2007).

Steinhauer notes (1996: 2), 'The evidence suggests that inequity, marginalization, and powerlessness more than economic deprivation aggravate poor families' distress.'

Point to Consider   1.1

Quebec's Structural and Strengths-Based Approach

In 1959, the fertility rate in Quebec was 4.0 children per woman; this fell to 1.47 by 1998 (Baker, 2005: 17), leaving Quebec with one of the lowest birthrates in the world. Then, the structural and strengths-based approach was applied as part of the provincial government's poverty reduction plan. This plan included financial support for low-income families with children under the Parental Wage Assistance (PWA) program; accessible, quality child care (at a cost of $5 per day); and the Quebec Family Allowance. Structural supports were accompanied by a strengths-based approach to children, who were positioned as assets to the province (Baril, Lefebvre, and Merrigan, 2000). By 2002, the birthrate began to rise, and this shift continued. In 2007, 84,200 babies were born in Quebec, a startling figure that reflects the baby boom that began in 2002. The example of Quebec demonstrates that, with adequate structural and strengths-based support, adults can and will plan responsibly to become parents.

Children in poor families live on or beyond the edge of what most think of as 'normal' Canadian life. They are impacted by a social inequality that they do not understand, and they feel only that somehow they should be ashamed of their poverty. Two provinces do have poverty reduction action plans: Quebec (developed in 2004) and Newfoundland and Labrador (developed in 2006). Neither province is the wealthiest in Canada, but both have concrete programs to eliminate child poverty—programs that include dental care, child care, and early learning. The results already are making the lives of children in these two provinces healthier (Novick, 2007).

DSM-IV

The *Diagnostic and Statistical Manual of Mental Disorders*, fourth edition (DSM-IV), was published by the American Psychiatric Association in 1994 as a shorthand or reference text for mental health specialists and health care providers with extensive clinical training. The expert panel of doctors who revised the DSM-III to generate the DSM-IV were drawn from several branches of the traditional medical community, all of which use the biomedical model as their framework for assessment. This text's listing of 297 disorders was intended as a reference tool for the doctors' colleagues and was revised in 2000 as the DSM-IV-TR (text revision). Non-professionals were directed to consult the DSM-IV to obtain information only, and not for the purpose of making diagnoses. However, a diagnosis based on the DSM-IV soon became the basis for securing specialized services for the child or financial reimbursement for the child's medication. As a result, workers in education, child care, and social services began to use the text as their standard reference tool. In this way, the DSM-IV became a powerful structural determinant in shaping, funding, and delivering services for children.

The DSM-IV-TR (the current version in use) is structured categorically, and provides inclusive symptoms for each category. These symptoms are drawn from both scientific studies and conventional wisdom. The symptoms of ADHD (attention deficit hyperactivity disorder), for example, include inattention, distractibility, impulsivity, and hyperactivity. These are also 'symptoms' of average children inside a stuffy classroom on a sunny June day. ADHD includes many more symptoms and is a serious condition. However, choosing one symptom in order to label a child ADHD, for example, can be a misdiagnosis that pathologizes that child; the label connotes a sickness or deficit, and the child becomes known by the deficit above all else. This diagnosis tends to follow the child for years, subsuming both the child's identity and his or her capacity for change. As Ungar (2006: 295) observes: 'Interventions by professionals and the diagnostic assessments to which high-risk youth are subjected cause more harm than good when these labels become yet another barrier to a child's healthy constructions of self.'

Once a DSM-IV assessment of a child has been completed, the assessment tends not to be repeated. Tests are costly and, once a label is applied to a child, it is difficult to get funding for retesting. Because, for example, Colin feels distracted and fails to manipulate objects effectively in a testing sequence on the testing day, he may be labelled as 'delayed' and may carry this label for years. The boy hears the label repeated by the worker, foster parent, and other professionals and paraprofessionals, and may ask for details. The worker's response reinforces Colin's identification with the label, and causes him to behave in ways that are consistent with and that reinforce the original label. Colin is no longer Colin: he is a very delayed boy. As Colin reinforces the validity of the original label, the behavioural descriptors increase, and the assessors (adults) feel validated in their original diagnosis. In her institutional ethnography, Smith (1998) identifies this as a trick that professionals use to disable the child and to erode his or her self-esteem so that the child, in turn, becomes more pliable and easier to control.[7]

Rosenhan's (1973) research study in the mental health field demonstrates the application of this trick and illustrates the enormous power of labels. Rosenhan began by asking hospital staff volunteers from 12 different US hospitals to admit themselves to several local psychiatric hospitals, reporting to the admissions clerk that they had been 'hearing voices'. All but one of these eight volunteer participants, or pseudo-patients, were admitted to hospital under the label 'schizophrenic' rather than under their own behavioural descriptors ('hearing voices'). Once admitted to the hospitals, the participants behaved normally, read their books, and engaged in routines. All of them exhibited no signs of schizophrenia or abnormal behaviour. Despite this consistently normal behaviour, all of the participants continued to be diagnosed as 'schizophrenic' by staff nurses and doctors. They had difficulty getting out of hospital, and one of the participants was released only after 52 days of hospitalization. As so often happens with children, the biomedical model label caused others to view the research participants

Article 42 of the Convention stipulates that appropriate and active means be used to disseminate information about the principles and provisions of the Convention to those affected by it. However, most Canadian children are not aware of the Convention. The text is rarely displayed in daycares, schools, child welfare agencies, community centres, health-care centres, or family resource centres, and is seldom posted on any of the government websites for parents, children, and families. This omission is deliberate. Denying Canadians knowledge of children's rights also denies citizenship status for children. This denial of citizenship status is often alluded to by adults who call children 'future citizens' rather than current ones. Children in Canada may be citizens according to the law; however, they are not typically counted as part of the current body of citizens.

A decade after the Convention was adopted by the United Nations, Elections Canada and UNICEF organized an activity designed to inform Canadian school children about it by asking them to vote for their favourite Convention article. This was a token activity, supported by the federal government long after ratification. However, even this activity was resisted by certain Canadian adults. One school board trustee in Abbotsford, British Columbia, warned: 'It undermines the integrity of the family and involves children in a political undertaking. There is a gradual erosion of parental authority and this is one more step in that direction' (Howe and Covell, 2005: 3). Unfortunately, this reaction to the Convention seems to be both common and widespread among adults. The resulting lack of information about children's rights has had a negative structural impact on all Canadian children. The outcome of the Elections Canada vote by three-quarters of a million Canadian children in 1,900 schools was telling. The article voted 'number one' by Canadian children was the right to a family. Pretty radical stuff!

Certain articles of the Convention pose particular challenges in Canadian law.

- Article 12 (the right to voice an opinion and be heard), Article 17 (the right to access information), and Article 3 (the right to have one's interests prioritized over those of adults) all uphold children's civic rights to have information and participate in affairs that directly concern them. Article 12, for example, would suggest that five-year-olds who want to go to school for a full day have a right to speak. They may not know the implications of their eagerness to be in full day school with their friends, and they may not understand that full day school might mean giving up an afternoon nap. This right to voice an opinion does not imply that school boards and curriculum planners need to adjust the school day to accommodate these five-year-olds. However, Article 12 reminds adults that children also have the right to voice an opinion and, by voicing this, they have an opportunity to learn that multiple factors determine whether or not that opinion is heard.
- Similarly, Article 17 states that children do have the right to access information concerning themselves: school records, health records, and educational plans. Can a seven-year-old read and understand an educational plan? Perhaps not. Does the seven-year-old have the right to know that there is an educational plan signed by her or his own parent? Definitely.

- Article 17 challenges Canadian family law that recognizes the child's voice in custody rights awarded to parents. Custody is determined according to several criteria, of which one is the child's best interests. Children's expressed wishes regarding custody are given more weight as the child matures; however, this level of maturity is often difficult to determine, with age rather than maturity being the easier option. Teenagers, for example, typically have their expressed wishes considered, whereas 10-year-olds may not. Children would caution, 'Don't speak about us without us'. However, they are still used as window dressing at national conferences. They can participate in plays, choirs, and focus groups, but they cannot vote or make decisions on child protection, education, health, and welfare. Similarly, children do not actively participate on boards that determine the nature and quality of daycare, schools, recreation, or community health. And with regard to information access, children who are conceived by sperm donors do not even have the right to know the names of their fathers.
- Article 16 (the right to privacy) is contravened when children in schools are searched without a warrant, their bags and their lockers searched, and their personal diaries, letters, blogs, phone records, and emails scanned by caregivers, workers, or parents.
- Articles 19, 28, 37, 38 (the right not to be hurt or mistreated) are contravened when, under the Criminal Code of Canada, Section 43, children are assaulted under the guise of 'discipline'.
- Article 37 (the right to be incarcerated with other children instead of with adults, and to be treated with dignity) is contravened when Canadian children, under the Youth Criminal Justice Act, are not offered rehabilitative services and are incarcerated with adults because of the chronic national shortage of juvenile detention facilities.
- Article 18 (the right to child care when parents are working) is contravened by the lack of universal, affordable, and accessible quality child care in Canada.
- Article 24 (the right to protection from environmental toxins) is contravened when Canadian children are exposed to pesticides, mercury, nicotine, and other toxins in the air, water, and food they consume.
- Article 34 (the prevention of sexual exploitation). Despite federal government brochures such as *What No Child Should Endure*, penalties for adults engaging in sexual activities with children are not consistently enforced, and a national registry of child sexual abuse offenders has not been established. Benjamin Perrin (2008: A3) summarizes our apparent attitude towards the sexual exploitation of children here and in other countries, arguing that 'A Canadian passport is essentially a get-out-of-jail-free card for people having sex with children overseas.'

Aboriginal children and those living in remote areas have even less protection under the Convention. These children often do not have access to local community health services, and some do not even have clean drinking water in their homes. Such conditions directly contravene Article 24 (the right to attain the highest attainable standard of health possible) and Article 27 (the right to an adequate standard of living).

Alarming current statistics (van Daalen-Smith, 2007: 78) reflect the reality of these unhealthy living conditions:

• The rate of SIDS (sudden infant death syndrome) among First Nations infants is 3 times the national average.
• The rate of FAS (fetal alcohol syndrome) among First Nations children is estimated to be 10 times the national average.
• The rate of Type 2 pediatric diabetes among First Nations children is among the highest in the world.
• The suicide rate for First Nations children is 6 times higher than the national average.

These statistics reflect abysmal circumstances experienced by these children, in addition to substandard early childhood education, schools and colleges, and recreational opportunities. These children in particular do not feel protected by the Convention.

A recent example of this deprivation of rights is the story of Jordan, a First Nations child born with complex medical needs who died alone in hospital when he was four years old. Jordan was a victim of jurisdictional disputes around the costs of caring for him. Despite the commitment of his family and community, Jordan was kept in hospital for two years while provincial and federal governments argued over his health-care costs. His family and his community, because they could not afford to pay privately for his health care, were not allowed to bring him home. This contravention of the Convention resulted in the framing of 'Jordan's Principle', a child-first document upholding a child's right to health care as a citizen of Canada. Jordan's Principle was unanimously supported in Parliament in December 2007, but at the time of writing (November, 2009) it has not been enacted as legislation that would protect the health-care rights of all First Nations children.

In 1993, the Canadian federal government declared 20 November as National Child Day to commemorate the passing of both the Convention on the Rights of the Child and the Universal Declaration of the Rights of the Child by the United Nations. On that day, all Canadian children are called on to celebrate their legislative rights. Critics suggest that Canadian children would be more likely to celebrate if they had a clearer understanding of what these rights are! The failure to implement the Convention has had a huge structural impact on the lives of Canadian children.

Structural Assets

Three structural determinants (poverty, the DSM-IV, and the Convention on the Rights of the Child) have been described in this chapter. Each of these determinants has something to contribute to our understanding about negative impacts on the child's overall health or wellness. Poverty affects both short- and long-term outcomes for children. The DSM-IV is being used in a way that unfairly assesses, labels, and, in some cases, overmedicates children. The Convention makes promises it cannot keep because

Photo 1.3 Jordan River Anderson (1999–2004).

corresponding legislation has not been enacted in Canada to provide enforcement of all of its articles.

Fortunately, Canadians also enjoy structural assets or health-enhancing resources that improve the child's overall outcomes. When an active, engaged, and competent child interacts with these structural assets, a positive outcome is likely. A child who has support from an adequate income, knowledge and advocacy skills related to basic Convention rights, and specific health supports to match specific needs, is more likely to be healthy and well. Benson (2006) and Scales, Sesma, and Bolstrom (2004) describe 40 developmental assets, 20 of which are external to the child and under significant control by communities. Central to these researchers' description is the belief that the child both affects and is affected by his or her surrounding structure. The assets they describe counter-balance or protect against poverty and other structural determinants that impede development. The scientific foundation for these 40 external and internal developmental assets, organized into 8 categories, is described in more detail in Scales and Leffert (2004). The 20 external or structural assets are listed in Table 1.1.

Support, empowerment, boundaries, and a commitment to learning: such qualities seem simple enough for any community to provide for a child. However, these structural assets are often lacking. The child does not feel community support, and does not feel safe in a community that is sexist and violent; where expectations for the child are low because of the child's ethnicity, race, or ability; and where commitment to meeting the child's learning needs is lacking. This range of structural assets

Table 1.1   Structural Assets

Asset	Examples
Support	Family support, positive family communication, other adult relationships, caring neighbourhood, caring school climate, and parental involvement in schooling
Empowerment	Community valuing of children, view of children as resources, children's provision of service to others, and safety
Boundaries and expectations	Family boundaries, school boundaries, neighbourhood boundaries, adult role models, positive peer influence, and high expectations for children
Commitment to learning	Creative activities, children's programs, religious community, and time at home

Point to Consider   1.2

Children's Rights Programs

Provincial education programs that include the Convention have demonstrated cross-curricular educational benefits. In Nova Scotia, the health and social studies curriculum for kindergarten to grade six includes information on the Convention that has resulted in a wider understanding of citizenship responsibilities in these young children (Levine, 2000). In Saskatoon, at Princess Alexandria School, the Convention is the basis for a rights-based discipline policy. Schissel (2006: 150–3) describes an environment in which 'negative' behaviours are countered with options for the student so that the individual child has positive possibilities for personal growth and change: 'At a general level, the students are treated with the respect that adults, at least formally, are granted by society.' Because of the rights-based conduct policy, expulsion and suspension are not used; instead, the focus is on providing support to keep children in school for as long as it takes them to learn the elementary school curriculum. Children, thus, are acknowledged as having the right to an education.

does provide a framework for civic planning. In a country that respects and values its youthful citizens, the development of these assets is essential.

Structure and Strengths

The focus of the strengths-based approach is the child's ontogenetic potential: what the child can achieve rather than what the child has done wrong or what the child is lacking (his or her 'deficits'). The child's strength is measured holistically rather than in one or two domains, and represents the sum of the child's potential. The wisdom of the Medicine Wheel (see Chapter 3) informs the strengths-based measurement: 'Health means balance and harmony within and among each of the four aspects of human nature: physical, mental, emotional, and spiritual. Over-focusing or under-focusing on any one aspect upsets the balance of the four' (Harris, 2006: 123). This wellness approach stands in profound contrast to the traditional biomedical approach that looks for deficits in the child, or specific areas in which the child is lacking or deficient.

The primary deficits that the structural and strengths-based approach focuses on are the external structural deficits/deficiencies that hold the child back, impeding the child's wellness. The approach is based on the belief that the child has the capacity to make choices and is motivated to grow and to change, even under adverse conditions. Such conditions or experiences (structural deficits) can block or distort the child's capacity to choose and to change, but can also be a way to further strengthen resiliency.

In a sufficiently nurturing and supportive context, the child will develop resiliency and a capacity for change.

Peterson and Seligman (2004) use the word 'virtues' to describe the child's assets and strengths, including cognitive strengths, strength of will in the face of opposition, interpersonal strengths, civic strengths, strengths that protect against excess, and strengths that forge connections to meaning. By identifying these assets and strengths as virtues (rather than vices), Peterson and Seligman prompt workers to look for strengths in the child. In turn, the identification, acknowledgment, and reinforcement of such strengths empower the child to believe in the existence of positive solutions and opportunities for change.

This focus on strengths does not translate into the worker's repetition of 'good job' each time the child finishes a task, eats a snack, or complies with a request. The child is quick to spot the superficial nature of this overworked phrase. Nor does this focus deny the child's deficits, shortcomings, and weaknesses. The child has both strengths and weaknesses, like any other person, and to pretend otherwise is to be dishonest. As Fewster (2005: 3) notes, 'The cognitive trickery we use to "focus on the positive" denies our own experience, distorts our perception of the other, and places our curiosity in cold storage.' Instead, the worker is authentic, interested in the child, and ready to identify an asset or strength. The worker conveys this belief in the child by using supportive language such as the following:

- 'You came today, even though the bus was late and it was snowing. I'm glad.'
- 'How did you change the time on your cell phone? I don't know how to do that.'
- 'Did you manage to get the paper done on time? That took some organizing.'

Each statement is factual and honest, and each conveys a frank admiration for a task completed, a challenge overcome, a strength demonstrated.

Leadbeater (2004: 4) contrasts the structural and strengths-based and the biomedical, deficit-based approaches. The former supports the child and family, building on strengths and valuing resilience. The latter pathologizes families, isolating and punishing them for their weaknesses. Leadbeater provides examples of structural and strengths-based programs, such as excellent inner-city school academic programs that are offered to all children and that assume their competence and their potential for academic success.

Empowerment is fundamental to this approach. The worker assumes that the child is competent and fosters the child's strengths or assets and the child's ability to participate in interventions and to make decisions. This begins early. The worker provides empowering and stimulating experiences for an infant so that the infant feels free to explore and engage with the world. The worker responds to the toddler with reassuring looks, smiles, and warmth when the child completes tasks such as throwing a ball, closing a door, climbing a set of stairs, and so on. Instead of, 'Look out, you're going to fall' with its corresponding assumption of failure, the worker offers encouragement: 'One more step to climb!'

In addition, the child's opinions and preferences are recognized and heard, rather than dismissed and disregarded in favour of 'adult wisdom'. The child chooses solutions and takes responsibility for making these chosen solutions or new behaviours work. This process of empowerment affirms the child's sense of control and responsibility for change, but it demands both participation and leadership. Empowerment requires 'ownership' of both the problem and the solution—the sense of responsibility articulated in the Convention on the Rights of the Child. In effect, the worker says to the child, 'You are in charge of this. You decide where you want to go with this.' The choice of intervention or resources is in the hands of the one who is most familiar with both the problem and the behaviour: the child.

Structural and strengths-based interventions empower the child to make decisions and to move forward. When the child demonstrates a need to engage in physical play rather than sit at a desk for hours, the worker advocates for the child's acceptance into alternate, more physically satisfying programs. When the child talks about teasing by classmates, the worker listens and helps the child to reframe the teasing and devise new responses to it. The worker also addresses the structure and engages the school and classroom teacher in anti-bullying strategies. This does not diminish or excuse the child's responsibility for having hit others. On the contrary, this increases the child's responsibility to advocate for change and to make that change happen.

Structural and Strengths-Based Interventions

Structural and strengths-based interventions do what Senator Landon Pearson suggests in the epigraph to this chapter: they make the worker a partner with the child and change the 'me' to 'we'. Rather than assessing the deficits of the child and imposing remedies or medication on the child ('me'), the structural and strengths-based worker and the child ('we') collaborate to identify and assess both the structural deficits and the child's assets. The worker acknowledges the role that adults play in disempowering the child and works to correct this power imbalance. The worker also remembers that, when pointing out structural deficits, the other three fingers of the hand point backwards: the worker and the child together are responsible for advocating for structural change. Saleebey (2002: 13–18) summarizes this type of intervention beautifully:

Every individual group, family, and community has its strengths; trauma and abuse, illness and struggle may be injurious but they may also be sources of challenge and opportunity; assume that you do not know the upper limits of the capacity to grow and change and take individual, group, and community aspirations seriously; we best serve clients by collaborating with them; every environment is full of resources; and caring, care taking, and context count.

Consider Tammy, a young girl with language delays. The method of the deficits-based biomedical approach is to pathologize Tammy's language skills (screen for language deficits or delays) and assign a label or diagnosis. Perhaps the DSM-IV is used, or a speech pathologist applies a written or oral language test. Then Tammy is given medication, speech/language intervention, or extra tuition, while her parents are reprimanded, coached, or given instructions on improving their communication with Tammy. Tammy and her family, or Tammy alone, is fitted into an existing program. Scarcity of resources often means that the assessment and the intervention may not take place until months or years after the identification of the initial language delay.

The structural and strengths-based approach locates structural determinants that affect Tammy's language delay: access to communication opportunities, comfort within these conversations, and presence or absence of encouragement to talk. Tammy's access to communication opportunities may be curtailed because she is located within a poor neighbourhood and has caregiving responsibilities for younger siblings that prevent her from attending school regularly. She may feel limited in her access to her friends because she doesn't have a cell phone or computer with internet access in her bedroom at home. In addition, the racism in her school and in her pervasively white neighbourhood may inhibit Tammy, as a biracial girl, from engaging in conversations with neighbourhood children and having local friendships. Impacted by poverty and racism, Tammy struggles to have a voice. She struggles, not only because of the reasons for language delays within herself, but also because of the structural determinants or deficits that impact her life.

A key structural determinant may be the language assessment tool itself. These assessment tools have an inherent cultural, linguistic, and format bias. The assumption of such tools is that expressive language builds incrementally, and that word counts mark this development. Tools such as the Rosetti Infant-Toddler Language Scale, Receptive-Expressive Emergent Language Test, Preschool Language Scale, and others value expressive over receptive language skills in younger children. In Tammy's case, the assessor may be a speech/language pathologist, a psychometrist, or the classroom teacher basing her assessment on Tammy's contributions to class discussions. The tool, the assessor, and the assessment conditions all affect the result.

In contrast, the worker who takes the structural and strengths-based approach locates the cause of Tammy behaviour (delayed language) within this larger structure, pinpointing poverty, racism, assessment models, and school culture as specific barriers to this child's success. The identification of structural issues prompts the consequent intervention. Tammy has strengths: enthusiasm, health, intellectual ability, willingness to learn, strong interpersonal relationships within her family, and an engaged and concerned family. The worker reinforces and acknowledges these strengths. With a parent's collaboration, the worker can arrange for child care that frees Tammy to join an after-school social group. The family, Tammy, and the worker plan to engage the school in an anti-racism program that includes racial pride activities as part of the curriculum. Tammy gets a chance to speak, and so her language develops.

This structural and strengths-based approach is quite different from one that labels Tammy or blames her parents, reminding them to sign off on her homework and read her stories every night before bedtime. By locating structural determinants for the language delay, the child and the family can reposition themselves within a larger world. They can begin to see that the child is not the problem: the source of Tammy's language delay is in a larger structure that can be changed. Structural and strengths-based interventions have the potential to support all children affected by similar structural determinants.

In another example, a teacher diagnoses six-year-old Tyler as being hyperactive and recommends to the parent or caregiver that Tyler be given the stimulant medication Ritalin. The intervening worker does not dispute the teacher's diagnosis and the parent's frustration, or in any way excuse Tyler's aggressive behaviour. However, before intervening or medicating the child, the worker conducts a structural and strengths-based assessment that reveals the following:

- Tyler's ability to communicate verbally with a wide, age-appropriate vocabulary;
- Tyler's ability to listen effectively for up to five minutes (normal range);
- Tyler's above-average psychomotor skills;
- Tyler's basic understanding of school rules and consequences;
- Tyler's strong family system and parental interest;
- the above-average socio-economic status of Tyler's family;
- a supportive learning environment in the classroom and the school;
- positive teacher–student relationships in the classroom; and
- a well-developed and age-appropriate peer group at school.

These nine identified strengths prompt corresponding strengths-based and structural interventions. Each one matches the assessed strengths of Tyler, his family, and his school community, and takes full advantage of these assessed strengths. Tyler signals to the worker a readiness to change—a readiness prompted by lunch hours spent in the principal's office rather than outside, and parental anxiety and stress at home. He is seen to be competent and inherently capable of finding solutions to problems.

Through structural and strengths-based interventions, Tyler is empowered to take ownership over both the problem and the solution. These interventions are developmentally appropriate and correspond to Tyler's assessed strengths. Tyler will make changes by

- practising positive language around feelings ('I am angry', 'I am sad', and so on);
- practising receptive language skills around aggression and hearing what friends say;
- participating in physically demanding games in an after-school program with slightly older children who already know and practise turn-taking and teamwork;
- taking on a classroom role to help the teacher to record everyone's behaviour on a chart;
- taking part in an in-home behaviour program for everyone in the family that complements and reinforces the behaviour program in the school; and
- participating in recreational activities that support sharing and co-operation.

Point to Consider   1.3

A Community Faces Poverty

In 2005, the Municipal Council in Hamilton, Ontario, acknowledged that 20 per cent of the city's population—roughly 100,000 people—were living in households subsisting below the poverty line. Instead of taking the 'charity' approach and setting up new food banks and clothing distribution posts, the Council asked for solutions from the people in the poorest neighbourhoods. The goal was to make Hamilton the best place to raise a child. The people in the poorest neighbourhoods identified specific projects they felt would result in better outcomes for children. Their expertise was acknowledged and valued and formed the core of the Hamilton Roundtable for Poverty Reduction (HRPR). Some of their early initiatives were:

- the COPPERS program, in which police officers read to children in an inner-city school;
- Kids Unlimited, a program of mentoring and of providing food, clothing, and activities;
- the Mohawk College renewal of classrooms in a community centre.

These three projects, among others, were undertaken by people in the poorest neighbourhoods, together with people from outside these neighbourhoods. This shared goal and shared power resulted in new relationships and community collaboration within other areas of mutual interest. In a community focused on poverty as a structural determinant of child health (Chamberlain and Weaver, 2008), the poverty rate was lowered significantly.

These behavioural redirections are not punishments; discipline or learning is being practised in an educational sense. Each intervention acknowledges Tyler's strengths in communication and socialization, and takes advantage of the pre-existing structural supports for change. Each of these interventions is controlled by Tyler, who takes responsibility for the change. The structure adapts to support this change. The child, even at six years of age, can control the timing and the amount of change, and can continue learning in school without medication and without a label.

The most successful structural and strengths-based interventions are simple. They involve a worker changing an uncaring and immovable structure to a caring one by showing consistent interest in a child's life. Robbie Gilligan (2006: 21) tells the story of his friend, Debra Fearn, who grew up in foster care and later went on to become a university professor. Debra reflects on the structural and strengths-based intervention in the educational system that helped her to develop high self-esteem during her life in foster care. One teacher made this difference:

She saw a spark in me and for the next seven years ensured that the spark became a flame that did not extinguish itself. She believed in me, and gave me courage and a belief in myself that could have easily been lost along the way. When I failed Maths and French . . . , she ensured that I received extra tuition after school, and she gave me the belief that I would be successful the second time around. . . . What makes her stand out in my mind is that she cared for me and she liked me.

This intervention may seem too simple: 'she cared for me and she liked me'. But decades later, and more than 20 workers and 12 foster homes later, this intervention is what Debra remembers from her childhood. Her strength was supported and encouraged by one teacher who gave her the specific attention that she needed at the time and made those structural adjustments (e.g., arranging for tutoring) to enable her success. A lack of recognition and attention leads to a sense of invisibility for a child; many children with difficulties talk about feeling 'invisible' or 'not heard'. Indeed, research by Ann Masten (2006) suggests that the most important structural and strengths-based intervention is a strong relationship with a caring, prosocial adult.

What are the distinctive qualities of these caring and prosocial adults? They almost always share the same culture and gender as the child. They are skilled at taking a structural and strengths-based approach—working to change systems rather than assessing, changing, or blaming the child. They choose to spend time with the child. Their intervention usually takes place during a few hours each week over an extended period of time and takes the form of a mutually enjoyable activity. The effect on the child of having a relationship with a caring and prosocial adult is described by Gilgun (2002: 70): 'Young people can turn out well despite adversity when they have long-term relationships that promote belonging, when they consciously emulate positive role models, and when they have personal, familial, and community resources that support positive behaviour.'

As a result of such an intervention, the child is more likely to complete high school and enter college or university (Langhout, 2004). The child in foster care tends to achieve in these ways when caregivers take a structural and strengths-based approach. They place a higher value on emotional and social well-being than on school performance (Barber and Delfabbro, 2004). This type of intervention sounds familiar: Debra Fearn (Gilligan, 2006: 21) would understand why it works so well!

Structural and strengths-based interventions reflect a balance of power between adult and child, with perhaps more power on the child's side because the child is the decision-maker. Consider, for example, an intervention with Tibo, a young offender who engages in self-harm as well as abusive behaviour towards others. A structural and strengths-based assessment of Tibo reveals the following:

- a youth detention system that lacks educational or remedial programming;
- a surrounding societal association of youth with crime;
- a lack of appropriate and supportive state care for children;
- Tibo's ability to deal with an attachment injury from early childhood;

- Tibo's age-appropriate cognitive ability and communication skills; and
- Tibo's relationship with his brother, who visits regularly and demonstrates support.

Tibo has been able to deal successfully with the absence of a consistent caregiver during his last 14 years in foster care. His achievement needs to be recognized and acknowledged first. When his immediate family, peer group, and worker recognize his success in dealing with this early attachment injury, they may also be able to support his attempts at problem-solving. Tibo may want to meet with past care providers to express his anger. He may want to write to them, or even lay abuse charges against them. His active decision-making replaces helplessness with hopefulness and acknowledges his strengths and potential for success (Masten, 2006).

What we know about successful interventions is that they are structural and strengths-based and planned to match the needs of the individual child. Effective interventions are based on a belief that the child is competent, has the personal resources to change, and will change when structural supports are adequate. The worker respects both the strengths of the child and the child's capacity for change and identifies to the child the structural supports needed to support the child's decision to change.

Summary

The structural and strengths-based approach to working with children differs significantly from the traditional biomedical or deficits-based approach, which usually begins with the identification of a behaviour problem. The child is constructed as a problem and is assessed, and the usual intervention is a requirement for the child to change. The structural and strengths-based approach, on the other hand, assumes that the child is competent and able to problem-solve with an adult in order to make changes. These changes can be structural and, in advocating for and making structural changes, the child is empowered to continue problem-solving. This chapter introduces three particular structural determinants that directly affect the lives of children in Canada and elsewhere. Poverty is an overriding factor, causing children to miss out on structural supports and opportunities and, in some cases, even the basic necessities of life. The second structural determinant is the *Diagnostic and Statistical Manual of Mental Disorders*, fourth edition (DSM-IV-TR), which offers a stark contrast to the structural and strengths-based approach in its diagnosing and labelling of children's behaviours as the result of disorders. Finally, the Convention on the Rights of the Child frames all of the basic rights of children, but the lack of legislative application in Canada of this important document illustrates why children's legal rights are so often neglected. In subsequent chapters, we will see the structural and strengths-based approach in action as we learn to listen to children and to understand their behaviours. Keep in mind these three structural determinants as they also circumscribe work with children.

Review Questions

1. Describe an example of a structural and strengths-based approach to a toddler who continually runs away from a caregiver.
2. Name the eight structural determinants of health identified by Statistics Canada's Population Health project.
3. Why is poverty the most important structural determinant for children in Canada? Give examples.
4. What is the National Longitudinal Survey of Children and Youth (NLSCY)? Name three major findings of this survey.
5. How is the DSM-IV-TR used, and what are the inherent drawbacks of this diagnostic tool?
6. Contrast the deficit approach of the biomedical model with the structural and strengths-based approach. Provide an example of how you might use these two approaches in working with a 15-year-old girl who regularly engages in unprotected sex with older men.
7. List Peterson and Seligman's six groups of assets or virtues, and give examples of these assets.
8. What does changing 'me' to 'we' mean?
9. Why do some workers prefer the traditional, deficit-based approach? Give reasons to support your opinion.
10. Describe the qualities of Gilligan's caring and prosocial adults.

Discussion Questions

1. 'Empowerment' is a term often used in the helping professions because one of the goals of caring for others is to support them in ways that move them into independence and self-actualization. How can you create an empowering relationship with children? Is this something you might want to do? How might the goal of empowerment affect your work with children?
2. Do you think that children have too many rights in Canada today? Which articles of the Convention on the Rights of the Child are too liberal? Give examples to support your opinion.
3. When working with children like Colin and Tyler, described in this chapter, how would you engage the family and teachers in the structural and strengths-based approach?

Chapter 2

The Social Construction of the Child

daddy says the world is
a drum tight and hard
and i told him
I'm gonna beat
out my own rhythm

—Nikki Giovanni, 'the drum'

Google the word 'child' and you will find screens of definitions and descriptions. Definitions of 'child' vary according to the social location of the definer, usually an adult, who decides the age limits, descriptors, and behaviours that combine to form the social construction of a 'child'. In one social location, the definer may construct the child to be property of the family and may see children as persons under the age of 10. In another, the child may be viewed as a citizen of the world with universally acknowledged rights. In Canada, the social construction of 'child' continues to evolve as our understanding of the definition, boundaries, and dimensions of childhood changes.

The social location of the definer reflects the socio-political constructs of the time. In a period of pioneering and settlement, a child is a valuable property who can work in the fields, cook, and clean. In more affluent times, a child is a cherished accessory to be cosseted, trained, and valued for 'refined' accomplishments. In this chapter, we will trace the social construction of the child through a century and a half of Canadian life. This history is not a comprehensive account of childhood and children, which is the subject of many books listed in the references (Hulbert, 2003; Janovicek and Parr, 2003; Kail and Zolner, 2005; Stearns, 2006). Instead, this brief review deconstructs the social construction of children in each period to uncover socio-political underpinnings, boundaries, and dimensions.

During the first 50 years of this period (1850–1900), the Canadian child was positioned as valuable property. Families were large, infant mortality rates were high, and every hand in the family was needed for survival. In the next half–century or so (1900–1950s), the child was positioned as vulnerable and needing moral correction, training, and education. From the 1960s onwards, the child was positioned as who fails to thrive, or the child with a disability gets less attention and less sustenance than the child who can contribute to the family pot. In times of affluence, on the other hand, children are better appreciated and cherished. The child in both cases has the same personal qualities, but the social construction of the child characterizes the child in tough times as inessential (another mouth to feed) or in easier times as essential (warm, cuddly, and part of the family).

The meaning, social significance, and experience of childhood also vary among generations and among cultures and belief systems. A mother's childhood may have been quite different from the childhood that her own child experiences; for example, a street child in Ecuador (in this instance, the mom) will have experienced a very different childhood from that of her child raised in Canada in an affluent neighbourhood. Children and families are shaped by the culture in which they are situated and, at the same time, they reproduce that culture through the way they operate and behave in their daily lives.

The social construction of the concept of childhood is controlled and sustained by adults, who position themselves as socially, politically, and economically superior to children. Adults decide which persons are to be categorized as children, and how these persons are to be described. After all, children do not vote or pay taxes or hold positions of political power. They are dependent on the actions of parents, guardians, or the state acting in the place of a legal guardian, and they usually are described, therefore, as vulnerable, dependent, and helpless. This description also validates the positioning of children as recipients of adult care even after they are well beyond their early infant years.

Adult power is reinforced when the child is described as irresponsible—or even as playful or fanciful. When a child is asked to tell a story or to offer an opinion, adults often automatically filter the content or dismiss it completely in their official reports. When a child testifies in court, this testimony usually is questioned solely on the basis that the person offering it is a child. As James and Jenks (1996: 329) comment: 'Children's words may continue to be viewed with suspicion or indifference by an adult, as in cases of child sexual abuse where age, rather than experience, may still often be deemed the more important indicator of a child's ability to tell, or even to know, the truth.'

Perhaps the most damaging descriptor applied to children, and the one that permeates most of the early childhood literature, is 'developing'. Children are socially constructed as incomplete persons who will be complete only when they have achieved adulthood. They are seen as 'human becomings' (Garrett, 2003: 26) rather than as human beings. This perceived quality of incompletion is considered a deficit, a negative. In fact, many of the adjectives used to describe childhood and children—'innocent', 'ignorant', 'incompetent', 'vulnerable'—have negative connotations. Innocence suggests naiveté; ignorance, a lack of knowledge; incompetence, a lack of ability; and vulnerability, powerlessness. The 'science' of child development taught in colleges and universities maintains that healthy development results in a child's becoming a responsible adult. Unhealthy development, on the other hand, may result in a child remaining a child, which is presented as a decidedly inferior position.

In this state of incompletion and learned helplessness, children may be deprived of their rights (see Chapter 1); and of taking responsibility for their actions. They may be offered choices about clothing and food—whether to wear the blue or green shirt or to eat one sandwich or two—but they are prevented from contributing to major decisions about housing, education, health, family structure, or home location. Children are positioned as needing competent and knowledgeable adults to speak for them, to protect them, and to make decisions 'in their best interests'. These knowledgeable adults typically are a child's parents or the state acting (through teachers, daycare workers, social workers, legal representatives, counsellors, and so on) in the role of the parents (**in loco parentis**). Adults decide what children should do at given times: what they should eat, how they should play, with whom they must live. Adults hold this power or responsibility because they are older and perhaps wiser and also because they have been socially constructed as competent.

Even very young children are quick to grasp this power differential and to understand the real meaning of 'best interests'. As one young person remarked (Lambe, 2009: 11), 'While there are social workers, foster parents and extended family members who make great efforts to help young people understand that they have been removed from their families "for their own good", they typically feel that they are being punished for the abuse they have suffered. After all, it is not the parents who are removed from everything that is secure and known; it is the young person who must shoulder the burden of loss and family separation.'

The French philosopher Michel Foucault (1977: 140–8) describes the ways in which adults control children through routine. **Routine**, the regularity and rhythm in a child's activities and tasks, is dictated and imposed by adults to suit their own social needs. Children are required to eat, sleep, wash, and excrete at specific and regular times, on the premise that this routine is essential for every child's healthy growth and development. Routine is 'good' for the child. However, this adult-imposed routine confines the child's body and may impede healthy growth, as well as teaching the child to mistrust and disregard the feeling of natural bodily rhythms. Inevitably, routines constrict the child and undermine both self-confidence and the inner sense of limits that provide a foundation for personal responsibility.

Foucault describes how this happens in the child's classroom. School is presented to children as a learning experience. However, Foucault suggests that school is socially constructed by adults as a way for children to learn to obey, accept, and conform to a series of disciplines that reinforce adult power. The child learns at an early age to behave according to rules established by adults in school, no matter what the rules are or how meaningless and trite they may be. The child may be asked to face the front, put up a hand, and sit up straight; the one who conforms is the one who will be called on, whether or not she has the right answer, and who will be given the teacher's approbation. The message given to all of the children is: what is to be learned (i.e., the math lesson) is less important than the child's obedience and submission to adult power. As Jenks (2005: 81) notes, 'The whole premise of adult interaction with the child, even often in pleasure, is control and instruction. All conditions combine and conspire to that end'.

Those children who do not conform to adults' rules—and who thus fail to fulfill the role socially prescribed for them—are punished and labelled as non-children. Children who run away from home, for example, are called 'street youth' even at 11 or 12 years of age. Children who injure other family members are called 'delinquents' or 'young offenders'; others are labelled 'brats', 'deviants', 'monsters', and 'not children at all'. Such was the case with the two 10-year-olds in the United Kingdom who murdered Jamie Bulger,

Photo 2.1 Michel Foucault (1926–1984).

a toddler, in 1993. These children were vilified and their parents denounced in court and by the media. The boys were described in court as 'monsters', and their act seen as 'incomprehensible' by a society nurtured on the idea of a fairytale version of childhood. These boys, like the street youth and the delinquents, were impacted by family poverty, lack of community support, inadequate and inaccessible schooling, a culture of violence, and isolation. When they missed school their absence was barely noticed. When they roamed shopping centres their presence was unwelcome. When they returned to their neighbourhood they were met with poverty and family violence. As Jenks (2005: 121) remarks: 'Not only did the Bulger murder give rise to a broad public debate about the nature of childhood, but it may also have depotentiated the ideological role which childhood has traditionally played in public perceptions of children.'

When children act as persons—demonstrating that they have the power to make decisions and act independently—they challenge the prevailing social construction of childhood. Twelve-year-old Jasmine Richardson did this in 2006 in Medicine Hat, Alberta, when she helped her 23-year-old boyfriend to murder her parents, Marc and Debra, and her brother Jacob. Tried under the Youth Criminal Justice Act as a youth instead of as a child, she was convicted, and much was made of her relationship with her boyfriend and her sexual activities, both of which put her outside the fairytale version of childhood. Jasmine was described in the press as 'depraved' and 'a monster', but never as 'a child' or 'a little girl' despite her young age and diminutive size. As with so many of her predecessors, Jasmine was impacted by a community in which she had no place. She embraced a Goth culture that isolated her from her Medicine Hat classmates, and chose a much older boyfriend and an internet community, both of which further contributed to her social isolation.

Kelly and Totten (2002) argue that children who commit such assaults are categorized as 'youth' and tried under the Youth Criminal Justice Act because they do not fit

Group Exercises 2.1

Meeting the Child

The brief visual and auditory experience of this large-group exercise demonstrates how the position of children as vulnerable and helpless is socially constructed.

The exercise begins with one volunteer who sits in front of the group and takes on the persona of the child. The group members are asked to print on a sticky note the first word that comes to their minds when they think of a child. The group members then affix their notes to the volunteer while saying their words. This part of the exercise should be done quickly to avoid group members' searching for politically correct phrases or words. Some words, such as 'innocent', 'young', 'helpless', 'vulnerable', and 'cute' will be repeated. When all the words are said, the volunteer should be covered with sticky notes.

The group leader then asks the volunteer how it feels to be described in this way. The volunteer may remark on how demeaning this exercise feels, and how the repetition of particular labels is hurtful. The leader then thanks the volunteer, perhaps patting his or her head or hair. The volunteer may spontaneously react to this; if not, the leader asks the volunteer how it feels to be touched this way by a stranger. This leads to a discussion of why children's personal space often is invaded by adults. The discussion can be enlarged to include social construction; the repetition of words (labels) is part of this social construction, as people begin to associate these words with children. The group members may want to repeat this exercise to deconstruct the labels. This time, the participants may choose to use only strengths-based words to describe a child. The exercise is repeated, with the volunteer being asked to compare experiences of being labelled 'helpless' versus being labelled 'strong'. During the deconstruction, the group leader does not touch the volunteer or invade the volunteer's personal space. Instead, the volunteer is respected as a person with the right to space and dignity.

our social construction of children. Their acts are planned and deliberate, showing that they are powerful persons who can act independently without the direction and control of adults; in short, they are human beings rather than 'human becomings'. Schissel (2006: 13) goes further in describing Canada today as a child-hating country. When children act independently as persons, he notes, they are moved to another category (youth), or simply described as monsters and aberrations. Omar Khadr knows this. His non-conforming actions as a child soldier led him to lose his Convention rights and, instead, to be incarcerated in a brutal US-run adult prison at Guantanamo Bay, Cuba, in 2001. Only 15 years old, deprived of family and of any children his own age—deprived of a trial, in fact—this Canadian child was left outside of Canadian society and, at the time of writing still lives in an adult prison.

Photo 2.2 Newspaper stories suggest that this 12-year-old is not a child at all.

The social construction of childhood positions children as passive victims of abuse or as wide-eyed innocents who dream of being adopted. As Fewster (2002: 18) argues, 'By definition, childhood is a diminished state—interesting only as a preparation for adulthood but not to be taken seriously.' However, the reality is that children are not property to be protected, admired, or warehoused by adults. They are not inherently sweet, innocent, or playful, but are persons with a full range of emotions who can act independently—including ways that are not expected and sanctioned by society. Children are not lesser, incomplete entities that are in the process of developing into the 'better' and complete state of adulthood; they are growing persons who have voices, intellects, and opinions that need to be heard.

The Marginalized Child

Histories of Canadian childhood (e.g., Janovicek and Parr, 2003) contrast the stories of mainstream children with those of children marginalized by the socio-political constructs of race, ability, language, class, culture, and ethnicity. These childhoods have been, and continue to be, very different from the mainstream. Marginalized children have confronted bias and stereotyping from infancy, and often are perceived stereotypically as representatives of a group rather than as unique individuals or children. Their stories have only begun to be heard, but they help us to understand the difference that marginalization makes in the social construction, and the lived experience, of childhood.

In the late nineteenth century and through much of the twentieth century, while most mainstream Canadian children were dealing with discipline and work at an early age, their First Nations peers in northern and western Canada often were worse off—being forcibly taken away from their families and placed in orphanages and residential schools. Their birth names were replaced with numbers or English names, and their home clothing was replaced by uniforms (Sinclair, 2009). Slowly, through imposed changes in name,

Photo 2.3 Omar Khadr at age 14.

hair and clothing style, language, and religion, these children experienced **deculturation**, the process of having one's culture systematically devalued and stripped away (see Chapter 5). Some children died in the process, often by suicide; others escaped, only to be rounded up again and punished (Schissel and Wotherspoon, 2003; Davis, 2009). Every one of the remaining survivors carries memories of this dehumanizing experience. Despite this well-known history and the modern understanding of it, however, more First Nations children are in state care today than at the height of the residential schools era (Blackstock, 2008). In British Columbia in 2006, for example, over half of the children in foster care were First Nations children (Bennett and Sadrehashemi, 2008: 5).

Even more severely marginalized were the children of First Nations mothers and white trader fathers, as they were made to feel that they belonged to neither culture. Girls often were indulged by their white trader fathers; but boys tended to be shunned by them and described as 'wild as an Indian'. The mothers, whether married to the trader fathers or not, occupied a tenuous and usually inferior social position, their loyalties divided between their partners and their children, each of a separate culture. The children, too, held divided loyalties, and had difficulty fully identifying with either of the cultures that infused them. As Pollard (2003: 65) remarks, 'Métis offspring of the traders challenged the dominant culture and often consciously chose to reject white society in favour of perpetuating a [distinct] cultural identity which they retain to this day.' This cultural identity, however, still causes them to be denied some of the government services available to First Nations children, and to be equally excluded from programs for mainstream children.

Point to Consider   2.1

Auton v. British Columbia

Connor Auton, a British Columbia toddler, was diagnosed with autism in 2000. His parents were surprised to find out that their son's applied behavioural analysis (ABA) and intensive behavioural intervention (IBI) therapies, while recognized as valid and reliable health care for autism, were not funded by the government. So they, along with several other parents, brought a class action suit against the government of British Columbia. Their suit was impacted by many layers of often conflicting legislation, including the Canada Health Act, the Constitutional Act, the Medical and Health Care Services Regulation (BC), the Interpretation Act (BC), and the Medicare Protection Act (BC).

The British Columbia Supreme Court agreed that early intensive intervention using ABA/IBI therapy was essential to Connor's health and well-being, and cited the Convention on the Rights of the Child in their decision. Articles 23 and 28 of the Convention specify children's right to health care and educational services that provide appropriate supports for children with special needs. However, this ruling was overturned by the Supreme Court of Canada because the therapies were not considered 'core service' provided by 'health care practitioners'. Despite the negative impact of the ruling on Connor and other children with autism, it did affirm that children have the same health care rights as adults. This equalization of status, at the same time, positions children as needing to have money in order to pay for health care needs such as ABA/IBI, dental work, eye care, and so on. Because labour laws do not allow children to work to earn money (and children in any case cannot enter the workforce as it is constructed), such a ruling once again forces children to be completely dependent on adults for health care.

As Canadian immigration expanded to include people from all parts of the world, children of particular non-European backgrounds also were ostracized and marginalized. In British Columbia, Chinese-Canadian families provided labour, taxes, and service, but their children were shunned in the school system (Janovicek and Parr, 2003). Despite their being second-generation Canadians, they were called 'Orientals' and categorized as inferior. Stanley (2003: 126) notes, 'In British Columbia, white supremacy was often expressed in the notion that B.C. was, and should be, a white man's country.' These beliefs were put into action in 1922, when the Victoria School Board forcibly removed Chinese-Canadian children from their classes and marched them to Chinese-only schools.

If race, ethnicity, and language were barriers for children in late nineteenth- and early twentieth-century Canada, so was class. The children of lone mothers and of the poor were marginalized by mainstream society and socially constructed as morally tainted. In a society dominated by conservative, intolerant mores, a child born to a lone mother was labelled a 'bastard'—a product of sin who was undeserving of title rights or of inheritance rights. Poverty was viewed also as resulting from sinful acts, and the poor were depicted as lazy, drunken layabouts. Their children were perceived as products of sin—as the undeserving poor destined to survive or not as determined by mainstream society. Such social reformers as Helen Gregory MacGill and Emily Murphy (of the Famous Five[1]) linked illegitimate babies to mentally unfit mothers and advocated for the forcible sterilization of women deemed 'mentally defective'.

Then, there were the children marginalized on the basis of ability. Until very recently, children with developmental disabilities were either institutionalized or home-schooled instead of being integrated into the mainstream educational system, under the assumption that their disability was contagious. Owen (2008: 165) describes this institutionalization of children: 'They were subjected to medical experimentation, substandard living conditions, and, involuntarily, sterilization. They were also over-medicated and victimized through abuse, neglect, or cruel and unusual punishment.' Similarly, children with visual, ambulatory, hearing, or learning needs were encouraged to attend special schools and institutions, usually located in rural areas far away from their home cities. Owen and colleagues (2008: 163) describe this situation as ongoing to the present day: 'The rights of children . . . with . . . disabilities to live in their family homes, to have access to education or educational support systems, and in some cases to life-saving medical treatment remain issues of controversy.'

Children marginalized on the basis of race, ethnicity, culture, class, or ability nevertheless are aware of the experiences of children in mainstream society. They watch and wonder at the inequality of their treatment. They may try to fit in with the mainstream by hiding their ethnicity, language, or disability. They may protest—only to be punished in an adult detention facility. They may seethe with silent anger throughout their childhood years. Each of these potential reactions is unique to the child and the child's social location. That such behaviour is a reaction to marginalization needs to be acknowledged and understood before we begin to work with a child on the margins.

The Economically Valuable Child (1850–1900)

In nineteenth-century Canada, when childbirth was difficult and infant mortality rates were high (one out of five children died before the age of one), very young children were socially constructed as dispensable (Knapp, 1998: 318). This construction enabled mothers to accept the continual loss of their babies. Those children who did survive their first five precarious years were considered economically valuable and were put to work in the family and sometimes in the community. Work, rather than school, was regarded as the best education for children at the time. In 1850, Ryerson noted that there were 'nearly one hundred thousand children of school age in Upper Canada not attending any school' (Davey, 2003: 108).

Childhood was viewed both as a time of innocence and as a time of waywardness, and children were thought to be vulnerable to corruption. Chunn (2003: 192) remarks, 'All children were now perceived to be simultaneously innocent and evil; in danger but also dangerous.' Work, it was thought, could cure a multitude of sins, from laziness to delinquency to sexual promiscuity. Children required moral and physical structure and care, which were provided by hard work and by the family. Social order was tied to the traditional family, with father as breadwinner and mother as homemaker, and the parents, especially the father, had property rights over their children.

Those without a family, or those whose parents were unavailable, were expected to get their moral order and guidance solely from work. Under Britain's Poor Law, 80,000 poor British children—some orphans, others separated from their parents—were transported to Canada between 1880 and 1930. They were placed with Canadian families as farm labourers and as domestic servants, forced to toil without pay because it was thought that this work would be an education for them and would redeem them from the sin of their poverty. Poor Canadian children were expected to work, too, and work they did, enduring long hours of toil while their pay was handed directly to their owner-parents. In 1890, 21.5 per cent of the miners in Nova Scotia were boys under the age of 18, some as young as 8 years, and all were involved in back-breaking and isolating labour in the mines. Farmhands in the West were no better off, working from before dawn milking the cows until after dusk, bedding these same animals. Seeding, harvesting, logging, washing, and building: all were children's work on the farm (Janovicek and Parr, 2003).

In the cities, poor children were put to work early and routinely, and their wages were expected to help support the family. It was taken for granted that the child's wages would belong to the parents, just as the child did. There were not many factory jobs for children, but girls found jobs in domestic service, and boys found jobs as messengers and newspaper sellers (Janovicek and Parr, 2003). Baker (2007: 76) comments: 'As soon as working-class children were old enough, they were expected to contribute to the family economy in some way, first helping around the house and garden and later contributing their labour or wages to support the household. . . . In other words, childhood . . . was not much different from adult life in nineteenth-century low-income families.'

In Owen's perspective, children who could not work were just another mouth to feed. Those who were seen as 'retarded' or disabled, and who were therefore unable to engage in conventional forms of work, were put to work in freak shows, orphanages, and houses of prostitution. Every child was required to have an economic value, and those who did not were allowed to quietly slip away or starve (Owen, 2008: 166).

The Vulnerable Child (1900–1950s)

These attitudes towards children remained prevalent into the twentieth century, and some hold attitudes about the evil in children today. However, the socio-political changes at the end of the 1800s were significant and impacted or changed the social

Photo 2.4 Nineteenth-century line drawing of young children working in the mines.

construction of children. Canada had become a country in 1867, and between 1898 and 1914 the Canadian economy boomed as never before. Many Canadian families moved from farms to cities where there were jobs that paid well in the steel and iron industry, manufacturing, banking, and other services. In 1881, the numbers of persons employed in agricultural and non-agricultural pursuits were almost equal. By 1911, the number of persons employed in non-agricultural pursuits was double the number in agricultural pursuits (Statistics Canada, 2009).

This economic and geographic shift had two effects on the social construction of children. The first was that the harsh treatment of children was more visible. Strangers now saw the cruelties inflicted on children that previously were kept within the circle of the family. Children living and starving on city streets were re-labelled as street urchins, but this did not end the scrutiny; some Canadians began to question the appalling conditions in which some children lived.

The second effect was a direct reaction to the new urban economy. Children who could handle small motor parts and detail work were competitors for jobs; they were cheaper to employ and less apt to complain, and so seemed a good bet for employers. However, children soon would be edged out of a labour market that was bursting with new immigrants to Canada. Through a slight shift in their social positioning, children could continue to be constructed as valuable to the family, while they were expected to do daily family chores (housekeeping, child care, cooking, laundry, gardening). However, their work outside the home could be replaced by compulsory schooling and instruction. This first was positioned as a means of protecting them from the immorality, sin, and dissolute behaviour to which they were vulnerable; then, as training along the industrial model for the assembly lines they were expected to service.

Educational reformers spearheaded campaigns to prevent very young children from working, to implement sex-specific schooling for girls and boys, and to regulate the leisure activities of youth. This social construction of the vulnerable child kept the highly paid urban job market in the hands of adults and successfully created jobs for teachers, principals, and school inspectors. This new industry of educators was honed in just a few decades.

In 1900, the average daily attendance rate (among those enrolled in school) for the whole of Canada was 61 per cent. Moreover, most children stayed in school for only a few years, leaving at age 9 or 10 when they were needed to work at home. Education was administered locally, and compulsory education acts varied from coast to coast. In 1921, in Ontario, the Adolescent School Attendance Act increased the age of compulsory school attendance to 16 in urban areas (with some exceptions). This change reflected the strength of the economy and of the education movement as much as the strength of the social construction of the child as vulnerable and needing guidance.

Compulsory education for children increasingly was accepted by most families who saw that literacy could be a ticket to the well-paid urban jobs. If their children had these jobs, they might also help out the family as the parents aged. Improved levels of hygiene in hospitals led to lower infant mortality rates, and mothers began to vest more care and affection in their infants. Stearns (2006: 56) notes: 'With fewer children overall and with each young child far less likely to die, emotional investment in the individual child rose.' Lucy Maud Montgomery's famous Anne books illustrate this social shift. Anne Shirley, a plucky Canadian heroine for children in *Anne of Green Gables* (1908), later relinquishes her dreams of being a writer and leaves her post of principal at Summerside High School for the higher dream of being a mother with her 'prince', Gilbert Blythe, beside her. Her motherhood is not seen as a relinquishment of dreams but rather as the high point of her life. When Anne's second child is born, she tells Marilla, 'The best dream of all has come true' (245). In the early twentieth century, motherhood was constructed as more fulfilling than any career, and the child was positioned as vulnerable and at risk of going astray without maternal care and moral guidance.

Late nineteenth- and early twentieth-century psychologists and psychiatrists such as G. Stanley Hall, William Healy, John Watson, and Sigmund Freud warned that maternal neglect could cause terrible damage to the child. By the 1940s, Dr Benjamin Spock and others were encouraging mothers to become more involved in their children's lives, so as to better guide and educate their children. Dr Spock's message of maternal involvement in their children's lives was echoed in Dr Ernest Couture's *The Canadian Mother and Child*, first published by the Canadian Minister of Health and Welfare in 1940, and reprinted nine times up to 1991. The message was clear: there were no bad children, only bad mothers.

This construction of the mother's role and the child's vulnerability was given credence by attachment theorists such as John Bowlby and Konrad Lorenz (see Chapter

4), whose research indicated that early bonding or attachment with the mother was the basis for a child's health and emotional wellness. A child with a healthy attachment had a chance to succeed; a child who missed out on such bonding was said to suffer 'attachment injury' and to be less likely to succeed. The child was thus positioned as vulnerable and needing the secure attachment to a nurturing mother, either a birth mother or an adoptive one.

Socio-political events reinforced attachment theory and the message conveyed by *The Canadian Mother and Child*. Soldiers returning from World War II took the jobs women had held during the war and this was seen as only right, considering the soldiers' sacrifices overseas. Daycares that had flourished during the war years were closed, and new government family allowances offered a further financial incentive (albeit small) for mothers to stay home and do the child-rearing. Attachment theorists, politicians, and economists were united on this front: children belonged at home in the nurturing arms of their mothers.

Marriage rates rose, the average age of first marriage and first birth became lower, and family size increased. Mothers were encouraged to become involved in the 'scientific management' of their vulnerable children. *The Canadian Mother and Child* advised: 'The first principle to bear in mind in training children in good habits is regularity. This applies, as you already know, to the matter of sleep, feeding, cleanliness, and also to correct toilet habits' (166). This regularity or routine, said to be for the child's well-being, allowed the mother to plan her day: early toilet training meant less diaper washing; regular naps meant free time to sort laundry and clean the house; and solitary play let mother continue to do her housework without having to play with her child. Then, as now, research studies of children often served adult purposes first.

The Child as Social Capital (1960s to the present)

In the first half of the twentieth century, traditional Christian morality dominated family life and government, and politicians used this morality to justify their laws, their tax increases, and their treatment of the poor. This shared and widely understood morality was the glue that kept the construction of the vulnerable child together. The post-war child of the 1950s was still seen as morally vulnerable, liable to fall into evil ways, immorality, and poor habits without the nurturance and guidance of a mother. In the 1960s, this glue began to lose its strength, and this social construction came unstuck.

The 1960s were a time of unprecedented numbers of teenagers (the baby boom), and of prosperity, social revolution, political protest, and experimentation with drugs and sex. Many mothers at home had begun to question the role of full-time parent, and to want the consumer goods that two income earners could afford. At the same time, a burgeoning market economy enabled full participation by these baby boomers, both men and women. There were more opportunities for women in the workplace, and Bonnie Fox (2001: 163) traces women's response to these jobs and changing roles. She

a switch from separation to inclusion: 'The fact of the matter is no medical diagnosis can tell what a child's abilities are to learn' (O'Donnell, 2009). This statement may be a justification of spending cuts or a thoughtful re-direction of educational funding. However, it is clear that the emphasis remains on the child as social capital, an investment with dividends.

To further prepare children for their participation in a capitalist, free-market economy, they were groomed simultaneously as consumers. As Stearns (2006: 128) notes, 'At some point in the later twentieth century, parents in most places began to believe that providing goods and good times for their children was a vital part of their role, and they experienced real guilt when their capacity seemed inadequate.' As children received more, they craved more, encouraged by television and other media advertising, and this craving was given structural support with lists of 'essential' sports equipment, 'essential' school supplies, and buying seasons such as 'Back to School Days'. In a country in which 20 per cent of children lived below the poverty line, the answer from charities was a toy mountain rather than affordable housing and adequate social assistance.

The child constructed as social capital is a 'six pocketer' who receives cash from the pockets of a minimum of six adults: mom, dad, two grandmas, and two grandpas. The child has financial resources and an acquired taste for consumer products. According to *YTV Tween Report 2008*, Canada's 'tweeners' (8- to 14-year-olds) spent some $2.9 billion of their own discretionary income in 2007, the average child spending $1,154.84 that year in 'throwaway products'. In addition, the report documented the $20 billion 'kidfluence', the influence that the Canadian child had over family purchases that were made by time-stressed and multi-tasking working parents.

Rather than contributing to family income as in earlier days, the contemporary Canadian child drains that income—and the income of taxpayers without children, too. Such costs play a part in the reactions of some adults who have restricted their child-bearing. Canada's birth rate has been in free fall since the baby boom of the 1940s and 1950s, with the 2008 birth rate being 1.58 children per woman, far less than the two children needed to replace two adults.

Lawmakers separate some children from the boundaries of childhood into categories called 'youth' or 'adolescence'. These boundaries are historically situated—intended to serve adult interests at a particular time in the economy or social climate—and socially constructed. The construction of these boundaries is explored in the next section.

The Boundaries of Childhood

The construction of the age limits demarcating childhood changed in Canada over the course of the twentieth century. In the nineteenth century, 10-year-olds were considered fully capable of being employed as adults for 12-hour work days outside the home. Today, such participation in the workforce is not expected of a 10-year-old child, although some child actors still work for lengthy periods of time, and labour laws vary across Canada (see Chapter 1).

The constructed age limits that define childhood are not based on biology. On the one hand, they are culturally determined, reflecting the culture of society and the family. On the other hand, they are co-relational, as one age limit for an activity (working, smoking, driving) affects the age limit for a related activity. Being a child allows a person to engage in certain acts and not others. Being a youth rather than a child has similar co-relational effects.

A 'child' is defined variously as a person who is under the age of 6; as a pre-pubescent child, or under the age of 13; or as a not-yet-adult, under the age of 16. Under provincial adoption law in most provinces of Canada, an adopted person (regardless of age) forever remains a 'child' of a parent in not having rights to birth information if their parent forbids disclosure. These different upper age limits, from 6 to 60, affect the child's access to legal rights and social services, to information, and to bridge confidentiality hardly suitable to an adult. These age limits affect the boundaries of the worker–child relationship. When an adult discloses abuse to the worker, the worker listens and counsels. When a child does the same, the worker is bound by law to break confidentiality.

Adults decide on the age parameters of the category of 'child', decisions said to be based on what is best for children. However, it often seems as though the categorizing meets adult needs rather than those of the children. Whether childhood is constructed as ending at age 12, 14, 16, or 18 depends on which construct benefits the adults most. For example, when the labour market is full (as was the case in Ontario and New Brunswick several years ago), mandatory schooling was extended to 18, thereby keeping children out of the competition for jobs. When the need for seasonal farm help is high, as in the Quebec fruit and vegetable market, there is no labour law regarding age, and even the youngest children can work in the fields for pay.

Childhood may begin in utero, as some health professionals suggest; or, it may begin after birth. Age limits at either end of childhood are an outcome of deliberate socio-political and economic decisions that have profound effects on the children within and outside these age limits. Where childhood begins and ends is very important to the issue of the child's social location and experience. Table 2.1 provides an overview of various constructions of the 12-year-old in current Canadian legislation.

Lower Age Limits

Canadian law does not recognize a child as a person until that child is born. From the time of ossification, or bone formation (approximately eight weeks after conception) until birth, the developing prenatal organism is called a fetus rather than a person or a child. The fetal period is marked by continuing, rapid growth of the specialized systems that emerge during the embryonic phase. A one-inch embryo at 8 weeks, the fetus develops to have sex organs by 12 weeks, hair by 16 weeks, eyes by 24 weeks, and so on.

Under the law, decisions during the first nine months of fetal growth are solely the prerogative of the woman carrying the fetus. She decides whether or not to participate

Table 2.1 Constructions of the 12-Year-Old in Canadian Legislation

Criminal Code of Canada, Section 43	May be spanked by a parent or an adult in a position of authority in order to be disciplined or corrected.
Youth Criminal Justice Act	Included in a category called 'youth' with persons up to the age of 17, and can be incarcerated. Can apply to have a lawyer appointed by the court.
Canada Health Act	Can obtain a therapeutic abortion without parental consent.
Child Welfare Acts (provincial and territorial)	Can be removed from the family if seen to be at risk of abuse and/or neglect, but cannot press charges against the alleged abuser.
Social Assistance (provincial and territorial)	Cannot receive social assistance until age 16 unless the child is a parent.
Bill C-2 (Legal age of consent to sexual activity)	Cannot consent to sexual activity until the age of 16.

in prenatal care. She decides how much alcohol and drugs the fetus will consume, whether or not the fetus will be deprived of oxygen in the blood, what stress and risks the fetus will have to manage, and what food the fetus will have. She chooses to use vitamin supplements or not. She chooses to increase or decrease the risks of disability in her fetus. She can also decide whether to remove the fetus through abortion at any stage of fetal growth. She makes all of these decisions for the fetus until birth, when the child becomes a legal person (Chamberlain, 1995).

For the early months during the nine-month gestation period, the woman may be unaware that she is pregnant. If she is aware, she may not be planning to carry the fetus through to birth, or she may not be planning to care for the child after the birth. During her pregnancy, she may be drinking, doing drugs, eating little, and may be under severe physical and emotional stress; she may be alone and without support. This situation, in August 1996, was that of a Winnipeg mother of three when she came to the attention of Winnipeg Child and Family Services. Two of the woman's three previous children had been born permanently disabled and were permanent wards of the crown. Superior Court Judge Perry Schulman ordered her held in residential treatment for her glue sniffing. However, the courts' *parens patriae* jurisdiction (the power to act as a child's parent in order to intervene with an abusive or neglectful parent) was successfully contested on appeal as such intervention would contravene the woman's rights under the Canadian Charter of Rights and Freedoms. As a result, the woman was not detained, and she continued her previous addictions. Her child was born prematurely and was developmentally delayed. As this case demonstrates, the only right recognized by the courts is that of the already born person; courts no longer have *parens patriae* jurisdiction over unborn children.

This legal position on the age at which childhood begins is contradicted by other cultural beliefs and medical practice. The fetus is more photographed and scanned now than ever before in history. Mothers are advised to avoid drugs and alcohol, take folic acid and multi-vitamins, increase calcium intake, listen to classical music, avoid stress, and get regular exercise while carrying the fetus. The woman

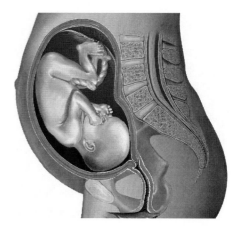

Photo 2.5 Six-month-old fetus.

carrying the fetus is told that her pregnancy term comprises the first nine months of childhood, and that these nine months are critical to the child's development of organs, cognitive and physical skills, and a healthy attachment. The study of fetal learning has become a science, and prenatal stimulation is considered to be a way to enhance the future intelligence of the child.[2]

The contradiction between the social constructions of fetus as active learner and fetus as passive tissue affects the social and legal perceptions of what constitutes the first year of the child's life. Does the year end at 12 months after birth or does it include the 9-month fetal stage and end at 3 months after birth? How this first year is defined may determine whether the mother can be held accountable for prenatal stimulation or the lack of it. Which definition is accepted also determines the point at which the child is considered to become a person under Canadian law, and therefore to have legal rights.

Although the Convention on the Rights of the Child recognizes the child as a person in the first year of life, Canadian law does not. If a child is killed in the first 24 hours of life, the legal term for the act is 'post-natal abortion' or 'neonaticide'. If the child is older than a day but younger than a year, the act is called 'infanticide'. Neonaticide is typically punished with a conditional sentence or probation. Infanticide carries a maximum five-year punishment. The act of killing a person, however, is called 'murder' and carries the much more severe maximum punishment of life imprisonment. Of the 33 child killings in Canada in 2003, almost half (42 per cent) were considered to be either neonaticide or infanticide. It would seem that children in their first year of life are deemed expendable, despite current cultural beliefs, medical practice, and the Convention on the Rights of the Child.

Parents who adopt a child accept the child's genetic background, type and amount of prenatal care, and experiences in early development, and must conform to adoption agency standards of parenting until the adoption probation period is over. Once this period ends, the adoptive parent is free to withhold birth family and medical information from the child. The parent may also deny the child information about the adoption itself. Even though the child is not the adoptive parent's child genetically, the new parent is encouraged by adoption workers to develop a sense of entitlement or ownership over the child.

The terminology of entitlement and ownership used in the adoption process is a throwback to the time when the child was the family property: the valuable Canadian child of the nineteenth century. Currently, a child arrives in an adoptive family without legal birth ties and, when there are ties, these are maintained or severed according to the adoptive parent's preferences. As Dickerson and Allen (2006: 10) note, adoptive parents are advised to 'weigh the responsibility you feel to protect the child from the birth parents with the risks to your relationship if you do not. If you do not know the identity of the child's birth parents, you must decide whether to assist the child in any efforts to locate them.' The actions of both adoptive parents and birth parents—and the experiences of their children—are affected by what the parents perceive to be the age at which a child becomes a person. The birth mother who neglects her infant and is put on probation when her eight-month-old dies may have regarded her daughter as a neonate rather than as a person. The adoptive parent who sees the eight-month-old as starting life on the day of her adoption may decide to withhold information about the previous eight months, and the child may never know when and how her life as a person actually began.

Upper Age Limits

Just as the argument over the beginning of childhood has continued over the years, so the debate over the upper limit of childhood persists. Some workers, legislators, counsellors, and judges hold that childhood ends at puberty, which is perceived to happen at a younger age in Canada—once 13, it is now considered to be 12 (Steingraber, 2007). Other adults, primarily parents and educators, tend to believe that childhood ends when public schooling does; they mark the occasion by holding graduation ceremonies and by giving keys to the house and assigning additional responsibilities to the young persons in their care. The age considered to be the upper limit of childhood is important as it relates to the legal rights of children. Because the rights outlined in the Convention on the Rights of the Child extend to age 18, denying a person these rights when that person is 12, 14, or 16 denies that person the full legal protection to which she or he is entitled as a child.

Some legal experts contend that children should be held accountable for their crimes, even when they are younger than 12 years of age. Relatives of persons who have been murdered by young children in Canada and elsewhere usually support this call for culpability. In contrast, others argue that the constructed stage of childhood should be extended, and that, for instance, children should be required to attend school beyond age 16. Add to the discussion the voices of youth calling for more rights and ownership,[3] and the controversy increases.

The age of majority in Canada is either 18 or 19, depending on the province. In Alberta, Saskatchewan, Manitoba, Ontario, Quebec, and Prince Edward Island, the age

Table 2.2 Legal Rights of a 16-Year-Old in Ontario

Area of daily life	Has the right to . . .	Does not have the right to . . .
Health	Smoke cigarettes in public places	Buy a package of cigarettes until age 19
Education	Leave school in all other provinces and territories, except New Brunswick	Leave school until age 18
Social	Marry with parents' consent; leave home without parents' consent	Marry without parental consent; work during school hours
Finance	Apply for and receive Social Assistance as a single parent or under special circumstances only. In both cases, social assistance is paid to a trustee through Ontario Works, and is not paid directly to the 16-year-old.	Work full-time (compulsory schooling until age 18); get financial assistance or temporary residence in a foster home from child welfare; be admitted to many municipal homeless shelters until age 18
Civil rights	Apply for information under the Freedom of Information Act	Get birth information until age 18 if adopted or in state care; vote until age 18

is 18; in BC, Nova Scotia, Newfoundland and Labrador, Prince Edward Island, New Brunswick, the Northwest Territories, and Nunavut, it is 19. However, each province and territory has its own definition of the age range comprising childhood, and separate legislation and ministries to govern the welfare of children. Some provinces deem a person under the age of 16 to be a child; others stipulate that a child is any person under the age of 21. In some provinces, children are provided with legal counsel, while in others their wishes are represented by adults, usually workers in the child welfare system. Although a child is entitled to a personal advocate or lawyer when parents divorce, relatively few children in Canada make use of this resource, partly because the federal, provincial, and territorial advocates for children work at arm's length from the children they serve, and partly because few children are informed by their parents' lawyers that this free legal resource exists for them. Currently, no legislation compels lawyers to give children of divorcing parents the information that they can request counsel (Brownstone, 2009).

Even within a particular province or territory, a child's legal status is complex. Table 2.2 sets out the contradictions in the legal status of a 16-year-old in Ontario.

Although the age of majority in Canada is clearly set at either 18 or 19, the extent of parental duties towards children between the ages of 16 and 19 remains uncertain due to inconsistencies in federal and provincial legislation. In Ontario, for example, a child under the care of parents still defers to parental decisions until age 16, and a child in foster care defers to the legal guardianship of the state until age 16, when he or she legally can leave the foster care system. At the same time, however, Canadian federal law requires parents (or the state in the role of the parents) to provide for their children until they are 19 years of age. A child of 16 may leave home contrary to parental wishes, but the parent may still be liable for that child's living costs and accrued debts (Cottrell, 2003: 4).

A further complication is that introduced by the Youth Criminal Justice Act (YCJA), which removes children aged 12 and older from the category of 'children'. However, Section 61 of the YCJA permits each province and territory to set an age at which young persons between ages 14 and 16 can be sentenced as adults for specific crimes. In one province, a 14-year-old is tried under the YCJA; in another, the same child faces an adult hearing and adult sentencing. This type of discrimination on the basis of age is specifically forbidden by the Convention on the Rights of the Child, the internationally binding law that stipulates that all persons under age 18, in *all* nations of the world, are children.

Summary

This chapter positions the Canadian child in a historical context. One social construction of the child has evolved into the next, up to the current Canadian construction of the child as a social investment. Although most children are viewed this way today, children who are new to Canada (immigrants and refugees), children with different abilities, children who live in reserves and rural areas, and children who live in poverty, all are treated as deficits; they are marginalized and largely forgotten in the language of investment.

Also discussed in this chapter are the age limits of childhood—specifically how variations in legally specified age limits affect the child's access to certain activities, placements, rights, and resources. Now that we are familiar with the ways in which the various constructions of the period of childhood affect the child's social location, we will examine how child development is socially constructed.

Review Questions

1. What is social construction, and how and when does it typically begin?
2. Describe how the category of 'adolescence' came to be used, and what effects children experience as a result of being included within this category. Is there a difference between adolescence and youth? Explain.
3. What does the phrase 'human becomings' mean, and how does this concept affect everyday life for children?
4. How do children learn to be helpless? What are the structural determinants for this learning process?

5. Name five groups of Canadian children who are marginalized, and explain the impact this marginalization has made on their lives.
6. How did government encourage women to rejoin the workplace in the 1960s and leave the care of their children to others?
7. What are the cultural factors influencing the social construction of when childhood begins and ends?
8. How would you differentiate among neonaticide, infanticide, and murder?
9. How does the Youth Criminal Justice Act affect the social construction of the upper limit of childhood?
10. Describe how legal positioning of a 16-year-old in Ontario can be confusing, and give three concrete examples of this legal confusion.

Discussion Questions

1. Deculturation of some children happened in the past in Canada. Explain why or why not this still happens in Canada, giving examples to support your explanation.
2. What do you think the lower and upper age limits of childhood should be in Canada? How does your personal culture (family, ethnicity, spirituality, value system) influence your understanding of these age limits?
3. How do you feel about the 1996 case of the pregnant Winnipeg mother being held in custody because of her addictive behaviour while pregnant? Should the state be afforded this kind of authority? Discuss.

Chapter 3

Developmentally Appropriate Practice

I'll bet that boy's father wishes he had a little girl who fingerpainted and wiped her hands on the cat when she was little and who once cut her own hair so she would be bald like her uncle and who then grew up to be seven years old and crowned herself with burrs. Not every father is lucky enough to have a daughter like that.

—Beverly Cleary, *Ramona and Her Father*

In the passage above, the seven-year-old speaker, Ramona, clearly knows who she is, even within the context of a society infused with a gender construction that places girls in curls and dresses rather than burrs and pants. Many of the children with whom we work do not have Ramona's high self-esteem and sense of gender equality. They have been impacted by a developmental perspective that prescribes what they can achieve at each age and stage, and a gender construction that is equally limiting. The developmental perspective imbues childhood with a mechanical predictability: at age two, the child does this; at age five, the child does that. At the same time, the developmental perspective prompts workers to provide certain play opportunities at certain ages, and to take advantage of critical learning opportunities: time-sensitive periods for acquiring competencies. In this chapter, we will explore the developmental perspective, its meaning and its strengths, and we will also explore its impact on the social construction of childhood.

Developmentally appropriate practice is the provision of structural and strengths-based supports that meet both the individual and developmental needs of the child. This practice is based on close observation of the child's culture, interests, social location, and overall **development**. The worker needs to first consider the two dimensions of developmentally appropriate practice. One of these is age appropriateness, which refers to an awareness of the general and predictable sequences of development that occur in the physical, emotional, social, and cognitive domains. Knowing this typical developmental sequence helps workers listen to the child effectively, understand the child's play, and plan developmentally appropriate interventions. A second dimension is individual appropriateness, which is grounded in the recognition that each child experiences a unique timing of growth and changes, and has an individual culture, temperament, ability, learning style, and family. These individual differences require an individually directed and unique response from the worker. Individual differences are why child-initiated and child-directed interventions are both developmentally appropriate and in the interests of the child: they match the unique needs of an individual child at a particular time.

Understanding child development entails understanding the child's structural needs and critical learning periods, as well as recognizing the strengths and abilities of the particular child at each age and developmental stage. Structural and strengths-based assessment acknowledges that developmental stages are guiding markers only, not strict *requirements*, and that each stage is complete in itself rather than a step on the way to a later stage. When critical learning periods are undermined or when milestones have not been reached, appropriate structural and strengths-based interventions may be needed so that the child can achieve optimal well-being. These interventions, designed to meet the individual and age needs of the child, necessitate a revision of traditionally defined developmentally appropriate practice that was informed only by the developmental perspective.

We begin this chapter with a critique of the developmental perspective on the child. A cornerstone of this developmental perspective is the concept that there are three **domains** or aspects of the child to take into account: the physical, the cognitive, and the socio-emotional. In this chapter, we introduce a fourth domain of spirituality from Medicine Wheel teachings. This fourth domain balances the child's other three domains, infusing them with a necessary spirituality or connectedness with one another. This fourth domain also informs our understanding of the child as a whole person who has equally important physical, cognitive, socio-emotional, and spiritual domains.

All four domains include critical learning periods, opportunities for the child to either feel strength and success or experience powerlessness and failure. In these learning periods, the child also internalizes the prevalent gender construction with all of its implications for sexual orientation and gender roles. At these times, the worker who understands whole child development, critical learning periods, and social construction can support the child's healthy development in all domains. The worker who follows the developmental perspective, on the other hand, may impede or damage whole child development and certainly will not understand Ramona's observation that 'Not every father is lucky enough to have a daughter like that.'

Objectives

By the end of this chapter, you will:

- Understand the impact of the developmental perspective on both children and the adults who work with children.
- Identify developmental milestones and critical learning periods, and what children need at each critical learning period, particularly as they understand their own gender and their own sexual orientation.
- Demonstrate your understanding of developmentally appropriate practice.

The Developmental Perspective

The **developmental perspective** on the child views the child as evolving or developing in a natural, orderly progression (in stages). This perspective maintains that particular milestones need to be reached before the child can move from one stage to the next. The perspective was initiated by naturalist and evolutionist Charles Darwin, who based his study *Biographical Sketch of the Infant* (1877) on the daily logs he kept during the infancy period of his firstborn child, William. In these logs, Darwin recorded William's reflexes, first movements, and reactions. He positioned his son as somewhere between a person and an animal, thus advancing his evolutionary theory that people and animals had a common ancestor. From this particular example of one infant, Darwin generalized to all, hypothesizing that child development was linear and evolutionary.

This positioning of the child as an object to be studied allowed Darwin to ignore William's cries in order to record his stamina and vocalizations. He perceived his son as *developing into* a person rather than living as a person. William would become a person later,

Photo 3.1 Charles Darwin (1809–1882).

once he was fully developed, and then his cries (and words) could be listened to and considered. Darwin's thinking about infants was not dissimilar to that of most parents of his time, who likened infants to little bunnies, chicks, and kittens. Infants were objects of study rather than subjects, and their growth and survival were precarious. A high infant mortality rate was a fact of life in the late nineteenth century (see Chapter 2).

Evolutionists continued to hypothesize that evolution or development was an organizing principle for childhood, and that all children developed in stages, each stage building upon the previous one. Darwin (1809–1882) studied his son William; Sigmund Freud (1856–1939), his daughter Anna; and Jean Piaget (1896–1980), his daughter Lucienne: each theorist was a father, and each observed his own child in order to generalize about all children,

G. Stanley Hall (1846–1924), considered to be the first developmental psychologist, was one of the first professionals to study children in a laboratory. Alfred Binet (1857–1911) and Theodore Simon (1873–1961) used a similar laboratory setting to develop cognitive skill tests that defined and bracketed developmental stages. Arnold Gessell (1880–1961) further supported the developmental perspective through several longitudinal studies that compared age-related differences in socio-emotional, cognitive, and motor skills among children.

Lawrence Kohlberg (1927–87) used only males to test his theory of a six-stage, three-level, developmental sequence of morality. At Kohlberg's pre-conventional level, physical consequences determine what is good or bad: the child avoids what is 'bad' because of the punishment factor (fear of being punished). This is a learning stage

Note From the Field   3.1

Being Bad

The worker in the Head Start nursery school becomes increasingly frustrated by the toddlers who do not listen when she tells them that their behaviour is 'bad'. She begins to think that they want to be bad or that they enjoy being bad, and often calls them naughty or mischievous. Her frustration shows at the end of the day when her voice tone and volume rise. She often feels that she is yelling at the toddlers, and wonders if her care is any better or worse than the care provided by their parents. These morally dichotomous terms ('good' and 'bad') are part of this worker's spirituality and culture, and she finds it hard to understand why these toddlers, unlike the children at her Sunday School, do not try to be 'good'. By the end of a year with this worker and her moral teaching, the children will have understood that they are bad when they do not do what an adult (in this case, the teacher) tells them to do. These children will also be well prepared to comply with the demands of a pedophile, who will build upon this grooming of obedience to adults.

Table 3.1 Piaget's Stages of Development

Stage	Age	Characteristics
Sensorimotor	Birth to age 2	Knowledge of the world is based on senses and motor skills. By the end of this stage, the child can generate mental representations.
Preoperational	Ages 2 to 6	Child learns how to use symbols (words, numbers) to represent aspects of the world, but relates to this world only through his or her own perspective.
Concrete operational	Ages 7 to 11	Child understands and applies logical operations to experiences in the present.
Formal operational	Age 12 +	Child speculates on the future and thinks abstractly.

during which the child is taught certain moral lessons. It leads to a second level, the conventional one, at which the child sees that it is 'good' to please or help others even if the action is not rewarded; doing one's duty is seen to be good. Practice at the second level leads to a third, post-conventional level, at which the child comes to understand that what is 'right' is a matter of conscience in accordance with universal principles. One stage leads to the next in Kohlberg's developmental perspective on morality.

Perhaps the best-known developmentalist was Piaget, who divided **cognitive development**—the evolution of the organizing and thinking systems of the brain—into four stages that built upon one another: sensorimotor (birth to age 2), preoperational (ages 2 to 6), concrete operational (ages 7 to 11), and formal operational (age 12 and above) (Piaget, 1929). Table 3.1 provides a brief summary of these four stages of development.

At the sensorimotor stage, the child looks for an object only if it is visible. When an object is removed from sight, as in the peek-a-boo game, it ceases to exist for the child. At the preoperational stage, the child begins to look for a hidden object and realizes that an object still exists even though it is hidden from view. The child starts to anticipate the effect of one action on the other at this stage; seeing a raised hand, he or she may anticipate a slap if that has already been experienced. The child acquires symbolic thought and begins to use words and numbers. One afternoon when she did not have a nap, Piaget's daughter Lucienne said to her father, 'I haven't had my nap so it isn't afternoon.' To Piaget, this demonstrated Lucienne's preoperational stage of transductive thinking. She saw that two things were happening at the same time, so assumed that one thing caused the other. Some adults may remain at this preoperational stage if they have a cognitive delay.

Thinking is further developed at the concrete operational stage when the child begins to be able to understand that things change: the leaves turn colour, water becomes ice, and some days *are* different from others. When Lucienne reached this stage, she began to realize that the afternoon still existed even though she had not had a

Photo 3.2 At the sensorimotor stage the child experiences the colour, texture, smell, taste, and sound of the leaves.

nap. Later, at the formal operational stage, the child can hypothesize or imagine change and think in abstract terms. The child may plan an event in the future, or consider a moral dilemma.

While Piaget's taxonomy is useful for understanding a child's frustration around change and transitions, it also is obvious that a very young child may think in all four ways during a single day, even when that child is, in Piaget's terms, in a preoperational stage. For example, the child may explore autumn in a sensorimotor way by throwing fallen leaves in the air and experimenting with them, hypothesizing the idea of gravity, even though the word is not in his vocabulary or understood.

The developmental perspective on the child became accepted as fact—and as the basis for modern pediatric science, education, and child psychology. This perspective affected the social construction of the child (see Chapter 2), and all of the laws, services, and rights surrounding the child. It influenced judges to disregard the testimony of pre-pubescent children who were considered to be only at Kohlberg's level of pre-conventional morality, and influenced child welfare services to withhold information from children perceived as unable to understand abstract concepts because they were still in Piaget's concrete operational stage.

The developmental perspective on the child helped adults to study and interpret children's play, but also has led to serious misunderstandings of this same play. It influenced workers to provide basic services and withhold others until the child reached the appropriate 'stage' or was 'ready'. This developmental perspective on children's care and services continues to guide decisions about which services are to be offered and when, despite cultural bias and the underlying flaws in its logic. The developmental perspective's cultural bias emanates from its origin in European theorists' in-home studies of their own children. Initially, Asian, South American, or African studies were not done, nor were large population studies. Most of the first developmentalists were white, Western men who observed their own children and generalized from the particular. Piaget, for example, cites the example of his daughter Lucienne when stating that the concrete operational thought of a seven-year-old differs from the preoperational thought of a four-year-old. Although these early in-home studies later were corroborated by wider, somewhat more inclusive studies, the objects of study (the children) continued to be mainly white, middle-class children in two-parent families who shared a common language and culture. In Kohlberg's case, the objects of study all were males. There was little to no diversity in the test sets.

The Eurocentric bias evident in these early studies continues to permeate the developmental perspective. Workers who use the developmentalist approach measure every child against the Eurocentric model of the well-developed child, a model that simultaneously advocates and condemns independence in the child. On the one hand, independence is considered an asset and a strength—a position drawn from the Eurocentric idealization of individualism and autonomy rather than co-operation and community. Judith Jordan (2005: 80) notes: 'The job of socialization in this model is to bring the dependent child into a place of separate, independent adulthood. These standards apply to all children, but especially to boys.' 'Walks independently' and 'plays independently' are developmental **milestones** to be achieved, whereas 'shares a toy' and 'recognizes community caregivers' are considered neither assets nor strengths.

On the other hand, this model also positions independence as a deficit. For example, independent toileting is discouraged and is perceived as anxiety-producing and stressful for children until two to three years of age—perhaps in part because of the interests of the billion-dollar business built around disposable diapers and later toileting. Both business and culture determine this developmental milestone. As LeVine and New (2008: 53) caution: 'Infant care is a universal human concern, but the terms in which it is conceived and conducted vary both across cultures and across the generations.' The developmental perspective fails to account for such variations.

Kelly et al. (2006) record the effects of this Eurocentric cultural bias on the assessment of young children. Their study of nine-month-old children across three cultural groups demonstrates that children of non-European races and ethnicities are assessed as 'not meeting their developmental milestones' when the assessors use tools based on Eurocentric developmental milestones. The non-European nine-month-old children are considered to be in an inferior position, and their caregivers and communities are perceived as guilty of neglect for not supporting their child's development. Eurocentric developmental milestones can be used by child protection workers to justify removing these children from their supposedly neglectful caregivers and communities.

The cultural bias of the developmental perspective is compounded by the flaw in its logic that positions children as underdeveloped or incomplete persons who are developing in a structured, linear progression, with one stage leading to the next. The idea of linear progression makes sense to some extent, and certainly reflects human growth patterns. The child coos, babbles, and then says his or her first word. The child rolls, wiggles and squirms, and then crawls. However, this linear perspective also positions adults as the finished, or fully developed, result. Children are placed in the default position of undeveloped or underdeveloped persons. They are perceived as incomplete versions of adults, dependent on adults for optimum development; conversely, children who 'fail to meet their milestones' are described as slow to develop, delayed, retarded, or abnormal.

This emphasis on linear progression does not take into account periods of stability, consolidation, or natural plateaus in which little to no change takes place in a child's skill level. Nor does it recognize the recurrence of socio-emotional states—a recapitulation of an earlier stage necessary for emotional recovery. For example, a child may return to thumb-sucking, breast-feeding, or cuddling in order to make sense of the birth of a sibling, a transition to daycare, or the sudden absence of a caregiver. **Developmentalists** call this activity 'regression', a term that again implies that all child development is linear and aimed at reaching adulthood.

In its emphasis on the achievement of milestones, the developmental perspective takes into account only those environmental forces that directly affect the child: parental caregiving, early feeding, teachers' scolding, and so on. Larger structural determinants, such as social systems and culture, are not considered—a limitation in scope that ultimately weakens this perspective. Although the developmental milestones of this perspective may prove useful in the diagnosis of specific areas in which the child may need structural intervention, it is important to remember that these milestones are culture-specific and constructed rather than based in objective fact. Even supposedly physiological milestones (e.g., 'eats a variety of foods') may have cultural aspects and, therefore, influences. Children unfold rather than develop, and each skill acquisition is a change rather than a stage leading to adulthood.

The Whole Child

A cornerstone of the developmental perspective is that development occurs in three domains: the physical, the socio-emotional, and the cognitive. In the physical domain, the child develops in stages from sucking to drinking, from crawling to cruising. In the socio-emotional domain, the child develops in stages from egocentrism and a short attention span to an interest in social play and a longer attention span. In the cognitive domain, the child develops from sensorimotor play to formal operational thinking. The three domains of development are interconnected: the cognitive affects the physical and socio-emotional and is, in turn, affected by the physical and socio-emotional. An infant who is not able to roll and squirm will not engage in the exploratory play that is basic to developing language skills; as a result, language skills in the cognitive domain will suffer. On the other hand, an infant whose socio-emotional needs are met and is flourishing will have the trust and confidence to explore the environment and will develop more skills in both the physical and the cognitive domains.

The division of child development into three domains reflects a Eurocentric and scientific perspective that does not include spirituality. The Medicine Wheel teachings describe four domains of the child, adding a spiritual domain that informs and breathes through the cognitive, physical, and socio-emotional. These four domains of the child position the child as complete, a whole person rather than a developing one. The child is a gift from Mother Earth and, as such, is not to be thrown away, rejected, or changed. The spiritual domain (in the East) is the spiritual energy that flows from Mother Earth to Father Sky, connecting the child to the wholeness that is life, the land, the ancestors, and the community (Blackstock et al., 2006).

The First Nations view this Medicine Wheel as a sacred circle that is present in everything that breathes, in the seasons, and in the stages of life (Gilgun, 2002). The circle represents balance, wholeness, harmony, and equality. If one part of the circle or wheel is flattened or damaged, then the wheel cannot turn smoothly, and disequilibrium results. As shown in Figure 3.1, the child is in the middle of the four-segmented wheel, and develops in all four domains through reflection, listening, action, and communicating. The North domain represents wisdom and understanding, strength, and endurance. The South represents power, learning, personal growth, and mastery of skills. The East represents connectivity and bonding, and the sense of belonging. The sun sets in the West, which represents uniqueness. All of these domains are interconnected: the child experiences life in all four while simultaneously affecting life in all four. The child, the gift from Mother Earth, is at the hub of the wheel.

When a child becomes distracted, impulsive, addicted to drugs or alcohol, or violent, the Elders follow the Medicine Wheel teachings to bring the child back into the wholeness of life and the circle. The child is placed in a circle of caring, composed of the community that cares for the child. The child absorbs the energy of that circle and the strength of the community, past and present, through sacred ceremonies and work with the Elders. This spiritual domain of connection to the earth and to nature has been shown in many studies to have a healing or therapeutic effect on children. Louv (2005: 49) cites recent studies from Cornell, for example, which demonstrate 'that nature can help protect children against stress, and that nature in or around the home appears to be a significant factor in protecting the psychological well-being of children.' These studies corroborate the truth and power of Medicine Wheel teachings and the importance of including the fourth domain of spirituality when working with children.

Patterns of Growth and Development and Critical Learning Periods

The terms 'growth' and 'development' are often used interchangeably. However, there is a difference in their meanings: growth refers exclusively to physical changes, whereas

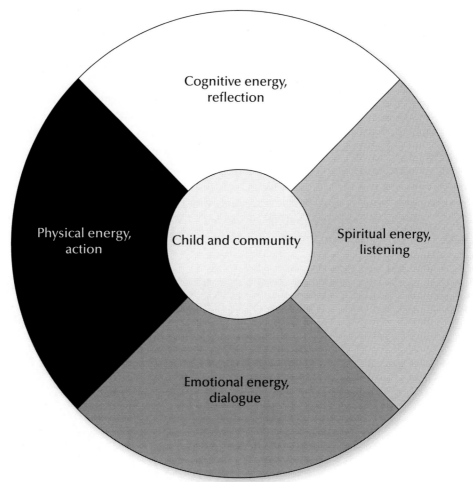

Figure 3.1 Medicine Wheel Domains

development refers to changes in all domains. The infant's body may grow physically, and gain weight and size following a genetically preset timetable, but, because of genetic mapping, he or she may be developmentally delayed in any one of the physical, cognitive, spiritual, or socio-emotional domains, or in all four. The worker who understands the patterns of child development, the critical learning periods, and the milestones of development can recognize such a developmental delay.

Development is about simultaneous change and continuity. The child changes or develops, but he or she remains the same person throughout this period of change. The pattern of development in the child can be mapped as a series of questions about where, what, who, and why. The first question the child seems to ponder is, 'Where?' The child wonders, 'Where am I?' 'Where is my food?' 'Where is the warmth?' The child explores the world, often encapsulated in the mother's breast, first through smell, then taste, then touch. The infant sniffs until the breast is found, latches and sucks, and then nuzzles closer for more. This is the earliest stage of sensorimotor 'play', through which the infant senses the world and moves to find it. Through this play, the infant begins to develop a sense that the world is responsive. In Erik Erikson's terms (see Chapter 4), the child is beginning to develop a sense of trust in the world.

The next question that emerges in the child's developmental pattern is 'What?' The child asks the questions, 'What is this toe?' 'What is this blanket?' 'What is this finger?' The infant explores him- or herself in an attempt to discover what the body is and how it feels. The infant inserts the thumb into the mouth, or pushes the finger toward the bottle, or squirms in a wet diaper. The infant is no longer constrained by the womb and now begins to bend arms and flex feet. Gradually, the infant begins to take charge of the self and to discover body parts. At the same time, the senses reveal a world of blankets, sunshine or snow, lights that flicker and fade, harsh noises, and throbbing heartbeats. The 'What?' question is both asked and answered in every breathing moment of the infant.

Photo 3.3 Toes are tasted, felt, and smelled in the sensorimotor stage.

As the infant becomes more mobile and is able to roll and then sit up, he or she interacts with the environment more closely. People move into the infant's vision and then fade or disappear; they identify themselves as mother, boy, uncle. In time, the infant grows into a toddler who hears words, makes comparisons, and continues to self-explore. This brings us to the toddler's question 'Who?' The toddler wonders,

'Who can hold my hand?' 'Who can bring me water?' 'Who can find my wagon?' The toddler develops a sense of gender, ideas of family, a feeling of race and ethnicity, and a glimpse of friends. This developing self-concept is verbalized when the toddler proudly announces, 'Me Josh' or 'Me big girl'. This self-concept widens through exploratory play, parallel play, and then group play as the child develops an idea of who he or she is in comparison to others. The young girl takes note of how caregivers respond to her and her playmates. Are boys responded to differently? Are boys liked? Is the smaller, brown girl liked? The toddler listens attentively to these cues and begins constructing a concept of 'who'.

It is only much later, after many experiences with persons and the environment, that the child begins to ask the question 'Why?' The version of this question may be elementary at first—'Why do we have to go?'—but it continues to be asked in many ways, and achieves a depth in middle childhood as the challenge, 'Why am I not allowed to go?' The child begins to question boundaries, limits, and the socio-political constructs of the environment. The child has moved very far from infancy's narrow focus on the mother's breast.

Growth and development take place concurrently in most infants' lives. When a baby is born, the head is large (one quarter of the body's size), and the brain is close to the surface of the baby's skull. **Fontanels**, or spaces between the bones in the skull, allow the head to be compressed in the birth canal while ensuring that the brain is protected. These fontanels also allow space for the baby's brain to grow further, and they gradually disappear as the small bones of the skull connect together to form the unified skull.

The infant's brain is genetically programmed to produce more synapses than it will ever use. These synapses, or connections between individual nerve cells, are formed and become permanent during the first few years of life, affecting the development of vision, speech, and thinking. These years of intense brain activity form a **critical learning period** during which the child's developing brain has exceptional plasticity, or is open to stimulation. Important windows of opportunity governing cognitive and socio-emotional skills are programmed to close by the end of the first three years; in short, this is a 'use it or lose it' period for the child.

The pattern of infant development is **cephalocaudal** (from the head downward) and **proximo-distal** (from the midline outwards). The large head of the infant, which requires such care and support, moves first, and then the body starts to roll and squirm. Similarly, an infant's arms move before the hands, the hands before the fingers; the legs move before the feet and the feet before the toes.

When caregivers recognize and understand these patterns of infant growth and development, and recognize that the early years are a critical learning period, they are more likely to advocate for structural support to ensure the infant's optimal health. This is described in Table 3.2, which indicates the requisite structural supports for the infant's optimal growth and development.

Point to Consider   3.1

The National Longitudinal Survey of Children and Youth

The National Longitudinal Survey of Children and Youth (NLSCY), launched in 1994, is the first truly national assessment of the wellness of Canadian children. This survey assesses whether or not Canadian children are meeting their developmental milestones as these milestones are currently set, and which structural determinants most influence their growth and development. Children in all 10 provinces and 3 territories were initially surveyed in 1994, resulting in data from some 26,000 Canadian children from birth to age 11. By Cycle 6 of the survey (2004), this first cohort ranged from ages 10 to 21. The early cycles produced significant data such as the following:

- Poverty has an overriding impact on the healthy development of children—a greater impact than parenting style, neighbourhood, school, or many other factors that were previously considered to be most significant.
- One-quarter of Canadian children already have academic and/or behavioural and/or socio-emotional problems by age 11, a much higher percentage of children than in most countries with comparable economies.
- More and more children are enrolled in child care. In Cycle 1 (1994–1995) 42 per cent of children were in child care; by Cycle 4 (2002–2003) this rate had increased to 54 per cent.

As each cycle is analyzed, we learn more about which structural determinants affect Canadian children most. This survey provides an essential baseline for all projects and programs that include Canadian children.

Gender construction refers to the process through which children learn the cultural norms, expectations, and behaviours that have been socially constructed for males and females. The two sexes are presented as a dichotomy—one in opposition to the other and one inherently 'stronger than' the other. Gender construction produces **gender stereotypes** of strong males and weak females, active males and passive females. These agreed-upon or socially constructed patterns of expected behaviour serve to reinforce the relative and dichotomous power of girls and boys. Because gender affects self-concept, peer and family relationships, school performance, and plans for the future, the process of gender construction—or the dominant gender discourse—affects child development. In this sense, gender becomes something that is *done to* children; in other words, and as identified by Health Canada's Population Health project, gender construction is a structural determinant of children's health or wellness.

Even in the earliest stages of a child's infancy, gender construction happens through verbal and non-verbal messaging. Parents may express joy or sorrow when they learn their infant's sex, and their initial reaction can frame their child's emerging gender identity. The parent may express delight: 'Oh, a girl!' On the other hand, the parent may smile and say sadly, 'Oh, another girl'. The newborn does not understand the words yet, but reads the body language, and hears the tone and the underlying meaning. The newborn has been experiencing this parent for many months and, literally, knows the parent from within.

Field (2007: 148) cites several studies of gender construction as it relates to infants. She estimates that by 12 to 18 months, the infant understands gender construction and its inherent power differential. One of the studies Field cites involves having an infant match images of female and male faces with other objects shown on a computer screen. The infant is given a gender neutral prompt to do the match and, in most cases, the child matches objects such as fire hats, hammers, bears, and fir trees with the male face.

How does the infant learn or absorb this gender construction and sort out the power differential at such an early age? Parents, caregivers, extended family, and society at large convey gender expectations through the way they relate to infants, as demonstrated by a recent study of parental expectations (Mondschein, 2000). When asked to assess the crawling ability of their infants, mothers overestimated the ability of their sons and underestimated the ability of their daughters. In actual performance, a non-parental tester assessed the crawling abilities of the sons and daughters as identical. Eventually, as they develop, the sons and daughters will attune themselves to the higher and lower expectations of their mothers and the prevailing gender constructions, whatever they may be in a particular community.

The solitary play of infants involves hours of physical self-exploration as the child touches and explores genitalia, as well as toes and fingers. The infant also observes gender roles in caregivers. Infants are attentive especially to other infants and watch how other children play. They begin actual parallel play as toddlers around age two, and the child plays alongside other children and observes their toilet patterns, play episodes, and language. The toddler typically touches other toddlers' bodies, testing for strength and softness, and searching for similarities and differences in exploratory play.

This exploration of self and other results in a rudimentary understanding of gender difference, and the confident toddler will announce, 'Me girl!' By now, the dominant gender construction is absorbed. A little girl has learned to be clean and neat and dressed beautifully in order to be praised as a girl. A little boy has been told to be brave and 'not a crybaby' in order to be praised. Young boys are urged to climb and run and throw, while young girls are urged to ask for help.

As the child grows, this social construction of **gender roles** continues as the preschooler develops an understanding of gender identity, his or her own and that of other preschoolers. The young child easily identifies and begins to seek gender-specific play and play materials. Adults in the child's life, particularly family members, may label this choice of play and play materials as 'strong' or 'weak and silly'. Consider the following case study described by Smidt (2006: 98):

> Johan is four years old. . . . He loves nothing more than to dress up in the clothes in the dressing up box. And most of all he likes to dress up in a particular pink dress and drape a purple scarf over his shoulders and totter around in shoes that are too big for him. But he will not do this after lunch and when asked why he explained that he didn't want his mum to see him dressed like that because 'it's girly and I'm not a pouf'. He fears his mum will tell his dad.

Johan wants to explore what it might feel like to be a girl just as he explores what it might feel like to be a knight or a robber. But Johan has already internalized and absorbed the prevailing gender constructions. He understands that the important adults in his life would disapprove of his exploring the girl role, but they would praise his exploring the firefighter role. Gender constructions are solidly fixed in this boy's four-year-old mind, and he recognizes the social disapproval that might occur if these rigid constructions are questioned or transgressed. Sanctions against gender nonconformity begin early in the child's life. By middle childhood, children engage in social or group play, and they tend to form peer relationships with same-gender peers in the ongoing development of gender self-identity. Not only adults but also peers now have the power to denounce play as silly or to support play as fun and healthy.

During middle childhood, it is more probable for boys to engage in physical aggression and physically interactive play.[1] The 'boy code' pushes them towards extremes of toughness and aggression. As Jordan (2005: 80) notes, 'Shame-based socialization for boys directs them towards being strong in dominant-defined ways: unyielding, not showing vulnerability, and displaying a narrow range of affect.' Canadian child incidence abuse statistics show that boys are more likely than girls to be victims of physical abuse and more likely to witness domestic violence. They are also more likely to carry a label of a conduct disorder or of ADHD (attention-deficit hyperactivity disorder), and more boys than girls are medicated in middle childhood (Potter, 2004).

During this stage, girls form peer relationships with other girls and are often themselves victims of relational aggression from other girls. Girls are less likely to be involved in competitive sports and are often positioned as weak, vulnerable victims. Girls tend to excel in school in expressive language skills, and in co-operative games and clubs.

When children move into their teenage years, they return to interacting in mixed-sex groups and they continue to explore gender roles and gender relationships. At this time, they may also act upon their sexual orientation, forming sexual relationships with their own sex or with the opposite sex. This activity tends to be covert because of homophobia and social sanctions regarding premarital sex, sexual touching, and **contact comfort** (Johnson, 2008). The teen years are characterized by a lack of contact comfort from peers and a lessening of contact comfort from parents and caregivers, who may feel constrained by their children's prepubescent body changes and growing interest in sexuality. This lack of positive physical contact may contribute to the aggression, isolation, and anger that seem synonymous with the teenage years.

During these years, boys typically form the largest component of conduct disorder classrooms and treatment foster homes. The Statistics Canada (2004) report *Education Matters* notes that the gender gap in school achievement continues to widen during the teen years, with more boys than girls dropping out of high school and more boys than girls failing literacy tests. Boys are more likely to engage in risk-taking behaviours such as drinking, fighting, or doing drugs; those who don't take risks may be called 'fraidy cats' or accused of being 'afraid of the cops'. Teenage boys are more likely than girls to die from accidents, suicide, or homicide, and they may try out violent behaviour using weapons (Meichenbaum, 2006).

Teenage girls also engage in risk-taking behaviours, although these tend to be within sexual relationships, and typically involve either unprotected sex or sexual experimentation with transitory partners. Boys typically enjoy being with groups of other boys, but girls tend to feel less loyalty to other girls, often competing with them and engaging in relational aggression. Although girls form a small minority (20 per cent) of young offenders, they are more likely than boys to be involved in truancy, to run away from home, and to engage in certain crimes such as prostitution (Kelly and Totten, 2002). Body image has greater importance for girls than boys, and this focus on body image increases in adolescence as entry to desired peer groups may be dependent on body image. During the teen years, girls are more likely than boys to endanger their health by extreme dieting practices; to be diagnosed with eating disorders; to experience internalizing mental health problems, such as depression and anxiety; and to attempt suicide (Weir and Wallington, 2001).

Jordan (2005: 82) summarizes these gender role differences in describing how adolescents react to stress. She notes that boys tend to take the 'fight or flight' approach, either running away or confronting stress directly through physical aggression and fighting. Girls, on the other hand, take the 'tend and befriend' approach, and use social support to deal with stress. These opposite reactions to stress reflect the dominant social gender constructions. Girls are taught in society to care for, nurture, and communicate, whereas boys are taught to stand alone, fight, and conquer. Workers who understand these gender constructions as structural determinants bring this understanding to their behavioural interventions.

The deconstruction of gender involves a number of structural determinants such as media, class values, sport and recreation, educational norms, legislation, and cultural norms of beauty. A worker can frame a gender construction within any or all of these structural determinants so that the child can begin to understand how a particular behaviour is gendered. When working with a child who has anorexia, for example, deconstruction may include looking at how females are depicted in the media and how females are culturally positioned as vulnerable, less than worthy, and body-centric. In the case of a child who is engaging in violent gang activity, deconstruction can include looking at how media depicts boys moving in packs and engaging in risk-taking behaviours that are a rite of passage to 'being male'. This deconstruction helps the child to understand more clearly how gender role scripts affect behaviour in a society in which gender constructions can devalue a person's sex and/or sexual orientation. Positive gender constructions of strong and caring males and females can be carefully introduced by the worker to replace the negative gender roles that boys and girls typically are expected to play.

Group Exercise   3.1

Words of Hate

In this group exercise, each participant is given a blank card on which to write what he or she considers the most disturbing or hurtful word or phrase. In small groups, the participants look at the unsigned cards and prioritize them, putting the group's choice of worst word at the top of the pile. Each small group then shares their selection with the larger group.

Over the last few years, the words of hate chosen by participants have become increasingly virulent and racist. However, the top words of hate selected by female-dominated groups have been 'fat' and 'ugly'. This choice is even more significant when the prevalence of other racist, sexist, and homophobic words in the piles is considered. This is an effective reminder that words commonly considered offensive within a society are not equally offensive to all people, and that other, more body-centric, words may hurt more.

Sexual Orientation

Sexual orientation refers to one's erotic attraction towards, and interest in developing a sexual relationship with, members of one's own or the opposite sex. A **heterosexual orientation** refers to an erotic attraction to, and preference for developing sexual relationships with, members of the opposite sex. A **homosexual orientation** refers to an erotic attraction to, and preference for developing sexual relationships with, members of one's own sex. Heterosexual children may be called 'straight'; homosexual boys may be called 'gay' or 'queer'; and homosexual girls may be called 'lesbians' or 'dykes'. A **bisexual** orientation refers to an erotic attraction to, and preference for developing sexual relationships with, members of both sexes. Then, under the **transgender** umbrella are included transexuals, crossdressers, intersexuals, performers, and gender benders. Homosexuals, bisexuals, and those under the transgender umbrella are referred to as **two-spirited** by First Nations and, increasingly, by other Canadians also.

A child is born male or female or intersex. In later life, the child may choose to have his or her sex medically changed. However, the majority of infants of a particular sex grow into adults of that sex and remain so throughout the life cycle. A child may also decide to alter the expression of his or her sexual orientation, stifling what feels 'natural' or modifying it to suit others. A child may experiment with sexual relations with the same sex or the opposite sex or both. The way sexual orientation is expressed changes as the child develops relationships and understands the prevailing social climate. Sexual orientation has been described as both genetically determined and as a lifestyle choice, this duality reflecting the nature versus nurture debate that dominates the discourse about many spheres of human behaviour.

Psychologists, sociologists, and neurologists have not reached a consensus about what causes an individual to develop a heterosexual, bisexual, transgender, gay, or lesbian orientation. Is a child born heterosexual? Does a child become heterosexual through affiliation with the dominant sexual lifestyle? Research on possible genetic, hormonal, developmental, social, and cultural influences on sexual orientation has yielded no definitive answers to such questions. Many Canadians feel that both nature and nurture play a role in determining sexual orientation. At the same time, most Canadians also feel that they have little personal choice about their sexual orientation. Statistics Canada reports that 1.3 per cent of Canadians aged 18 to 59 identify themselves as homosexual, 0.7 per cent as lesbian, and 0.7 per cent as bisexual (Canada, 2003, Cycle 2.1). However, these percentages are tiny in comparison to the 10 per cent estimate of some gay and lesbian advocacy groups.[2] The wide gap in these statistics reflects the lack of reliable research in this area. The subject of sexuality, sexual feelings, and sexual orientation remains controversial territory in the area of child study.

Some young children may feel an attraction to the same sex at a very early age. Just as heterosexual children begin to develop 'crushes' on children of the opposite sex, homosexual children begin to develop the same type of crushes on children of the same sex. It is quite common to hear stories of gay and lesbian children who start to develop attractions to people of the same sex and then realize that this attraction is more than a 'friendship' attraction. In the National Film Board of Canada film *Out: Stories of Lesbian and Gay Youth*, Mark recalls seeing men in the swimming pool change room when he was five years old and realizing that he was sexually attracted to them. While this attraction is usually not acted on until puberty, many children may, in fact, experiment with sexual games and role play at a very young age. They play out sexual roles with other boys and girls of the same age, but these typically involve touching, hand holding, and kissing only.

At the same time, even very young children soon recognize and acknowledge the socially dominant sexual orientation and, regardless of their own sexual orientation, they usually try to conform to the dominant construct of heterosexuality. This is easier to do because the behavioural role models dominate, and heterosexuality is more socially acceptable. Boys will talk about being 'daddies' and girls will play out being 'mommies', with both sexes assuming that their partners are of the opposite sex. Homophobic views also start forming early in life. Barrie and Luria (2004) point out that, by middle childhood, children use labels such as 'fag' and 'queer' as insults generally, as well as for boys who do not conform to gender stereotypes.

Despite the heterosexuality prevalent in Canadian society, some children recognize in middle childhood that the dominant sexual orientation that they are expected to identify with doesn't represent who they feel they are. These children will choose to identify with whatever gender attributes are most comfortable for them. Gay and lesbian children will often begin to identify with attributes of the opposite sex; a little girl may dress like a cowboy and play with cars, while a boy may like to dress up in feminine clothing and play with dolls. Sometimes, these attributes are closely linked to the same-sex attraction they are experiencing, or they may, as mentioned above, simply be an exploration of others' gendered roles. In identifying with attributes of the opposite sex, these children are, in a sense, creating their own sexual orientation. By not conforming to the socially constructed notions of gender, these children are creating a third gender that they can identify with that exists outside the conventional norms of heterosexuality.

This is not to say that all children who identify with a third gender will later identify as gay or lesbian. While some children who engage in gender experimentation at a young age do in fact identify as gay or lesbian later in life, many children who later identify as heterosexual will also experiment with gender construction. Such experimentation demonstrates that these children—regardless of their ultimate gender identification—do not feel strictly bound by the social codes of gender and are more willing to accept and identify with experiences and attributes that fall outside the limits of the sexual orientation norm.

Social cues affect every aspect of a child's development. When cognitive excellence is emphasized, for example, a child will see academic work as a positive and will tend to want to read and write at an early age. Similarly, the social cues of sexuality and sexual orientation can shape and influence how a child behaves. Attraction to the same sex is inherently different from the type of attraction that is inculcated in many Canadian families. Heterosexual parents do not always overtly teach that homosexuality is wrong; however, they covertly and subtly suggest that homosexuality is a second, rather than a first, sexual choice. When a child identifies with attributes that are outside the dominant sexual orientation construct, he or she also recognizes the strong negative social reaction to this identification. It is not uncommon to hear stories from the gay and lesbian community that involve children being socially reprimanded for making choices and engaging in behaviour that is outside the bounds of the strict sexual orientation code. Sometimes the reactions the child experiences are volatile and can cause emotional as well as physical harm to the child. When children exhibit signs of same-sex attraction, they may be punished, mocked, or chastised by heterosexual parents and guardians—punitive and shaming actions that reinforce the social constructs and diminish the developing self-esteem of the child.

As the child realizes that his or her own sexual orientation is outside the mainstream and therefore marginalized, it also becomes clear that this 'difference' can alienate and upset family members, teachers, and friends. The child may become a victim of bullying, homophobic 'jokes', and exclusion by peers. Because sexual orientation is so much a part of self-identity, the shame and guilt of being different becomes internalized and associated with the self. The child develops a self-concept of being unworthy, isolated, a freak, and may try to hold back, disguise, or hide any expression of sexual orientation at all. Because of this suppression of sexual orientation, the child often lags in developing a viable social reference group and socialization skills. Without a peer reference group and positive role models, the child may become even further isolated. This isolation can cause the child to spiral into depression and can lead as far as suicidal ideation; gay and lesbian children in Canada are estimated to account for approximately 14 times more suicides than their heterosexual counterparts (Dorais, 2004: 9–10).

Sexual activity usually begins with the onset of puberty, although full sexual activity (intercourse) may not happen until adulthood. This healthy sexual activity is part of a child's socio-emotional development and a way for the child to develop a fuller awareness of his or her sexual orientation and sexual relationships with others. Although delay in sexual activity is not itself a risk, confusion as to sexual orientation can delay self-acceptance and self-actualization. Sexual orientation is as much a part of self as cognition, physical ability, and spirituality. To deny or distort sexual orientation is to deny an essential part of the self.

Impediments to healthy sexuality include structural determinants such as culture, heterosexism, and religion, as well as mesosystem determinants such as sexual abuse. The cause of child sexual abuse is not structural: it is the pathology of the perpetrator who is sexually aroused by children and acts on this arousal. The majority of known perpetrators are within the child's family circle; 'stranger danger' is less prevalent. This compounds the abuse because those within the family circle are purported to be safe and caring persons. When these persons sexually abuse the child, any basis for trust in the world is shattered.

A child who is sexually abused or assaulted is typically groomed by the perpetrator to believe that she or he is a willing participant in the abuse. A very young child may be told that he is too pretty to resist. An older child may be told that she has asked for it. Grooming is part of the sexual abuser's repertoire and wreaks untold emotional damage on the child victim. Part of that emotional damage is loss of trust and part is confusion as to healthy sexuality and what that entails.

Child sexual abuse intervention requires specific skills and expertise in this field (Rycus and Hughes, 1998) and is typically a lengthy intervention. Prevention work happens through the structural and strengths-based intervention of the worker's full support for the child's sex, sexual orientation, and healthy sexuality. Such acceptance and support are modelled in the First Nations community as described proudly by one two-spirited youth: 'The two-spirit being is a higher being and I am supposed to have a higher wisdom' (Barbara, 2004: 12). The worker may strengthen structural supports for a child's sexual orientation by doing any of the following:

- providing information about community and national role models with a variety of sexual orientations;
- valuing visuals and media that depict families led by both homosexual and hetero- sexual individuals and couples;
- accepting and validating individual sexual orientation;
- challenging homophobia and homophobic 'humour';
- modelling positive and affirming gender constructs.

Because sexual behaviour and sexual orientation are very private parts of the child's life that are not often demonstrated publicly, the worker is sensitive to this privacy, supporting the child in all aspects of development and celebrating the child's unique and special qualities. This implies full acceptance of the child's whole self and full support for the child's healthy sexuality.

Summary

This chapter explores the characteristics of developmentally appropriate practice, via a critical discussion of the developmental perspective on the child. We acknowledge that this perspective has strengths. It cautions workers not to teach infants to walk at nine months unless the child is ready to, or to 'share' at 24 months. It reminds workers how interrelated the physical, cognitive, and socio-emotional domains are when the infant is starting to babble and to explore. The developmental perspective has weaknesses, however—primarily in its linear logic, which positions a child as an undeveloped version of an adult, and its Eurocentric and scientific bias, which emphasizes only three domains, each with specific milestones, neglecting spirituality.

By recognizing the linear logic as a weakness and by expanding the three domains to four, and so including the spiritual domain, we expand the developmental perspec- tive to encompass the whole child and we ground this perspective in Medicine Wheel teachings. This expanded developmental perspective on the child positions the child as a gift from Mother Earth and as the centre of the Medicine Wheel, connected to community as well as to family.

In the next chapter, we will apply our critical and expanded understanding of the developmental perspective on the child to the subject of attachment. We will ask ourselves how important attachment is to the overall physical, cognitive, socio- emotional, and spiritual development of the child. Our focus will not be limited to the caregiver–child relationship, but will widen to include the child–caregiver–community relationship as well. Specifically, we will examine the importance of healthy attachment to the overall wellness of the child, the self-confidence that Ramona expressed in her pride regarding her gender. This healthy attachment sets the child's life course, a fact that makes it imperative for the worker to intervene when unhealthy attachment is diagnosed.

Review Questions

1. What is the flaw in logic in the developmental perspective on the child? Explain.
2. How did the cultural bias in the developmental perspective form? Is this bias prevalent today? Why or why not?
3. How are the four domains of development interrelated?
4. Describe how patterns of development are both cephalocaudal and proximo-distal.
5. Name and explain Piaget's four stages of cognitive development.
6. What are critical learning periods for children, and what happens when these periods are missed?
7. How is development both co-relational and cultural? Explain with reference to walking.
8. What is the difference between sex and gender, and what is meant by gender construction?
9. When do children become aware of their gender, and when do they become aware of their sexual orientation?
10. How can workers support positive gender roles for children?

Discussion Questions

1. When planning a play area for school-aged children, how does your support for the children's sexual orientation guide your planning process? Do you find this support difficult to offer because of your own sexual orientation, or because of your beliefs about the sexual orientation of others?
2. Children who have to flee their home country often suffer developmental delays as a result of this trauma. Their language skills may lag, or their social skills may suffer. How can their optimum development be supported when they reach Canada? You may want to visit programs that welcome refugees in your own area, and explore the supports that they offer to children on their own and children in families.
3. Consider the developmental milestone of independent toileting. When is this milestone reached, and how does this milestone reflect cultural values? Is it important for children to reach this milestone before they begin preschool? Why or why not?

Chapter 4

Attachment

You cannot touch love, but you can feel the sweetness that it pours into everything.

—Helen Keller, *The Story of My Life*

W hen we think of attachment, we may picture a mother in a rocking chair singing a lullaby to her sleeping baby. This is an appealing image, but it does not necessarily illustrate attachment. The mother's singing may be for her own amusement, and the child may be an unconnected part of the musical moment of the mother as she rocks. The child may look into the mother's eyes and see loathing, and may try to cuddle into her body and feel only bitter rejection.

Attachment begins to develop during infancy, when the infant is distressed or feels threatened and the caregiver responds to this stimulus of distress with love, nurturance, and consistently responsive care. The attachment relationship develops over time as the infant and the caregiver interact. The caregiver with whom the infant forms attachment may be a mother, a father, a nanny, an extended family member, or a community group—any caregiver who is attuned to the infant and responds consistently, attentively, and lovingly. This synchronous response provides the infant with a secure emotional base for exploring the wider world.

Because research on the subject is relatively new, the lifelong importance of healthy attachment is only now being fully realized, and it is still undervalued and misunderstood by some workers. Though the impact of attachment on life success is still being researched, much of the evidence points to this impact being deep, dramatic, and sustained. This chapter introduces the key researchers in the field, many of whom are Canadians, along with some of their significant findings.

Early attachment affects behaviour, growth, and the formation of intimate relation-ships throughout life. Workers must understand how attachment develops and how they can best intervene when symptoms of unhealthy or insecure attachment become evident. The knowledgeable worker can intervene in a structural and strengths-based way to restore feelings of attachment and security, and to heal early attachment inju-ries. This chapter describes some interventions that are effective.

Objectives

By the end of this chapter, you will:

- Understand the importance of healthy attachment for the child.
- Identify the causes and symptoms of insecure attachment.
- Demonstrate how to intervene effectively in the home and outside the home when a child has attachment injuries.

Research on Attachment

In the early 1930s, Konrad Lorenz (1903–89), an Austrian zoologist, studied the bond that baby chicks formed with their mother, and noted that they appeared to be pre-programmed to follow her after birth (Lorenz, 1970–1). Lorenz theorized that the chicks' **imprinting** on their mother—their spontaneous attachment to her as the source of their nutritional needs—could be transferred to another figure. He tested his theory by removing the mother immediately after birth and replacing her with another moving object, after which he observed that the chicks followed the moving object as they would follow a mother. This imprinting worked only if applied in the first week of the chicks' lives, during which Lorenz could imprint himself or a mechanical object, and the chicks would follow. This pattern of imprinting has subsequently been observed by other biologists and environmentalists who find themselves caring for newly born mammals and birds. These newborns imprint on the caring human, attaching themselves easily to the consistent and responsive caregiver.

Harry Harlow's (1905–81) later research with mammals (primarily rhesus monkeys) in the 1960s and 1970s revealed the flaws in imprinting theory and the effects of **maternal deprivation** (Harlow and Harlow, 1962, Harlow and Suomi, 1972). Newborn monkeys that Harlow studied preferred the comfort and warmth of non-lactating, terrycloth mothers over lactating, mechanical wire mothers. The newborn monkeys would literally starve themselves to death in their search for contact comfort and nurturance. Those who were not comforted, and were fed only by a mechanical mother, grew into socially crippled adult monkeys. Exhibiting hostility, aggressive behaviour, depression, and self-destructive habits, they were unable to read social cues or to solve problems and, as adults, they were unable to mate (Kraemer, 1997). Food from a non-responsive dispenser did not replace the emotional benefits derived from contact comfort. Even more worrisome was the fact that monkeys exposed to maternal deprivation for over 90 days (six months in human-growth terms) could not be comforted. Their hostile and aggressive behaviour persisted even when they were systematically treated with an intervention of contact comfort.

The terms **attachment** and **bonding** were coined first by John Bowlby (1969) when he describes the socio-emotional or affective bond that develops between the infant and the primary caregiver. He postulates that all infants instinctively seek attachment with caregivers who provide basic physical needs, emotional comfort, security, and protection. Bowlby also argues that attachment was an evolutionary survival mechanism in that the search for such a connection prompted the infant to seek nourishment from the attachment figure, and likewise prompted the attachment figure to provide nourishment to the infant. Bowlby (1988: 27) defines attachment behaviour as 'any form of behaviour that results in a person attaining or maintaining proximity to some other clearly identified individual who is conceived as better able to cope with the world.' Bowlby's description of this proximity-seeking behaviour helps to explain why a young child also can form an attachment with an abusive adult. The adult wielding abusive control over the child nevertheless appears 'better able to cope with the world' and is able to provide the short-term nurturance or protection that the child needs, while simultaneously abusing the child. Bowlby explains that attachment can be unhealthy, and also describes how such unhealthy attachment gradually becomes the internal working model of intimacy for the child. Hence, unhealthy attachment can extend across generations as one insecurely attached caregiver wields power over an infant, producing another insecure attachment.

Vera Fahlberg (1988: 13) explores this interactive dynamic of attachment, describing healthy attachment as an affectionate bond between two individuals and demonstrating through her work with adoptees that attachment affects the child's lifelong socio-emotional development: 'A strong and healthy bond to a parent allows a child to develop both trust in others and self-reliance. The bond that children develop to a person who cares for them in their early years is the foundation of their future psychological, physical, and cognitive development and for their future relationships with others.'

The Canadian researcher, Mary Ainsworth, devised a procedure known as the 'Strange Situation' in order to investigate and classify attachment relationships (Ainsworth, 1978). The Strange Situation comprises a series of experimental episodes, each about three minutes long. First, the mother and infant enter an unfamiliar room filled with interesting toys; next, once the infant is settled, the mother leaves the room briefly; and, finally, she returns to reunite with her infant. During these three episodes, the experimenter observes the infant and records the infant's responses to the mother's presence and absence.

The results show that most of the infants seem to be securely attached to their mothers. They relate to their mothers through warm interactions; they use the mother as a safe base for exploration; they protest and cry upon separation; they show pleasure when the mother returns; they are easy to console; and they clearly prefer the mother to a stranger. These infants are considered to have healthy attachment. However, some infants display a variety of conflicting behaviours, both in the presence of their mothers and when separated from them, that suggest anxious or insecure attachments to their mothers. Through the Strange Situation, Ainsworth develops a taxonomy of insecure attachment, classifying attachment according to degree (from least to most severe) as avoidant, resistant, and disorganized.

In 1997, Elinor Ames used Ainsworth's taxonomy to identify early attachment injuries in Romanian children adopted by Canadian families. These children displayed indiscriminate friendliness towards strangers as well as other characteristics of insecure attachment. Her research pinpoints the cause of this insecure attachment to be early maternal deprivation in Romanian orphanages. Like Harlow's monkeys, these children had been given dry diapers, bottles of milk, and warm cribs as infants, but they had lacked early emotional nurturance.

Canadian adoption research confirms Ames's findings. Descriptions of 'searches for birth mothers', 'attachment injuries', and 'reunions with birth parents' in the adoption literature (Cech, 2000) clearly signal the deep and long-lasting effects of early maternal deprivation. As Webber (1998: 72) notes, 'The inner lives of those who've been rearranged by adoption have nothing to do with the families who adopt. The drive to seek and hold on to the truth of one's beginning exists only for the people essential to the moment of delivered life.'

Although not always working directly with children, Sue Johnson, director of the Ottawa Couple and Family Institute, studied the long-term damage caused by attachment injuries in individuals who sought to maintain their adult relationships. Using **emotionally focused therapy**, which she developed over decades of working with couples, Johnson (2004) describes the 'music of the attachment dance' and the contact comfort needed by adults with attachment injuries.

Attachment research also has been carried out by Diane Benoit and her colleagues at the Hospital for Sick Children, in Toronto. In studies of mother–infant interaction, Benoit (2005: 2) identifies maladaptive behaviours in children that result from insecure attachment. She is also able to identify caregiver behaviours that contribute to this insecure attachment, which include 'failing to keep a child safe, failing to comfort a distressed child, laughing while the child is distressed, mocking or teasing a distressed child, asking for affection and reassurance from the child, or threatening to harm'. The antecedents to the maladaptive behaviours of the children in Benoit's studies clearly are caregiver-centred.

Healthy Attachment

Infants will attach themselves emotionally and psychologically to a primary caregiver, provided that the caregiver is consistently responsive and nurturing. This attachment to a source of benefit offers a distinct survival advantage: the attachment figure provides the essentials for life, of food, water, and warmth. However, the meeting of attachment needs continues beyond infancy. A bond of trust with a caregiver who consistently does provide the essentials for life is the basis for an individual's mental model of self-esteem and health. A feeling of attachment answers two questions: Am I lovable? and Can

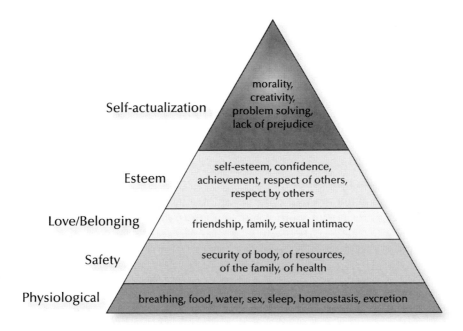

Figure 4.1 Maslow's Hierarchy of Needs

others be trusted to supply my essential needs? The securely attached child feels worthy of love and is able to trust others.

Sometimes called a 'secure-base relationship,' healthy attachment is fundamental to the overall growth and development of the child. The sense of emotional safety derived from healthy attachment provides a secure and dependable emotional base from which the infant can explore, experiment, and develop the self-confidence, self-reliance, autonomy, and resiliency needed to cope with future stresses. Abraham Maslow (1943) describes this need for a secure and dependable emotional base in his five-level hierarchy of needs (Figure 4.1). He identifies the most basic needs as physiological. Once these needs are met, the next human level of needs is for safety and security, followed by love and belonging. Maslow's hierarchy provides a template for the importance of healthy attachment as the foundation of an individual's eventual development of self-esteem at level four and self-actualization at level five (and for self-transcendence, level 6, which he added later in his life).

Psychologist Erik Erikson's psychosocial development model similarly complements attachment theory. Erikson (2000) identifies eight stages of psychosocial development that human beings go through from birth to death, the first two of which take place in early childhood. According to his model, the first stage—in the first year of life—is the critical learning period for developing trust in the world, a sense that the world is safe. The next stage, when the child becomes a toddler, is a critical learning period for independent decision-making. Erikson's model suggests that without a solid foundation of trust the child cannot move forward to the second stage of being an independent decision-maker.

A healthy attachment is one of the strongest protective factors for a child and can outweigh a constellation of risk factors. Securely attached children who are raised in war-torn countries, in abject poverty, and amid constant chaos can develop into successful, optimistic adults. Their secure attachment outweighs the poverty, stress, malnutrition, disease, and turmoil of their early years. Secure attachment promotes resiliency, is associated with school success, and reduces the risk of depression and other behavioural disorders. In their longitudinal study of children at risk, Marsiglia and Kulis (2009: 89) note that 'a distinguishing factor shared by the individuals who showed resiliency was a close long-term childhood relationship with a caring, responsible parent or other adult.'

Healthy attachment is also fundamental to the development of communication. Babbling, cooing, vocal interactions, and eye contact with caregivers are the first stages of language development. Infants use this rudimentary language to indicate their need for food, sleep, and comfort, and the attentive caregiver soon learns to respond to this infantile language. Within a few weeks, the infant's cries become differentiated, and the caregiver can recognize what each cry means and respond appropriately. When this happens, the infant feels heard and begins to understand and imitate the rhythm of conversation. The caregiver will pause and the child will react; the caregiver will hum or sing and the child will respond to the rhythm of the words. As response triggers language, more language develops; this language development is dependent on healthy attachment.

In her early research on attachment, Ainsworth (1978) found that children who were securely attached also were able to be more caring and empathetic towards others. They did not have to worry about their own safety, so they had more energy and concern available for others. Through positive relationships of caring, affection, and protection with a responsive caregiver, the child begins to feel valued, worthwhile, respected, and wanted, and is secure enough to reach out to others. Healthy attachment is thus related to higher self-esteem, openness to experiences and people, and an internal locus of control (Johnson, 2004). The child begins to feel part of the larger culture of the caregiver, and gradually absorbs the attitudes and values of this culture. On the other hand, the child with an unhealthy attachment has less cultural identification and affiliation, and so develops poor self-image and low self-esteem.

The young child with a healthy attachment trusts and wishes to please the responsive caregiver. This desire to please is a significant motivator for the child to learn and to explore the world. The securely attached child engages in activities such as ball tossing, running, swimming, and reading as a means of further engaging with the caregiver and developing this trusting relationship. The child develops social skills—sharing, co-operation, and negotiation—through play with the caregiver, and is encouraged in this skill development; for example, many children would never attempt to swim (or would attempt to swim and drown) were it not for a proud, cheering, and encouraging caregiver. The reciprocity that infuses this relationship is evident, as the confidence with which the child explores the water, the playground, and the slide is nurtured by the responsive support of the caregiver. As each skill is acquired, the child's confidence and feelings of competence grow.

Healthy attachment also forms the basis of the child's internal working model of intimate relationships later in life. **Intimacy** can be described as feelings of closeness and connection, of being bonded to another person. This other person alleviates attachment fears and opens up possibilities for acceptance and responsiveness. In an intimate relationship, securely attached adults can expose their vulnerabilities because they already have a secure base and high self-esteem.

How do we identify healthy attachment? Unfortunately, observations such as the following are unreliable indicators even though they are commonly believed to demonstrate how attached a child is:

- 'Look how she cries when her daddy leaves the daycare!'
- 'Oh, aren't they sweet! They do everything together!'
- 'He just lights up when his mama comes into the room.'
- 'Look you. She's laughin' up a storm. I guess she jus' loves her nana!'

A child's response of crying, laughing, or being silent may or may not indicate healthy attachment. Nor is healthy attachment an inevitable outcome of a relationship in which a child and a stay-at-home parent do everything together. As noted earlier, the mother rocking her child in the rocking chair may in fact hold an infant who is insecurely attached to her.

Healthy attachment can be identified when an infant under stress seeks proximity to and contact with the caregiver, and the caregiver responds with reciprocal body language. Through this harmonious and instantaneous sequence of responses, called **synchrony**, the caregiver achieves a state of **attunement** to the child's needs over time. The caregiver's behaviours of feeding, holding, nurturing, massaging, smiling, cuddling, and talking to the infant reinforce the infant's attachment to the caregiver. And, at the same time, the infant's responses to care, including cooing, smiling, cuddling, and becoming quiet when held, stimulate and strengthen the caregiver's attachment to the infant.

Healthy attachment also can be observed when a young child deliberately chooses interactions with the caregiver that are contact-maintaining and proximity-seeking, and which include social referencing. In contact-maintaining interactions, the child seeks out physical contact with the caregiver, turning towards her,[1] gazing at her, crawling towards her, and cuddling into her body. The child gazes into the eyes of the caregiver, and in that reflected loving gaze begins to develop a sense of self. The child seeks the touch, smell, and sound of the caregiver, and is soothed by the feel of her, the smell of her body, or the sound of her voice. The child moves towards the caregiver or reaches out to touch her fingers or hair.

Photo 4.1 This boy sees himself reflected in his father and both express joy in their attachment.

Proximity-seeking is evident when the child deliberately moves into the area occupied by the caregiver or brightens when the caregiver moves into the child's area. The child may turn his or her head at the sound of the caregiver's voice, seeking to meet her gaze. The proximity of that gaze provides the child with a sense of security and comfort in stressful situations.

The child's engagement in social referencing is a third indicator of healthy attachment. **Social referencing** is the child's action of looking first to the caregiver to read cues regarding a new event or a new person in the room. If the caregiver becomes tense, the child reads that cue and then becomes tense or fussy or cries. If the caregiver smiles at the new person, the child relaxes, smiles, and opens up to that person, too. This early learning of social cues through social referencing is a safe learning experience that encourages the child to explore beyond the known and into the unknown. Through social referencing, the child with a healthy attachment learns how to explore the environment beyond the caregiver in order to distinguish between safe and unsafe situations.

Insecure Attachment

Attachment injuries happen in the child's microsystem—the intimate relationship between child and caregiver. When the synchronous, prompt response to a stimulus that characterizes secure attachment is lacking, insecure attachment begins to develop.

Each time a stimulus from the child (that is, an expressed need) is met with no response or too slow a response from the caregiver, an **attachment injury** occurs. Each attachment injury or wound builds on the previous one; thus, insecure attachment develops. It is important to recognize and try to understand the cause of the attachment injury, not in order to assign blame but in order to heal the wound.

All infants need consistent nurturance, but some may have difficulty expressing this need. For example, infants with autistic spectrum disorder, communication delays, brain injury, or infants who have experienced prenatal exposure to alcohol or drugs may not be able to signal their needs clearly. They may cry continually or not cry at all, sending to their caregivers confusing messages that may trigger no response or an inappropriate one. An infant who is unable to signal needs clearly, and who receives little or no response, gradually slows or stops signalling needs. The infant may simply stop trying to communicate—a response that leads to even more delays in language and other communication skills.

Even when the caregiver knows that the infant has a communication delay and responds appropriately to the infant's cries, the infant may misperceive the response or be unable to respond adequately. When the caregiver soothes the infant, the infant may scream or turn away from the caregiver. When the caregiver offers her breast, the infant may not be able to suck and may continue to scream with hunger and thirst. The caregiver may then adjust the response, trying different methods of providing care and attention. Sometimes, in a pattern of circular causality, the caregiver misreads the infant's cues and withdraws; and when the infant cries in response, the caregiver withdraws further.

On the other hand, the infant may be healthy and able to respond, but the caregiver may be unhealthy and unable to respond to the child's expressed needs. The caregiver may have mental health issues, addictions, postpartum depression, developmental delays, attachment injuries of her own, or may simply be overwhelmed by the demands of caring for an infant. When the caregiver does not consistently respond to and meet the needs of the infant or young child, the child suffers an attachment injury. Gottman (1997: 153) uses the term 'stonewalling' in reference to love partners who shut down emotionally and do not respond to each other's needs. This same stonewalling characterizes the caregiver who does not respond to the child. The caregiver may not know how to respond, may not have the affect to respond, or may respond in a way that the child perceives to be negative. In all cases, the child feels relationally deprived and, therefore, devalued. The child feels the importance of the relationship, but the caregiver does not respond to the importance of that felt need.

An infant may attack a stonewalling caregiver in a frantic attempt to be recognized and accepted. The infant may cry, thrash, or scream in a desperate attempt to get a reaction, any reaction. If the caregiver continues to offer no response or contact comfort, the infant may then withdraw, feeling loss, despair, and helplessness. Starving emotionally, the infant gives up on life. This emotional withdrawal can result in chemical, physical, and anatomical changes in the brain that can permanently damage the infant, resulting in non-organic failure to thrive or **growth-faltering**. The infant, like the baby monkey with the mechanical mother in Harlow's studies, receives food but fails to put on weight or become healthy. Children with diagnosed attachment injuries or with insecure attachment develop socio-emotional difficulties so deeply rooted that any change, even a positive shift to nurturing caregiving, is strongly resisted. Unfortunately, Harlow was correct about the long-term damage caused by insecure attachment.

The mesosystem in which the caregiver and the infant are situated also can impede the development of attachment. Relatives and the caregiver's partner(s) may make disparaging remarks about the infant, the caregiver, or the relationship. They may caution the caregiver not to pick up and soothe her infant. They may call the caregiver inadequate, a 'lousy mother'. Colleagues, neighbours, health practitioners, and employers, too, may criticize the caregiver's parental capacity, making the caregiver even more unsure of how and when to respond to her infant. This feeling of inadequacy may prompt the caregiver to pass around her infant from babysitter to babysitter, with each change in caregiving style further confusing the infant. All of these mesosystem factors affect the development of the attachment relationship.

Macrosystem factors also have a significant effect. Structural determinants include parental value systems, child welfare systems, war and violence, sexism, racism, and socio-economic factors. For example, parental value systems that encourage harsh discipline prompt caregivers to ignore, punish, or neglect the child when the child communicates physical or emotional needs through crying, fussing, or moving. This inappropriate, abusive caregiver response triggers insecure attachment in the child. Miller (2005: 204) documents the long-term effects of such attachment injuries on the child: 'The love of formerly abused children for their parents is not love. It is an attachment fraught with expectations, illusions, and denials, and it exacts a high price from all those involved in it.'

Child welfare systems inflict attachment injuries when they remove children from their attachment figures (see Chapter10). The child who is removed from the home and placed in foster care typically mounts an angry protest. As the protest subsides, the child succumbs to a despair that looks like classic depression. Infants who are separated from their birth mother and adopted by a stranger, for example, show signs of this anxiety, anger, and depression. Regardless of how this loss is explained later by the adoptive parent, the young child feels 'rejected, betrayed, and abandoned by birth parents' (Feeney, 2005: 45). This attachment injury is compounded when a child is moved from foster home to foster home and has only brief, interspersed access to the original attachment figure. Trocme (2002) has documented the attachment injuries and disorders caused by early, prolonged, or traumatic separations from the primary caregiver.

War and violence also separate children from their attachment figures and from the communities of their birth. While some children are able to recover from such trauma through access to counselling and support, consistent parenting, and nurturing communities, as well as through their innate resilience, other children do not recover.

Like the child in Yann Martel's novel *Life of Pi* (2001), they drift alone on the ocean of relationships, trying to find nurturance in the temporary caregivers of their lives.

Sexism and racism are other structural determinants of unhealthy attachment. The newborn reads disappointment in her caregiver's response to her sex or his race. The caregiver may regard the female sex as inferior or brown-skinned people as less valuable than white ones. The newborn reads body language much more accurately than adults do, particularly when the body belongs to a caregiver on whom the infant totally depends.

Then, there is poverty. Parents living in poverty may be juggling several day and night jobs; they may be forced to move continuously to find affordable housing; they may not have access to quality child care because of the cost; and they may lack healthy peer relationships and recreation. They may not have time to respond to their child's needs and, even when time permits, the response may be inadequate because there is just not enough food in the cupboard. Poverty is an overriding structural factor that directly impacts the development of healthy attachment between a child and parent.

 Point to Consider   4.1

Attachment Development through Video

An infant's optimal mental health is nurtured within relationships with sensitive, responsive caregivers. 'Seeing Is Believing' is a video-recording strategy used by nurses, educators, and mental health professionals with First Nations families, mothers with addictions, families identified as abusive or neglectful, and families of preterm infants (see Sameroff et al., 2005). The program helps parents to identify their baby's cues, and to recognize their own strengths in responding sensitively to those cues. After video-recording the parent–infant interaction, the worker then watches the video with the parent, asking questions to help the parent discover the meaning of behaviour as seen through the infant's eyes.

Insecure attachment has three levels of severity—from avoidant, to resistant, to disorganized. All insecure attachment is cause for concern; however, insecure-disorganized attachment is the most damaging because of its deep, long-term effect on the child. The insecure-avoidant infant has already learned in the first few weeks of life that the caregiver is not to be trusted. When the infant cries, the caregiver does not respond or responds inappropriately. This caregiver is not a safe base, and the insecure-avoidant infant responds in a self-protective way by ignoring her. When the caregiver leaves, the infant protests briefly; when she returns, the infant shows little or no signs of pleasure. The infant gradually learns to detach from or avoid the caregiver. As the insecure-avoidant infant grows and becomes verbal, the child continues to show little affect when the caregiver comes and goes. The child does not differentiate between caregiver and stranger, kissing and hugging either of them when required, but with little or no enthusiasm. The child may answer 'Whatever' when asked to choose an activity, clothing, or food. The child develops the response of detachment to cope with an early attachment injury and an insecure base.

The more significantly affected insecure-resistant infant demonstrates confused behaviour, alternating between anxiety and resistance. The infant becomes severely agitated and anxious and may cry continuously when the caregiver is out of the play-room. However, when the caregiver returns, the infant continues to cry and cannot be comforted, alternately clinging to the caregiver and pushing her away. As the insecure-resistant infant grows and becomes verbal, the child tends not to develop social relationships or engage in social play with peers. The child appears fearful of new experiences and changes playmates often, never developing close friends or a stable social group. This unconscious and unspoken strategy insulates the child from potential disappointment and further attachment injuries.

At the most severe end of the attachment injury spectrum, the insecure-disorganized infant displays very confused and contradictory behaviours in reaction to the chaos and danger posed by the caregiver. This infant develops reactivity and a series of rapid reflexive responses to imminent danger. The infant may exhibit intense anger, followed suddenly by a dazed appearance. When held by the caregiver, the infant may cry continuously, with stiff body and arched back. The infant may show signs of fear and scream intensely when the caregiver enters the room.

As the infant grows and begins to walk, he or she may try to leave the room with a stranger or whoever appears to be most attractive at a particular moment. The child prefers high-risk activities and has little sense of personal safety. Later, the child may gravitate to gangs and other attachment-disorganized children with similar attachment injuries. This coping mechanism affords a temporary feeling of safety with like-minded peers who also avoid close emotional relationships.

Feeney (2005: 45) describes insecure-disorganized attachment injury as 'fearful, the most negative attachment pattern.' In her study of adults with attachment problems, she discovered that 72 per cent of the fearful group had been adopted as infants. She notes that this group of adults continue to suffer from their early attachment injuries. They attach easily to strangers, much as they did as infants, but they find healthy attachment to be elusive and have difficulty forming intimate relationships with other adults. They also block out huge periods of their childhood, remembering little.

Without an appropriate intervention, the insecure attachment developed in infancy will persist throughout childhood. Hamilton (2000: 690) observes: 'Although change in this internal working model is possible, over the course of early childhood the internal working model becomes less flexible and consciously accessible and so may be less susceptible to change.' As a result, some or all of the following behaviours may develop:

- social withdrawal and hesitancy to participate in interactions and activities;
- poor problem-solving skills;

- avoidance of any intimacy;
- hostility and aggressiveness towards others;
- lack of respect for the property of others;
- superficiality in relationships and rejection of any affectionate overtures;
- a pervasive lack of trust;
- a strong need to control and to manipulate others;
- bed-wetting and poor hygiene skills;
- volatile anger, hostility, and cruelty to animals and to other people.

These behaviours may also be observed in deeply troubled children who are securely attached. At times they may vandalise property, for example, despite a secure attachment to parents and to community. However, it is the constellation of behaviours, and their pervasiveness, that characterizes insecure or unhealthy attachment.

The insecurely attached infant has a coping strategy that is both defensive and protective: ignore the caregiver and relate on an equal basis with both the caregiver and any random stranger. This infant develops into an anxious child who blocks emotions and feelings and avoids emotional ties to others. Unattended attachment injuries can interfere with and even stop the child's development and wellness. Attachment injuries, although less visible than physical damage, are probably the most difficult childhood injuries to heal.

Attachment Injuries and Deculturation

Attachment injuries usually are described as having been inflicted by the primary caregiver. However, they can occur when the primary caregiver is the community and the child is removed from it by child welfare agencies, religious groups, or private adopters. Richard Foot (2008) describes the contemporary enthusiasm of non-Inuit Canadians from the south for adopting Inuit children, and the attachment injuries that result. Beth Brant, a Mohawk writer born in Ontario in 1941, describes the process of deculturation that many Native Canadians have endured in 'A Long Story' (2005), in which she recounts her removal from her community, followed by her daughter's similar removal: 'They said it was in her best interests. How can that be? She is only six, a baby who needs her mothers. She loves us' (p. 146). The pattern of attachment injuries is perpetuated as children are removed from communities, are raised by culturally dissimilar caregivers, become emotionally distanced themselves, do not attach to their children, then have their children removed and placed with culturally dissimilar caregivers.

The histories of both Inuit and First Nations children have been recounted in the records of residential schools, foster care and adoption agencies, and Canadian political texts. In his report on Indian and Métis adoptions and placements Senior Family Court Judge E.C. Kimelman (1985: 185) refers to the perpetration of 'cultural genocide' and describes a situation in which 'Cultural bias is practised at every level, from the social worker who works directly with the family, through the lawyers who represent the various parties in a custody case, to the judges who make the final disposition in a case'. But the attachment injuries and deculturation these children have suffered are perhaps best described through the storytelling tradition of Native culture. For this, we turn to Jeanette C. Armstrong, an Okanagan born in 1948 in British Columbia, who tells the story of a coyote trapped in a hallway in a city building. Someone has mistaken the coyote for a dog and let the coyote into the building, not recognizing that the coyote is an outdoor animal,

Photo 4.2 A coyote on a rooftop, alone and far from the pack, gets ready to jump.

a free spirit. The coyote, trapped and cut off from all that is familiar, becomes fearful, anxious, and disoriented, searching for a way to escape to the outside and return to his pack (community). The coyote finally rides up to the roof in an elevator, and then jumps off the roof rather than go back down in the elevator into a building that inspires such fear. Armstrong (2005: 242) describes 'the coyotes hanging around in the cities these days. Nobody wanted them there, so nobody made friends with them, but once in a while they made the papers when they did something wrong or showed up, trotting along Broadway, cool as could be.' Here, the coyote refers to the transplanted child moving on the margins between cultures, gaining attention only through misbehaviour, and ultimately turning to death for escape. In this story, Armstrong strongly criticizes the removal of children from their birth community and culture, illustrating that, for Native Canadian children, deculturation results in an attachment injury.

Attachment injuries involving deculturation also are inflicted on children who, after being partly raised in another country, are transported to Canada, losing their language, culture, country, and birth family in the process. The child loses not only a primary caregiver but also a base for the internal working model of culture. If the child is removed to a community with a different culture, as so often happens, the child becomes culturally confused and the internal working model begins to deteriorate and may collapse (Le Mare et al. 2006). Such deculturation occurs through private adoptions that involve the purchase[2] of children from countries around the world, mainly from South America and Asia, although some European nations such as Romania and Russia have provided children for private adoptions. In countries such as India, Korea, China, Kenya, and Chile, groups have organized to protest this export of their children. Birth families of adoptees have formed the majority of these groups, some asking for their children to be returned, and others questioning why they have never heard from their children after the adoption. Other nations have stopped the practice of inter-country adoptions amid charges of corruption and child exploitation.

This tragedy of deculturation is best articulated by the adopted children themselves, who describe their anger and their attachment injuries. Not only do they feel torn from their birth family; they also feel torn from their culture and their home country, as expressed in the following poem by Kevin Minh Allen of the adoptee group Transracial Abductees (2008):

Middle-class wives
can't get enough of these infants.
So adoptable, adaptable,
so contractually obligated
to fit neatly in a grateful paradigm.
After their husbands hand over the check
that greases the palms of the minister of interior,
who dropkicks the orphans over the border,
these sunburnt women catch them in their gardening hats
and shine them on their aprons,
like so many apples in a bowl.

In *Life of Pi* (2001), Canadian novelist Yann Martel illustrates the importance of attachment in the lives of children who lack a stable cultural base. Martel, who has described Canada as the best hotel in the world, moved from country to country with his peripatetic parents throughout his early life.[3] However, he retained his attachment figures in the same way that his protagonist, Pi—a child adrift on the ocean without family or friends—retains his attachment to Richard Parker, a tiger. Richard's consistent presence heals Pi's attachment injuries caused by the sudden death of everyone in his family. Though Richard may not be cuddly, the tiger is stable, consistent, and attuned to Pi. As a result, the resilient Pi survives, even when his symbolic figure of attachment lopes into the jungle: 'Then Richard Parker, companion of my torment, awful, fierce thing that kept me alive, moved forward and disappeared forever from my life' (p. 316).

This story and the story of its author are quintessentially Canadian tales. They echo the stories of many new Canadian children who are adrift and unable to communicate in their new land. However, these resilient children can survive if they have a healthy attachment to a consistent and responsive caregiver.

Attachment Interventions

If a child's attachment is insecure due to caregiver behaviour, attachment interventions in the home can support positive changes in this behaviour, which in turn affect the behaviour of the child. This does not mean that caregivers need to be 'perfect parents'. Winnicott, an early attachment theorist, suggests instead a model of 'good-enough mothering', which he describes as 'devotion': an imperfect but adequate provision of emotional care that is not damaging to the child. He was convinced that mothering could never be perfect because of the presence of a mother's own emotional needs, and notes that 'The good-enough mother . . . starts off with an almost complete adaptation to her infant's needs, and as time proceeds she adapts less and less completely, gradually, according to the infant's growing ability to deal with her failure' (Winnicott, 1953: 94).

Update Winnicott's model by revising the word 'mother' to 'parent', and good enough parenting still promotes healthy attachment today. Supported by his extensive psychoanalytic work with adults and children, Winnicott's research offers all parents hope that they can attach to their children despite having personal emotional needs or inadequacies. Affection and love cannot be taught, but, through attachment interventions in the home, an emotional bond between caregiver and child can be nurtured over time.

The worker's first step is to explore the caregiver's own attachment injuries, if any. The caregiver may have been abused or neglected as a child, and may never have developed a healthy attachment to a primary caregiver. She may have suffered an attachment injury when a beloved parent died or became seriously ill; may have had an absent parent, an emotionally distant parent, or a parent who really did not want to be a parent; or may have been removed from her early caregiving community. All of these possibilities can be explored through a slow and gentle conversation infused with affirmation and support. The following example illustrates how a dialogue between worker (W) and caregiver (C) might begin:

W: In the past, parenting was not always a choice. It was what people just did. What was it like for your parents?

C: I don't really know. I don't see what that has to do with my son's being so difficult and fussing all the time.

W: Well, sometimes we as parents give messages that are the opposite of the messages we want to give. We need to find out where those messages start. Sometimes they go back to when we were just newborns ourselves. Can you think back to those first few years of your own life? Who was in your home then?

C: My mom and dad. We were a normal family. Pretty typical, really.

W: So you were the first child, yes?

C: Yes, my mom had a miscarriage and then got pregnant with me. She was so happy to have a daughter.

W: A miscarriage?

C: Well, not really. Actually it was a stillborn, I think. Oh, no. My older brother died a month after he was born.

W: Oh, oh. The death of a first son.

C: I never thought of it that way. You see, my parents never talked about it. Never even had a funeral.

W: Never talked about it with you?

C: Actually, they didn't. It was one of many things we never talked about. That, and the fact that they had only one daughter. I think my dad always regretted never having a son.

W: Never having a son?

C: Well, you can't really count their first baby. He was only a month old.

W: A month old.

C: I guess. The same age as Cameron.

W: And you are home just like your mom was at home.

C: Actually, she wasn't. She went to work just after I was born.

W: So, who looked after you?

C: I don't know. A lot of different babysitters, I think. I only remember one really mean one, though.

This conversation about early childhood begins with a description of a 'pretty typical family' and evolves into an uncovering of emotionally stressful events that echo through the generations. The worker listens to the mother and affirms each remembered event, contextualizing the mother's experience within a larger discourse about attachment figures, loss, grief and unattended grief, and the long-term effects of early attachment injuries.

When a young child has attachment injuries, the worker sometimes meets with the child outside the home. This choice acknowledges both the caregiver's request for help for the child and the child's anger with the caregiver. If the caregiver–child relationship is ever to be mended and re-established, both the caregiver and the child need to identify and work through their own early attachment injuries and the impact of these injuries on their relationship. The parallel adult–worker and child–worker meetings are not about blame; they are about recognition and acknowledgment and relationship work. Interventions with caregivers can happen in the home, but interventions with children are often best situated outside the home or outside the scene of the injury.

The worker who intervenes needs to understand the causes and effects of attachment injuries in order to recognize the grief expressed in the behaviours of the child. Attachment work is a long-term process, and the lengthiest part of the work is relationship-building. The insecurely attached child has learned not to trust adults who say they care, and not to express emotions to anyone. This learning is pre-verbal and has been imprinted on the child's mind during early infancy. The worker can explore the possibility of unlearning, but must recognize that this goal will be achieved only through healing experiences, not through words. The intervention therefore needs to be experiential.

With each loss experienced during childhood, the child's capacity to trust diminishes. A parent may die, then the substitute caregiver may leave, then a family member to whom the child is attached may become ill. Throughout these experiences, there may have been many words of reassurance, but the child feels only loss. 'I care about you' is followed by 'I am leaving you'. Each loss builds upon previous ones. Attachment interventions do not minimize these losses or try to undo them; the worker knows that the loss of a primary attachment figure is traumatic to a child and is likely to result in irreversible emotional scarring. The child has missed out on safety and security in

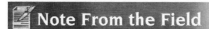

Note From the Field   4.1

When Love Is Not Enough

Brodzinsky (1998) presents the case of an adoptive mother and her seven-year-old adopted daughter, Susan, who was placed in her adoptive home at the age of 13 months. Before she was adopted, Susan's infancy was marked by attachment injuries, and she was therefore attachment-disorganized and demonstrated stiffness and inability to respond. Her adoptive mother felt that her love could change this, so she destroyed Susan's social history (the record of her abusive past) and surrounded her with cuddling and warmth. Brodzinsky quotes the mother's description of Susan's response to her parents' care:

> Susan never seemed to warm up to us. From the very beginning she resisted being held and comforted. She would go stiff when we tried to cuddle with her . . . even now she doesn't come to us when she gets hurt. . . . I feel that the only time we exist for her is when she wants something . . . then she gets all friendly and sweet but we feel the falseness. Even after all this time, she doesn't feel that much for us or really care about us. (p. 101)

As Susan grew, her untreated attachment injuries festered. They were not openly acknowledged and attended to by her new parent, so Susan did not go to her adoptive mother for affection. Her adoptive mother reacted by feeling hurt and unloved, and by withdrawing emotionally from Susan. She labelled her daughter as manipulative and began 'blamestorming', perceiving the child as the cause of the family's problems. This adoptive mother's anger and blaming further reinforced her daughter's mistrust of adults.

In working with these clients, Brodzinsky used a strengths-based and structural approach that included educational, psychological, and physical strategies. Susan and her mother were educated as to the cause and effect of early attachment injuries, and Susan's mother in particular was educated about the responsive caregiving and contact comfort necessary for building attachment with her daughter.

The psychological intervention work Brodzinsky did with Susan led her to reconstruct her early infancy through pictures and drawings, and through hearing about her social history. Susan's mother lived in poverty and was unable to care for Susan. During her first year, Susan was placed in a series of inappropriate foster homes, in one of which she suffered emotional abuse from a caregiver with mental health issues. This reconstruction of events positioned Susan's narrative within a context of poverty and class issues over which she had no control. Through autobiographical reasoning, Susan began to understand that she was a wanted and loved child; her birth mother did love her but was unable to care for her.

Note From the Field   4.1 continued

The physical interventions in this case involved Susan's mother learning to play in response to Susan's verbal and non-verbal cues. Susan's adoptive mother learned how to have fun with her daughter again. She began to choose to spend time with Susan and to play with her, and this play time helped to rebuild the relationship between mother and daughter.

Adoptees like Susan can recover from early attachment injuries, as demonstrated by Harlow's early attachment studies (Harlow and Suomi, 1972). Harlow's monkeys, having suffered severe attachment injuries due to being raised without contact comfort by mechanical mothers, were placed in a cage with a 'therapist monkey' for one hour a day, five days a week, for six months. The therapist monkeys offered physical play and cuddling to the monkeys reared in isolation from physical contact. By the end of the six-month period, these highly damaged monkeys had recovered and their social behaviour was close to normal. Attachment interventions over the next 30 years confirmed these results as workers intervened to restore the healthy attachment of children.

childhood, and has survived by not expressing emotion and by avoiding further injurious encounters with caregivers.

The worker can begin by acknowledging the resiliency and strength necessary for such survival, and by honestly confirming that the child does not want the meeting and does not trust the worker: trust needs to be earned. The worker may avow, 'This is your time to use as you wish. I am here to listen.' The child will test these words over many meetings, and the worker's predictability and consistency is critical.

In the silence that will likely begin this first meeting, the worker can offer a non-threatening structure or a scaffold: 'I have heard that you lived with your mom when you were a baby.' This scaffold opens the worker to being corrected by the child, much as a teacher corrects a student. This equalizes the power dynamic at the onset, and puts the child in the leadership role. The worker then scaffolds the correction: 'Thanks for setting me straight on that.'

The worker validates the child's resiliency and strength throughout the first meeting, remarking on the child's ability to survive, problem-solve, create a life. The worker incorporates as much of the child's own language as possible to keep the dialogue meaningful and open; for instance, the worker may say, 'Yeh, I'm onto that' rather than use professional jargon. The worker can also use crayons and paper, drawing in response to the child's instructions. These drawings can become positive images for the child: genograms to map family connections; sociograms to map current and potential social supports; or lifelines to graphically plot important dates and events.

Point to Consider 4.2

Continuity of Attachment through the Generations

Bowlby (1969) postulates that the condition of secure or insecure attachment extends through the generations, as insecure caregivers struggle to form a secure attachment with their infants. His thesis has been tested using the Strange Situation procedure, the Adolescent Attachment Interview, and the Adult Attachment Interview. Instead of limiting their focus to individual responses or actions, all three methods of assessment consider the patterns of response between caregiver and child.

Hamilton (2000) showed how these patterns indicate a person's state of mind with respect to attachment. In her research with mothers, she used the Adult Attachment Interview in classifying feelings of attachment as autonomous, dismissing, preoccupied, or unresolved—four classifications that map onto earlier classifications of infant attachment as healthy, avoidant, resistant, and disorganized.

It is important to refer to the work of Bowlby and Hamilton when planning attachment interventions with adoptive mothers who are locked into a pattern of anger and 'blamestorming' with their older adopted children. These adoptive mothers may not have had the chance to grieve their infertility and feelings of loss around birthing. Their adopted children may not have had the chance to grieve the loss of their birth families. These early and primal losses, repressed by both for so long, need to be expressed before the healing and the nurturing of healthy attachment can begin. Expressing and listening forms a new pattern of responses that may feel awkward at first—anger and blamestorming are the more familiar and comfortable mode. However, by expressing to each other unresolved feelings of loss, both mother and child can begin to empathize with each other and to work towards a healthier attachment.

Children with attachment injuries typically describe their family members as 'weird' or 'crazy'. The worker affirms and repeats these descriptors and writes them down on the genogram as the child instructs. Together, the worker and the child slowly reframe the family. The worker may tell a story about other families or friends with similar attributes that can be seen as positive. The weird sister who changes jobs all the time, for example, can be reframed through a story about a co-worker who does the same thing in order to learn more. This exercise is not intended to excuse or rationalize the caregiver's behaviour or minimize the child's pain. Instead, the reframing may support and broaden the child's understanding of early attachment injuries and encourage his or her expression of feelings, probably non-verbally at first, about those injuries. The worker supports the child in naming the pain and acknowledging its effect, and when the child is ready, the worker can provide support as the child confronts family members and begins a different, more open relationship with past and present caregivers.

Foster Care

Another intervention that workers use with children with attachment injuries is to place children in foster care. The rationale commonly offered is that foster care providers are better able to develop the healthy attachment that the child's primary caregivers did not, and that a stable placement with a nurturing foster caregiver can help to heal attachment injuries. In defence of this position, a long-term and stable relationship with a caring and responsive person has certainly been shown to help a child recover from early attachment injuries (Kaufman and Heinrich, 2000).

However, the attachment-injured child who is moved to foster care is more likely to experience a series of placements, or **foster care drift**, than a long-term and stable placement. Such moves happen for many reasons, most of which are attributable to adult decisions or needs: the foster parent may move to a smaller home or another jurisdiction, may become ill or have a family member who is hospitalized and requires additional care, or may die or experience the death of a family member. In some cases, foster parents have expertise with a limited age range of children, and the child 'ages out' of the home. In other cases, a child's brothers or sisters are in another foster home, and the child is moved to be reunited with them. Sometimes a family has too many children for the space available in one foster home, so the children are divided, then reunited, then divided again. If some of the children return to the home of their original caregiver and others in the family stay in foster care, the siblings may never overcome their anger and hostility towards those who 'get to go home'.

Such experiences in the foster system only worsen a child's attachment injuries. As Webber (1998: 39) notes: 'Little wonder kids risk developing attachment disorder. It may start in the womb, but it certainly comes from an early childhood spent like a rubber ball. Being kicked around can, understandably, turn a kid off love. They start to view caregivers as disposable, interchangeable parts, and themselves as all they've got.' Though the circumstances resulting in a move from one home to another may have nothing do with the child's behaviour, the child typically experiences the move as another rejection. The child may feel 'not good enough' for the family or unloved by the foster parents. The child may self-identify as a problem or a 'bad kid' who has to be moved. With each relocation to a new foster home, the child becomes more certain that the problem is internal rather than external, and the original attachment injury is compounded.

The child in foster care also has to deal with separation from parents, brothers, and sisters who are still alive and who may live in the same district. This loss of connection can be even harder to accept than the more common loss of parents through death. Children in foster care know that their parents are continuing to live and survive without them, and this knowledge only deepens the attachment injury.

Photo 4.3 Smiles, sunshine, and rainbows may hide the loss of one child to foster care.

Too often, the foster care intervention is an attempt to erase a child's family from his or her life. The child is told to forget a cousin or grandmother and to move on to more positive relationships, on the basis that these relatives can never change their behaviour. In arguing for long-term placement, the worker assures the child that the abusive mother will continue to be abusive, regardless of the life experiences and education she may have. These, attempts to dismiss family members from the child's life also dismiss potential lifetime sources of care and support for that child. In addition, denying the possibility that family members can change implies that the child, too, is unable to change or develop.

In a British Columbia study of children in foster care (Jones and Krak, 2005), the children declared that their workers would not listen to them and that they did not feel heard by the system. Their multiple placements made them feel that they were not a real part of any family. At the same time, almost all of the children in the study identified their birth family as the primary object of attachment and expressed a wish to find their birth families, despite their histories of suffering abuse and neglect in these same families. This instinctual wish for a family and for some secure attachment, even when that family is abusive, neglectful, or emotionally distant, is well documented (Blackstock and Trocme, 2005).

Children in foster care face a heightened risk of social isolation. Their restricted social network tends to be formal, including adults such as a worker, foster parents, or a tutor—people who are paid to help them and support them. Informal social support, including childhood friends, neighbours, and relatives, are wholly absent from their lives. The lifelong network of birth family relatives—cousins, aunts and uncles, grandparents—is broken, and foster children assume the transient social identity of a 'child in care'. The loss of extended family to the personal identity is itself an attachment injury.

Customary Adoption

A traditional structural intervention used within First Nations communities is customary adoption and kinship care. Generations of First Nations and Inuit mothers have occasionally given their babies to sisters or other women in their families or communities. The birth mothers may have felt unable to care for their newborns or they may have felt empathy for a sister or aunt who had no children of her own to raise. This has been and remains an open social practice, one that is woven into the texture of communities, and one that reflects an inherent belief in the child as a gift to the community rather than the sole responsibility of parents. As the Royal Commission on Aboriginal Peoples (1996: 231) states, 'Children hold a special place in Aboriginal cultures. According to tradition, they are gifts from the spirit world and must be treated very gently lest they become disillusioned with this world and return to a more congenial place. . . . They bring a purity of vision to the world that can teach their elders. They carry within them the gifts that manifest themselves as they become teachers, mothers, hunters, councillors, artisans, and visionaries. They renew the strength of the family, clan and village and make the elders young again with their joyful presence.'

Customary adoption is described as a process of making relatives rather than losing them. For this reason, a First Nations child may happily identify two women as mother, and may feel secure knowing that the entire community is a caregiver, as described by Beth Brant earlier in this chapter. Elders and other adults in the community feel equally empowered to guide a child of their community, through showing, listening, gesturing, or relating stories from the past.

Customary adoption does not attach blame or guilt to the birth parent, the adoptive parent, or the child. The child's relationship with the birth family is not terminated; nor is there any change made to the child's name. The birth family may not have the resources to care for the child at the time of the adoption, but the emotional connection between that family and the child is preserved. The adoption is finalized in a traditional ceremony that recognizes the status of the child as the responsibility of a caring community that includes extended family, the band, and the clan. Honouring the child as a gift from Mother Earth, the community members dedicate themselves to the care of this very special child whose best interests are seen to be the same as those of the community as a whole.

Customary adoption has long been a tradition in Canada, and is now commonly practised by the Yellowhead Tribal Service Agency in Alberta and the First Nations Children Society of British Columbia. These two agencies have been leaders in facilitating customary adoption and showing how to intervene to promote healthy attachment between the child and the child's community. The role of community in developing healthy attachment is vital, as this account of two Inuit who spent seven years in a residential school explains: 'When finally they were allowed to return home, their families took them immediately onto the land in what Theo describes today as a rescue mission. Over a series of years, he recalls, "They turned us back into Inuit men"' (Davis, 2009: 209).

Summary

Tracing the development of early attachment between the child and the caregiver or community of caregivers, this chapter explores the actions and contexts that help or hinder this relationship. The importance of the secure emotional base that attachment provides is evident in the contrasting descriptions provided here of the child with a healthy attachment and the child with an insecure or unhealthy attachment. Interventions both in and outside the home can help to build secure attachment or to repair the injuries caused by an insecure attachment. So much in a child's life depends upon healthy relationships, and one of the most important bonds can be that between the child and the worker. For this relationship to be healthy, it must be built on congruence, respect, and empathy, as accompanied by the cultural competency demonstrated by a caring and supportive worker.

Review Questions

1. When and how does attachment begin?
2. Name three researchers who have studied attachment and their contribution to this theory.
3. Explain the Strange Situation procedure.
4. Why is healthy attachment so important for human socio-emotional development?
5. Compare and contrast the three kinds of insecure or unhealthy attachment.
6. What three behaviours of a young child indicate that there is a healthy attachment between the young child and his or her caregiver?
7. What is synchrony? How does it develop between two persons?
8. Name three causes of attachment injuries.
9. What is meant by the 'reciprocity of relationship' between a caregiver and a child? How does the story of Susan illustrate this dimension of relating and the ways in which it affects attachment?

10. Name three possible interventions either in the home or outside the home that can help to heal a child's attachment injuries.

Discussion Questions

1. How can structural determinants be altered to encourage the development of healthy attachment between caregiver and infant? Are there programs that facilitate such change?
2. Do you think it is possible to heal attachment injuries that occur in the first year of life? What evidence do you have that this is either possible or impossible?
3. Healthy attachment is considered the basis for forming healthy adult relationships. Reflecting on your own experiences, do you think this is true? Why or why not?

Chapter 5

Relationships

Uncle drummed and everyone sang as Solomon lifted the mask to his face and danced. Beneath their feet the spring sunshine warmed the ground and woke a dormant maple seed. As Solomon danced above, the tip of a root sprouted below and pushed into the loamy earth. 'Ahhh,' whispered the cedars to each other. 'A new beginning.'

—Andrea Spalding, *Solomon's Tree*

This scene from *Solomon's Tree*, Andrea Spalding's children's book about a Native Canadian community, takes place after the Elders ask the young Solomon about the condition of his maple tree, and he shares his grief for his broken, dead friend. The Elders' active listening empowers Solomon to find a pathway to recovery. Solomon watches, learning, as the Elders make a mask from the dead branches. Joining in the task and making a mask to fit his own face, he lifts it and dances, thus finding a new beginning.

In 1940, psychologist Carl Rogers set in motion just such a new beginning for social services when he challenged the traditional dynamic between worker and client. Working *with* clients rather than telling them what to do, he positioned them as equals—as persons with rights who were deserving of respect. Like the Elders in Solomon's community, Rogers led from behind, listening with congruence, empathy, and respect. He defined in a moment healthy working relationships.

The strength and wisdom of this respectful, communicative approach to relationships, with roots in both Native Canadian and Rogerian practice, seems obvious, yet it continues to elude the authoritarian worker who takes the approach of helper–helped and giver–receiver. The worker who assumes the superior position of helper feels validated by this elevation, even though it forces the client into the inferior position of being helped and receiving services—and in the case of the child client, of needing to be saved by an adult 'expert'.

In this chapter, we will explore the Rogerian worker–client relationship and analogous Native Canadian healing practices. Both operate within the legal boundaries of consents and confidentiality; as complex as these boundaries are, both approaches demand openly shared information that sometimes challenges these boundaries. This journey may feel strange and unsettling to those more familiar and comfortable with authoritarian approaches. Such workers often cite structural barriers to the Rogerian relationship: heavy caseloads, overriding legislation, confidentiality requirements, agency protocols. Others will cite the covert barriers of their own bias, insecurity, and fear—an unwillingness to relate openly and equally with the child and to give up the powerful position of expert. Such workers may lack cultural competency, and so assess and evaluate the child and the family according to the yardstick of their own personal culture. The Rogerian relationship challenges this mode of assessment and the helper–helped power dynamic that ultimately entraps both the worker and the child in the 'helping prison' described by Ram Dass (1997: 122–52). The Rogerian relationship takes a rights-based approach that is not easily adopted by workers who do not understand and accept the rights of the child.

The rights-based approach that informs Rogerian practice and Native Canadian tradition empowers the child to embrace personal change and move forward in the dance of life. This chapter concludes with a description of how this approach is exemplified in community capacity-building, through which the child can experience learning without being taught, just as Spalding's Solomon is able to do within a community that cares. If both overt and covert barriers are openly and honestly challenged, community capacity-building can support the child as a person and a valued participant within the community.

Objectives

By the end of this chapter, you will:

- Understand how the worker's cultural competency is fundamental to developing healthy working relationships with the child and the child's family.
- Identify Rogers's three key elements in these relationships.
- Identify how consents and confidentiality can become legal and legislative barriers to these relationships.
- Demonstrate how you could plan and participate in a community capacity-building activity that involves children as equal and valued participants.

Healthy Working Relationships

In the biomedical, deficit-based approach described in Chapter One, the worker identifies and assesses the child as being at risk or having problems. Sometimes this is done in response to a third party telephone call, and sometimes in response to a school or health report. The worker visits the family home, not to establish a relationship but to gather further evidence against the family. The worker speaks *to* the family members rather than *with* them, and assesses the family situation, clipboard in hand. Henry Parada (2002: 106) describes this authoritarian power construct: 'An assessment is already made, and the purpose of meeting the family is to corroborate the assessment.' The worker's preconceptions and bias colour a home visit during which the worker collects 'facts' or reality bites about the family in order to corroborate the pre-visit assessment. The positioning of the worker as the expert keeps both the power and the solution with the worker rather than the family, who must conform to the dictates of the worker.

The worker is part of an agency and a larger, more powerful structure, and brings to the child's home the protocols, systems, and power of the agency. DeMontigny (1995: 220) describes the relative power of the worker: 'Although social workers may not command the power of some professionals, compared with the power of most Native clients, single-parent women, welfare clients, and members of racial minorities, they have considerable power.' The worker plans the intervention, sometimes in collaboration with the parents and sometimes not. The worker bases this intervention on pre-existing assessments of the child, applies the intervention to the child, and then assesses the result. Adjustments follow, and the intervention is reapplied or a new intervention is tried based on the 'expert assessment' of the worker.

The worker may have good intentions, and may want to be a helper. However, these intentions and these wants are worker-centred: they are based on the premise that the worker holds the solutions or remedies to the family's problems. Such help is grounded in the worker's control of the situation and is inherently disempowering for the child and family. This approach reinforces the traditional power dynamic between helper and helped and teaches the child and the family to feel helpless simply because they have been put into the role of being helped. Blackstock and colleagues (2006: 5) quote Milloy in commenting on the well-documented damage done in residential schools to Native Canadian children who were put into this role of helplessness by workers who had 'good' intentions:

> Doing 'good' is apparently better than doing 'nothing' well—and so hangs the tale of the residential school system and the child welfare system too, which could only ever afford child protection (removal of children from their families), rather than prevention activity (building up families). Those good people constantly lobbied for better funding but rarely made any structural critiques and thus they became fellow travelers of a system they did not approve of and earned the ill feeling of those to whom they delivered second-class service.

However well-intentioned, this type of approach, rooted in control, tends to hurt children rather than to help them (deShazer, 1984). The child, re-victimized by the helping adult, feels diminished by the directions and the restrictions and by the implication that he or she has nothing to contribute to the relationship with the worker.

Photo 5.1 The soccer coach builds on the strengths and hopes of the players.

The child therefore resists the restricting, limiting 'help' being offered and instinctively looks for a window of escape. This traditional intervention model can be likened to the wheel in a gerbil's cage: it goes around and around as the worker chases the child in circles, gaining little ground.

Compare this result to the working relationship developed within Rogerian client-centred practice—a relationship based on mutual respect and shared power and control (Rogers, 1951: 41). In the Rogerian approach, the worker presumes that the child has the inner strength for healing and growth and can be an active and equal participant in planning the intervention. The worker's techniques and expertise uncover this strength and affirm it. A respectful sharing of viewpoints and searching for solutions takes place rather than a struggle between the two parties for control and domination. The child is the focus of the planned intervention, and the improvement of the child's welfare is a mutual goal.

Chang (1998: 254) likens the relationship between Rogerian worker and child to that between a player and a coach, a relationship in which the coach learns as much as possible about the player—his or her strengths, hopes, and worries—in order to build on the player's strengths. The player is already on the team and the coach wants only the best, or optimal success, for the player.

More than just a shift in perspective, the Rogerian model demands a complete change in power dynamics in that it is based upon congruence, empathy, and respect, all of which are attributes of power sharing. **Congruence** refers to the alignment between words and deeds, between what the worker says and what the worker does. No promises are made about confidentiality, resources, or care that cannot be kept. **Empathy** refers to the worker's ability and willingness to understand what the child feels and thinks, and to communicate this understanding to the child. **Respect** is demonstrated by the worker's acceptance or unconditional positive regard for the whole child. Rogers (1951) maintains that these three worker attributes, discussed more fully below, are essential to a healthy working relationship between worker and child.

Achieving congruence is not easy because it demands that the worker be both genuine and self-aware: 'The feelings the therapist is experiencing are available to him, available to his awareness, and he is able to live these feelings, be them' (Rogers, 1980: 115). The worker tells the whole truth to the child and does not keep secrets, candidly acknowledging when the law requires that confidentiality be broken, even when this broken confidentiality angers and disappoints the child. Because many of the laws related to consent and confidentiality do not respect the child as a person, congruence is difficult to fully achieve. The following are some examples of congruent worker statements:

- When you say 'secret,' I cannot keep a 'secret' because the law sees you as a child. If your secret harms you or someone else, or if it is a secret about abuse or neglect, then the law requires me to tell someone. Let's look at the secret together; then we can identify who has to be told.
- I am making notes on what you are saying and I am going to share these notes with you. Then you can sign them by printing your own name and today's date at the end of the notes. That lets me know that you and I both understand what is in these notes.
- Your birth mother's file is not open to me or to you at this time, but I can try to help you to get the information you need in other ways.
- If you tell me you have been hurt or that you are hurting others or yourself, I have to let another worker know. That is the law. You and I can talk to that other worker together.

All of these examples of the worker's congruence may provoke the child's anger, distrust, and sadness. The child may become silent, leave the room, or shout at the worker. However, such congruence is fundamental to a healthy working relationship between the worker and the child as equals and as partners in seeking solutions.

The second worker characteristic Rogers insists on is empathy, or warmth and responsiveness. These qualities encourage the child to freely express feelings of hatred, envy, remorse, guilt, anger, and resentment, even when these feelings are described by others as wrong, bad, cruel, or shameful. The child may express dissatisfaction with parents or teachers, but the worker unconditionally affirms the feelings the child expresses, and does not respond by arguing or defending the child's parents or other professionals. Instead, the worker responds with empathy, placing the child's dissatisfaction within a structural construct. The worker may say, 'Exams and tests can be really stressful' or 'Social housing is just not adequate for families, and forces them to squeeze more people into one apartment than can really fit that space'.

This type of relationship is unlike more traditional ones in which a worker may dismiss or disregard the child's feelings, or attribute a specific value to these feelings. The traditional worker may suggest to the child that she or he move out of the home (into a foster care situation) or stay in the home and obey the caregiver's rules at all times. The child-focused worker does not offer these types of suggestions and does not advise or pressure the child to take any particular course of action or to adopt worker-created solutions. Rogers (1951: 41) describes the merits of this empathetic approach: 'In the emotional warmth of the relationship . . . the client begins to experience a feeling of safety as he finds that whatever attitude he expresses is understood in almost the same way that he perceives it, and is accepted.'

The third crucial characteristic of the Rogerian relationship is respect: the worker's unconditional positive regard for the child as a person, not as a vulnerable innocent or property of the family or social capital (see Chapter 2). Respect is not the same as the overly sympathetic, often patronizing, indulgent praise sometimes heard in adult–child situations: 'Oh, aren't they sweet'; 'What an adorable child'; 'Kids say the darndest things!'. Instead, respect entails the worker's caring and appreciation for the child as a unique person. Pearson (2008: vii) describes this deep valuation of the child: 'Respecting children goes beyond merely listening to what they have to say. It means hearing their words with your eyes, your ears, your heart, and your undivided attention. It advocates using the voice of children to inform action.'

The respectful worker is emotionally constant and responsive to the child, matching activity type and level to cues provided by the child. The worker practises a responsive approach grounded in attunement or interactive synchrony, engaging when the child is ready and beginning at the child's interest and developmental level. When the child signals the need to disengage, the worker supports this need and does not impose adult plans or solutions on the child. Respect entails working *with* the child rather than *on* the child.

Congruence, empathy, and respect are interrelated, overlapping in a child-centred focus that is very similar to the traditional Native Canadian way of working with children, based on Medicine Wheel teachings. Describing this approach, Gilgun (2002: 68) notes, 'The framework assumes trust, mutuality, and reciprocity between young people and the persons to whom they relate.' To return to the example of Andrea Spalding's novel, when Solomon's maple tree dies and he is devastated by the loss, the Elders of his community hear him and do not judge his grief as silly, foolish, or childish. Instead, they ask open, respectful questions in order to understand the boy's feelings, such as 'Did your tree have a voice?' and 'Did your tree smell nice?' (Spalding, 2002: 17).

Solomon's community works with his grief, encircling it with spirituality and a love for Mother Earth. Through the empowering and very physical experience of creating, alongside his community, a mask from his tree, Solomon is able to transform his grief into something more positive that will help him move forward. As he lifts the mask to his face and dances, a new maple tree sprouts from the seed of his old tree, symbolizing the life connection between Solomon, the Elders, the community, and the earth.

In this client-centred, collaborative practice, advocated by Rogers (1951), Ram Dass (1985), bell hooks (1994), and Paulo Freire (2000), the key element is mutual respect. As hooks (1994: 54) notes:

> Authentic help means that all who are involved help each other mutually, growing together in the common effort to understand the reality which they seek to trans-form. Only through such praxis—in which those who help and those who are being helped help each other simultaneously—can the act of helping become free from the distortion in which the helper dominates the helped.

In client-centred practice, the child experiences a sense of emotional and physical safety that encourages further self-exploration and reflection. Freire (2000) calls this exploratory process **conscientization** and encourages people to develop an under-standing of their collective oppression through learning about structural impacts on their lives. Conscientization normalizes personal difficulty, connecting it to difficulties experienced by others who are equally oppressed. This approach is not too abstruse or theoretical for children because it is grounded in their experience of mandatory schooling, curfews, and apprehensions. Children can understand how the structure (education, poverty, foster care, gender roles, power constructs) affects both their behaviour and the behaviour of all children in a country that does not uphold interna-tional law as stipulated in the Convention on the Rights of the Child.

As Rogers (1951) notes, boundaries are crucial to the healthy relationship between worker and child. Agreed-on boundaries circumscribe the relationship and help the child feel physically and emotionally secure. These boundaries establish that the worker–child relationship is safe and is limited by time and space and the regularity of meetings. If the worker crosses these accepted boundaries, the child begins to feel unsafe. The worker who extends the meeting time, for instance, because the child is upset or wants to play longer in the play therapy room, is jeopardizing the established limits and safety of the relationship. The worker who needs to be admired by the child and asks the child for praise ('Do you like coming here?') threatens these same bound-aries, as does the worker who offers personal affection to the child ('You know what? I really like you. You are my friend.').

Establishing and maintaining boundaries in the worker–child relationship shows respect for the personhood of the child. The legal concept of fiduciary relationships (related to employment for pay) acknowledges the issues that may arise regarding boundaries. Because workers influence the lives of children, they are held to a higher standard in fiduciary relationships with children and are solely responsible for maintaining professional boundaries. Subsections of the Code of Ethics for the Canadian Association of Social Workers (2005) prescribe the following worker responsibilities regarding trust and boundaries:

2.2.1 Social workers do not exploit the relationship with a client for personal benefit, gain, or gratification.

2.4.1 Social workers take care to evaluate the nature of dual and multiple relationships to ensure that the needs and welfare of clients are protected.

2.5.1 Social workers avoid engaging in physical contact with clients when there is a possibility of harm to the client as a result of the contact.

2.6.1 Social workers do not engage in romantic relationships, sexual activities, or sexual contact with clients, even if such contact is sought by clients.

This code of ethics is a guideline only, not a legal document. Words such as 'romantic' (2.6.1), 'possibility' (2.5.1), and 'nature' (2.4.1) are inherently ambiguous, and indicate the difficulty of enforcing prescriptive codes. The effectiveness of such codes relies on trained workers applying the principles in a thoughtful and ethical way, as described by Wharf and McKenzie (2004: 160): 'Our vision of the professional is one who surrenders the desire to control while acknowledging that there are some limits imposed by legislation, by budgets or, increasingly, by time. These professionals welcome the contributions of those being served and work hard to establish relationships characterized by partnership.'

Cultural Competency

At a meeting with a new client, a worker may see a child whose culture is similar to his or her own, or a child whose culture is dramatically different, even antithetical to the worker's. Each child brings a personal culture and a family culture to the first meeting. How a worker responds to that culture and establishes the base for the relationship that will develop—whether healthy or unhealthy—is determined by that worker's level of **cultural competency**.

Culture has an enormous influence on who and what we are—on every action and decision that we take and every relationship that we enjoy (Cech, 1991). The construction of our own culture begins from the moment we are born, and continues to develop through family life experiences, travel, community influences, ability level, socioeconomic status, exposure to violence and war, religion; in other words, our culture is multi-faceted and is always changing. The child carefully constructs a personal culture, and experiences it as unique and different from the cultures of others. This personal culture is tied to self-worth: if society values the child's culture, the child feels valued,

Point to Consider   5.1

Cross-Cultural Factors

The *Negotiating Resilience Research Project* developed by Ungar and Lieben-berg (2008) of Dalhousie University demonstrates the cultural bias that perme-ates many communities. This project examines resiliency factors of children aged 13–15 years who are in transition between two (and sometimes more) culturally distinct worlds. One child with a physical disability is being educated among able-bodied children; one First Nations child lives off-reserve in an urban and largely mainstream urban environment; one multi-ethnic child negotiates her identity in an ethnically diverse community; and a child refugee without family is situated in a family-based community. Ability, spirituality, ethnicity, race, family, language: all these and more are components of culture. The children in this study try to fit in with other children in their respective communities, while still holding on to their own distinct personal cultures, but these children are met with systemic cultural bias in each of these Canadian communities.

and if society misunderstands, ridicules, or hates the child's culture, the child feels marginalized and diminished.

Each child's culture is unique to that child. It reflects the child's family culture but is not identical to the culture of other family members. Brothers and sisters may appear to be very similar in mores and traditions; however, their individual interpretations of family culture make them behave in slightly different ways as they develop their own personal cultures. One child may embrace the religion of the family, while another child rejects it. One child may absorb the pacifist norms of family behaviour, while another child chooses more aggressive norms and mores.[1] In addition, the child's culture changes continuously through exposure to different religions, values, peers, and life experiences.

If the child's culture is both unique and continuously changing, then, we may wonder, what is the point in workers learning about it? Surely by the time we learn about a child's culture, that culture will have changed! How can we expect to be a 'cultural expert' about so many individual cultures in a family? And how can we achieve cultural competency in a worker–child relationship when we do not know what the child's personal culture means to the child?

The answer to all of these questions is simple: we must listen to the child, who is the expert in his or her own culture. Culture affects behaviour and is viewed through behaviour. We can learn about the child's constantly evolving culture from the child, using our own culture as our reference point and acknowledging that every word, action, or behaviour of the child is filtered through our own cultural bias. The child is our doorway to cultural competency, and cultural competency is the essential framework for a healthy working relationship. So, we listen.

Achieving cultural competency does not entail knowing everything about the culture of the child, but it does involve knowing as much as possible about one's own culture. When the worker intervenes with a child who is in the program because of 'obesity', for example, the worker filters the concept of 'obesity' through his or her own personal cultural bias. What does obesity look like to the worker and how does the worker describe it? Does the worker even consider obesity to be a problem? Think of the variety of culture-specific descriptors for obesity: 'pleasingly plump', 'healthy', 'fat', 'disgusting', 'curvaceous', 'well-rounded', 'full figured'. Each of these descriptors reflects the personal cultural bias of the person who uses it. When the worker understands and acknowledges this fact of personal bias, he or she is more culturally competent to support the child's view of obesity (as the child understands this term).

Personal bias is constructed over a period of years through life experiences, and it affects the worker's appreciation of the child. A bias towards small children, for instance, may prompt the worker to remark: 'Isn't she too cute? I just love that little girl. I'm going to bring her out some little shoes the next time I visit.' Another child in the family who is tall beyond her years may get little or no attention from the same worker. Bias thus causes the worker to favour one child over another.

Bias can also cause the worker to misinterpret the child's messaging. The worker may value close body proximity, for example, and seek to be close to the child and family and to share their personal space. When the child steps back or rejects this physical proximity, the worker may experience this as a rejection and may perceive the child as shy or fearful of adults. Another worker may view the child's direct eye contact as disrespectful and challenging, and may perceive such a child as bold and aggressive. The worker who is culturally competent is aware of personal bias and the multiplicity of possible cultural behaviours, and so is less likely to attribute the wrong meaning to the child's cultural mores.

Bias can be even more evident in the worker's response to a family's cultural values. In many ethnic cultures, the family comes first, and family members feel that attention to the individual, particularly to a child, is a sign of weakness or sickness. 'Think about the family and not about yourself' may be an important aspect of the family belief system. This includes keeping family matters private, respecting elders and their wishes, and putting the needs of the family first. The culture of the worker and the agency, however, may value individuality and place importance on the individual, causing the worker to complain, 'How can they be so selfish? Why don't they see that their child's needs should come first?' The worker can thus culturally misinterpret the family's means of caring for the child, and may describe the child's frequent babysitting chores as inappropriate or even abusive.

Ethnic culture affects the family's relationship with the worker, and also affects who in the family participates in this relationship. While Canadians from some ethnicities

Photo 5.2 Each child brings a unique culture to the worker.

value independence *from* the family, those from other ethnicities value interdependence *within* the family. Some families may expect parents to come to a meeting with the child, some may expect the child to come independently, and some may expect all extended family members to be involved. For example, family interdependence and the participation of all family members may be particularly important for Canadians who are of Middle Eastern or Asian descent, and for Native Canadians. This respect for extended family members, which applies even to those who are no longer living, is described by Calvin Morrisseau, a Native Canadian writer (1998: 90): 'When we understand "all our relations," we will know our ancestors are just as much a part of us today as when they were physically walking Mother Earth. In this sense, we are never alone. Our relations are still present to help us.'

Privacy is another value strongly affected by culture. A child whose culture values privacy for oneself and in family matters may be silent, guarded in relationships with strangers, and may avoid personal disclosure. When the worker tries to establish a warm and caring relationship, the child may interpret this as an invasion of personal privacy and as an insult rather than as an invitation. The child may feel that it is culturally inappropriate to be friendly, open, and unguarded with the worker, who is a stranger and culturally different. The child may perceive such a worker as a trickster who is trying to deceive or ensnare the child. The child may avoid a warm handshake or greeting, and may prefer to call the worker by a last name, or as 'Teacher Sue' rather than as 'Sue', for example. If workers are personally biased towards the 'Dr. Phil' style

Group Exercises   5.1

Welcome to My Home

This large group exercise begins with pair-sharing and ends with large group sharing to create a webbing map of culture. In this brief yet powerful exercise the large group discusses the components of personal culture, why each culture of each person in the group is so distinct, and how cross-cultural miscommunication can happen.

The exercise begins with participants pairing up with participants whom they do not know well. The leader then prints on the board some components of a home visit: rules in the home, rooms for visitors, food and drink, other people in the home, pets.

The leader explains that each participant will offer an overview of these home visit components prior to the other participant visiting the home. The leader explains that this overview will be brief (five minutes), and may involve questions and answers.

At a signal from the leader, the exercise begins. In five minutes the leader signals the participants to switch. In this way, both participants have the opportunity to describe their homes to each other. In five minutes the leader signals the pairs to stop for a debriefing.

At this point the leader collects the components of the home visit from the pairs. These components may include rules and mores, customs, manners, beliefs, and lifestyles. Then, the group leader asks pairs to identify if their home visits were identical and, if not, what made them different. These differences are added to the webbing map of culture that is emerging on the board in front of the large group. Finally, the leader asks which rules, customs, or habits might prove problematic or puzzling to others. Those components are then circled on the board. This exercise not only prompts discussion of cross-cultural misunderstandings but also leads to a greater understanding of the depth and expanse of personal culture.

of casual openness in which intimate thoughts and activities are discussed and shared with strangers, they may describe children who value privacy as distant and closed, or fearful of adults, or they may interpret this cultural value of privacy as a possible indicator of child abuse.

The personal bias most detrimental to a healthy working relationship is expressed in the worker's bold assertion, 'I have no bias. I treat everyone the same.' A worker who makes this claim tacitly denies having either a personal culture or a workplace culture. Instead, such a worker *does* treat every child the same—as if the child is culturally the same as the worker and the workplace. The worker judges all families by the

Point to Consider   5.2

Language and Culture

The Aboriginal Healing Foundation (Chansonneuve, 2005) reminds us that Aboriginal children in residential schools were robbed of their home language. This cultural damage compounded the injuries of removal from family and community and traditions. Today less than one-quarter of Aboriginal persons speak an Aboriginal language. For the non-Aboriginal worker this means that the process of building trust with the child and family will be lengthy. There will be many 'first meetings' and many silences. Many Canadian deaf children also attended residential schools in which their deafness was seen as a deficit. They were encouraged to lip-read and to speak orally in order to fit in with mainstream, and many today feel caught between the deaf world and the mainstream, while fully belonging to neither. Today deaf children often are bilingual, speaking both ASL (American Sign Language) or LSQ (Langue des Signes Québécois) and oral language.

Language and culture are inseparable. When children are stripped of their language, or made to feel their language is inferior, they carry deep scars. The culturally competent worker acknowledges these cultural injuries in the first meeting by acknowledging first language and its importance in the child's life.

yardstick of his or her personal culture, expecting families to conform to worker and workplace culture rather than vice versa. This covert action denies and denigrates the child's culture, labelling it as inferior to the culture of the worker and the workplace. Such workers bring to the child and family the bias of authority and the controlling culture of the workplace. This added level of bias affects the working relationship and may prompt the worker to threaten the family: 'If you don't co-operate, we'll have to amend the service plan.' Other workers, confronted with a family culture they do not understand, may impose their **monocultural bias** on the family: 'They need to be told what they're doing wrong; otherwise, we'll take their kids away. They need to learn what we do in Canada.'

What *do* we do in Canada? As Driedger (2003: 12) remarks, 'Since "official" Canada was largely north European, white and Christian for a century, it should be not surprising that Canadians have a great deal of ambivalence about others who are different.' Traditional approaches to counselling are white, male, Eurocentric, and middle-class in origin and practice (see Chapter 3), and still appear suspicious and alien to those who are not white, male, Eurocentric, and middle class. Other marginalized individuals and families may avoid pursuing counselling, even when their children's behaviour appears problematic. They may believe that, because of their language or their cultural beliefs, their concerns will not be understood by the worker who counsels them. Stigmatized by their poverty, illiteracy, or employment status, they may feel so culturally distanced already that they wish to avoid any contact with professionals.

Those who do come to counselling often do so unwillingly, forced by social agencies, child protection services, educational professionals, or family members. Their expectations are that the counselling will be traditional and, therefore, largely ineffective. They tend not to reveal their family situation to the worker for fear of being misunderstood, of being judged incompetent, or even of losing their children.

Another dimension to this lack of trust is the bias of the child and of the family that has been carefully constructed over many years. A grandmother who has experienced 85 years of the social construction of her culture, for example, may resist the worker in an instinctive strategy to protect her grandchild and her family culture. She may refuse to let the worker into her home, refuse to talk to the worker, exhibit anger and verbal hostility, deny the existence of any problems, attribute blame for family problems to someone or something else, miss scheduled appointments, and/or openly threaten the worker. Such resistance is to be expected. A stranger from another culture who challenges the family's way of life and their love for their child may be experienced as a threat, regardless of how sensitively the worker begins the relationship. One of this grandmother's cultural values may be that children must respect their elders. Confronted by a grandchild who does not respect her, who interrupts her, or who even dismisses her, she may feel ashamed, hurt, or angry. She may feel culturally obligated to teach her grandchild how to behave, and so may hit or spank her grandchild and shout a warning. The grandchild may express anger, distrust, or hatred of that grandmother, but that grandmother is still a part of the child's life, past, present, and future.

The worker's culture, on the other hand, may prescribe very different attitudes towards elders and towards spanking. In such a situation, the worker is required to investigate the grandmother as a potential abuser of her grandchild. However, before intervening with the grandmother, the culturally competent worker pauses, acknowledging both personal bias and the bias of the grandmother. The grandmother may have had previous negative experiences with educational and social welfare systems, and may assume that workers are not to be trusted. 'They are just part of the system', she may think. 'They say they are here to help, but really they're just here to catch us and get our kids into the foster homes.' Just as the construction of the grandmother's culture has been lengthy, so is the deconstruction of this culture a long process. The culturally competent worker recognizes this fact in planning interventions that are culturally appropriate, long-term, and respectful of the child and family.

Cultural competency entails awareness of personal bias and how it affects our acceptance and understanding of the culture of others. Each child and family who arrives for the first meeting with a worker comes through the door bringing a specific personal culture. This culture may bear no resemblance to what the person's skin colour, name, or religious affiliation suggests. *All* counselling is multicultural in that all individuals think and behave according to their own personal culture, and, as Shebib (2007: 303) notes, 'within-group cultural differences may actually exceed between-group differences.' This cultural distinctiveness of all persons needs to be acknowledged at the first meeting of worker and child. The honest acknowledgement of the dissimilarity between the two participants begins a dialogue that positions the worker as the learner, listening carefully to the child, who has the personal cultural knowledge fundamental to building relationships with others. The child becomes the cultural expert rather than the one being helped.

Consents and Confidentiality

The capacity to consent and the rules of confidentiality are determined by legislated age limits, both upper and lower. These age limits vary among the provinces and territories; and even within an individual province or territory, professions and colleges dictate varying age limits for access to service and interventions. This variation and complexity can confound workers trying to explain to children why a service cannot be offered and how age limits affect service (see Chapter 2). Children who need the service may respond angrily and question the worker's congruence. In this way, legislation affecting children in turn affects the healthy working relationship between worker and child.

In Ontario, for example, the child welfare system requires children of age 7 and older to provide written consent to being adopted, and children of age 16 and older to provide written consent to leaving the foster care system. Both consents, one at age 7 and one at age 16, have life-changing effects. In the first instance, the child consents to severing all ties with all members of his or her family of origin, including extended family. In the second instance, the child consents to losing all child welfare services, which include counselling, housing, financial support, and educational funding, among others. That these consents are required and are considered valid—one at age 7 and one at age 16— demonstrates the variation in age determinants of capacity for consent in Ontario.

The adults in the child's life—guardians, parents, or the state acting as guardian— typically have first rights of consent. When a child approaches a worker without parental knowledge or consent, this action is considered to be **implied consent** to treatment. However, the law generally supports parents and guardians who forbid counselling of their minor[2] children, except under extenuating circumstances; this law takes precedence over agency practice and all codes of ethics. This is why workers usually try to obtain **express consent** from the adults in the child's life unless danger to the child may result from doing so. A child's safety could be jeopardized, for instance, in cases in which the parent is alleged to be an abuser. If the parent is informed that the child has sought help, the parent may further harm the child. Federal law also recognizes **mature minors**, children who are considered to be able to fully understand the implications of treatment. In most provinces and territories, mature minors can consent to non-therapeutic treatments such as termination of pregnancy, blood donation, cosmetic surgery, and provision of contraceptives (Rozovsky, 2003).

A child may give express or implied consent to therapeutic treatments such as counselling or guidance. However, the child's right to confidentiality may not be honoured if he or she talks about having been assaulted, as assault of a child is criminalized as abuse, and provincial law demands that abuse, unlike assault, be reported. This duty to report suspected child abuse supersedes the worker's ethical and legal obligation to maintain a client's confidentiality. The consequences for a worker failing to report suspected child abuse vary provincially, from no fines in Manitoba and New Brunswick to fines of $10,000 and six months in jail in British Columbia and Newfoundland.

Consents and confidentiality are not the only areas of the child's life affected by legislation. Federal legislation affecting children includes the Youth Criminal Justice Act, Canada Health Act, Controlled Drug and Substance Act, Canadian Food and Drug Act, Criminal Code of Canada, and those laws governing marriage, divorce and separation, **child support**, and **child custody**. Provincial and territorial laws govern matters of child welfare and child care in each province, as well as health, education, parental leave, social services, and social assistance. Municipal and band laws govern local policing and the provision of subsidized housing, shelters, and daycare spaces. These three legislative layers sometimes conflict or contradict, as, for example, in the case of Conor Auton (see Chapter 2), in which provincial financial constraints denied a federally legislated service.

The boundaries and extent of consents, confidentiality, and provision of service also are determined by legislation within associations that regulate the practice of professionals working with children and youth. Psychologists, psychiatrists, doctors, child and youth workers, social workers, parole officers, and early childhood educators are guided by their colleges and associations and their codes of ethics, and are often caught in ethical dilemmas posed by conflicting agency, union, and association or college rules.

A child may be monitored by many different people, such as a child protection worker, a foster care worker, a family physician, a psychiatrist, teachers, sports coaches, and foster parents. The child protection worker is trying to collect evidence; the foster care worker is allocating a per diem rate for the child's daily needs; the doctor is treating the child's injuries; the psychiatrist is assessing the child and perhaps beginning therapy and/or medication; the teacher is planning the child's upcoming test; the sports coach is wondering whether or not the child can make the next out-of-town sports meet; and the foster parent is wondering how to access information about the child's family history, health, or school records.

Legislation related to consents and confidentiality restricts the information available to each of these professionals and paraprofessionals. In addition, and probably more important for the child, each person has vital information about the child that can be shared. But they may not share this information, and one of them may function as a gatekeeper for the child's life, holding all of the information about the child and choosing which information to provide to which person.

Sometimes, to ensure the child and family's confidentiality, agencies, associations, colleges, or unions may prohibit the sharing of information about the child with the foster parent. As a result, the foster parent has only limited information on which to base daily decisions made on behalf of the child. Child welfare agencies operating within the same city may be restricted by agency policy and may not even be allowed to share information with a worker at another agency in the same city who is investigating the abuse of another child in the same family.[3]

The counselling records of parents can be shared with child welfare workers only with the parents' consent; without this consent, the worker needs to apply to the courts. Child abuse registries that list child abusers and document abusive acts operate in some provinces and not in others, and access to these registries is limited. To this date (September, 2009), there is no national child abuse registry in Canada. The child may sign a letter of consent to the sharing of information about his or her abuse, but the child's consent may not be considered valid, and the parent may refuse consent and override the child's consent. This failure to grant the child's rights can result in the child's feeling unsupported and receiving inappropriate and poorly timed services, or even being put in an unsafe situation. It would seem that legislation enacted to protect the rights of children sometimes results in these same rights being compromised or denied.

Community Capacity-Building

Community capacity-building develops healthy working relationships between the child and the community—relationships that can have a positive structural impact on the child. Rather than focusing solely on a specific child within a neighbourhood, this approach views the child's neighbourhood itself to be at risk. The goal is to improve the neighbourhood, changing it from a risk factor to a protective factor, and thereby to improve the child's chance of living a healthy life within it. This approach has developed in reaction to traditional modes of community social service work: short-term programs and targeted interventions. In these well-entrenched approaches, government funds are directed towards specific groups in need, such as young single mothers, low-birth-weight infants, children with language delays, and teens at risk of suicide. Professionals deliver the programs to those community members who are identified by other professionals, and the programs are evaluated by the participants who, grateful for the attention, snacks, free childcare, and other benefits, usually respond positively. However, when the funding dries up, the programs end, the professionals leave, and the community returns to its former status.

Community capacity-building, on the other hand, is a process of building on individual and community assets that begins *inside* the community. Community members identify a focus or need: food assistance, safety in the neighbourhood, or after-school programs, for example. Next, they map their community's assets and strengths,[4] as this mapping will be the foundation of the capacity-building process, and lastly, they design a plan. The focus of this process is on capacity-building *of* the people, *by* the people, and *for* the people in the multiple levels of the community. The professionals participate in the process but do not direct it. They may provide resources if asked, but their participation is short-term, unlike the long-term participation of community members who have a vested interest in permanent and positive change in their own community. Community capacity-building is a new name for the traditional community-powered process of neighbours helping neighbours. When a school burns down in a community, the local residents get together to decide what to do to either rebuild it or relocate it. When a family moves into the neighbourhood, bringing violence and criminality with them, the community members meet to strategize how and when to speak to the family to change their behaviours or, at least, reduce their impact on the community.

However, community capacity-building is different from these more traditional approaches to healing and empowering communities. One difference is the way in which professionals are involved. In this bottom-up approach, the ideas, opinions, and expertise of professionals and community members are valued equally when decisions are made. Those who know the community best on a daily basis are seen to have important information, opinions, and observations. They have a vested interest in the welfare of the community and the children who live within the community, and they will live in the community long after the professionals have left. Selekman (2002: 138) describes the benefits of this approach: 'When I mobilize the family, with key members of their social network, and with the professionals from larger systems, I adopt a mindset that each of these participants is a potential ally and brings to the table a vast reservoir of strengths, expertise, and wisdom that can help us as a group to disentangle any family-helping-system knots that have developed.'

In community capacity-building, professionals are not involved in their traditional roles of assessor, planner, and funder—'office-bound, rules-driven, at arm's length from parents, families, and communities' (Barter, 2009: 275). In Barter's project in the Chalker House neighbourhood in St John's, Newfoundland, for example, the professional worker simply listened for the first year, sitting in kitchens and playrooms, while the residents spoke of their dreams and hopes, as well as their frustrations. Long hours of this kind of attentiveness in non-traditional settings (kitchens, yards, sidewalks) resulted in the development of relationships and long-term projects that were important to and driven by the residents of Chalker House rather than by the professionals.

A second difference between community capacity-building and other approaches to strengthening communities is the **collaborative practice** among professionals that characterizes this method. Traditionally, professionals use the **silo approach**, working in isolation with families living in isolation from other professionals. Professional collaboration is hampered by factors such as the competing interests of associations and unions, professional jargon and its misinterpretation by those outside of the profession, laws related to confidentiality, scheduling demands, distrust of other disciplines, and competition for funding (Dufour and Chamberland, 2003). Within the silo approach, each professional brings a particular expertise and a particular support or intervention to the community. Each professional identifies or diagnoses a deficit or problem and has a limited time and funding package to effect the 'cure'.

Because reports, assessments, records, and observations rarely are shared in this traditional, isolationist method of practice, the community and frequently the children within it endure continual examination but enjoy very little tangible and consistent support. When Matthew Vaudreuil died as a result of parental abuse in 1992, for example, he had been seen by many professionals in his community, each of whom saw a different side to this five-year-old boy. The coroner's inquiry into Matthew's death (the Gove Report) prompted Webber (1998: 43) to ask, 'How many helpers does it take to fail a child? Gove counted 21 different social workers and 24 doctors spread over 75 visits, resulting in 60 filed reports. The shocking thing is that this tally is noteworthy only for its averageness.' Matthew Vaudreuil was one of many children who was seen, yet overlooked, by *many* professionals and, ultimately, left to die. Community capacity-building counteracts these all-too-common results of the traditional silo approach by requiring collaboration among professionals.

Photo 5.3 Ken Barter, Memorial University of Newfoundland.

Finally, community capacity-building is different from more traditional approaches in its shifting of focus from a community's problems and deficits to its assets and strengths. This building process tends to happen in communities that are disadvantaged by oppression and persistent poverty. The reasons are evident: poverty tests any community network of relationships. People move in and out of the neighbourhood and tend to be juggling multiple, low-paying workloads. They lack community meeting places, transportation, and child care, so getting together to form relationships is difficult if not impossible. A history of structural oppression (short-term, deficit-focused interventions) further weakens these communities, keeping them politically and socially inactive.

Community capacity-building offers such troubled communities 'multiple perspectives and potential solution strategies' (Selekman, 2002: 151). In this positively focused process, traditional community culture is viewed as an asset and becomes the foundation for community activities which, in turn, provide opportunities for change for the community and the children within it. In essence, the community becomes a safe place for its members, in particular its children, who feel nourished and cherished and valued within a community that cares.

This approach ensures that the personal becomes political as real change happens on a community level. People in the community share stories and make connections.

Through their involvement with the community-building project and with one another, they begin to feel stronger and to see and to feel a belonging and a commitment to their community. Warry (2007: 152) identifies how community capacity-building works in many Native Canadian communities that have been ravaged by workers 'from the outside' over the years. Although he explains that the focus of the process is long-term and that the positive results may show only after a decade, the people in the communities feel empowered because the process puts 'culture and traditional values at the centre of contemporary efforts to rebuild communities'. This is the structural and strengths-based approach in action.

Community capacity-building projects in Canada that are federally funded by the Public Health Agency of Canada include prenatal nutrition programs and Native Canadian Head Start programs. Other community capacity-building is supported by private and public funds, donations, grants, and businesses: the Neighbourhood House project in Victoria, BC; the Chalker House project in St John's, Newfoundland and Labrador; the Whole Child Program in Whitehorse, Yukon; and Community Holistic Healing Circles in many Native Canadian communities. These projects and programs have already started to lower the numbers of reported child abuse incidents, and have raised health and wellness rates for children (Barter, 2005; Deslandes, 2006). Parents actively participate in these projects because they feel other community members value their talents and strengths. As they participate, they develop a sense of pride and belonging in their community, as well as relationships with other parents, neighbourhoods, and the professionals working alongside them.

An example of this approach at work is Ontario's Better Beginnings, Better Futures, a community capacity-building project that was started in 1991 in eight Ontario neighbourhoods. All of these neighbourhoods had been the subject of previous government interventions, in which much funding had been spent with little improvement. Peters (2005: 173) describes the resulting mood in these neighbourhoods: 'local residents viewed government programs and social services with skepticism, suspicion, or hostility.'

Better Beginnings, Better Futures began by asking community residents to map their community's needs in order to identify sustainable and long-term projects that could be managed by the residents themselves. Because the project's organization was bottom-up rather than top-down, the programs continue to operate beyond the funding period and are ultimately staffed by community people who have a local, vested interest. The professionalization of care is replaced by a community of caring for all children, caring that is non-professional and embedded in the neighbourhood. Quantitative data (Peters, 2005) supports the success of the capacity-building, including:

- A 10 per cent decrease in cigarette smoking by mothers;
- A greater feeling of safety and security in neighbourhoods;
- A decrease in children's anxiety and depression levels;
- More timely immunizations of children;

- A 20 per cent increase in 'excellent health' of children as rated by parents; and
- An increase in use of neighbourhood parks and recreational facilities.

Other similar projects demonstrate that community capacity-building, based on Rogers' model of congruence, empathy, and respect can work (Wharf, 2002). The key to the success of such projects is the achievement of consensus or a common values orientation, and an authentic sharing of resources, risks, and power. These same qualities are evident in the principles of engagement Wharf (2002) proposes for community capacity-building:

- Identify one outcome as the quality of relationships among members of the community.
- Assume the existence of common goals that all members of the community want to achieve.
- Respect the child's contribution to the community now and as it varies over time.
- Value each member of the community both as a citizen and as social capital.

Barter's (2009: 279) description of the Chalker House project encapsulates the asset-focused energy of community capacity-building, an approach that is 'not about change but innovation, not about welfare but justice, not about wielding power but discovering it, not about programmatic "fix-it" approaches but about distributive collaborative approaches, not about programs and services that are rule- and procedures-driven but about programs and services that are vision- and value-driven.'

The community is the meso-system in which the child lives, attends school, forms friendships, and engages in play. The community may value the child, listening to the child's needs, opinions, and observations, or it may disregard the child, valuing only adults and considering the child as unimportant, even annoying. Barter (2009), Wharf (2002), and Peters (2005) describe communities that work together to build the capacity for all community members, children and adults alike, to live better lives. This community capacity-building is a key protective factor if children are to have healthy relationships with one another and with adults—relationships that value the contributions of all community members.

Summary

This chapter examines the components of a more beneficial working relationship between the worker and the child. In this relationship, the worker, traditionally viewed as the helper, becomes the learner and the child becomes the teacher. The conventional power dynamic is reversed so as to create a more equal relationship based on the Rogerian tenets of congruence, empathy, and mutual respect. In a healthy relationship, the culturally competent worker is acutely aware of misunderstandings and miscommunication related to culture and tries to learn as much as possible from the child about the child's and family's culture. The worker is bound by legislation that regulates the information that can be shared, the services provided, and even whether or not the child can be served at all. The ongoing worker–child relationship is widened through community capacity-building to include all of the community who support the child. How this healthy working relationship unfolds is the subject of the next chapter, in which you will find a guide for the first worker–child meeting. Two valuable tools— genograms and case notes—will be explored, as well as potential dialogues, agendas, and financial supports for the family. More importantly, you will learn how to use these tools and your current skills more effectively to convert interviews into meetings.

Review Questions

1. Define a healthy working relationship between worker and child, and describe the components of this relationship as formulated by Carl Rogers.
2. How does the traditional power dynamic change in a client-centred relationship as described by bell hooks, Paulo Freire, and others?
3. How can a worker's good intentions get in the way of a healthy working relationship?
4. What is cultural competency and how does the worker develop this competency?
5. Does everyone have personal bias? Explain, giving examples.
6. Name five aspects of family culture that you would consider when striving to develop a healthy working relationship with that family.
7. Does a child's age determine his or her capacity to give consent? Provide examples to support your answer.
8. What are the three criteria a worker must consider in making the decision to break confidentiality with a child?
9. Which relationships are built and sustained through community capacity-building?
10. Describe the process of community capacity-building.

Discussion Questions

1. According to Carl Rogers, healthy relationships are built on congruence, empathy, and respect. Reflect on healthy relationships, both past and present, in your own life. Do they follow the Rogerian model? Explain, using specific personal examples.
2. Angelina is a 14-year-old student with a straight-A average in school. She is also on several sports teams and has a wide circle of friends. Angelina comes to you because she is pregnant and wants you to arrange an abortion. She does not want

anyone, especially her parents, to know about this. In responding to Angelina, how would you deal with issues of confidentiality and consent?

3. Suggest a community capacity-building project that might be beneficial in your own community. Who would be involved? How would you initiate such a project?

Chapter 6

The First Meeting

I spent the first day picking holes in paper, then went home in a smouldering temper.
'What's the matter, Love? Didn't he like it at school, then?'
'They never gave me the present.'
'Present? What present?'
'They said they'd give me a present.'
'Well, now, I'm sure they didn't.'
'They did! They said: "You're Laurie Lee, aren't you? Well just you sit there for the present."
I sat there all day but I never got it. I ain't going back there again.'

—Laurie Lee, *Cider with Rosie*

We laugh when we read about Laurie Lee's misunderstanding of the teacher. Then our laughter subsides. Did the child misunderstand the teacher, or did the teacher misunderstand the child? Was the child's first day at school ruined because a teacher did not communicate effectively? Like Laurie Lee, the children who come to us sometimes leave our first meeting saying, 'I ain't going back there again.'

Successful interventions are planned. The worker may meet the child in a drop-in centre, on the sidewalk, or in a shelter, or at a spontaneous meeting in response to a crisis. Before the worker meets with the child, the worker takes time to reflect. Informed action based on reflection, education, training, and sound practice principles is called **praxis**. Praxis is more likely to be helpful than an impulsive reaction based on sympathy or emotional reactivity. Sometimes stress can heighten our sensitivity, and sometimes stress just makes us stupid. When the worker is stressed in a crisis, the intervention can become misguided.

When the meeting is scheduled in advance, the worker has more time for praxis. There is also time for a file review, preliminary resource scan, telephone intake interview, consultation with a supervisor, and reflection on this combination of information. Previously completed assessments, case notes, school and health records, and diagnostic material can be evaluated for validity and reliability. The worker may reflect also on models of change to attempt to situate the child within the model. The transtheoretical model is examined in this chapter.

This first meeting or face-to-face encounter, whether or not in the home, is the beginning of a relationship. If the worker signals disinterest, disengagement, or a lack of understanding, the first meeting will likely be the last. On the other hand, the worker may convey empathy, openness, and a willingness to listen to the child. If so, the child will understand that a relationship is beginning, and the child may choose to enter into this relationship.

This chapter describes how to engage the child and possibly the child's family, and to begin this process of relationship-building. We will explore guidelines for the home visit, as well as the practical applications of these guidelines. We will identify tangible structural supports for the family. We will learn how to write case notes *with* the child; learn how to co-construct a genogram; and discuss how to assess those case notes that are already in the child's file.

Objectives

By the end of this chapter, you will:

- Understand the power dynamics that differentiate meetings from interviews.
- Identify key elements in successfully engaging children and their families when using the transtheoretical model of change.
- Demonstrate how to conduct an initial meeting with a child, and with a child and family, both in the agency and in the home.

Meeting or Interview

A 'meeting' implies a relationship of some equality. There may be a chairperson and a minute-taker, but the persons who are present usually are considered to be equals. We have a family meeting and each member of the family expresses an opinion or makes a recommendation. We have a community meeting and neighbours discuss what can be done about a proposed change in the community. Sometimes there are minutes taken of a meeting and, if so, these minutes are shared with everyone at the subsequent meeting and approved (or not) by them.

On the other hand, an interview is a way to collect facts. It is an 'us-and-them' activity. We interview an author to gain insight on a recently published book. We interview a criminal to gather evidence. We interview an applicant for a job to decide whether or not this applicant is suited for the job. On the basis of the facts gained at the interview we make a decision, assess the risk, or form an opinion. The person giving the 'facts' is in one position (usually subordinate, but not always), and we are in another position. An interview usually reflects a power imbalance.

The worker decides whether to 'interview' or to 'meet with' the child. The former places the child in the inferior position of being scrutinized or examined. The latter places the child in the position of participant. The worker's initial decision about the approach to take is crucial.

A worker who decides to meet with the child prepares by reviewing the child's file. This file contains information, or 'text-mediated reality', that was previously constructed during interviews by other workers. DeMontigny (1995: 26) describes this activity: 'People's lives, difficulties, conflicts, and problems provide raw materials to be inserted into professional frames and theories to produce the case. The transformation of the everyday into the extended discourses of professional social work comprises a taken-for-granted bedrock for social work intervention.' This file information is considered to be 'the truth', even though it is socially constructed and may not include the most relevant information about the child: those missing photos, personal notes, and journal entries.

This text-mediated reality in the file is commonly called a **case note**. A case note is meant to be an objective, simple, specific, honest, and accurate record of an event that is written, dated, and signed by the worker within 24 hours of the event. The case note is an important document that can be considered as evidence in court when the worker is subpoenaed, and can be the basis for a court **affidavit**. Because of its importance, the worker writes the case note carefully and deliberately rather than as a hurried after-thought at the end of a busy day.

Through the process of transcribing and categorizing the child's reality, a new, agency-centred reality is socially constructed. DeMontigny (1995: 64) describes this socially constructed reality: 'The text is a mask, concealing the embodied speaker who utters this or that claim. Through the text, social workers can promote their claims as though these were the universal wisdom of the profession in general.' The worker takes on the persona of a professional with universal wisdom, that combination of scientific fact and popular folklore. The worker, who may have never met the child before the event, speaks for the child, transforming the child's room into an 'unsafe bedroom' and the child's play into 'inappropriate behaviour' in the case note. This is done as part of the worker's professional role as interviewer and as demanded by the protocol of the agency. 'In all cases, the representation is designed by the conceptual organization of an institutional discourse to which the actuality it represents must be fitted' (Smith, 2005: 186).

In her institutional ethnography, Dorothy Smith (1998) describes three tricks that workers are compelled to play when they write case notes. The worker may not intend to deliberately trick the reader or the child, but the worker who is bound by agency policy and protocol has little choice. This protocol typically dictates case noting an interview in such a way that the reality of the interview and the reality of the child must be re-constructed.

The first trick separates what is said from its context: the child becomes either an acronym or a client. Seven-year-old Mohammed, strong and articulate and a defender of the family through their five years in a refugee camp, becomes M.R. His elder sister, raped at age six, becomes W.R. The child's manner of speech, beliefs, and emotions become secondary to the child's words as 'information'. A phrase or word from the child is pulled away from the facial expression, the commotion on the street that makes him apprehensive, or the sob. The phrase or word, the accent and intonation, are lost in the words on the page, and may even assume a meaning contrary to the one intended by the child speaker.

A mother may say, between sobs, that she once gave her child a spanking. The case note is written as follows: 'R.T. admits physical abuse (spanking) of B.T. on March 4, 2008.' That admission in the case note, coupled with the mother's struggle with alcohol and chronic poverty, may be enough for her children to be removed from her arms and from the home (apprehended).

The second trick is to categorize or assess according to agency protocol. The whole child is divided into risk factors, deficits, or domains, depending on the agency. A parent's self is organized to fit the mandate of the agency, whether it be child protection, mental health, or addiction treatment. A parent's choice to live in the woods is described by a worker as 'social isolation' and a 'risk factor'. A Mexican father's struggle to answer questions is recorded as 'low literacy level' and a 'parental risk factor'. Neither the smell of the pine forest nor the warmth of the Spanish language is captured in the case notes. These are impressions rather than facts, so they are not included.

A child's strengths, or those of the parent, are rarely captured in a case note because the notes are problem-oriented and are expected to pinpoint problems rather than strengths. The father's skill in carpentry and cooking is extraneous information for which no checklist line exists. There may be a line called 'adequate nutrition' on which the father may fail because there is no milk in the kitchen. There may be a line called 'living room safe for toddlers' that the father may also fail because he has left his hammer or sandpaper on the rug. The father's culinary and carpentry skills are not relevant to the case note or the assessment, so are not recorded. 'People's actualities become a resource on which work is done to extract formalized and highly restricted representations' (Smith, 2005: 186).

The Ontario Risk Assessment Model (2000) demonstrates this second trick. This Model presents 11 risk decisions with set time lines, plus a requirement that the worker rate the caregiver or parent on a Risk Eligibility Spectrum. If the caregiver rates a 3 or a 4, and if the cumulative risk factors are below 'the line', the child may be removed from the home (**apprehended**). This rating is extremely important in determining the future of the child. On the basis of the first meeting the worker must rate the caregiver from 0 to 4 on the CG4 as follows:

0   Very accepting of the child
1   Limited acceptance of the child
2   Indifferent and aloof to the child
3   Disapproves of and resents the child
4   Rejects and is hostile to the child.

Most parents have at some time acted in all five ways towards their children. A parent may resent the crying child early in the morning and be very accepting by mid-morning. If the child breaks a treasured gift, the parent may appear hostile or indifferent to the child. A parent may move from 0 to 4 and back again in one morning! If the parent's manifested feelings score 'below the line', then the child's place in the home may be in jeopardy and the child may be apprehended. The worker interviewing the parent might see any one, or several, of these manifested feelings and write a case note to support or justify the rating.

The third trick is to repeat the case note to the child so that the child begins to believe the case note rather than the reality of his or her daily life. The child who is called a 'slow learner' or a 'behaviour problem' in the case note begins to act according to what has been recorded (see Chapter 1). If the case note describes 'dysfunction', then the child begins to act out dysfunction every day so as to reflect what has been told about and to the child, and to make the case note seem more accurate. An event, a family dynamic, a behaviour: these are described according to the worker in a case note that gradually becomes more real than the actual event, family dynamic, or behaviour.

Barron (2000: 48) describes her review of the files of Canadian young offenders: 'The files contain massive amounts of information, ranging from youth risk assessments and custody reports to case management reports and daily program logs, providing a valuable source for understanding how authorities interpret the youth's behaviour.' Note Barron's deliberate wording. These very full files are a source for understanding 'how authorities interpret the youth's behaviour'—which is to say, the institutional construction of the youth's behaviour—not for understanding the behaviour itself or even the youth. 'When a youth has a behavioural problem it all has to be "chemical imbalance"; it has to be something wrong with the brain, not something wrong with their environment, or their resources that they're receiving, or their support' (Lambe, 2009: 22). When Barron meets some of the young offenders whose files she has reviewed, she encounters a very different reality. During her meetings the young offenders do not behave in the same way as they are portrayed in the case files. Barron describes the difference between the young offenders and the case notes, a dichotomy that affirms the power and control issues inherent in both interviews and case notes. The child behaves and the adult labels the behaviour and, in doing so, recreates the child. That this happens, whether deliberately or not, seems to be inevitable. The writers of the case notes are empowered to exert control over those about whom they write. The institutional context in which they work often demands that they become judges rather than helpers, morality enforcers rather than moral models of that honesty, empathy, and congruence called for by Rogers (see Chapter 5). Literature on workers within the child care system is rife with examples of worker dissatisfaction with the assessment and enforcer roles (Smith, 2009; Ferguson, 2008; Ruch, 2005).

After the file review the worker interviews the child, deciding what is in the 'best interests of the child' and sharing file information with the child only when the child is deemed to be 'ready for it' or 'able to understand'. The worker decides when the intervention will end, and the child cannot choose to discontinue the intervention. If the child does decide to leave the room and walk out of the interview, the child is 'apprehended' and runs the risk of being placed in a home or institution. All of this is done, of course, in the 'best interests of the child'.

In a *meeting*, however, both the method of recording and the agenda are jointly agreed on and approved by everyone at the meeting. The recording is still objective, but that objectivity is jointly monitored and jointly achieved. The recorder of the meeting follows these guidelines:

- Be concise, short, and to the point. Include exactly what has been seen and heard, nothing more and nothing less.
- Include direct quotations and a context for these quotations in order to give a fair representation of the circumstances in which the words were said.
- Do not include judgement statements or opinions about what has been seen and heard.
- Use accurate and concrete descriptors rather than relative terms such as 'dark' or 'normal'.
- Preface any feelings, assumptions, and perceptions about the client or the client's behaviour with qualifiers such as, 'appears to be' or 'seemed to be'. An example of such a descriptor is, 'Jake appeared to weigh between 52 and 54 kilos'.
- Check the recording with everyone who is present.
- If possible, have everyone at the meeting sign the case note as being an accurate and objective recording of the meeting.

Meetings, like interviews, are a way of collecting and sharing personal and subjective information. Everyone attending the meeting offers information and the information is shared, assessed, and acted on by the people who are present at the meeting. The agenda is not a secret one pre-determined by the worker. The agenda is open to everyone's input and is subject to change. The minutes of the meeting may look exactly like case notes of an interview, but they are co-formulated and signed by the people who are present as being a true and accurate record of the event.

The Transtheoretical Model of Change

Transtheoretical refers to the integrative nature of this model, which draws from many major theories of psychotherapy and behavioural change. This model reminds us that change is a process in life rather than an event. This process unfolds naturally as part of a hopeful future as well as in reaction to stressful events and interventions. A worker who understands the underpinnings of this model is more apt to recognize the child's location in the events unfolding around her or him and the child's capacity for change. The worker is more apt to identify which processes of change might be most useful for that child at that location and capacity, interpreting a child's reaction to a suggested program as a stage of change rather than simply as behaviour that is intransigently defiant or aggressive.

The transtheoretical model describes 10 processes of change, of which consciousness-raising is said to be the most common type (Prochaska and Norcross, 2007: 513). 'Consciousness-raising' refers to that cognitive process by which the child develops awareness of the need for change. This consciousness-raising may be developed through life experiences, worker intervention, peer interaction, parent discipline, teacher reinforcement, and so on, and at any or all of the six stages in the model.

The first stage of change, **pre-contemplation**, is said to occur when the child is not even thinking about change and has no intention of changing in the foreseeable future. The child may be meeting the worker involuntarily, or at the prompting of a teacher or guardian. The child may not be even considering or thinking about behaviour change at this point because the child does not see the need for any behaviour change.

The second stage is **contemplation**. At this stage the child appears to look at the possibility of change and to consider the advantages and disadvantages of such change. The child who asks questions about a suggested program could be identified as being at the contemplation stage. The child may not agree to participate in the program, but may show some interest in it.

In the third stage, **preparation**, the child begins to plan actual change. The child may appear to be ready to engage with a tutor, big brother, or a new foster home. This stage is characterized by action as well as contemplation. The first steps to making change are taken.

The fourth stage is **action** during which the child actually participates in the change process. In this fourth stage the child learns the specific skills that are needed to make the change. The child in the action stage begins to practise these skills.

The fifth stage is **maintenance**, a period in which the child consolidates the change into the daily routine, feeling more comfortable with the change on a daily basis. This stage involves actively learning how to make the change a regular part of everyday life. Finally, in the **termination** stage, the change is so much a part of the child's routine that it no longer seems like change. The child is no longer tempted to return to the previous behaviour, and no longer has to try to keep from relapsing.

The third dimension of this model is the level of problem or behaviour. Five levels are identified: situational problems, maladaptive cognitions, current interpersonal conflicts, family or systems conflicts, and intrapersonal conflicts (Prochaska and Norcross, 2007: 524–5). These levels are interactive: one affects the other. In addition, any problem or behaviour can be seen to originate at several levels concurrently, depending on the viewpoint of the worker.

This change model is useful to workers because of its clear and definable stages and its positioning of change as a decision-making process by the child. This change model is integrative and can provide an indication of how and when to intervene. 'Integrating the levels with the stages and processes of change provides a model for intervening hierarchically and effectively across a broad range of therapeutic content' (Prochaska and Norcross, 2007: 526). This model suggests that the worker and the child work in synchrony, the worker keeping step with the child at each stage of change.

However, the transtheoretical model also reflects the traditional bio-medical model. The illness, deficit, or problem is located within the child rather than in the structure around the child. It is the child who is expected to change, rather than the structure. As one child in a social change program wisely remarked, 'They said I had attachment disorder. Really, I had a life disorder. I attached accordingly' (Lambe, 2009:12). This model clearly identifies the child as the agent of change; if the child chooses not to change, then the child is stuck within 'the problem'. If the child does not react positively to the change suggested by the worker, then the child is seen to be at category (stage) one: pre-contemplation. At the same time, the child may also be labelled as 'resistant to change' which, roughly translated, means 'resistant to my program'. Like Piaget's stages, Erikson's stages, and Kohlberg's stages, the stages of the transtheoretical model are clearly defined and mutually exclusive spaces into which the child must fit. The program and the funding source do not adapt to the child; the child must fit into the program.

Another difficulty is that this model values active change above contemplation, acceptance, and integration of change. Change is positioned as a positive activity rather than an increasing commitment, as the child marches from contemplation towards action. Contemplation is devalued in this model by being restricted to stages one and two. When the child acts or superficially complies with the worker, the child is reinforced, so the child soon learns to adapt and perform. A child who moves into a treatment program may be neatly categorized as being in stage four of the change process: action. However, the child may actually be tuned out, and only getting on the bus because the worker (the power agent) has offered no other viable option. When the girl beside him offers him a hit (drugs), he is more than willing to take it. The body may be on the bus, but the spirit is not engaged in the change process at all despite the neat categorization in the case file. The child has not accepted and integrated the change into his daily life, despite his getting on a bus to attend treatment.

Dorothy Smith's institutional ethnography (2005) provides a lens through which to view Prochaska and Norcross's model of transtheoretical change. In this ethnography Smith differentiates between learning feminism and practising feminism, and the consciousness or mindset necessary in practising feminism. Readiness to change from learner to practitioner can be sudden, and can be prompted by life events or external pressures; the change may not be observable to an outsider, and may not proceed in discrete stages. Smith would say that the categorization of human functioning is inherently flawed because it does not take into account those internal processes that cannot be observed or categorized neatly. In the transtheoretical model the worker supposes that change is an observable *action*, and that progress is made when the child 'does something' such as program participation. This model may in fact lead the worker to ignore and, consequently, not support real internal change when it happens prior to or concurrent with an observable action.

Photo 6.1 On a train going nowhere or on the way to making a change?

Engaging the Child

Most children with difficulties do not seek out adult interventions or knock on the door of a worker or counsellor. Children who are being bullied by peers resist telling an adult for fear of reprisals by those peers and because they believe that action will not be taken to stop the bullying even when their stories are told. Children who are being abused or neglected resist telling adults because they fear being punished at home or, even worse, being taken away from their home, school, and community and put into a stranger's (foster parent's) home. Even when children do disclose abuse or neglect, they may tell several adults before this disclosure is acknowledged. This lack of real response, plus the fear of being punished, bullied, or removed from the home, discourages most children from disclosing or seeking out adult interventions.

Instead, the child usually is brought to the attention of the worker by another adult who is in a position of power (parent, police officer, teacher, guidance counsellor, group home staff). In deShazer's (1984) terminology, the child is the involuntary **visitor** who is brought to the worker by some social control agent. DeShazer's categorization of those seeking help from workers differentiates between 'visitors', 'clients', and 'customers' of adult interventions. He stresses the importance of the person's coming voluntarily and willingly as a **customer** to participate in the intervention for that intervention to be effective. Rogers (1951) concurs in his description of healthy working relationships and their equalization of power or power-with.

When the child is a visitor, a helper–helped power imbalance exists initially in which the helper (adult) holds all of the power. Because the child is a visitor, the child frequently will deny that there is a difficulty, even when the staff, who are in positions of power, identify one. Nico Trocme (2003) notes that children often deny their original disclosure when they are asked for details about the abuse or about violence in the home. Fear of reprisal, mistrust of adults, and suspicion of those in authority combine to make the child a visitor, rather than a willing participant in the meeting.

Note From the Field   6.1

Shifting Control

Jake is sitting in the meeting room when I arrive. His hood is pulled over his baseball cap, his body sprawled over the chair. He grunts in answer to my first few questions, then shuts down entirely. I let the silence settle for several minutes. Finally Jake asks, 'Can I leave now?' This is the opener that I wanted. Now that Jake is the questioner he can take some control. Now this first meeting begins to feel promising!

In addition to visitor status, the child, who has never met the worker in person, may be most familiar only with adults who control and hurt. These adults have been and continue to be the context for the child's daily life. The child may be dreading meeting this new adult (worker), and may even be physically sick with apprehension. The child's initial reaction is an important first clue in trying to get to know the child. The worker observes the child's reaction, listening carefully to the spoken and unspoken messages sent out by the child. The worker does not try to change, minimize, or dismiss these messages because they are very important first clues or indicators of the child's assets and strengths, and the child's understanding of adults.

This first meeting may take place in an agency meeting room, detention centre, restaurant booth, home, sidewalk, or hospital waiting room. I once met with a lone mother and her daughter for the first time in a vast, empty lecture room for a hundred people. Too often the surroundings of the first meeting are 'official' and, therefore, threatening: big office desks, hard chairs, two-way mirrors, and interruptions. All of these threatening messages convey the power of the agency and of the worker, and reinforce the powerlessness of the child. The worker's body language may be saying, 'I want to help', but the meeting space may be saying the opposite.

This power dynamic can change at the first meeting by the worker making sure that the large and threatening space is converted to a comfortable, private, and more secure one. The restaurant booth can become a cozy place to talk when the worker speaks quietly and orders comfortable and familiar (for the child) food and drinks that last for an hour. The sidewalk can become an open and relaxed meeting place if it is the child's

Photo 6.2 A no-home placement means no food, no warmth, no hope, and nobody to care.

home turf; the worker follows the child's lead because the child knows best where to sit and where to go for a quiet talk. In an agency or waiting room the worker has even more opportunity to soften the edges and the mood of the space. Cozy, comfortable cushions, chairs pulled together, and attentive concern for the child's comfort can convert an otherwise sterile room into a safe haven. If tables are pushed out of the way there may be space on the carpet for conversation. If the lights are dimmed rather than glaring, the blank, beige walls will soften.

The worker is part of that space and the worker's position, stance, and gestures can be threatening and confrontational, or comforting and open. The worker who is positioned in a lower chair, or even on the floor with the child, is immediately less intimidating to the child and to the family. When eyes meet eyes on a level plane, there is more chance to communicate freely than when eyes look down from five or six feet to a child lying on a blanket on the floor. If the worker cannot squat, then the worker can pull together two chairs so that, in the sitting position, eyes still can meet eyes. If the worker pauses to consider the child's feelings and is willing to meet the child at the child's physical level, rather than looking down at the child, some of that fear and trepidation and power imbalance can be reduced.

Equally important is an open, comforting body posture that communicates safety without the barrier of a desk, clipboard, briefcase, or paper. During the first meeting,

Note From the Field   6.2

Why Don't You Like My Kids?

Emily has started working in an ESL nursery school program and she really enjoys the diversity of children and parents. After a few months in the program, however, she notices that the mothers still have not accepted her, and seem eager to leave when they collect their children. She asks Maria, her supervisor, about this and is surprised by the response. Maria has assumed that Emily does not like the children. Further discussion reveals a cultural mis-understanding. Maria holds, cuddles, and hugs the children, unlike Emily who is aloof, more verbal, and less physically responsive. The children and their parents interpret this as Emily's dislike for them and their response is to imitate her aloofness and to stay away from her whenever possible.

recording materials such as paper and pen, laptop, and recorder are barriers to the relationship. The focus of a meeting is relationship-building before information-gathering.

The worker is a stranger who does not touch the child's body, hair, or clothing without the child's express verbal or non-verbal consent. Even if a request is made, the worker uses professional judgement before acceding to this request. If the child asks to be picked up or held, the worker can hold the child briefly, squat down to the child's level, or engage the child in comforting talk. Each of these responses is appropriate under certain conditions and with certain children; discretion is necessary. Each response demonstrates respect for the child and the child's personal space, as well as appropriate 'stranger behaviour' with children. The culturally competent worker reads visual cues from the caregivers and from the child as to the level and type of physical interaction appropriate to meet the child's comfort needs. The worker sits close to the child while respecting the child's personal space and need for movement.

One pre-schooler asked repeatedly to sit on my lap in the first meeting. Her request was neither a spontaneous response to an established relationship nor an immediate need for contact comfort, but a consistent and learned response to the sexual abuse she had suffered. She was used to being seen as an object of sexual pleasure for adults, and her behaviour had been groomed in this fashion. She routinely made this request to all of the adults in her home. While I understood the source of her anxiety and fear, I also understood that acceding to her request would only strengthen her belief that all adults took pleasure from her tiny body and that she was an object to be used for pleasure. Providing a lovely child-sized chair for her and having that chair close to mine gave her some feeling of safety, while still acknowledging that she was a separate person with a story to tell and a unique self to be respected.

Photo 6.3 Eyes meet eyes and smiles connect as this worker learns from her student.

The worker's clothing also sends a message to the child. The worker who wears loose, uncluttered clothing and appropriate footwear can squat, run, play, and move with the child. If the child is young and active, the worker does not wear dangling earrings or enticing rings. The worker's clothing sends a message that the child comes first. The focus is on the child, not on the worker's hair colour or fashionable outfit.

Vocal tone and rhythm can be more important than words. A high-pitched tone, raucous laughter, or machine-gun speech (a fast-paced volley of words) loaded with agency jargon can frighten the child (and everyone else) and exacerbate the child's stress. Too often, the worker is the loudest person in the meeting! The worker who modulates tone, rhythm, and accent can create an aural comfort zone for the child. The worker puts aside both professional jargon and 'baby talk' and uses appropriate and simple words that echo the words of the child. The worker is speaking to be understood rather than to coerce, mislead, impress, or intimidate the child.

Gestures can comfort or threaten. They are more forceful than words and are easily mis-interpreted. A gesture such as offering a chair to everyone but the child, for example, both disrespects and disregards the child. This gesture forces the child to sit or climb on a caregiver, or to sit on the floor. Offering a chair only to the women in the family and ignoring the grandparents or elderly members of the family is equally insulting. Then, there are the workers who arrive at a first meeting carrying their coffee cups. The worker drinks throughout the meeting, oblivious to the lack of refreshment

Group Exercise   6.1

Engaging the Child

This small group exercise is best done in groups of three to five people. In this brief yet powerful exercise the small group discusses how to engage an older child. One member of the group volunteers to play the older child, and the other members play the team members meeting the child for the first time.

The exercise begins with the volunteer stepping away from the group to prepare an improvised dialogue. This volunteer is given one of the following instructions on which to base this dialogue with the team:

- You have been suspended from school (Grade 5) for five days because you witnessed a bullying incident at school and did not report it. Both the bullies and the victim are classmates and friends of yours and you are not going to implicate them.
- Your 'best friend' in Grade 8 has been having sex with your current boyfriend so you trashed her locker and posted gossip about her on your Facebook site. You are two months' pregnant and have told no one about this.
- You are in Grade 12 and have been cutting yourself for the last year as a way of coping with the pressure about getting good enough grades for college from your father, who is a deputy minister. You have already been to two different psychiatrists about this and you are on heavy medication now.

At the same time, the team is given one of the corresponding instructions:

- Jeremy, 10 years old, has been suspended from school (not the first time) under the Zero Tolerance policy.
- Emma, a 13-year-old student, vandalized a classmate's locker and posted hate mail about her on Facebook.
- Amal is suspected of selling drugs to other Grade 12 students and has been diagnosed as possibly bipolar.

When the team is ready to begin the meeting, they call in the volunteer (older child) and engage in dialogue for five minutes. At this point the leader stops the action of all the small groups and begins a debriefing by asking questions such as the following:

- How did the team engage the child? Was this successful?
- From the child's perspective, how could the team have equalized the power construct right away? Did the team appear to be accusatory?
- What strategies work best to begin a meeting?

for the child and the family. If a worker cannot talk or listen without a drink, perhaps the child feels the same way. These forms of behaviour transgress basic etiquette and consideration for others; after all, providing water as a bare minimum for everyone in the room is just common sense. However, these insulting gestures are all too common and can prevent any relationship-building in this first meeting.

This first meeting is an opportunity to respectfully listen to the words and the body language of the child in the room. The worker conveys this respect for the child in any of the following ways:

- being silent and attentive when the child is speaking;
- smiling or nodding to indicate understanding of what the child is saying;
- appropriating the child's words whenever possible to ease the dialogue and to demonstrate respect for the child's choice of words;
- following the lead of the child in the conversation;
- offering a bathroom break to a child who is squirming or bouncing on the chair;
- offering a blanket or warm coat to a child who is shivering;
- offering a tissue to a child who is sniffing;
- indicating the clock in the room and the time that the meeting will be over. This gives everyone the chance to prepare for saying good-bye.

With spoken language, once again the key is to be child-focused and honest. Silence works, too. The respectful worker provides time and space to become acquainted with the child, listening to the child attentively and trying to read the child's body language and words. The worker acknowledges how hard it is for the child to be at the meeting:

- I'm glad you came up to see me today. How can I be of help to you?
- I know that your teacher has sent you here for an hour every Wednesday. It must be a real drag to be made to spend extra time after school with me. How can I help you to get your Wednesday afternoons back?
- I know that your parents told you to come and see me because of your grades. What do you want done about your grades/parents?
- The staff have asked me to speak to you about vandalism, but I am wondering who did all the damage in the recreation centre. Are you good at detective work? Do you know if the person left any clues?
- We have an hour to spend together today. How would you like to spend that hour here?

The message conveyed by these types of introduction is that the child, not the worker, owns the time. The child is in charge of the agenda for this meeting, and the worker is primed to listen. The worker assumes that the child is competent and can actively engage and look for solutions.

Honesty includes acknowledging that the child may have been a visitor many times before, or may have seen many other professionals and paraprofessionals. If such is the case, the child has had experience and may have some clear ideas on the most useful direction for this first meeting. The worker acknowledges that expertise and opens up space in the dialogue so that the child is empowered to advise the worker. The child is the expert on the presenting problem, too, and probably already has ideas about potential solutions. The worker can acknowledge and support that expertise by asking the child to clarify the meaning of words and the situation, or to explain the roles and relationships in the family. The key is to ask for and acknowledge the importance of the child's input:

- Can you think of anything else I should do differently with you?
- What other things did your counsellors do with you that turned you off?
- You say they really bugged you. What did they do that you didn't like?
- Where does your brother live now?
- What does that mean, 'hokey'?
- Can you download test papers before you even write the test?

Even very young children intuit when the worker is genuinely interested. If the worker is just making conversation and faking interest, the child will not respond, or may respond with the same level of superficiality as the worker. When the worker meets the child on an equal basis and looks to the child for information, advice, or expertise, the child tends to respond. This means being consistently genuine and honest, and may also include using the language that the child uses or using self-deprecating humour:

- Are you really able to draw caricatures of your teachers? I would like to see some of the ones you've drawn.
- Karate sounds like a really demanding sport. Maybe you would show me some of your moves at the next session.
- Did you sit through the entire film without leaving? You have more concentration than I do. I left after 20 minutes. Can you tell me how the film ended?
- Was the candy under the bed really attached to the carpet? How did you eat it that way?
- Wow! That family holiday sounds like a wild trip! Did you really leave all your luggage in the taxi?

These communication guidelines are simple steps and are basic to any honest working relationship. However, so often these steps are missed. I remember working with a child in a group home who remarked about her former worker, 'She didn't even know my name.' The worker had misread the file name and never checked with the child about her correct name. That hurts.

Genograms

When asked about family, an older child may respond, 'I have no family' or 'I am on my own.' This is not a lie. This is contextually true for the child. The child may feel alienated, abandoned, or dispossessed by family; as a result, the child states that he/she has no family. The child may have lived apart from family in a foster home or on the streets for many years, or may not have access to any information about the family's whereabouts.

This statement is a painful one because it reflects a loss. This loss is huge because it is a loss of family and a loss of childhood memories, too. This loss may engender in the child feelings of guilt and shame at not having a supportive birth family, or at having memories of illness, abuse, rejection, or death. These feelings and memories may prompt the child to refuse family involvement and to deny their existence. 'Family' brought the child to this point, and 'family' can't help now—so the child's statement may realistically express all of these negative feelings about the concept of 'family'.

The worker affirms the child's statement of current reality. At the same time, the worker puts this reality into a larger construct in order to try to decipher the covert or implied message. To feel totally unsupported by a caring family is a very challenging position for a human being at any age, let alone a child. It is alienating and confusing and very hard to bear. A child who replies, 'I have no family' can be viewed as showing tremendous courage in daring to make this very powerful first statement. In this statement is both a problem and a potential solution, and the child points the way.

The response or potential solution to this brave statement lies in helping the child to make a paradigm shift from 'no family' to 'family'. This shift can be made tangible and physical and visual. It does not mean crowding the meeting room with bodies of relatives, or telephoning all of the people listed as family in the child's file. It does mean crowding family names onto that flip chart paper, notepaper, or serviette during this and the next several meetings. At the first meeting the serviette may have only two names: the child and one family member who is remembered. This family member may be an aunt, younger brother, or cousin. Most children can recall and name one person from their family. At subsequent meetings that one person may become two because the remembered person is now married, has a child, or has a parent. Slowly the family emerges as uncles appear, grandparents surface, and a long forgotten and much disliked step-father is given a name.

The **genogram** is a case note of family relationships that can help the child to make that paradigm shift from family-less to family-full. It is not a genealogical description. It is not a confidential document that the worker constructs based on the case notes in the file. It is a shared case note that the child constructs with the encouragement of the worker. The child controls and directs the genogram, deciding who to include and who to exclude. This way of proceeding establishes an equal power dynamic between worker and child in the very first meeting. Instead of the child's looking to the worker for answers, the worker is looking to the child for information and direction. Equalizing of power also creates a problem-solving environment for the first meeting, and problem-solving is a positive and optimistic place to be.

There are many ways to draw a genogram and many genogram models. Because this is a case note, each one of these genogram models has similar characteristics of simplicity, clarity, and literacy. The genogram is simple because it is meant to be read easily by the child, the family, and the workers who may read the genogram in the child's file many years later. The genogram is clear because it is a structural signpost for the child and the worker and it must be clear to be read easily and correctly. Literacy follows from simplicity and clarity and, best of all, there are no words on the genogram except the names of people in the child's family. In this way any child can read the genogram even when linguistic barriers exist. The genogram is truly an open book if it is co-constructed honestly by the child and the worker.

The following are guidelines for a simple, child-directed genogram:

- Females are represented by circles and males by squares.
- The age of the person is put inside the circle or square, and the name of the person is put under the circle or square.
- Genograms are read from left to right, the oldest child in the family being furthest to the left.
- Marriage is shown by a solid line and a common-law relationship by a broken line.
- Separation is shown by one slash mark, and divorce by two.
- Dates of marriages, separations, divorces, and deaths are indicated only by the year; no days or months are indicated. Only the last two digits of the year are indicated (for example, 97).
- Pregnancies are indicated by a triangular shape.
- Death is indicated by an X and a date of death.
- The genogram itself is signed and dated.

Consonant with the child as the controller and the source of the information, the first picture on the paper is the child (a circle or a square) with the child's age on the inside and the child's name underneath. Then, the genogram unfolds and is drawn together, with the child as the authority spotting any mistakes, correcting lines of connections and names, adding people as they are remembered. The worker adds dates as the child directs, and simply configures the date from the child's memory of 'two years ago' or 'when I was eight'. Each direction is accepted and followed, although the worker may need to ask questions to clarify names, ages, and dates. The co-construction of the genogram is part of a slow and gentle conversation filled with affirmation and support. The following is one such dialogue between worker (W) and child (C):

C: I don't have any family.
W: Okay. I will put you in the middle with your age inside: 14, right?
C: Yeh, and I guess you better put in my brother Paul.

W: Okay. Is Paul older or younger?
C: He's 22 now. He's not the oldest, though. Ray is. He's 23.
W: Right. We can draw them both, too. No sisters, right?
C: Yeh, I have a little sister but she's with my dad.
W: And what's her name?
C: Celine.
W: Is she much younger?
C: She's only eight. I don't see her much, though. Really, she's just my half-sister; her mom was my dad's girlfriend before she took off.

The 14-year-old started this first meeting with the statement, 'I have no family.' That one declaration speaks volumes. It is a very brave assertion by a child who has survived alone and is still surviving without family. However, in less than a minute of dialogue that the child has controlled and directed, a family has emerged on paper. There are six family members identified: two much older brothers, a younger sister, a mom, a step-mom, and a dad. These six family members may not be the most important ones for the child; and they may have been sources for many of the child's problems. The really close ones may emerge later: an aunt, a grandfather, a half-sister who lives far away. But the structure of the family is emerging, and the lines of connections can literally be seen by the child and the worker together.

In such a dialogue the child may begin to want to talk about family, if only to correct the worker who is drawing the genogram. The child has all of the information and is clearly in control of the genogram. The child directs the telling of a story that becomes increasingly visual and rich with detail. As the worker and the child co-create the genogram together, they also re-capture the emotions, nicknames, and attitudes of family members. This shared case note—the genogram—slowly becomes filled with family, potential sources of problems and sources of solutions and supports, too.

A dialogue between worker (W) and child (C) during the co-construction of the genogram may sound like this:

C: That is my Aunt Martha. She was always bossy with me.
W: I'll write 'bossy' beside her name.
C: Yeh, that's right. She used to call me 'lazy'.
W: I'll write that beside you and put 'M' in brackets so I remember where that came from: Aunt Martha. Were there any other names?
C: Just Tony. He called me his 'princess'.

As the genogram emerges, the sources for many of the problems and hurts are visually identified, and the child sees the structure of the narrative emerge on the paper, much like a picture of family life. There may be a pattern of leaving the family. Dad's girlfriend leaves; mom leaves with a new partner; an elder sister leaves home to live on the streets. Other members of the family do not leave but stay to care for one another.

Why do they stay and what gives them the strength to survive the loss of another family member when that person chooses to leave the family?

Alcoholism may have permeated the lives of several generations; however, there may be one aunt who is not an alcoholic. In her case, what made the difference? Why did she not become an alcoholic? What can be learned from her pattern of problem-solving? Did she seek outside help? Did she get a job? Did she have a stable love relationship? What made the difference? The patterns of problem-solving within the family can suggest solutions that are more appropriate for the child's culture, needs, and lifestyle.

A child is more likely to pay attention to this family pattern of problem-solving because it is a familiar one to the child. This is not a story about a distant national hero or a character in a movie. This family relative who solves problems and who breaks the pattern is part of the child's own family. This relative is a relevant and valid role model for the child and, unlike all of the other strangers in the child's life, is physically linked to the child for life. Children instinctively recognize this in their patterns of behaviour in the adolescent years. Child welfare records show that most children leaving care at age 16 seek out birth family as opposed to strangers, even if the strangers (foster family, previous workers) have known them longer than birth family (see Chapter 10).

Identifying family is also a way to identify potential caregivers. Sometimes the solution can happen only with the support of the family, and only the child can identify that family member who can supply the desired support. Finding a family is finding a potential source of support as well as the potential source of the problem. Both solutions and problems come with the genogram, making this a very powerful way to begin the first meeting.

Consider Figure 6.1. Joey is the 11-year-old son of Darlene (42) and Brian (43). Darlene and Brian have been separated (one slash mark) since Darlene moved in with Amelia (22). Joey spends his week-days with his father, Brian, and spends his weekends with his mother and his mother's partner, Amelia. Joey also has a close relationship with his older step-brother, Ralph (18).

Joey identified five people in his genogram: himself, his mother Darlene, his father Brian, his step-mother Amelia, and his step-brother Ralph. The other people were added to the genogram by his mother who attended the meeting with him. She wanted to let me know more about Amelia, her current partner, who is acting as Joey's step-mother. She also wanted to let me know more about her other two children, Ralph (18) and Amanda (20) from her first marriage with Bob.

When Joey saw the other people being added to the genogram he became very interested. He asked questions about Bob, Darlene's first husband, and asked if his mom knew then that she liked girls. Joey and his mother began a conversation about relationships, a conversation prompted by the genogram, and a conversation that was not focused on Joey's school problems, the initial reason for the meeting.

This conversation revealed that Joey had experienced a lot of bullying at school because his mom was 'weird', and he had started avoiding school as a result. Joey's school problems turned out to be related to the homophobia that Joey was experiencing

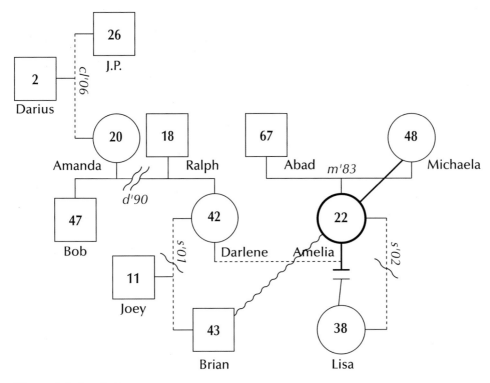

Figure 6.1 Joey's Genogram

at school, and his confusion over his mom's apparent change in sexual orientation. The latter subject was taboo in the home because Joey was perceived as being too young to know about sex. However, his school experience put him in the disempowered position of having some, but not all, of the information that he needed. The genogram helped to fill the gaps in Joey's family knowledge and, although he did not yet understand fully what sexual orientation was, he now understood who the people were in his family and how they were related. He also felt closer to his mother who assured him that he was her one and only little boy, and that she loved and cared for him.

Home Visits

Baby, the heroine of Heather O'Neill's (2006: 7) *Lullabies for Little Criminals*, describes her Montreal neighbourhood: 'That neighbourhood looked the worst in the morning. The street was empty and there was vomit on the sidewalk. All the colourful lights had been turned off and the sky was the color of television static.' Despite the lack of food, the rats, the squalor, and the drugs, her father Jules walks her to school every morning. Outside the school they 'gave each other seven kisses for good luck', and then he rushes home to shoot up more drugs. Her tone and choice of words, her defiance in the face of poverty, neglect, and abuse, are evident. A few hours on her street would educate the worker who wanted to get to know Baby.

The worker is lucky who gets these few hours on the child's street during a home visit. This contextualizes the child within a family structure that affects the child, supporting or stopping change, minimising or enlarging behavioural problems. The child's brothers and sisters may be at home, too, making this a family time. The worker catches a glimpse of how the child fits into the family and how family dynamics unfold. To make a change needs to be the child's own goal that is shared among the child, family, and worker. This homemade and shared goal is more likely to induce change than a solution that the worker brings from 'outside'.

The worker hears the sounds in the home, smells the cooking, and sometimes the unwashed laundry. The worker feels the mood of the home. The worker sees which rooms and which objects the child is allowed to access. The worker also sees where the child sleeps and eats and plays and where the child is not allowed to sleep, eat, and play. Sometimes a parent's office is strictly off-limits. Sometimes the dining-room is only used for company. Sometimes the television is the only piece of furniture in the living room and all the meals are eaten on the floor in front of the television.

These environmental factors that precipitate and perpetuate the child's behaviour are often more important than any parental description of either the behaviours or their attempts at managing the behaviours. Seeing the behaviour within the home environment explains how the behaviour works in the child's daily life, and why this behaviour continues. Whether stealing, bullying, self-mutilation, or some other reason for concern, many behaviours can be more easily understood during a home visit. The home that the family creates is a stage that shapes the behaviour almost as much as the family in the home does.

Home visits are effective because home is the natural, long-term support for the child. Because family is a lifetime relationship, the stronger the family is, the more potential support there is for the child. Home is the place the child returns to after foster care, and home is the place that either supports or undermines the child's growth and development. The home is the family's refuge or safe place even though it may not be safe for any member of the family. The home is also the place in which the child constructs meaning.

The worker's position is that of a visitor, a stranger in the home. There are boundary and cultural issues in every corner of the home. There are behavioural indicators in the space and the interactions that happen only in that space. There is family history here. If the parent stands when the grandmother comes into the room, the worker also stands. If the family members take off their shoes in the home, the worker does the same. These signs of respect demonstrate an initial acknowledgement of, and respect for, family culture.

While the worker is observing the family, the family is watching and taking note of the worker's body language; this includes how the worker gets to the home, where the worker parks, whether the worker rings the bell or knocks on the front door, where the worker chooses to sit, what the worker eats or drinks in the home, and what the worker wears. Some workers leave their coats on during the entire visit, while others wear their religious beliefs around their necks or dangling from their ears. This sends out a very loud cultural message to the family and certainly establishes clear and rigid boundaries. The worker's cultural and boundary messages impact the relationship with the family and any interventions that the worker may attempt.

One family that I worked with was more impressed with my mode of transportation than with any of the resources that I suggested. Because I took the bus to their home rather than a car, they welcomed me with warmth and friendliness. Taking a bus positioned me closer to their culture (they had never owned a car) than previous workers, and they opened up to me more easily. Telling me which bus to take home and the schedule of that bus positioned them as the smart ones, the ones with the information. They felt in control of the situation not only because it was their home but also because they knew more about the neighbourhood (and the bus!) than I did. I looked to them as a source of genuine and tangible information, first.

As a result of this positioning, each member of that family began to tell me a story about the family and their role in the family. Each member of the family had a presenting problem that involved another member of the family and each demanded an urgent solution, perhaps one that I had brought in my briefcase or that I could impose on them from my position of authority. But my briefcase had no magic pills, and my authority in their home would be temporary at best. The family member they identified would still be their parent, brother, or sister long after I had left the family. The solution lay within their family already and together we worked to locate it.

I listened carefully to their narratives. I watched as the parents looked at me, occasionally at their child, and never at each other. I watched the brother slip out of the room to do 'homework', and then watched as he slipped out through the kitchen door and into the street. I saw the crowded bedrooms and the empty cupboards in the kitchen. I watched and listened, and, in the end, we constructed a new family narrative together. This new and more hopeful narrative was their solution, not mine. It promised safety for each member of the family, and the solution worked for them in their family culture.

This was a healthy working relationship in which I played a dual role. One role was to demonstrate respect for family culture and validate family strengths. The strength might be simply providing ample bedding for each family member, or having a place cleared in the kitchen for the children to do their homework. I tried to learn as quickly as possible how the family dynamics worked in the home, and how these dynamics could be seen as strengths. My second role was as learner-teacher, trying to learn about the child's place in the family and demonstrating child-centred practice.

One lone mother I visited was working full-time outside the home in addition to parenting her nine children. She had schedules written in Arabic on her kitchen wall. They were as clear and well-constructed as any genogram from the case files. Her strength in organization was immediately evident to me and, when I praised her, her very tired eyes sparkled.

Her children's role in the family was evident, and each child had a place in the structure. The clash she had with her daughter emanated not from any deficit in the mother or the daughter but in the gender constructs within that structure. The daughter was chafing in her role as caregiver of younger siblings and was unwilling to continue in that role while her brother played video games and socialized with his friends. Moving the problem away from the mother and the daughter and into the gender constructs allowed these two women to reconstruct a family structure that felt and looked more gender-equal.

The home visit is a chance for each member of the family to develop better coping skills, communication patterns, parenting skills, and more realistic expectations around children (Dufour and Chamberland, 2003). The home visit may focus on the caregiving issues and may involve helping the parents to keep the home safe and clean for the child. Rather than teaching bedtime routine, the worker affirms the parent in the authoritative role and works with the parent for the constructing of that hour before the preschooler goes to bed. The worker quietly and calmly helps with the bathing or reading, firmly discouraging loud or boisterous play. The worker then sits with the parent quietly after the child is in bed, reassuring the parent that the child indeed will sleep if there is no loud activity or diversions happening in the living room.

The worker reassures and encourages the parent who feels incapable and overwhelmed by the stress of parenting. Behaviour problems, too many activities, clutter, poverty, and overwhelming chores are some of the factors that can deplete the physical and emotional resources of a parent. An exhausted parent does not need brochures and pamphlets to read. These only feel like more work on top of caregiving, and probably balancing one or several out-of-the-home jobs, too.

Having another adult with whom to share parenting concerns is a tremendous support for parents, particularly when that person is well-informed, respectful of the parent, and focused on the best interests of the child (Klebanov, 2001). The dialogue can happen naturally when the worker and the parent sort through food in the kitchen, keeping some food and discarding the food that may be harmful for the child. The dialogue also happens when the parent makes a list of fresh vegetables that the children do enjoy, and the worker supports the parent in finding these vegetables at low or no cost. Both adults have much to contribute to this relationship, and the respectful co-operation of both adults provides a model of caregiving for the child in the home.

Engaging the Family

How do we engage families? In the home visit just described I did not take the role of judge or of expert. I offered the mother information about the effect of pre-packaged candies and sodas on children, and together we made the choice to remove them from the family kitchen. The mother was in control of the kitchen, not I. I was the learner-teacher, and the family taught me a great deal. This respectful position of learner-teacher is essential in engaging the family. The worker does not take the place of the parents or undermine their authority in the home; nor does the worker join with the children against their parents or demonstrate superior knowledge. The worker respects the family as they are today and as they hope to be in the future.

Sometimes children bring toys to the worker on the first in-home visit and sometimes they hide under their mother's skirts. Sometimes children hold their arms out for a hug and sometimes they angrily run into their bedroom and slam the door. Children react in various ways to a stranger in their home, and their reactions depend on many factors: age, attachment issues, family structure and culture, role in the family, temperament, and personal communication style.

The parent may feel compelled to ignore the child, perhaps because the worker is in the home and the parent feels inadequate and 'under the microscope'. The parent may also fear the worker's disapproval for turning away from the worker's questions and turning towards the child. Part of child-centred practice is the acknowledgment of the child's needs, feelings, and opinions. Because these sometimes are expressed only through body language, the worker needs to pay close attention to the child and listen to the voice of the child. An infant's crying, for instance, can indicate a need for food, water, affection, or a change of clothes. If so, the worker needs to support the parent in responding to the child and naming the need or feeling so that the child's needs can be addressed. This is child-centred practice.

In a recent Ontario study (Dumbrill and Maiter, 2004), parents of children in foster care asked for three things from child welfare workers: to be listened to; to be given choice in their child's life; and to be allowed to participate with full information. Their three simple requests echoed the requests of parents in similar studies. Whether their child is in the home or not, whether they choose to parent their child or not, biological parents have a lifelong, vested interest in their child's future that no other person has. This lifelong connection may not be healthy and may feel like a stranglehold, but the connection counts for the child. In child-centred practice this connection counts for the worker, too.

Parents often feel like failures when outside help is needed. They feel powerless and diminished by agency intervention, and ashamed that their child is seen to be in need of outside help. They may need to process these feelings of guilt, anger, remorse, and disappointment with the worker. Parenting is socially constructed in Canada as a solitary responsibility and a natural outcome of birthing children. When parenting difficulties arise, this construction needs to be de-constructed so that parents recognize the structural determinants that impact their parenting.

The worker can help in this deconstruction by listening without being judgemental, then repositioning the parents as important components in the child's change. When the caregivers, guardians, or parents are co-designers and supporters of the child's change, any interventions with the child usually are more effective. Through this non-judgemental positioning, the parents begin to understand that the child's change implies family change, too, as each member of the family supports the family's solution to the presenting problem.

With worker encouragement and support, parents can share their expertise and life experience. If the parent identifies a bullying problem in the family, for example, the worker can ask the parent to recount her own experiences with bullying. A mother may talk about being bullied when she was a child, describing how she felt and how she reacted. This helps the worker to contextualise the problem. This also helps the children in the family to understand that their mother was once a little girl, too, with a past and with experiences and expertise from which the children can learn.

 Point to Consider   6.1

Traditional First Nations Healing Practices

Workers need to be aware of traditional First Nations healing practices that a child or family has used in the past or wants to use now. These may include:

- sharing circles;
- storytelling;
- such ceremonies as sweat lodges, pipe ceremonies, and potlatches;
- traditional role models such as elders, healers, and traditional teachers;
- medicine wheels.

These traditional healing practices may be more effective than the conventional approach of a worker or agency. At this first meeting the worker needs to iden- tify whether or not the First Nations child or family prefers to use traditional First Nations healing practices. This identification needs to be phrased positively with an affirmation of the value of healing practices and how long such approaches have been marginalized by mainstream Canada. The worker may want to ask directly at several points in the first meeting to ensure that the child and the family feel that these approaches are equally valid and reliable healing practices. More important is the worker's reaction to the family who requests traditional healing. The worker needs to bring in these resources and ensure that the family is firmly connected with traditional healers; in other words, a pamphlet or a telephone number is not enough!

Identifying structural factors that impact parenting can lead to a discussion of those structural determinants that could also support parenting. These include appro- priate, accessible, and practical financial resources to which the child is entitled; some are described in Table 6.1. There are federal, provincial and territorial, municipal, and Band subsidies, food bank support, and benefits. The worker can match these resources to the family so that only appropriate ones are offered. Quality, affordable, and accessible resources are more useful than a complicated pamphlet promising supports from a government office.

However, families do not always use these subsidies, supports, and benefits effectively or to the fullest degree. Some families accept persistent poverty on the margins rather than confronting forms and agencies. Almost half of the families who need food bank support never go to a food bank. Over half of the mothers who are entitled to Parental Leave under Employment Insurance also do not claim this benefit.

Distrust of authority, cultural and family pride, and accessibility can be barriers to accessing supports. If the parent has had negative experiences in the past with authority figures such as police officers, child welfare workers, and teachers, the parent is unlikely to want to seek help from these same authority figures. The parent may be afraid of going into government buildings and of giving the government personal information. The parent may feel that social assistance, immigration, or health benefits will be jeopardized by asking for other supports at the food bank, community centre, or drop-in. As a British Columbia researcher commented: 'A grandmother explained that she chose to avoid asking for needed services because she was afraid that the Ministry would become involved and apprehend her grandchildren from her' (Bennett and Sadrehashemi, 2008: 27).

Another barrier is the inability to speak and write either official language, a distinct barrier to either telephoning for help or to completing complicated on-line forms. If English or French is not the parent's first language or if the parent has limited vision, speech delays, hearing impairments, or low literacy, the parent may feel awkward speaking to officials or explaining personal difficulties. Translation services and cultural interpreters are sometimes available in hospitals and agencies; however, asking for these supports can be both stressful and embarrassing for parents.

Accessibility to supports means possessing and being able to use a telephone and a computer and a vehicle. Parents who are unable to pay telephone bills or who do not have a deposit for a telephone or a credit card for a cell phone do not have telephone access. These same parents may not have a computer in their home to easily access on-line information, documents, and forms. They may not have a vehicle to bring home groceries from a food bank, clothing from an agency, or a free washer and dryer from a donor. All of these accessibility barriers prevent parents from accessing muchneeded resources.

The worker may need to arrange for a van to collect the furniture and appliances. The worker may need to access translation services or a cultural interpreter to accompany the parent or to support the parent in completing forms. The worker may need to drive the parents to the family resource centre for their first visit. This practical support engages family in a genuine way, and is an extension of the home visit. In addition, conversations happen while driving in a car that happen nowhere else. Sometimes, when the worker is driving and unable to have eye contact with the parents, they will share memories, opinions, and feelings that they feel uncomfortable sharing at home.

Table 6.1   Brief Overview of Canadian Federal Programs for Children, 2009

Universal Child Care Benefit (UCCB) is a monthly payment of $100 per child made to all families who have children under six years of age.

Canada Child Tax Benefit (CCTB) is a tax-free monthly payment made to eligible families to help them with the costs of raising children under eighteen years of age. The CCTB may include the NCBS (National Child Benefit Supplement) and the CDB (Child Disability Benefit).

National Child Benefit Supplement (NCBS) is a tax-free monthly payment made to eligible families for each child who is under 18 years of age.

Child Disability Benefit (CDB) is a tax-free benefit for eligible families who care for children under the age of 18 who have a severe and prolonged impairment in mental or physical functions.

GST Credit is a tax credit for low-income parents with children under 19 years of age.

Child Care Expense Deduction (CCED) is a tax deduction for employed parents who have child-care expenses and receipts to prove these expenses. The CCED can be used for both regulated and unregulated child care, but cannot be used for parental care.

Adoption Expense Deduction is a tax deduction for parents who adopt children to help them cover eligible costs associated with the process of adoption.

Paid maternity and parental leaves are for parents covered by Employment Insurance (EI).

Family Supplements are provided by Employment Insurance to low-income families to raise the replacement level of lost income while parents are on parental leave.

Canada Education Savings Grant (CESG) provides grants to Registered Education Savings Plan (RESP) contributors until the beneficiaries reach the age of 17.

Children's Fitness Tax Credit lets parents claim up to $500 per year for eligible fitness expenses paid for each child who is under 16 years of age at the beginning of the year in which expenses are paid.

Aboriginal Head Start initiative provides supplemental learning programs for children and parenting courses for their parents.

Community Action Program for Children (CAPC) provides funding to community groups who deliver programs for children from birth to six years of age who are deemed 'at risk'.

Canada Prenatal Nutrition Program provides support for 'at risk' pregnant women.

National Children's Agenda provides Centres of Excellence for Children's Well-Being. These Centres strive to enhance the understanding of healthy child development.

Federal Child Support Guidelines ensure that family support obligations are respected.

Summary

We have considered many practical ways to engage with the child and the family. From an understanding of the power dynamics that differentiate meetings from interviews, you learned how to plan a meeting with a child, or a child and family. You learned how important your body language, tone, and attitude are in conveying your empathy and respect for the child. You also learned how to use genograms and case notes effectively in this first meeting. Both case notes and genograms depend upon your listening to the child: the gestures, the play, and the silences. This listening is a skill that will be explained in the next chapter, as we explore autobiographical reasoning and the slow and deliberate construction of the child's narrative.

Review Questions

1. Name three ways in which a meeting is different from an interview.
2. Which five guidelines should you follow when writing a case note of a meeting?
3. What are the three tricks that Dorothy Smith identified when describing a worker's writing of a case note?
4. Using deShazer's terminology, how would you change a 12-year-old visitor to a 12-year-old customer who wants to engage in a meeting with you?
5. Why might you choose to co-create a genogram with a young child?
6. What can be learned during a home visit?
7. Why would a family not welcome a home visit? Suggest three ways you can begin a home visit when encountering the family's initial resistance to your visit.
8. How would you model child-centred practice during a home visit such as the one described in Discussion Question 3? This mother has just had her first child and appears to be having some difficulties.
9. Name five potential sources of financial assistance available to a lone mother of an eight-year-old child who is in an after-school daycare program. The mother is working full-time outside the home but does not earn a living wage.
10. What does 'access to tangible support' mean? State specific ways in which you could increase a family's access to this support.

Discussion Questions

1. Have you ever reacted to a child's behaviour, then regretted your reaction? How might praxis change your interventions?

2. Draw your own genogram, then share your genogram with another student. What questions did that student ask that caused you to adjust or re-consider your genogram?

3. Acronyms are used to keep recordings brief for both the writer and the reader. Some common acronyms used are TM (telephone message), TC (telephone call), BM (birth mother), SP (service plan), LOC (length of contact), FP (foster parent), MH (mental health), PHN (public health nurse), and DOB (date of birth). Initials are also used to replace full names. Read the following case note and highlight any words or phrases that may mislead or trick the reader. Then rewrite the case note so that it resembles the minutes of a meeting, trying also to keep the case note brief.

> *26/01/08 10:40 a.m.*
> Visited T.R. as arranged on 12/12/07 per SP. T.R. is sleepy and is obviously still having drug problems. House still very dirty. Sufficient food but no jars of baby food as required by SP. Baby X (DOB: 10/08/07) sleeping in crib beside T.R.'s bed. Unwashed baby bottles still in kitchen sink; obviously she's overwhelmed by baby. T.R. admits to smoking joint one week ago. House stinks of cigarettes, and beer bottles lined up at back door. T.R. claims that ex-partner has not visited since New Years. TC to supervisor confirms that PHN visit confirmed for tomorrow at 11:00 am. Informed T.R., then left. LOC: 15 mins.

Chapter 7

The Child's Story

Grown-ups never understand anything by themselves, and it is tiresome for children to be always and forever explaining things to them.

—Antoine de Saint-Exupery, *The Little Prince*

A personal narrative develops and evolves as one experiences life and immortalizes segments of this life in memories. Each new experience becomes part of this life narrative, while some experiences are altered or discarded along the way. Telling the life narrative to others helps one to reflect on experiences and to make sense of one's life in the larger relational context.

When people relate family anecdotes or tell about experiences that reveal unusual twists and turns of relationships, they put these anecdotes and experiences into a structure or story. When listeners react to those stories with pity, anger, or joy, they observe such reactions and may adjust their stories accordingly. The next time the stories are told, they may leave out events, embellish them, change the names or dates, or put someone else or some other feature at centre stage. In this way our stories evolve and develop just as people do. A toddler tells a story quite differently when she becomes a pre-schooler, and adjusts her story again as an adolescent. These stories become part of her always-evolving life narrative which, in turn, begins to reflect self-image and self-concept as it is shaped and moulded by the surrounding structure.

Each member of a family has a personal story within the family life narrative. A father who experiences his child's first steps interprets this experience quite differently than does the older sister who watches these first steps. For the father this event might be like a miracle in his life, the moment at which his son begins to walk. For the sister this might be a moment to fear, a moment in which her little brother takes over the attention of her father and begins to get into all of her toys. The same family story, told by different members of the family, sounds quite different as each member tells it. Like witnesses at the scene of an accident, each person sees the same accident but each sees only certain elements of the accident, and experiences these elements in a personal way. Each witness tells the story from a personal perspective and through the window of his or her personal culture.

As the family evolves and as each member of the family grows and develops, the family narrative also evolves. Sometimes one unresolved problem piles on top of another, interfering with the narrative until the entire family narrative becomes problem-saturated. The family forgets about the good times, and the problem-saturated narrative becomes the dominant family narrative. Structural determinants are not identified and seen as oppressions. Instead, the family begins to own them, absorbing them into the family problem. At this point the family, or one member of the family, may turn to a worker for help with a presenting problem.

The worker listens. Listening is not an easy process. The AHA! Method guides the listening so that the worker can develop a connection with the story-teller. Through attentive listening the worker begins to understand the pain and sadness of the problem-saturated story. Structural determinants contextualize the story; these determinants are questioned and confronted. Specific challenges and problems are named and externalized in a metaphor, and the story is re-authored, name by name and experience by experience. The child and the family begin to move forward from a problem-saturated family narrative to a more positive one.

Objectives

By the end of this chapter, you will:

- Understand the difference between a 'story' and a 'narrative' and how auto-biographical reasoning creates this difference.
- Identify the difference between the presenting problem and the underlying problem.
- Demonstrate how to listen to the child's narrative using the AHA! Method.
- Demonstrate how to support the child's narrative through externalizing the problem or difficulty and identifying a metaphor for it.

Autobiographical Reasoning

As one grows and develops, a life narrative evolves. Each experience is a story of its own; when compiled and edited, these stories become the life narrative. These stories may be internalized and never told, or told much later, once a sorting process has identified the roles of the people in the story and the emotions behind the storyline. On the other hand, the story may be told right after the experience. As the story is told, it evolves. Each listener, each storytelling context, and each storytelling experience impacts the story. Each one of these stories—told, retold, and untold—becomes part of the life narrative.

Young children tend to tell stories about events in terms of what the people in the events look like. A young child may describe a teacher as a 'witch' and a neighbour as 'grandma'. The young child uses morally dichotomous terms that reflect a simplistic morality of 'good' and 'bad'. This unencumbered morality sees 'good' and 'bad' as contradictory terms with no room for ambiguity (Habermas and Bluck, 2000). The child calls the neighbour 'grandma' because the child associates the neighbour with grandmotherly qualities and physical characteristics. The child calls the teacher 'witch' because of her harsh words and demeanour. This 'mistake' is not lying or deception. This form of description is simple morality and pre-operational thinking at work. In Kohlberg's terms, pre-conventional morality is also at work (see Chapter 3).

Some of the child's stories, and some parts of the stories, are already metaphorical. Fantasy figures such as the good fairy, Santa Claus, dragons, and witches are blended together with the family dog in these stories, and all of the characters of the stories are considered to be equally real. The child demonstrates skill at engaging these fantasy figures to interact with the real persons or animals in each story. This skill also reflects the pre-operational reasoning of the young child. Like Piaget's daughter Lucienne, the afternoon does not exist when the child is not napping (see Chapter 3). The teacher lives in the school; the family dog may talk to the child at night; and there may be a monster under the bed.

School-aged children develop concrete operational thinking while they are developing complex language skills and a deeper socio-emotional understanding of people. They begin to reflect on the motivations of others and to see morality in less dichotomous terms. The 'bad' and 'good' of the young child are replaced by 'seems to be mean' and 'sometimes okay' of the older child. The child begins to construct more complex stories that reflect a deeper understanding of other people's motivations as well as a growing self-awareness. Fantasy figures begin to fade, especially in a social location in which reality is preferred and fantasy figures are positioned as childish or silly.

School-aged children also begin to try to connect the past events of their lives to the emotions surrounding these events. They sift through their memories, already faded by time, keeping some and discarding others, depending on whether these memories support their current ego identification. Sutherland (2003) calls these random memories 'the winds of childhood' and suggests that they are glimpses only, especially when the winds are from very early childhood. Children sift through them, trying to make sense of the present, or trying to adjust their present self to the remembered self. This reflective process is called **autobiographical reasoning**, and it usually begins in middle childhood when stories, past and present, are contextualized by emotional and moral reasoning.

An angry 12-year-old girl may look at her baby pictures and see only scowls on her tiny face. The pictures may remind her of the toddler tantrums she has often been told about by her parents. She begins to see herself as an inherently angry person. This becomes part of her own narrative. Similarly, a lonely 12-year-old boy will look at his camp pictures and only remember how much he hated camp. He will mentally discard

Photo 7.1 The lifebook records memories but she chooses which memories to keep.

the pictures of himself laughing with his bunk buddies. He will see the pictures from camp as further evidence that he is himself friendless or unsociable or different.

Children who suffer abuse, neglect, or trauma often blot out whole days or months of their life. Sometimes they cannot remember years. Jurek Becker, interned as a child in Ravensbuck and Sachsenhausen concentration camps, speaks of the effects of this forgetting: 'Without memories of childhood, it is as if you were doomed to drag a big box around with you, though you don't know what's in it. And the older you get, the heavier it becomes, and the more impatient you are to finally open the thing' (Miller, 2005: 84).

Michael White (1989, 2007) developed the theory that people's lives are actually shaped and organized by their life narratives. He came to believe that individual stories not only mirror the past but also shape the future as the child re-interprets the past through these stories. The angry girl sees her past as being full of anger, and sees only one future for herself, a future full of bitterness and anger. The lonely boy will push away classmates who call on him or ask him to join the team. He will see these friendly overtures as phony and shallow, because he is now convinced that he is destined to be friendless.

A family whose **dominant narrative** is that they are all 'losers' may only remember and recount their stories of failures and problems. Happy moments, family celebrations, jokes, and laughter are forgotten, suppressed, or minimized. This dominant narrative of 'losers' is repeated so many times and over so many years that everyone in the family now knows it, believes it, and behaves accordingly. The family gets stuck in its problematic narrative and the members mould themselves and their experiences to fit this narrative. If someone in the family has brief success, this is not celebrated. Instead, this is seen as an aberration, and a reason to turn away from that person until that person has another failure. The family narrative requires this reaction, and causes the family to feel too discouraged to move forward or to change. The family may feel that they can never succeed and can never alter their family narrative of being 'losers'.

This is a symbiotic process. The autobiographical reasoning of each member of the family both contributes to and is affected by the dominant family narrative. This dominant narrative tends to be generated from the dominant person in the family. If the family structure is hierarchical and patriarchal, the father may construct the dominant narrative of his daughter and may repeat this narrative until the daughter and everyone else in the family believes it. The father may repeat a problem-saturated story of his daughter, carefully constructing the dominant narrative of the daughter as 'stupid' or an 'idiot'. This same story and these same terms are repeated by the family power figure (father) until the dominant narrative is believed and ingrained and perpetuated, or at least not contradicted, by all of the members of the family including the daughter who now identifies herself as 'stupid' and an 'idiot'.

In this patriarchal family the narratives of the less powerful members of the family are often not expressed or, if they are expressed, they are not accepted. The brother, who no longer lives in the home, may not contribute to this dominant narrative of his sibling. This brother may have some very important and illuminating stories to tell about his sister, and his more positive stories could contribute to a richer understanding of his sister's behaviour. However, because he no longer lives at home, his voice is neither recognized nor accepted, and his sister's narrative is untouched by his contribution.

Another daughter in the family may have absorbed the dominant narrative that she also is stupid. She puts aside memories of successes and achievements, and instead remembers only failures. Moments of success at school are either forgotten or, once remembered, are dismissed as exceptions or aberrations. She may say, 'I've always sucked at school', and may not accept a tutor or an extra study class on the grounds that the dominant family narrative shows that such interventions are always unsuccessful. This maladaptive narrative becomes an obstacle to her health and wellness. The dominant narrative is constructed incrementally over the years and reinforces the negative self-concept of that daughter, too.

Many children construct life narratives that are negative and problem-saturated through this process of autobiographical reasoning. Their parents have repeatedly told them (or perhaps only once and it sticks!) that they are clumsy, so 'clumsy kid' becomes a persona in the older child's narrative. A sister may have taunted the child with the nickname of Plain Jane, so 'ugly me' becomes the child's dominant persona. Without anyone in the family to interject and offer happy stories and memories, the child may begin to reason that life has always been unhappy or problematic. An eight-year-old boy may say, 'I've never been good at sports'. A 13-year-old girl may say, 'My sister and I have always fought'. The child believes this narrative because it has been carefully constructed through autobiographical reasoning and it has been supported and verified by the dominant family narrative.

Structural oppression also helps to construct the narrative. Racism convinces a child that his race is tainted, unworthy, and insignificant. 'Ableism' oppresses the child with cerebral palsy, describing her struggles to play sport as clumsy, futile, and weak. Cultural beliefs about poverty tell the child in a poor family that he is a failure and that his mother is lazy or stupid because she is not rich. Gender construction convinces girls who like to build engines that they are 'weird' or 'butch'. Structural oppression, when not countered by community or family culture, continuously affects the child's autobiographical reasoning. There are exceptions to this, with politicians, media stars, community leaders, and teachers exemplifying their personal successes in countering structural oppression and an inherited negative narrative. A child may singlehandedly defy racial oppression when other family members accept it. A child may embrace the power of her gender and challenge gender constructs accepted by the family. A child may see a structural determinant such as ableism as a challenge and a problem that needs to be solved. Jason Kingsley and Mitchell Levitz do this in their book, *Count Us In*, in which they describe their experiences as persons with Down's syndrome. Despite medical advice to institutionalize them, despite exclusion from schools, committees, and sports activities, Jason and Mitchell pursued their careers as advocates that 'people with disabilities *can learn*' (2007: 27; emphasis in original). They countered the structural determinants and the inherited narrative to construct a more hopeful narrative for themselves that they are now able to share with others.

Children need to make sense of their lives, past and present, and so they engage in autobiographical reasoning. When they tell their stories they also conduct a backward search for memories that support their dominant life narrative. Memories are not so much retrieved as re-woven. The memories that do not fit either are not retrieved or are shaped to fit, re-woven into the dominant life narrative. Threads are added, weaving is tightened or not, and the tapestry emerges. Since children want to experience their own intentions as 'good', their re-woven stories justify their behaviours as being the only possible way to act in the circumstances; in other words, they 'did good'.

A 10-year-old girl who has not seen her father since she was a toddler and who really misses fatherly love and attention needs to make some sense of that absent father and to manage her own feelings about him. She also needs to make sense of and incorporate her mother's story of her father as an irresponsible and uncaring man. She suppresses her warm and intimate memories of her father; she may bury these memories so deeply that they are temporarily forgotten. They are certainly not retrieved for her dominant narrative. She begins to reason that her father abandoned her because he really did not care about her, a reflection of her mother's story of the uncaring husband and a way to deal with her own feelings of abandonment. She incorporates that story into her life narrative to make sense of the past and the present. If her father re-appears in her life when she is a teenager she probably will reject him because of this carefully shaped narrative. Her autobiographical reasoning tells her that her father is not to be trusted.

The adopted child needs to make sense of having been relinquished by her birth parent, so may gradually assimilate a social construction that mothers who relinquish their children are bad mothers who abandon their babies. She may also assimilate her adoptive parents' story that they 'saved her' or 'chose her', implying that her birth mother was hurting her or did not choose her. This feeling of rejection is too much for any child to bear, so the child carefully constructs a story in which her birth mother was bad and her current caregivers (adoptive parents) are good. This story becomes problematic as the child tries to reconcile being both chosen (wanted) and bad (she is her mother's daughter, after all). Should she eventually contact her birth family, her dominant narrative becomes further compromised. The child may be left with attachment injuries (Chapter 4) and a feeling of betrayal by all of the significant adults in her life. This feeling of betrayal has huge socio-emotional consequences as the child struggles to make these contradictory, constructed stories fit into her dominant narrative.

The child's narrative formed through autobiographical reasoning represents three lives: one that has been lived; one that has been experienced; and one that is being told. The life lived is what actually happened. The life experienced consists of the images, feelings, sentiments, desires, thoughts, and meanings acquired through living that life. The life being told is shaped by the structural context, the dominant family narrative, the contributions of others, and the cultural conventions of the story-telling. Out of all of these threads comes the child's narrative. As the worker carefully listens to this spoken narrative, the worker also attaches meanings and interpretations to the stories, and these spoken interpretations and silent responses contribute to the evolving co-construction of this narrative.

The Importance of Listening

There is a popular mythology that children are always listened to by adults. It is commonly suggested that adults spend too much time listening to children, and that adults should teach children not to interrupt. This socially constructed myth is the subject of many parenting advice books.[1] The deconstruction of this myth requires only a short period of observation.

Watch what happens when children talk to adults. In the home, children are told to wait, to listen, and to be quiet. When parents or caregivers do talk to children it is often to correct them, teach them, or control them. Sometimes they are ignored, sometimes misinterpreted, and often marginalized: 'Not now!' or 'Save that for later'. In school, children are told to listen to adults before speaking. Students' speech is circumscribed by adult dictums, and often limited to responses. If there is a discussion or debate, this speech has boundaries and marks are dependent on adherence to these adult-set boundaries. Parents, teachers, and workers ask children to speak about their mis-behaviours but rarely about their behaviours. Speaking about behaviours and feelings is typically confined to therapeutic settings, counselling, or social skills groups.

Photo 7.2 The multi-tasking adult has little time to listen and no time to hear.

Does the child's worker attentively listen when the child wants to tell a story rather than explain a misbehaviour or failure? A Canadian study of the foster care system concludes that this system is dominated by child protection workers who talk to and listen to the other adults first: 'It doesn't work because nobody has listened to the children' (Kendrick, 1990: 8). One of the largest studies of listening to children was conducted in Swedish child psychiatry sessions. This study (Cederborg, 1997) revealed that the 19 therapists (workers) spoke during 37.5 per cent of the sessions, parents for 56 per cent of the sessions, and the children for the remaining 6.5 per cent of the time. These percentages present a stark contrast to the stated intent of child psychiatry sessions: listening to the child!

The results of these two studies resonate with most workers. Despite agency procedure and the worker's stated intentions, there is little time allotted for actively listening to the child. Workers have the language skills, authority, and comfort with the conversational process to construct and control the dominant narrative. There is no space in this narrative for children to speak, except to confirm or to deny the dominant narrative, so children's voices and stories often are not heard. A Canadian boy in foster care spoke to Fay Martin (2003: 267) about the effect of this situation on his life: 'Do you have any idea how hard it is to be always watched and never seen? To be constantly analyzed and never understood? That right there, that's loneliness.'

Michael White, David Epston, David Nylund, and other narrative therapists have championed clinical, educational, and community approaches for listening to the child's narrative. In Michael Ungar's story of Christine (2006a: 8–11) he describes the active listening done by Mr Makhnach, a teacher who, 'listens as Christine tries on her new identity as social activist, educating her educators about the realities of today's youth. Mr Makhnach gives her space to speak, to play the expert rather than the problem kid.' Mr Makhnach takes time to listen. He co-constructs the narrative with Christine through his active listening and, as a result, Christine begins to believe in herself and to actively engage in school.

When a teacher, parent, or worker asks the child to journal, have a chat, or describe an event or a feeling, and the adult really takes the time to actively listen or to read the journal, the child may initially feel very uncomfortable. For most children who are used to explaining their mistakes, mis-behaviours, and failures, this is a new and strange experience. If the adult persists, the child may begin to trust and may respond with a tentative story. When the adult affirms rather than judges or scolds the child, the child may continue that story. This listening without interruption is crucial for the child: 'We need to empower children such that they can tell of their experiences within the context of interviews that acknowledge the distinctions between life as lived, experienced and told' (Westcott and Littleton, 2005: 153).

Listening must be open and unbiased rather than directive and judgemental. The worker has no hidden agenda of trying to convince the child to make a particular change in direction. Instead, the worker is trying to understand the truth from the child's perspective. This attentive listening is empowering because the child is the expert on the story, and controls its shape and content. The child is the teller, not the one being told (how to behave, what to do, where to go).

The power of this listening process is described by Carl Rogers (1980: 154). His colleague conducted a research study on visual perception that involved interviewing students regarding their visual perception history, their reaction to wearing glasses, and so on. The researcher listened to the students' replies with interest, but made no judgements or comments on their replies. When the research interviews were completed, a number of the students returned spontaneously to thank the researcher for all of the help he had given them. Although he had not given them any overt support or direction whatsoever, he soon realized that his active and interested listening was seen by these students as helpful, even though his intent had been to gather information rather than to help. The impact of active listening on the participants' lives was enormous!

At the beginning of term my graduate students do a half-hour assignment. They listen to two stories on film, one told by a 10-year-old girl and one told by a 12-year-old boy. Their reactions to the stories and their attentive listening is filmed, and they are given a mark on the basis of their filmed listening. Their only instruction is to listen attentively to the stories as they would in their professional capacity as workers.

Group Exercises 7.1

Telling Left from Right

Most people feel that they are active listeners, particularly when their daily job involves listening. This large group exercise dispels this myth in a few minutes. The large group stands in a circle, and each person has a pen. The group leader first asks if everyone knows his or her left and right. A show of hands usually confirms that everyone does know left from right.

The group leader then explains that a story will be read slowly. Each time the participants hear the word 'right', they must pass their pens to the right. Each time the participants hear the word 'left', they must pass their pens to the left. Then the group leader slowly reads the following story:

'Most children know that the right thing to do when there is only one cookie left is to share what's left with the right friend. But what if there are three cookies left and four friends? Who knows the right thing to do? If it's left to some right-thinking children, they will share what's left. But others will think, 'Right! I'm not sharing, no matter how many cookies are left'.

When the pens are returned to their 'rightful' owners, the participants can discuss why, even when they are told which words are important, it is still difficult to attend to the story, to listen and pick out the words. How much harder is it when the child speaks and all of the words that are spoken are potentially important!

My students bring to this exercise several years of curriculum work incorporating the theory and practice of attentive listening. They have already acquired many listening skills: how to focus on the client, lean forward, demonstrate empathy, and keep their body language open and comforting. Yet over half of the students fail this assignment! This result shocks them and rivets their attention towards the material in this chapter.

The 10-year-old girl tells a story about being sexually abused by her father. Although none of my students speak, their body language speaks volumes. Some bodies convey shock, disgust, anger, horror, and uneasiness; others convey sympathy and a desire to stop the story and comfort the little girl. If this were a real interview rather than a video, their body language would prompt the girl to feel guilty, ashamed, diminished, and unworthy. The girl would probably either stop telling her story or change her story, if only to comfort and re-engage the adult listener.

The girl's story is immediately followed by the boy's story. The 12-year-old boy tells a story about doing poorly in school. Without words, many of my students convey disinterest in this story, and some even convey disgust at the boy's weakness in the face of such a seemingly minor problem. Compared to incest, who really cares about poor grades? Their minds appear to wander and they appear to be out of step with the boy's story. As a result, in a real interview setting the boy would begin to feel ashamed, diminished, and unworthy. The boy would probably either stop telling the story or change the story, if only to elicit support and attention from the adult listener.

Because the mark is based on filmed evidence, the students do not complain too loudly. The film corroborates their mark. After several screenings, the students begin to be able to identify and evaluate their own body language, their expressions and their posture. They see that flicker of disgust and disinterest in their eyes. They soon grow to understand the effect that their body language has on any interaction with a child.

So the first and most important lesson is accepted: listening to a child is a skill. It is a learning process for the worker and it can be an empowering process for the child. Watching Elders work with youth in a healing circle is enlightening. They listen with their bodies and their minds. They tune into the thoughts of the youth as well as the others, past and present, in the circle. While we cannot pretend to be Elders, we can learn from them. Harris (2006: 125) reminds us: 'Traditional learning processes are holistic. . . . Learning and healing go hand in hand, and that learning is based on watching, listening, and doing.'

Fewster (2002: 18) cautions: 'However simple it seems, listening to another human being may be one of the most difficult tasks that we will ever embark upon. And, for most of us, listening to one of our children may border upon the impossible.' Now the real work of change can begin for the students. I call this an AHA! moment which is the precursor to being open to learning the AHA! Method. Now we can begin to **A**ffirm, **H**ere and now, and always be **A**uthentic (AHA!) when listening to the child's narrative.

The AHA! Method: Affirming

Childhood is imagined to be a carefree time: children play and children are happy. Advertisements of Canadian children generally portray giggling, laughing children in pleasurable situations. The adult role is to protect this pleasurable state, and to bring smiles to children's faces. Frowns, tears, and depression do not fit into this social construction of childhood, and children learn early in life to hide and suppress such feelings. When children do express negative feelings, workers often respond with words of cheer and hope. They twist the negative into a positive in an effort to show the brighter side of life, the optimistic side. They want to solve the problem, to make the child smile if only for a moment. It just feels like the right thing to do:

- 'Tomorrow everything will be fine.'
- 'It doesn't matter that you failed. What is important is that you tried.'
- 'You look lovely, with or without the new outfit.'

On the other hand, the worker who affirms the pain, misery, and loneliness of the child does not try to change or minimize these feelings in an effort to make the child smile. Instead, the worker affirms and validates the importance of these feelings, whatever they may be, and how disturbing, disgusting, or odious they may seem. This **affirmation** says that the child's feelings are important, and that the worker respects and values these feelings. The child does not have to pretend to be someone else or to feel something else or be happy. This non-judgemental affirmation of the feelings behind and in the words encourages the child to share more of these feelings.

A girl may tell the worker, for instance, that she is afraid her hospitalized mother will die. This is not the first time that she has told anyone about her fear. Her only mother is dying! She has lived this fear, then reflected on it and recounted it during sleep, play, and at school. She has said the words so many times and in so many ways to relatives, friends, and other professionals. When she has expressed her fear that her mother will die, however, her relatives and friends may have misinterpreted, dismissed, or even laughed at her emotions. In an effort to make her smile or make her feel better, they have offered her unsolicited advice, fantasy, or mini-lectures:

- You're not really afraid, are you? Your mom is in the best hospital in the city.
- That's just silly! It's so silly to be afraid.
- That doesn't make sense. Your mom is going to get better.
- I'm sure you don't mean that. You're a big brave girl.
- What I hear you say is that you believe your mother is going to die.

These replies either misinterpret what the girl is expressing, or dismiss her emotion. Through these replies and these reactions from adults, the girl begins to doubt her own feelings and to be unsure of how and when to express her feelings. She learns that she is weak or simple-minded, making her unable to understand her mother's health situation. Most of all, she learns that her darker emotions, such as fear, are not to be expressed because these emotions are usually wrong and will be met with sarcasm, derision, and advice. It is safer for her to keep these emotions bottled up inside and not express them.

The affirming worker, on the other hand, affirms the child's expressed emotion rather than soothing, changing, or dismissing it. The worker asks questions only to clarify the emotion, not to lecture, dismiss, or blame. The girl is given time to say that she is afraid her mother will die and then to explain her fear and her sadness. She uses this time to describe her fear in its entirety, from beginning to end without interruption.

The worker is a curious listener, affirming and clarifying strengths whenever they appear in the speaker's narrative. This affirmation supports the girl as she begins to trust her own feelings and as she gains a new sense of emotional knowledge, control, and responsibility. Fear and uncertainty about her mother's dying are replaced by feelings of her own competence and strength in expressing this fear. The worker's affirmation assumes that she is strong and competent and controls her own life narrative.

John Gottman (1997: 69–70) provides a personal example of the power of affirmations. On a long airplane flight with his two-year-old daughter, Gottman realized that he had packed his daughter's favourite toy, Zebra, in the checked luggage, rather

Photo 7.3 Hearing the feelings behind the words means taking time to really listen.

than bringing Zebra on board. When she asked for the toy he explained this luggage situation slowly and carefully to his daughter. His daughter rejected his lengthy and careful explanation. She turned away from him and began to sob even more loudly. She continued to ask for Zebra, wailing and moaning, and the other passengers started to look at Gottman in disgust. Even more agitated, he tried a different strategy. He stopped talking and really listened. What he heard in his daughter's wails was loneliness; she was missing the comfort of Zebra. When he affirmed this feeling of loneliness to his daughter and expressed empathy, she immediately quieted and, within a few minutes, soothed herself to sleep.

The worker checks out the child's emotions before affirming them. Does the girl fear her mother's death, or does she dread it? Gottman asked his daughter if she felt lonely because Zebra was in another part of the aeroplane. He didn't tell her that she was lonely; he asked her. When the child identifies and names the emotion, the child is the controller of the story and the emotion. The worker listens and affirms the emotion expressed by the child. This affirmation in turn strengthens the child's self-esteem as the child takes charge over the emotion by naming it. Carl Rogers (1980: 142) summarizes this skill of affirming: 'It includes communicating your sensings of the person's world . . . frequently checking with the person as to the accuracy of your sensings and being guided by the responses you receive. You are a confident companion to the person in his or her inner world.'

The AHA! Method: Here and Now

How is it possible simply to listen without offering advice, judgement, and direction? After all, isn't that our role, to counsel and to advise? Don't the families come to our office to hear our input and advice? The empowerment model suggests not. The families and the child already have the solution to their problem within them. Our role is to actively listen in the here and now, supplying information and resources when asked in order to coax out their personal solution and their unique strength in advocating for structural change

This is not easy. When a child relates a story, praxis often takes over. The worker is listening while reflecting on similar stories told by other children in the past, or while anticipating potential supports, programs, and plans for the child, all at the same time. The worker is not in the here and now, and the child is quick to sense this. When the worker drifts to the past or to the future, the child recognizes this drift by stopping, adding an unrelated event, or trying to switch topics.

Listening in the here and now means being fully present in a particular situation. It requires active and engaged attention and continual practice. Try concentrating on listening alone for the next five minutes. Listen to your breathing only. Now listen to other sounds. Do not think about the time, or about what you will do after these five minutes. Do not compare this activity to past attempts to meditate or reflect. Stay in the moment. This is not easy.

The worker who is available here and now focuses on the words and the emotions behind them as expressed by the child's gestures, posture, pauses, tone, cadence, and expression. The worker listens and does not express shock, sympathy, or sorrow. Chang (1998: 255) remarks: 'In the context of conversations with adults, children are quite sensitive to their conversational partners, and begin to anticipate their listeners' needs when they converse. They engage in metacognition, that is, they evaluate what they are saying and check that it fits with criteria about the purpose and context of conversation.' The child who is telling the story watches the worker's eyes, body, and comfort level for cues on how to change the story or when to stop the telling. A worker's raised eyebrows, slight frown, or drifting attention may cause the child to withhold parts of the story or to change the remembered events.

Being here and now with the child is where the worker needs to be, not mentally planning the upcoming intervention. When the child says that homework is difficult, the worker listens to the sadness and frustration but does not race ahead to planning potential tutors, eye tests, study areas, cognitive assessments, and teacher consultations. The worker listens attentively to the child's body language and all that it discloses. By staying in the moment, the worker demonstrates respect for the child and genuine interest in the child's story.

The AHA! Method: Authentic

The Rogerian worker–child relationship (Chapter 3) is based on the worker's being authentic, honest, and congruent. Authentic listening also is basic to the AHA! Method. The worker who respects the child as a person does not fake interest in the child but is genuinely curious, interested in knowing more about the child and about the story that the child is telling. The worker leans forward and listens carefully to the child's body language, the child's silence, and the sound of the child's words. The worker's total presence conveys genuine curiosity and affirmation, a powerful combination that supports the child's telling, and prompts the child to tell even more.

This means reflecting the story back to the child in a positive and curious way. The child tells the worker about an everyday event, then lapses into silence. The worker reflects on the everyday event and may ask, 'What are you feeling now?' This is not 'psychoanalytic' probing, or a trick question designed to unmask contradictory or negative feelings. This genuine question expresses the worker's interest in knowing. In answer to this question, the child may express an emotion or thought about the event. The worker may then reflect, 'Where does that come from?' Once again, this is not a scripted question devised beforehand. This is an authentic question that expresses the worker's interest in what the child sees and feels and thinks about those things. This authenticity supports the child's role as the teller and the one in control of the life story.

Children spot pre-scripting, dishonesty, and pretension very quickly. They see it reflected when the worker says to them:

- 'I know how you feel.' This intimate understanding of feelings around a child's past is unlikely in any case, and may dismiss the story as a common experience.
- 'That's just what I would do.' This fake attempt at forming an alliance denies the fact that the worker is an adult in an office in an agency, and the child is living on the street.
- 'You can take as long as you like.' This contradicts the schedule set at the beginning of the meeting, and is a fake attempt at an alliance.
- 'How are you?' Every child knows the expected response. Even toddlers learn to hide their emotions because emotions make their caregivers sad or upset. It is better just to pretend to be cheerful, optimistic, and unfeeling. Then nobody is upset.

The worker who is honest and authentic asks authentic questions and shares information if and when it is needed. The worker does have information and knowledge that may support the child in finding a personal solution and re-authoring the narrative. The worker is honest and ensures that the child has complete and accurate information to support this re-authoring.

The following are some examples of information that may be helpful to offer when a child is telling a story or explaining a feeling to the worker. These are examples only, and they may not be relevant to every child in every case. Other information may be more important for the child to have, such as the contact information for an ombudsman or a children's lawyer. The key is to offer accurate information when it is needed and as it can be received. If the worker is unclear about legal, financial, or educational resources, the worker is obligated to find out the correct information and transmit that information accurately and completely to the child.

- Child abuse is an abuse of power and is wrong. Adults do not have the right to hurt children just because they are bigger and more powerful than children.
- When a child is abused or assaulted it is never the child's fault.
- There are alternate homes available for children. If you cannot live in your own home with your own family, you do not have to live on the streets.
- Mental illness is not contagious. Because a family member has mental health issues, you will not necessarily develop the same mental health issues as you get older.
- Death is part of life. It happens. Because you wanted someone to die, or wished that person were dead, does not mean that you caused that person to die (or to get sick).
- Nobody deserves to be healthy or deserves to be ill. You are not ill because you are evil or bad. Illness happens to people.
- Poverty is not your fault. There are many children in Canada who live in poverty. The parents of these children may work very hard, may be kind and caring, and highly educated, but they still live in poverty because they are not paid a living wage and because we do not know how to control the big picture of how money is flowing. This does happen in Canada.

Such information may be needed for a particular child who is telling you a story. If so, this information needs to be shared with words that are appropriate and meaningful for that child. This information-sharing is just as important as the information-withholding demanded by confidentiality. Both are ethical requirements of any worker who listens to the child's story.

Because the child may have heard contradictory information for many years, this new information may not really register with the child or be accepted. Child abusers, for instance, may have influenced the child for years with the tale that the child seduced them or made them become predatory. In such cases it is important that the worker repeat the correct information in different ways, check that the child understands and absorbs the information, then listen carefully to ensure that this new information is integrated into the child's narrative. If not, the worker needs to repeat the information in another way until it is fully absorbed and integrated into the narrative.

Countertransference

The AHA! Method of listening to the child's story helps to elicit emotions underneath the story—the anger, sorrow, pain, and feelings of loss and betrayal. The worker who tunes into these emotions from the child's frame of reference can support the child in naming and articulating these emotions and what they evoke.

This can be painful for the worker as well, especially when the worker is feeling emotionally fragile or vulnerable. At such moments the worker may cross that boundary of the healthy working relationship and use a personal frame of reference to listen to the child's emotions; in other words, the worker may 'appropriate the child's emotions'. This can happen when the worker personally identifies with the child's pain and wants to make it go away, or when the child's story evokes in the worker a repressed personal memory with all of its accompanying emotion. **Countertransference** is an interactional process in which the child's narrative stimulates the worker's unconscious and dormant thoughts, emotions, and psychic memories, and the worker responds by projecting these same thoughts, emotions, and psychic memories onto the child's narrative. This is a subtle symbiotic process that can happen without the worker or the child planning for it or consciously wanting it to happen. The worker and the child are most likely not even aware that this process is taking over the child's narrative and changing it. The worker may project guilt onto the child and the child conforms, re-shaping the narrative to match the guilt from the worker. The worker may project anger and fear onto the child, reshaping the narrative. The obvious detriment to a child already burdened may not appear immediately in the working relationship; but the child will start to feel to some extent responsible for the worker's guilt, anger, and fear. Fewster (2002: 19) describes this worker–child countertransference simply: 'As we look after them, so they must look after us.'

Because this process is so damaging to the child, and because it impedes the authentic re-authoring of the narrative, the worker needs to be aware of and guard against the subtle power of countertransference before listening to the child's story. Being aware of both countertransference and of one's personal emotional wellness can help to prevent this process from happening, which is why most workers make use of supervision or work in treatment teams rather than alone.

In the following example of countertransference, the worker (W) appears to be listening to the child (C) but is actually processing personal emotions. The worker crosses the boundary of the relationship very early in this meeting. When confronted by the reflecting team or the supervisor, the worker may defend this early boundary-crossing as an empathetic response or an emotional scaffold for the child's telling of the story.

C: I've always known my mom didn't want me.

W: Oh, that's not true. Every mom wants her baby. She just might not have had the resources to look after you.

C: You mean she couldn't look after me?

W: Maybe. But she loved you.

C: Hmm . . .

W: How do you feel knowing that?

C: Well, I guess I could answer her letter then. Maybe I owe it to her.

Because of the countertransference that is happening here, the child cannot explore personal feelings of loss, rejection, and betrayal. That exploration is shut down by the worker almost immediately. The worker is insistent that all mothers love their children, which may simply be a careless remark reflecting popular 'mother mythology'. Or, the insistence may come from the worker's own attachment injuries, guilt, or anger. Whatever the source, the worker projects this belief onto the child, compounding the complexity of feeling that the child has expressed. Now the child can add the worker's emotional baggage to his or her own current emotional state.

It is natural to have feelings of despair, hopelessness, sadness, anger, shock, blame, embarrassment, or sympathy when hearing a child tell a story. These human reactions are engendered by the child's story, and they can be used constructively in the listening process. Being aware of these reactions is the key to active listening. The worker tries to distinguish between his or her personal feelings, the child's feelings, and the unconscious feelings (in both) evoked by the child's story.

When the worker is self-aware, the worker can internally name and distinguish these feelings while the child is speaking. The worker can name sorrow and be aware that this sorrow comes from an abiding concern for the child, a recognition of the story's sadness, or a memory of a similar event in the worker's own past. This recognition and naming of feeling allows the worker to use that feeling constructively and consciously. This process of exploring feelings in the story (listening and telling) is continuous and helps to prevent countertransference from impeding or infecting the child's re-authoring of the narrative.

The Presenting Problem

Serious problems arise out of traumatic events such as death, natural disasters, war, and illness. Less serious problems evolve from ordinary events at times of transition in the family. A parent loses a job; parents split up or re-marry; a baby is born; a brother leaves home; a child starts school: these all are transition times in the family life cycle. At these times the adults in the home shift in how they think, act, and interact with the children in the home, and the children respond accordingly.

Parents, caregivers, or teachers typically describe the **presenting problem** as the *child's* problem, usually in terms of misbehaviour. Such behaviour rarely is the essence of the problem, but it has become stressful enough for the child to be at this first meeting, willingly or not. Workers who are quick to assess and prescribe may unconsciously support the parents' identification of the presenting problem. Ram Dass (1997: 60) describes this: 'In comes Mary Jones, hurting real bad. As she sits across the desk she suddenly becomes Mary Jones, "schizophrenic". With a flick of the mind, we've turned a person into a problem.'

The worker may quickly recognize that the presenting problem is not the central problem, but the worker also is able to hear about the pain and sorrow that this presenting problem is causing the child and family. So the worker listens to the description of the problem from the perspective of each person who comes to this first meeting. Asking about this presenting problem lets the child and the teacher or family know that the worker does take this problem seriously and first wants to hear each person's description of the problem. This takes time because the worker needs to understand what the presenting problem feels like for each person, how it affects his or her daily life, and how it evolved; in other words, the worker needs to understand and be attuned to the frame of reference of each person involved in the presenting problem.

The presenting problem may be chronic absenteeism from school, and the first meeting may be the result of a call from a parent, school principal, or teacher. Descriptions of this problem will vary according to the person's relationship with the problem in the past and the present. An older brother who enjoys school may describe his little sister's chronic absenteeism from school in this way: 'She never goes to school.' The little sister may describe her absenteeism as: 'I never go on Fridays because Fridays suck.' The parent may present quite a different picture of the problem: 'She's only missed a few days this term. I don't know what the big fuss is all about.'

It is important to attentively listen to both the body language and the words that each person uses to describe the presenting problem. Words are value-laden and culture-specific. A mother may describe her daughter's attitude to school as 'lazy'. The daughter may describe her mother as, 'always in my face'. Both mother and daughter are describing their own feelings and their own values just as much as they are describing the presenting problem. The worker appropriates the daughter's words in responding: 'How do you know when your mother is in your face?' A response to the mother may be, 'What does your daughter do when she is lazy?' Using the actual words of the family member is a way for the worker to further understand their underlying meanings. These meanings are part of the family culture that the worker needs to know about in order to establish a relationship with the family.

It is even more important to listen to and appreciate the body language, and not mis-interpret it or ascribe a value to lowered eyes, hugs, or seeming non-responsiveness. One parent may look at the other parent, waiting for a signal before describing the problem. The child may look only at the floor. Body language dictates who sits next to whom in the family and who looks at whom, and body language reflects the family's culture.

The parent may avoid looking at the child and look only at the worker. Other family members may do the same, seeing the worker as a safe haven, an authority figure and potential ally against other family members. This worker-directed gaze can become a controlling pivot around which the meeting circles; this is often called the **maypole style of communication**. Sometimes the worker will try to diversify the dialogue by asking each family member to describe the problem from another family member's point of view, or to address their questions to other family members. This changes the maypole style to a **floating style of communication**, which is not worker-centred but is member-centred, each family member speaking directly to the other about the presenting problem.

Note From the Field   7.1

Be Direct!

Rogerian techniques such as paraphrasing and using reflective statements may not be appropriate with families whose cultural values dictate more direct confrontation. These families may feel that non-directive techniques (paraphrasing, reflection) are sneaky and deceptive. Take the case of Clement and his son Peter. Clement brought Peter to the worker for help because Peter's graduation from high school was in jeopardy. During the session the worker used reflective statements and paraphrasing in an attempt to understand this school situation from both Clement's and Peter's points of view.

Although Peter became increasingly more responsive during this meeting, Clement became increasingly irritated. He interrupted the worker several times, asking what the point of the questioning was when it was obvious that Peter was simply not applying himself in school. The worker in turn became irritated with Clement, feeling that he was an **authoritarian** parent with little concern for his son and with little patience or interest in the process.

However, Clement's personal culture valued directive statements, rather than the non-directive methods used by the worker. This cultural clash stopped the meeting in its tracks. Clement and Peter left before their hour was over, and Clement vowed not to seek outside help again. When a cultural clash is minimized or ignored, the child or the parent may shut down and stop communicating. The cultural clash may result in this being the first and last meeting with the child.

The worker may say to the older brother, 'How do you think your little sister sees her absence from school?' Or the worker may ask the child, 'What do you think your mother knows about your attendance at school?' Asking family members to relate the problem from another person's point of view in a culturally sensitive way expands the family's understanding of the problem as well as the worker's understanding, and also begins to illuminate several potential solutions.

The worker may also use reflective statements with the daughter such as, 'I hear you saying that school is always boring. Is that right?' These statements are not a technique. They are a way of honestly finding out more about the presenting problem from that person's point of view. This reflective statement incorporates the child's own words and is another way of understanding the meanings of those words. What does 'boring' mean for the child, and what does it mean for her mother?

Equally effective is paraphrasing in which the worker tries to summarize a family member's story, then asks for clarification. The worker may say to the mother, 'So when you get home at six o'clock, your daughter is always doing her homework. This tells you that she has been to school?' This is an authentic way to check out the mother's meaning. She can correct the worker, adding details, changing key words, so that the worker can understand more clearly what the family dynamic is when the child is at home and the mother is still at work. Changing perspectives, using reflective statements, and paraphrasing help both the worker and the child to get a clearer picture of how the problem is seen by everyone and how it affects everyone in the family.

This is often a moment of realization (AHA!) for the family. They realize how each member of the family has been concerned about the problem, and that each person is not alone with the worry and the stress. They realize that the problem does not belong exclusively to any one member of the family and that this problem has a multitude of meanings, causes, and solutions. They may begin to realize that they need to work on the problem, or that the presenting problem that brought them here is not really the problem they share. All of this can be accomplished while the worker is listening attentively to the family's description of the problem.

Externalizing

When self-identity and self-esteem become inextricably linked with the problem, the child becomes the problem. A boy may self-identify as 'a bad kid' or 'a drinker'. His family may repeat this label, supporting it with several problem-saturated stories of the many times he drank excessively.

Externalizing places the problem outside of the child. The child is not the problem. The problem is the problem. When the problem is 'out there' rather than within the child, the story-telling soon naturally separates from the negative experience and the emotions that surround it and becomes less stressful and threatening for the child. This disparity or distance leaves the child temporarily free from the problem. The child is seen as a person with strengths and assets, rather than as a problem or a failure. Now the child is able to have a relationship with the externalized problem instead of being defined as the problem.

Externalizing allows 'alcohol' to be changed, lost, or removed from its current position of power in the family. This emotionally distant relationship decreases conflict over who is responsible for the problem. It stops the **blamestorming** that problems often trigger, with one person assigning blame to the other in a spiral of accusations. Instead, the child can begin to look at the problem from the outside, as can other members of the family. The problem can now be changed, lost, forgotten, or put aside. It can also be solved!

The worker's first step is to try to understand what the problem looks like and feels like so as to co-create with the child a **metaphor** for the problem. This external symbol or metaphorical representation of the symptom (problem) is an expansion of Bruner's (1986) narrative metaphor and of Michael White's (1989) externalization of the problem. This metaphor is chosen by the child, or the child and the family, and reflects the child's understanding of the problem. The child may repeat a word several times when describing the problem, and this word may become the metaphor for the problem: 'Scaredy Cat' or 'Mr Blow Up' or simply 'Anger'. This metaphor prompts the worker's description of the power dynamic and its effect on the child: 'So Anger has been convincing you to scream and throw yourself down on the floor, yes?'

An older child may describe getting drunk on the week-ends, joy-riding with friends, and being grounded by parents. The worker listens attentively, using reflective statements and paraphrasing to find out more about these events and the feelings that they evoke. The child may use words like, 'high', 'wicked', 'crazy' or 'messed up'. One word may continue to recur in the story-telling, and the worker and the child may agree to use this recurring word as a metaphor for the presenting problem. 'Crazy' has been convincing the child to get drunk on the week-ends.

This metaphor puts the problem or difficulty outside of the child and the family. So Jordan is no longer a drinker or a drunk; Crazy is interfering with or controlling Jordan, and convinces him to do 'bad' things. But Jordan is strong, and the reflecting questions affirm this strength: 'When have you been able to withstand Crazy? How have you been able to beat him in the past?' A question for Jordan's parent might be, 'What has Crazy told you to think about your son?' This sets up an adversarial posture towards the problem, a posture shared by parents and child. Jordan has a relationship with Crazy and can now talk to Crazy, manage Crazy, or just tell Crazy to go away for a while, at least until Jordan graduates from high school. Jordan and his parents may be able to get rid of Crazy if they work together as a team to defeat Crazy.

By putting the problem outside of the child and positioning the problem as an externalized metaphor, the child can now be seen as a person rather than as a problem. Strengths can be identified, potential assets for combatting the problem. Crazy is making Jordan sleepy, stealing the money from his bank account, and hassling his parents. Crazy exists outside of Jordan and is not part of him. Jordan can take time away from Crazy, and can choose to deal with Crazy in his own way. Jordan and his parents can decide to tackle Crazy together with the worker, or by themselves as a family. Crazy has caused them to suffer; however, they have survived as a family in spite of Crazy. On the other hand, Crazy may be associated with a peer group that Jordan prefers to his parents. Jordan may opt to stay with Crazy and his peer group. He may leave his parents, physically or emotionally or both, in order to spend more time with Crazy. His parents are then left with many options, one of which is to bring Jordan and Crazy to an addiction specialist who is more familiar with Crazy and more able to work with Jordan to relinquish Crazy on whom he now depends. Because Jordan has externalized the problem he may be less likely to see his parents' concern as a personal attack and more likely to see this concern as a concern about Crazy.

Michael White demonstrates how to use this externalized metaphor in his classic story of Sneaky Poo (1989: 10–11). The parents express frustration and anger over their son's apparent encopresis or lack of control over his bowel movements. The boy is equally frustrated and anxious. Both the parents and their son decide upon the metaphor, 'Sneaky Poo', to describe the problem that sneaks in to interfere with their family life. This problem has started to take control of their family.

By identifying this power dynamic through creating a metaphor (Sneaky Poo), the family can look at the power dynamic and begin to regain control over their lives. It is no longer the boy who is the problem. In fact, the boy is an interesting and much loved person. The real problem is Sneaky Poo. Now the boy, his parents, and the worker together think about ways to deal with Sneaky Poo. Externalizing helps the child and his parents conspire together to trick Sneaky Poo into leaving, and they eventually eliminate it (pardon the pun) from their lives.

Contextualizing

The systems approach, developed by Bronfenbrenner in 1979, provides a structure in which the worker can contextualize the narrative. The worker can situate the child's life narrative, and each particular story told by the child, within the ecological environment that impacts the life of that child. This ecological environment was described by Bronfenbrenner as a set of nested structures extending far beyond the immediate experience of the child, each nested structure inter-related and connecting with the other, and each indirectly influencing the life of that child (see Chapter 1).

Contextualizing situates the child's narrative within a larger social construct or structure. This structure can both create the child's problems and support the child's solutions. The child's life narrative of addiction, vandalism, truancy, and violence can be contextualized within societal bias, support, funding, legal interventions, and culture. This context not only places the narrative within an explanatory macro-system but also suggests potential solutions within that structure.

The worker who contextualizes the child's narrative understands this dual role of the structure. Structural oppression, for example, impacts the child's ability to participate in placement decisions when the child is being placed in a group home. At the same time this oppression can be challenged through the office of the children's lawyer, a challenge that is empowering for the child and may result in a more appropriate placement than another group home.

The worker contextualizes the story of a girl who meets with him because of her shoplifting arrest. She tells her story and, as the worker listens attentively, she adds more details. The girl talks about her need to fit into her group, all of whom are middle class. The girl's family is struggling financially and the girl cannot afford designer jeans. Shoplifting is her solution, and her gateway to her peer group. She talks about the sexy, peer-approved clothing and, as she talks, she begins to question both the gender construction and the economic disparities between herself and her peers. The worker supports this structural contextualizing, adding information when asked. Contextualizing shoplifting does not diminish or eliminate the girl's responsibility for this illegal act, but it does place shoplifting within the oppressive social construct of her peer group that requires young girls to dress in certain ways.

The structural approach re-defines the child's story within a social framework. Media messages encourage children to drink alcohol, for example, as a gateway to adulthood and as a way to be socially acceptable. Contextualizing alcohol consumption helps a boy who drinks to see this as an effect of structural determinants and structural oppression, rather than as a personal deficit or weakness that is genetic and can never change. This boy may oppress others because of his alcohol-saturated narrative, while at the same time he is equally oppressed by media messaging, peer influence, and an inability to gain entrance to 'adulthood' without drinking alcohol. Multiple oppressions combine to keep the boy disempowered despite his fleeting moments of getting drunk and feeling powerful.

Contextualizing is an empowering process in which the child begins to understand a structural context and feel responsible for changing this context. The girl who shoplifts does not use phrases such as, 'gender construction'. However, she does begin to understand, in describing her need for peer-approved clothing, where the messaging for the clothing originates, and she feels her own power in challenging this messaging.

A young child may not fully understand socio-economic and political ideologies. However, this child does understand the feeling of powerlessness, and can begin to understand that this feeling is not a personal deficiency but is an effect of structural determinants. Contextualizing can emerge in a slow and gentle conversation filled with affirmation and support between the worker (W) and the child (C):

W: I know several other guys who've skipped school. They tell me it's boring.
C: Yeh, it sure is.
W: I haven't been to a high school here. What's it like?
C: You don't have any control. All day long they tell you what to do.
W: They?
C: The teachers, the secretary, the principal. You got no power, no nothing.
W: No nothing, yeh?
C: It's just how it is.
W: And that's okay?
C: Yeh, I guess so. I guess that's boring, too, just to accept.
W: What wouldn't be boring?
C: Maybe to run my own school, plan my own classes, be my own man . . .
W: Could you do that? Would that be allowed?
C: I knew a kid who did that.
W: Yeh, how did that happen?

The worker asks a series of simple and honest questions in order to find out and piece together the child's story. These questions allude to structural determinants and the potential for structural change. The worker is not in a high school every day and is curious to know what that context feels like for the child. This question triggers the child's self-reflection as the child tries to make some sense out of the problem (truancy) within its larger context (power and authority).

Contextualizing is a way for the child to understand that the situation or problem is not always a reflection of personal psychological, developmental, or moral deficits. Instead, truancy can reflect the child's resiliency in the face of adversity. 'The pre-delinquency discourse pre-empts discussions about unfair social structures, about exploitative adults, and about irrelevant or unworkable institutions' (Wotherspoon and Schissel, 2001: 329). Contextualizing prompts a child to identify and challenge structural oppression and to form meaningful solutions that really work within the child's life. This empowering process supports the child's position as the controller and the director of change. The child is responsible for the change, not the adults.

Re-Authoring

Children naturally link together the events or stories in their lives according to a theme. The theme may be failure, and events or stories are told that show the child failing in school, friendships, family life, or sport. The theme may be ugly, and the stories all illustrate how ugly the child is, irregardless of the clothes or the situation. When the dominant narrative supports this negative perception and problem-focused linking, any strengths or positive stories are suppressed, minimized, or forgotten.

Re-authoring a narrative asks children to link together the events or stories that are uplifting or positive in order to form an alternate narrative. Re-authoring is an opportunity for the child to remember and recount these positive events; in short, to own them. The child can recall moments of strengths, and personal assets that helped to resolve difficulties. As each moment of strength is recalled, the child feels more and more empowered. Success builds upon success.

The worker encourages this re-authoring by prompting the child to reflect on the past and to explore its multiple layers. An angry girl, for example, may be asked about being hurt as a toddler, 'When that happened to you, did you feel anything else?' She may insist that she felt only anger at the time. Gradually, however, she recollects and shares other emotions such as sorrow, distress, and loneliness. Each emotion is explored with the worker, and memories of loneliness and sorrow resurface, as well as the girl's skill at managing this sorrow and loneliness. A story of anger begins to evolve into a story of resilience and strength in the context of early childhood abuse. Autobiographical reasoning changes the memories, as well as the current feelings attached to these memories, into an alternate narrative.

Re-authoring has helped adult survivors of violence, war trauma, rape, and domestic abuse to regain personal strength. While not minimising these acts of violence, the worker can support adults to identify the survival skills they used in facing violence and to use these skills in re-authoring a future life narrative. Workers with children have done the same through play therapy (see Chapter 8) in which children explore memories and the emotions connected with them by literally re-playing them in the security of the playroom. The sheer frequency of a person's verbalizing of a traumatic event, the more dissipated the emotions surrounding it. This repetitive telling to a safe and supportive listener can alleviate the depth or vertical effect of trauma. Rycus and Hughes (1998: 374) describe this in their treatment of children who have been sexually abused: 'Simply talking about an issue reduces its threat and brings considerable relief. This is often a necessary intervention for persons who have been subjected to an exceptionally traumatic situation.'

To elicit memories of skill and strength, the worker may use the miracle question, a question that was developed by family therapists such as Insoo Kim Berg and her husband, Steve deShazer. The miracle question asks what life could look like without the current difficulty, bringing the child back to a remembered life before the difficulty or forward to a potentially less difficult life. The miracle question acknowledges the strength of the child in imagining and creating solutions. This may be the first time that the child has been asked to suggest solutions, so the child may not have an immediate answer. The child has been living within the problem so long that a different problem-free life may be difficult to envision.

If the family is involved in the re-authoring, this may be the first time that a brother or sister has been asked for input about the situation, so that brother or sister may also need time to reflect before responding. The first family member may suggest a solution that appears to be muddled or confused. The worker may need to draw out the details of the potential solution, encouraging that family member to paint in the details.

Sometimes no one can envision a miracle, or even remember an exception or a positive memory. They only continue to talk about the problem because this is the most familiar and comfortable subject for them. They are heavily invested in the dominant family narrative and the **homeostasis** this narrative brings to their family. A solution means change, and change is hard. In these difficult moments, when a miracle seems too out-of-reach and hard to envision, the worker can ask any of the following exception questions to try to locate situations or moments when the narrative was not problem-saturated:

- Can you remember a time when you were feeling differently?
- On a scale of one to 10, with 10 being how you feel today, can you tell me about a time when you felt at a five?
- Are there times when you feel less angry about all of this?
- When was the last time that you had a better day than today?
- What was different about that day that made it better? Where did it happen? What were you doing? Who was there with you?

These exceptions probably contain the seeds of solutions to the problem, but the child needs time to recall and recognize these exceptions as potential solutions. Each exception can prompt feelings and emotions that have been suppressed or forgotten, as the child struggles to identify potential actions to re-author the narrative. Once an

Group Exercises   7.2

Asking for a Miracle

This small group exercise is an opportunity to practise the miracle question and to experience the complex child–worker dynamic that is prompted by this question. In this practical exercise each group member has the opportunity to watch the evolution of the answer to the miracle question in the empowerment dynamic.

This exercise requires one member to play the part of the child and one member to play the part of the worker. The member playing the child silently reflects upon a particularly difficult situation that a 10-year-old child might be experiencing, and details this situation internally until it feels comfortable. When this is done, the member signals the worker to ask the miracle question. The other group members make notes throughout the ensuing worker–child dialogue, observing in particular:

- What encourages the child to reflect on the situation?
- What stops the process?
- What changes the locus of control from worker to child?

The exercise begins by the worker asking the miracle question: 'Suppose when you wake up in the morning your problem has disappeared. What does your morning look like?' The member playing the child responds and a dialogue unfolds. After two or three minutes have elapsed, the group leader asks all of the groups to stop and de-brief, using the above three questions as a guide for the de-briefing. When the groups appear to have finished de-briefing, the answers of all the groups are collected, and a guideline to the miracle question is developed from the group feedback.

exception is identified, the story around the exception can be remembered and developed. The specific exceptions are not important; it is their meanings that make the re-authored narrative so positive for the child. Re-authoring has layers of meaning and messages for the child. Each layer begins with details. The details are vivid and concrete. They are also fluid; they expand and contract as more details are added, and some are discarded. Slowly the child re-authors a positive narrative that is quite different from the problem-saturated narrative of the past.

The Re-Authored Narrative

Externalizing, contextualizing, and re-authoring are used simultaneously with the AHA! Method. Externalizing, for instance, helps to contextualize. Simple externalizations such as, 'getting rid of Anger', help to affirm and contextualize the child's temper or anger. This anger can be looked at on its own with all of the memories, feelings, and emotions around it. This anger can be seen as a legitimate response to an oppressive structure. Contextualizing anger is part of the child's gradual re-claiming of both the problem and the potential solution, or the re-authoring of the narrative.

A common difficulty with older children is skipping school. Parents may identify their child as lazy, sly, lying, or worse because the child skips school. The child may describe skipping school differently. The worker does not know if skipping school is a reaction against school, the people in it, classmates, teachers, or a cry for freedom and the lure of the streets. The story of skipping school belongs to the child who alone knows what is happening in the story. The parents may guess, as might other family members and the worker. Only the child knows, consciously or not, what is really driving the action.

The worker gradually elicits the story from each member of the family, as well as the feelings around the story for each person. The child listens, and adds some detail. A problem-saturated story spills into the room, and the story involves blamestorming as each person in the family blames the other. The presenting problem may be truancy, but the real problem is much more.

The worker supports the re-authoring of a new narrative through first externalizing the truancy, using the child's suggestion of 'Headache' as the metaphor. Having 'Headache' stops the child from going to the school door. Headache stops the child from getting out of bed to go to school. In describing Headache, the child tells stories about school failure, boredom, bullying by older students, and a teacher who sometimes yells. All of these concrete details help to create a picture of Headache that stops the child from attending school.

The worker, the parents, and the child begin to contextualize Headache. Through active questioning the worker finds out that Headache is worse before the child gets to the school yard. Then, Headache actually stops the child from going to the school door. Once the child turns around and walks towards the park Headache gets lighter and weaker and eventually goes away completely. The schoolyard has been identified, with all of its terrors, loneliness, and alienation.

The worker uses exception and miracle questions to pinpoint days when Headache does not hurt as bad; the child's strengths in resisting Headache when it starts; previous school experiences that were positive, and previous neighbourhoods in which the family lived. One parent remembers a favourite teacher, and another parent recalls the child's previous classmates at a birthday party. The child remembers a tutor and a school award from the past. Together these memories and feelings weave into a re-authored narrative full of hope, promise, and optimism.

The re-authored narrative offers choice: a new school, a new neighbourhood, a different class, a friend in the class, a supportive teacher. There are now many choices and many potential solutions to Headache. Having control of this expanded menu, the child chooses to discard Headache and walk a different walk. With the clear memory of past strength and present friends, the child is now in control and feels empowered to take charge, and is supported in this by a positive adult role model within the school and a new route to take to school. The worker congratulates the child and the family in finding their own solution and their own re-authored narrative.

Summary

This chapter introduced you to the AHA! Method of listening to the child's story. How this story changes shape through autobiographical reasoning, and how it changes into a re-authored narrative through externalizing and contextualizing was also explained in this chapter. When you understand the changes that take place as the child speaks about emotions, experiences, and memories, you begin to understand also the difference between the presenting problem in the story and the actual problem that lies within or behind the story. The presenting problem is usually a behaviour. The meaning of that behaviour is different for the worker, the child, and the family of the child. Our next chapter will explore how these multiple meanings unfold during play in the choices of play materials and play episodes. As we listen to the child's language of play we will take another step towards understanding how children construct meanings in their lives.

Review Questions

1. Do young children lie when they tell stories about their daily life? Give examples to support your opinion.
2. Explain how autobiographical reasoning works with children.
3. What is a dominant family narrative, and how does this affect the child?
4. Do adults typically listen to children's felt emotions? Give examples to support your opinion.
5. What is countertransference and how does it happen?
6. What are the three parts of the AHA! Method, and how would you put them into practice?
7. How might a worker show his authentic curiosity in the child's story?
8. Describe the use of a metaphor in externalizing.
9. Why is contextualizing so important when listening to the child's story? How might you contextualize a child's story about being bullied in school?
10. What are the steps in re-authoring and why is this so important for a child who feels overwhelmed by the presenting problem?

Discussion Questions

1. Recall one of your own life events that included other members of your family. Ask each member separately to describe the same event to you. Are their descriptions similar? What do you conclude about yourself, your family, and each member of your family from doing this exercise?

2. Sutherland describes 'winds of childhood' and suggests that the child sifts through these winds in developing the narrative. Which winds of childhood have you discarded in your personal narrative, and which have you kept? What influenced you to make these decisions? Do you feel you may have lost the veracity of your narrative through this process?

3. Use the AHA! Method to listen to someone telling a story. What part of the method was most difficult for you? Did anything surprise you when you used this method? What did the person telling the story notice about your active listening? Did the person find your body language and use of silence helpful or not?

Chapter 8

Listening to Play

I tried to teach my child from books,
She gave me only puzzled looks.
I tried to teach my child from words,
They passed her by, oft unheard.
Despairingly I turned aside, how shall I teach this child, I cried?
Into my hands she placed the key. 'Come,' she said, 'and play with me.'

—Anonymous

Toys are the words of children, and play is their grammar. Children express ideas, opinions, stories, and feelings more easily and naturally through play than through written or verbal communication. A toddler acts out frustration by smashing paper boxes. A preschooler tries to make sense of her parent's discipline by scolding or spanking her doll. Play provides a common language for the child's evolving life narrative, and the worker creates a respectful context for this language of play by shifting from words to toys, from language constructs to play episodes. The worker attempts to hear, understand, and interpret the child's play episodes in order to understand and explore the ideas, memories, and feelings of the child.

Play therapy sometimes is confused with other therapies such as pet therapy, dance therapy, art therapy, and riding therapy. Some of these therapies are legitimate and helpful, while others lack professional status and accreditation. Because of this confusion, play therapy has also been critiqued as a fraud and a pretense, a false therapy created by early childhood educators who crave some professional legitimacy. Play therapy has also been associated with puppet play, prompting some puppeteers to call themselves 'therapists'.

The theoretical framework of play therapy distinguishes it from the simple observation and planning of children's play that is done every day by parents, caregivers, and early childhood educators. This theoretical framework imparts a meaning to every choice of word, play material, space, and silence. **Play therapy** is an approach to working with children through play towards their self-realization. The underlying assumption of play therapy is that children will play through their conflicts, difficulties, problems, and feelings, and arrive at a psychologically satisfying (to them) resolution.

We will begin with the theoretical foundations of play therapy, as it is these theories that guide our interpretations of play. These theories also suggest either directive or non-directive play therapy, depending upon the child and the presenting problems. Understanding the history of play therapy, and the motivations of these early theorists and practitioners helps to locate play therapy in a continuum.

Play therapy unfolds in three stages, each with specific goals and roles. A dynamic evolves within each of these stages making each one essential to the overall working relationship and resolution. Some workers begin their meeting with play therapy, while others use play therapy only when the child's behaviour escalates. Some workers engage both the child and the caregiver in play therapy; others meet with the caregiver separately; and others use play therapy effectively with adults. This multiplicity of applications expands play therapy beyond crisis intervention and trauma work, and into those everyday patterns that echo the deeper (intrapsychic) struggles that emerge in the playroom.

Objectives

By the end of this chapter, you will:

- Understand the difference between playing with children, watching children play, and play therapy.
- Identify the goals and roles at each stage of play therapy.
- Demonstrate how to set up both a directive and a non-directive play episode for a child.

The Meaning of Play

Play is activity that is usually pleasant and voluntary, or chosen by the child. Playing the piano is **play** until it becomes forced and compulsory practice. Throwing a ball is play until it involves the stress and routine of baseball practice. **Play episodes** are specific, time-limited units of play that have a beginning and an end. Drawing a picture can be described as a play episode that may last a few seconds or longer. The length of the play episode depends on many factors such as the child's age, interest and motivation, and the attractiveness of the play materials.

Children make meanings through their play, acting out everyday life, fears, problems, and relationships that they know. They usually do not make any ongoing interpretations during their play, and tend not to make links between individual play episodes. A child may occasionally wonder aloud, 'Why did I do that?' However, a child rarely interprets the play episodes or reflects on the motivation behind a particular choice of play material. The play simply happens as a regular part of everyday life.

Play is said to progress in stages that correspond to cognitive and socio-emotional development (Piaget, 1929; Russ, 2004; Schaefer and Kaduson, 2006). The infant is said to engage in solitary play, exploring his/her own self and objects within easy reach. The toddler is said to engage in parallel play in which children play beside each other. They do not actually play together, but seem to enjoy playing alongside each other. Each child watches the other, and each watches what the other child is doing.

Some theorists argue that infants also enjoy parallel play and being alongside other infants whom they observe. Kail and Zolner (2005: 213) summarize the findings of these theorists and add the following description: 'Two 6-month-olds will look, smile, and point at one another. Over the next few months, infants laugh and babble when with other infants.' They contend that there is actually no stage of solitary play, and that this stage is a social construction designed to allow parents a respite either from playing with their infants or from bringing them into contact with other infants (Chapter 2). However, infants also seem to engage in playing with self for extended periods of time without expressing a need for more social play.

The next stage of play is said to be group or social play in which children play with other children, interacting and sharing play materials and play spaces. At this stage, adults typically expect that children demonstrate sharing and co-operation; however, these activities are not essential for group play. Group play is a time for learning social skills such as turn-taking, negotiating, decision-making, and following rules, but without the precondition of sharing and co-operation.

Typically, a child may engage in solitary play, parallel play, and group play all on the same day. A child may kick a ball in the yard, then kick the ball alongside a friend who is skateboarding. The two children may then join other friends to kick the ball in the yard or skateboard together. Whether play is solitary, parallel, or group, the child is learning and developing skills, as well as being impacted by such structural factors as bias, violence, gender construction, and oppression. The child is both acting and being acted on during play.

Play is pleasant and voluntary, but it is also the child's work. Children typically encounter their world in an experiential way, then in a cognitive way. In this experiential process they imitate the meanings of the daily life they have experienced. They arrange plastic cars outside a toy garage just as they have watched their parent's car waiting outside a garage. They put plastic food in a toy refrigerator just as they have seen their babysitter do. They hand out papers and pencils to their friends and make them sit at desks just as they have seen their teacher do in a classroom.

Play is also the way that children figure out how their bodies work. They stretch, climb, run, toddle, grab, pull, and push, exploring the limits of their strength and agility. They run until they are exhausted; then they feel their hearts pounding. They jump over and into puddles and streams until their shoes are soaked. They throw leaves

Photo 8.1 Group play is a chance to test ideas, behaviours, and personal limits.

into the air until their arms ache. They slide over ice and snow, feeling the difference in friction, and testing their limits.

Play is a way to relate with others, to see what other children do when they are bitten, pushed, hugged, or ignored. Children watch other children, even when they are just infants. Their eyes follow the faces of other infants, and they relate. Later, they will put these same children into wagons, boxes, and strollers, listening to them and watching them. They will play with them, arguing, taking turns and taking toys, possibly achieving enough consensus to play longer.

Adults set up play and watch children as they play. Adults try to keep play spaces safe so that children are not injured. They supervise the play and try to manage children when they play with one another. Adults are responsible for supplying safe play materials and safe play spaces. When a young child is injured during play, typically the adult supervising the play is called to account.

When adults supervise play they also interpret it. They may attribute qualities to certain children based on their play: 'Ooo, isn't she strong!' They may attribute emotions to certain children: 'He looks scared, doesn't he?' They may also attribute motivations for play: 'I think they want to hurt her.' These interpretations of play are based on the structural context of play, the cultural bias of the observer, the observer's understanding of play, and the child's own verbal and body language. One adult may see play as fun, while another adult sees the very same play as risky and dangerous.

Watching children play is part of play therapy. The difference lies in the intent, training, and theoretical framework of the observer. The adult who engages a child in play therapy is curious about the meaning within the play in addition to the meaning of the play. The adult recognizes that play has a meaning for the child, and wants to uncover that intrapsychic meaning in order to support the child's socio-emotional development. Play therapy is much more complex and multi-layered than simply observing and supervising children who play.

This difference in intent, training, and theoretical framework is fundamental and pervasive. This difference translates into deliberately choosing a play space and play materials that match the needs of the child; engaging the child in a Rogerian, child-centred relationship; meticulously observing, noting, and interpreting all of the child's communications during play; and supporting the child therapeutically during the process and when the child chooses to make changes. This is highly skilled work which requires sound clinical practice as well as an understanding of child development and the theoretical foundations of play therapy.

Play episodes are deliberate and focussed. This is solitary play: the child plays alone, occasionally assigning roles to the worker. The play space is set up specifically for play therapy. Each play material in this play space is chosen deliberately by the worker, and there are sufficient play materials so that the child can choose, direct, and control the play episodes. This play is quite different from pure relaxation or from the expending of energy. It is not the play that children do to find out how their bodies work or to develop their psychomotor skills: swimming, skating, running, or skipping. It is not the play children do to engage with other children: soccer, computer games, or hockey. Nor is this spontaneous or reactive play that happens when a child tries to catch a bubble or to kick leaves into the air. The *meaning* of the play in play therapy, or the motives and intent within the play, is the subject of play therapy more than the development of the child's psychomotor skills, expressive language, or strength. The intra-psychic world of the child is more important here than the child's ability to catch and throw, or play a co-operative game.

This meaning within the play may be obscure to both the child and the worker and may be difficult to uncover, unravel, and identify. When the worker senses the meaning behind the play and begins to reflect on a possible interpretation, the child is likely to withdraw from the play and choose another activity. The worker needs to be acutely sensitive to every aspect of these minute seconds of absorbed play (play episodes) that signal a deeper meaning for the child. Many layers need to be removed before these deeper meanings can be deciphered. It is this interpretation, or de-layering, that is the core work of play therapy.

Theoretical Foundations

Play therapy draws on many theories of learning, development, and relationships. It requires, at a minimum, a thorough understanding of child development as well as psychoanalytic theory, family systems theory, cognitive-behavioural theory, and object relations theory. Each theory is a belief system that some workers may embrace and follow, while others rigorously deny and do not use in their practice. No single one of these theories can explain the whole child or the whole play episode, but each theory helps to unravel the many messages that the child sends to the worker during these play episodes.

Psychoanalytic theory understands play as a vehicle through which the child makes sense out of repressed memories, dreams, and the unconscious. Play provides a means for the child to articulate dreams and fantasies in the sand tray or play house, and to work out the meanings of these dreams and fantasies. The child can play out the conflict between superego and id so as to gradually develop the ego strength necessary for self-reliance. Anna Freud (1935) and Melanie Klein (1965) demonstrated this superego–id conflict almost a hundred years ago (1921–45) when they applied psychoanalytical techniques in their work with children, using play as a substitute for the free association work done in psychoanalysis with adults. Instead of saying a word to a child and then asking the child to freely associate another word with it, they placed materials (words) in front of the child and observed how the child used the materials in play (spoke). Klein called this 'play analysis' in reference to the need for analysis, or the close observation and interpretation of play. Like Anna Freud, she made minute notes on the child's body language and verbal language during the play episodes that she constructed and observed.

Virginia Axline also applied psychoanalytic theory, using play with children to uncover their repressed memories and emotions. She describes an example of this psychoanalytic technique in her book, *Dibs: In Search of Self* (1964). In this account of a worker's relationship with a young boy, Axline demonstrates how the worker's psychoanalytic understanding of the child (Dibs) develops through close observation of the child's play and close reading of the child's silences. At the beginning of their play therapy sessions, Dibs rarely speaks to Miss A (Virginia Axline). Instead, he arranges the play materials in the room and explores paint, sand, and water. During these play episodes Dibs begins to uncover his thoughts and feelings, all of the emotional hurt he has experienced in his family life: 'Then he turned toward the sand, dug a hole with his hands, and buried the soldier. On top of the mound of sand he placed a toy truck. Without a word, he made this graphic statement to dramatize his feelings' (p. 114). Dibs repeats this particular play episode in several sessions until he can make sense of his feelings within this play. Axline uses psychoanalytic theory to uncover or interpret these feelings. Why does Dibs choose a soldier and why does he bury this soldier? Why does he choose a truck? Miss A puzzles over these deliberate choices of materials and play episodes. Dibs himself plays; he does not stage the play or act it out to impress Miss A. He plays, and Miss A struggles to understand and interpret this play.

She begins to theorize that Dibs is playing out his unpleasant childhood experiences in order to come to understand them and deal with their emotional impact. Dibs expresses both his problems and several potential solutions, from burying the soldier to keeping him. The play seems to demonstrate Dibs's feelings of anger, shame, and alienation, and eventually results in uncovering secrets that even Dibs's parents do not know. Axline demonstrates the conflict between Dibs's id and his superego, a conflict that Dibs resolves through his play as he gradually acquires control of his ego or self. When the play therapy sessions end, Dibs leaves Miss A as a more confident and secure boy, ready to assert himself in the family and to make changes in his life: 'He had learned how to be himself, to believe in himself, to free himself. Now he was relaxed and happy. He was able to be a child' (p. 214).

Another way to interpret this same play is through the lens of **family systems theory**. This theory sees the family as a whole unit rather than as a group of individual members. The role of the family members is to keep this whole unit intact and healthy rather than for each member to pursue individual goals. The behaviour of one family member affects the whole system, and the system is only as strong as its weakest member. Family systems theory explores the boundaries, communication lines, life cycle, and dynamics of the family as a whole unit.

Through the lens of family systems theory, Miss A (the play therapist) is able to understand Dibs's play as his way to making sense of the patriarchal structure of his family. The dynamic of a distant and disappointed father, frustrated mother, and idealized sister plays out in the sandbox. Dibs tries to make sense of his father's aloof demeanour. Dibs calls on memories of a gardener who cares for him, a grandmother who believes in him, and children in the daycare who sometimes play with him. These memories contrast with the current harshness of family life as he is experiencing it before and after the play sessions.

Equally important is an understanding of **cognitive-behavioural theory**. Cognitive-behavioural theory suggests that all behaviour is learned and purposeful, and suggests that the child learns to self-regulate behaviour through play. The child is given positive reinforcers for desirable behaviours, and negative reinforcers (discipline) for less desirable behaviours. By testing limits to experience and understanding 'natural' consequences for behaviour, play becomes a way to act out aggression safely, without the fear of being punished or admonished. Without adult intervention or discipline, the child can yell, scream, throw toys, and hit play materials. The child can explore the limits of this behaviour to the extreme, and look for more satisfying and less exhausting ways to express anger and stress. Through the full exploration of the range of feelings engendered by this behaviour, the child can learn to self-regulate behaviour rather than relying on traditional external controls such as the lock on the door and the isolation of the bedroom.

Axline (1964: 156) observes of Dibs: 'He was learning through experience that feelings can twist and turn and lose their sharp edges. He was learning responsible control as well as expression of his feelings. Through this increasing self-knowledge, he would be free to use his capacities and emotions more constructively.' Free from the locked room and the icy and disapproving stares of caregivers, Dibs learns to manage his own behaviour more constructively through acting out this behaviour in role-play with figurines. He learns how children can interact with other children in more productive (for him) ways. He learns to assert himself and to re-claim his identity within the family, and he begins to speak to his parents rather than yelling, crying, or refusing to speak.

Winnicott (1953) develops play therapy further through the lens of **object relations theory**. The term, **object relations**, refers to those relationships with important people in our lives, and the continuing impact of these relationships on our lives. Object relations theory suggests that we relate to other people based on expectations formed by earlier relationships, or our internalized object relations. Winnicott feels that the child self-discovers in relationship to other people and their expectations. Object relations is a bridge between psychoanalytic theory and family systems theory. It also is basic to attachment theory and the belief in the importance of lifelong emotional attachments to a significant person (Chapter 4). Object relations theorists believe that interpersonal relationships—or object relations—motivate or drive child development. They also believe that object relations start to develop at the very beginning of life.

Winnicott sees play therapy as a medium for exploring these early relationships, and the significant caregivers in the child's life. Winnicott uses both directive and non-directive play therapy, and explores various media in his play therapy sessions with children. His focus is always the child's relationships to others and what these relationships, or object relations, mean for the child. He echoes the Rogerian child-centred approach when he observes of his own work (1953: 89): 'The significant moment is that at which the child surprises himself or herself. It is not the moment of my clever interpretation that is significant.'

 Point to Consider   8.1

The Canadian Association for Child and Play Therapy

In 1986 the Canadian Association for Child and Play Therapy (CACPT) instituted the first certification in the world for play therapists, a multi-year certification process involving field practice, study, and lectures. Subsequently, the Canadian Play Therapy Institute (CPTI) began training programs in play therapy. By the 1990s Play Therapy International (PTI) had formed, and today counsellors, social workers, nurse practitioners, and child welfare workers incorporate play therapy techniques into their work with children and families. What began as an intervention used solely by therapists, psychologists, and psychiatrists with very young children is now an intervention used by workers in many fields with multi-faceted goals and a multiplicity of techniques.

Roles

Play therapy is the dynamic that evolves among three elements: the child, the worker, and the medium of play. This dynamic is ever-changing in response to changes from the child, worker, or medium of play. The child may make a change in the play; the worker may ask a question; or the play medium may change shape, size, or dimension. As each element changes, so does the play. Understanding the role played by each element is important in understanding this dynamic of play therapy and how it can work most effectively for the child.

The child plays the role of the central player and the focus of the intervention in both the directive and the non-directive models of play therapy. The child is the controller, manager, and director of play. The child leads the play, and the worker listens to the play. The worker does not question, critique, change, or stop the choice or direction of the play.

In directive play therapy the worker chooses the play materials and sets up potential play episodes before the child arrives in the playroom. The worker may arrange a scene in the sand table or set out particular colours of paints on the easel. The worker may select certain figurines and put them into the playhouse. When the child arrives for the session, the worker leads or directs the child to interact with these specific materials, and the child follows this initial direction and engages in certain kinds of play. The worker may prompt the child to change the play or suggest that the child enact certain emotions. However, the child is still the central player and chooses how to play with the materials and what the play episodes will be.

In non-directive play therapy there is less preliminary set-up of the playroom and the play materials are more varied and abundant, allowing for ample choice by the child. When the child arrives for the session, the worker does not suggest a particular play material or play episode. Instead, the child chooses the materials and the direction of play. The child may paint with one colour throughout the session, or the child may change play episodes in rapid succession. The worker does not prompt, suggest, or lead the play, or restrict the choice of play materials. Non-directive play therapy is said to be a longer process because it is less directed at the presenting problem; however, there is insufficient research to support this contention.

In both directive and non-directive play therapy, the worker establishes a non-judgemental, safe and secure environment in the playroom that encourages the child to role play, paint, draw, or colour a picture of friends or family, or create a diagram of a route to school, a household plan, or a dinner table setting for the family. The child assigns roles to the worker or the play figurines, and the child decides when and how the play episodes will evolve. When the child invites the worker to be a play partner and join a particular play episode ('Come and play house with me'), the worker takes up a role in the play and does not question the play episode, offer suggestions, or ask for a different kind of play. This immediate, almost synchronous, worker response reinforces the child's position as the director and controller of the play.

The worker playing house immediately assumes a role: mother on the telephone, baby on the floor, parent making dinner. This role reflects the worker's therapeutic goal, but fits in naturally with the play. The worker playing school can be a student in the class, another teacher helping to clean the board, or a busy janitor. If the child says, 'I'm the daddy. You're the baby', the worker immediately joins the play by lying on the floor, curled up like a baby. The worker does not ask the child about the kind of baby, the age of the baby, or the name of the baby. These questions would only impede the natural flow of play and the play script. Virginia Axline (1964: 15) observes this child control and direction in her story of Dibs: 'I wanted him to take the initiative in building up the relationship. Too often, this is done for a child by some eager adult.'

Jim Wilson (2005: 90) describes a play therapy session with a six-year-old girl who is brought to see him because her parents are going through a divorce and are concerned about their daughter's behaviour. Both the little girl, Clara, and her mother take part in the play therapy in the playroom. The mother's goal is to know how Clara is feeling about the divorce. Her preconceived expectation is that Clara will go to the figurines in the playhouse, or role play the mother, or hammer out her anger with the drums in the corner. Wilson convinces the mother beforehand, however, that Clara must choose, control and direct the play, and that they (Wilson and the mother) must follow this direction. Clara tells Wilson and her mother to be quiet because they are going to play school. Clara takes up a piece of chalk and goes to the blackboard in the room, assuming the role of teacher. Wilson and the mother immediately sit down with books and role play being students who are reading and writing. Then Wilson (student) puts up his hand to ask the teacher (Clara) a question. Clara allows Wilson to speak. Wilson stands and asks the teacher what parents should do with their children when the parents are going through a divorce. The teacher (Clara) explains to her student (Wilson) that parents should focus on fun things rather than divorce talk. The teacher tells student Wilson that children are tired of being asked questions about divorce all the time. In this way Clara the teacher conveys her message clearly to her mother and to the worker. She can speak in her role as teacher because the other two elements—the worker and the play medium—are in place and in role.

The role that the worker plays in the playroom depends on the worker's theoretical framework. A worker who observes the child from a psychoanalytic framework may focus on the child's dreams and fantasies, and the meanings that these have for the child. A family systems worker may provide family figurines and dress-ups that correspond to the child's family, and may focus on the child's role within that family. The cognitive-behaviourist notes the presence of certain behaviours and provides materials that relate specifically to these behaviours. The worker grounded in object relations theory is sensitive to attachment injuries and how these play out during the session. The worker's theoretical framework orients the way the worker observes, understands, supports, and interprets the intrinsic meaning of the child's play.

Play Materials

The third element in play therapy is the play itself, those play episodes that involve the child's deliberate choice and manipulation of play materials. The child uses these play materials to communicate emotions, feelings, and memories to the worker. Choosing and displaying the play materials in the playroom requires much preliminary thought and reflection by the worker. It is not a random or hurried choice. The following are some examples of play materials and the reasons for including them:

- keys and locks to provoke feelings about boundaries and freedom;
- sunglasses and hats that permit the child to speak and act safely without making eye contact;
- puppets with movable mouths to encourage the child to make the puppets speak;
- small people figurines to prompt role play involving persons in the child's life;
- small animal figurines to prompt the connection of animal attributes with people and remembered events;
- art materials to stimulate visual, non-verbal expressions of feelings.

Because play materials have such an important role in prompting play, these play materials must meet strict criteria. These play materials must be simple and safe. They must not be too complicated or difficult to manipulate; the development of cognitive or of fine motor skills is not the purpose here. A cash register, for instance, is a simple prop rather than a working register that rings and adds and is full of coins and bills. A cash register stimulates memories and feelings about money and purchases, rather than numeracy skill development. The figurines are attractive and unbreakable, and they represent everyday persons rather than media stars. There are no building toys, puzzles, noisemakers, or matching sets. Each play material has a therapeutic purpose and is carefully chosen. Each one has purpose in prompting the child's remembrance of an event, person, emotion, or feeling, and there is enough variety of materials to prompt this role play. This variety of materials can be described as 'art', 'aggression', and 'anywhere'.

The 'art' materials encourage the child to express emotions and feelings through sensorimotor play. The child expresses the unspeakable by drawing it or painting it or creating a sand pit. The variety of art materials matches the needs and interests of the child, the boundaries of the playroom, and the comfort level of the worker and may include paint, modelling clay, sand, playdough, water, paper, and markers. Some workers become anxious when water drips on the floor or paint is spilled. These workers are best to choose art materials that match their comfort level so that they can comfortably observe and, if invited, participate in the child's creative process. The purpose of these materials is not to stimulate artistic expression or the creation of works of art: a wonderful painting, or a fine clay sculpture. What is created is not important here. What is important is the emotion felt and expressed during the creative process.

The second category is 'aggression'. This category includes materials that help to elicit and support the child's search for power and control, or the child's need to express anger, hurt, or loneliness. Aggression materials include toy guns, handcuffs, locks, keys, ropes, rubber knives, masks, puppets, inflatable punching bags, hammers and blocks, people and animal figurines, beanbag chairs, drums, and pillows. These materials invite the child to actively bang, push, punch, hit, and thrust without actually hurting anyone.

Photo 8.2 Deliberate choices make this play space a battleground of emotions.

They invite the child to act out injuries, and to act out remembered aggressive events.

The third category is called 'anywhere' and includes props that reflect the child's daily life: stroller and doll, bendable doll, rag doll, plastic figurines of animals and people of all ages, kitchen furniture, plastic food and dishes, cars and trucks, medical kit, school kit, purse, briefcase, lunchbag, and cellphone. These materials prompt the child to act out everyday events; to speak on the cellphone, to put the dolly to bed. The child chooses the most appropriate material then customizes it. The bendable doll may be given a name of a sibling, and put inside the play fridge, or locked inside the briefcase. The child acts out the meaning of family dynamics and intrapsychic losses and crises through these items from everyday life.

The play materials include figurines that represent people, emotions, or events in the child's life. These figurines are sturdy, unbreakable plastic and are replicas only. The black policeman figurine may not look like Alec, the child's father, but may have a quality (stern face, uniform, slim build) that reminds the child of his father. This figurine provides that necessary distance between the child and his father to allow the child to explore the emotions surrounding this father figure and the events surrounding his father and himself. The child controls the play by manipulating this figurine in a sand table, on a rug, or on a table, or by pounding the figurine into clay or play dough. These categories intersect and combine. The child can pound, squeeze, and hammer play dough as a way to express anger and aggression. The child can bury animals in the sand and cover the sand with water, making a mud grave for the animals. The child can handcuff the rag doll. The categorization of play materials is not to suggest separate areas or separate activities. This categorization serves as a reminder to include play materials from 'art', 'aggression', and 'anywhere'.

Another play material can be provided solely by the worker: sonorous vocalizing or harmonic patterns in a minor key. If the worker is confident and comfortable with this simple a cappella vocalizing, the worker can use this vocal music to provide the safety and security needed for the child to express emotions, experiences, and feelings from infancy. This body music includes humming, clicking, throat singing, grunts, groans, and tonalities, all in a tempo that matches the tempo of a human heartbeat. This music is the traditional lullaby, a repetitive, almost droning, incantation, a melody made solely with body sounds rather than with words. It replicates that early, pre-verbal, time between mother and child, and evokes memories of early childhood. The harmonic patterns of this lullaby have been shown by Dr Mark Tramo of the Harvard Medical School (2009) and others to trigger the auditory cortex in the brain, evoking powerful emotions in the listener.

O'Callaghan (2008) calls these harmonic patterns 'lullaments', a combination of lullabies and laments. The lullament may also be a way for the worker to directly connect with the child, and establish trust in the first stage of play therapy by sending out a powerful message of affirmation and empathy. O'Callaghan's research of the therapeutic qualities of these 'lullaments' demonstrates that they can soothe a frightened child, de-escalate an angry child, or relax an anxious child. This is a connecting lullaby rather than disconnecting popular music, and can be a powerful tool in object relations work and the uncovering of attachment injuries.

The playroom with its play materials and authentic worker is a safe space for remembering and re-connecting dreams, fantasies, and memories. It is neither too large and empty, nor too small and cramped. The room is attractive, cozy, and private. Because there are safe boundaries the child is not put into the conventional position of begging for a toy to take home, an extra five minutes, or a candy. The rules are clear: the toys stay in the playroom, the play lasts an hour, and everyone stays safe. These boundaries create a space in which the child can play freely without worrying about the play being stopped or criticized. All play is accepted within the three rules. The child is free to toss up the sand, to throw the dolly against the wall, to knock over the cradle. In play therapy all of this can be done without an adult disapproving, scolding, or intervening.

Relationship-Building

Most play therapy interventions have three stages: relationship-building, chaos and struggle, and resolution. The child may go through one or two stages, then stop or withdraw. The child may go through all three stages in a short six-month period. Alternatively, the child may remain at the first stage for a year, going back and forth, and taking time to settle into that stage.

The first stage is the exploratory one of relationship-building between the worker and the child. Because the focus of play therapy is the child's self-realization, the worker needs to attend to the child's first three levels of need (see Figure 3.7). These include physiological needs (food, water, sleep), safety and security needs, and the need for love. While the worker is not responsible for feeding the child, the worker is aware of the child's physical comfort level. A child who is thirsty or who needs to urinate cannot relax and engage in play. A child who is afraid of the worker, the room, or the materials in the room also cannot engage in play. A child who feels that the worker

Photo 8.3 Reflections.

actively dislikes, disdains, or feels antipathy towards him or her is unlikely to want to engage in play. These three basic needs must be attended to first as part of relationship-building.

Children do not generally want to play in unfamiliar, strange, or frightening spaces, so the worker's calm, confident, and relaxed manner helps the child to feel safe. The worker invites the child to play and to use all of the play materials in the playroom and does not hide anything in the room. There is a clock in the room and, at a natural juncture in the play, the worker tells the child when the play time will end. If there is a two-way mirror in the room for observation, the worker tells the child about it. This may be the first time that the child has been allowed to freely and fully explore touching, choosing, and moving play materials. If so, the child needs time and space to adjust to this new experience and to test its limits. The child may select one toy, drop it, then go to the next toy, drop it, and so on until all of the toys are scattered in the room. The child may move, hide, or throw figurines. The child may choose to paint, then model clay, then play in the sand table, then play with puppets, all in rapid succession. The child may approach the sand table and scoop out the sand, throwing it all over the floor. The child needs to find out which toys are safe, how safe the worker is, and how safe the place is. This feeling of safety and security is fundamental to the relationship.

Unlike most adults, the worker does not rush over and scold the child, nor does the worker rush over to sweep up the sand and put away toys. The worker is more intent on the meaning within the play than the clean-up of the room. This reaction may puzzle the child who is expecting a reprimand or a scolding. The child may become confused, even angry at this upset of homeostasis, and may increase the volume of disequilibrium, throwing more sand and scattering more toys. This testing of the boundaries of the relationship can include questioning, playing with and discarding toys, trying to leave the room, or ignoring the worker by sitting all alone during the session. The following is a dialogue about safety between the child (C) and the worker (W):

C: Can I take one of these teddy bears home?
W: No, the teddy bears stay in the playroom.
C: *plays out aggression and anger with the puppet*

W: It seems really hard for you when you want the teddy bear and can't take the bear home, but all the toys stay here in the playroom. The bear will still be here in the playroom when you come back next week.

C: Can I stay longer today to play with teddy?

W: No, you are staying only for one hour.

C: *rolls on floor and kicks*

W: I'll help you know the time to go home by reminding you five minutes before the hour ends so that you will know that our play time is almost over.

If the child chooses to sit all alone in a corner of the room for several sessions, the worker can try to involve the child in the play materials. The worker may pick up a puppet who makes friends with the child, then introduces the child to the other puppets, encouraging the child to dialogue in the puppet play. The worker may show the child a figurine of an adult and ask the child if that figurine looks like her teacher. Alternatively, the worker may offer the child a bag of figurines and ask the child to find one figurine that looks friendly, mean, or angry. This directive approach can be dropped as soon as the child engages in play. If the child chooses to speak to the worker in this first stage, the dialogue between the child (C) and the worker (W) may proceed like this:

C: What does this (toy) do?

W: This toy can do many things. Toys can be whatever you like.

C: Why is this (toy) here?

W: This toy is here because I enjoy playing with it.

C: Why do you keep that broken one (toy)?

W: I know it is broken, but I still enjoy that toy and I want to keep it.

This may be the first time that the child has encountered an adult who simply listens then answers, and who does not try to teach, correct, question, or make demands. There are no mini-lectures in the playroom. The child needs time to adjust to this feeling of freedom and this new equal power construct in order to take on a more active role. The worker affirms the child's exploration of the relationship and the space, and ensures that the child knows that there are safe boundaries for this exploration in the following ways. The worker shows the clock on the wall and explains when the play time ends, or has a timer in the room that rings five minutes before the end of play time. This time is explained so that the child can understand that the full hour belongs only to the child and to no one else. These firm, consistent, and non-punitive boundaries help to create a safe and secure place in which the child can say the unspeakable and express the inexpressible. The child can scream or tantrum or roll on the floor, and feel safe knowing that the worker will not contain, restrain, or punish.

During the first play time, the worker usually asks the child to close the playroom door. This is a thoughtful and deliberate request that lets the child know that the door is not locked and that the child is the door-keeper. The child can open and close the door at will. The reaction to this request is significant. Some children initially run out of the room into the corridor with the expectation that they will be chased and reprimanded. They may repeat this action many times until they understand that they won't be chased, punished, or scolded for running away or opening the door. When this trust is established over several sessions, most children choose to stay in the playroom for the entire session.

The playroom rules are not posted or printed, but are introduced through the natural course of play, using words that match the vocabulary of the child:

- no hurting—only pretend hurting
- no taking toys home

The worker may add, 'If I think that you are not safe or someone else is not safe, I have to tell someone.' When the worker states this rule, the child often asks if parents are going to find out everything that is said during the session. The worker is honest and direct and uses the child's words to establish the privacy and confidentiality of the relationship. The child can tell the parents about what goes on in the playroom, but the worker does not do this unless the child is at risk of being injured or abused. The child will usually test these rules in order to verify the worker's congruence. The situation is different, of course, when the parents are involved in the play therapy as part of their own development. The parents may be in the playroom as Clara's mother was, or the parents may observe the child and the worker through a two-way mirror. The child is told if the parents can see the room, the child, and the worker. The child may ask further questions about this; however, usually the interest in the play materials is strong and the child chooses to play instead. The child's need to explore the playroom, materials, and play boundaries comes first, and soon the child is engaged and oblivious to the parents who watch through the two-way mirror.

Chaos and Struggle

The second stage—chaos and struggle—is the beginning of the healing journey. This movement to the second stage is not planned and deliberate. It evolves naturally from the child's acceptance of the worker and trust in the relationship, and it only happens when the child is emotionally relaxed and ready to really engage in play.

In this second stage the child enters into fantasy play that externalizes the pent-up emotions and memories of the past. The child may regress to the developmental level of the original painful event or incident. A 10-year-old boy may curl up on the couch like a baby or begin sucking his thumb or a bottle. An older child may begin talking

Note From the Field   8.1

The Runner

What does the worker do when the child is a runner? In a room with no locked door, how does a worker ensure the safety of the runner? These questions are often asked when setting up the playroom because the open door is an enticing part of this playroom, particularly for a child who has been confined, restrained, or chased by adults.

There are three parts to the answer. The first is that the playroom is in a building which typically has a waiting room, corridors, heavy exterior doors, and other impediments to running out into a dangerous parking lot or street. If there are no impediments, some can be added, such as a second adult or a buzzer system on the exterior door. The second part to the answer is that being chased may be an established part of the child's culture. Whenever the child has run, the adult care-giver has chased the child. In the playroom, the child is confused when the worker does not chase the child. When the worker consistently does not chase the child, the behaviour of running is gradually extinguished, particularly when there is a positive reinforcer (play materials) for not running. The third part of the answer is the playroom. The security, warmth, and attractiveness of the playroom naturally counterbalances the discomfort, uncertainty, and confusion of running. When the worker confidently and consistently implements all three parts of this answer, the running gradually diminishes, and fades then stops.

like a baby, using infantile expressions and babbling. The worker listens to and affirms these expressions of pain and longing, and continues to reinforce the safety and trust that has been established.

In the chaos stage the child imposes no order on the toys or sand and the play appears to be unfocused. The child acts out struggles with figurines or puppets to confront caregivers and to re-align relationships with family and peers. During these struggles, battles are waged. At the beginning there is no winner. Soon, however, the fighting becomes more intense and organized, and a winner (the child) emerges.

Elizabeth Newson (1992: 104) describes a second-stage episode with an older child who announces that he is going to 'muck around'. When the worker asks him if he wants to build his world at the sand table he chooses two cars—a police car and an ambulance—and throws them into the sand table with the words, 'That's my world!' Newson identifies what a strong message is conveyed in his deliberate choice of these two specific cars, as well as in the boy's decision to throw the cars rather than to place the cars.

At this second stage the parents observing their child through the two-way mirror can watch the chaos and the struggle without becoming physically involved in the play or feeling responsible for controlling or disciplining this play. This safe emotional distance lets the parents observe the play and reflect upon their dominant family narrative and their child's role within that narrative. The parents are a necessary part of this co-creation process as they will support (or not) the child's re-authored narrative when the child leaves and goes home.

Jim Wilson (2005: 95–7) tells a story about using the two-way mirror to involve parents in such a co-creation process with their son, 'the boy who lost his laugh'. This little boy, Alan, had been identified as a bully at school and is brought to play therapy because his parents see him as aggressive. Alan initially acts out this dominant family narrative, throwing toys and trying to break them. Once he has built a relationship with the worker, however, he begins to act out his sadness more than his aggression.

On the other side of the two-way mirror his parents begin to see their son more objectively as a very sad boy who is unable to smile. He is no longer a bully or aggressive. He is a child who has literally lost his laughter. Their son is their only surviving child; their first child, a daughter, died shortly after her birth, and the parents' grief has become the dominant family narrative. Because the parents observe this and make this interpretation themselves, they take charge of the change process and are invested in it. They are now able to see what Alan needs, and what they as a family need, too. They are able to plan, control, and direct an intervention to re-discover their joy and laughter.

Resolution

The third stage is the termination or resolution stage. Play therapy is a process that results in a change of direction or behaviour, and the loss of old habits or behaviours or ways of relating to others. The homeostasis or equilibrium of these old behaviours is broken, and the child must grieve this change before moving forward. The child begins to integrate the power of the session and the re-authored narrative into daily life with the family. At the same time the family is re-integrating a more powerful child into the family, a child who may react differently to family dynamics, norms, and rules. The family narrative needs to accommodate this changed child, and the family members need to shift to make room for this more hopeful and optimistic family member.

The worker begins this third stage by reinforcing and affirming the child as an integrated and strong person, and reminding the child of the progress that has been made. The focus is on the strengths that the child has demonstrated and the changes that have occurred. At this stage the child may decide to tell parents or caregivers about the play therapy sessions. The child may deliberately do this telling in front of the worker when the session ends as a way of demonstrating ultimate control over the confidentiality. The child watches the surprised reaction of the parent and, in this reaction, develops a renewed feeling of confidence and control.

Both the child and the family may resist the end of play therapy. This resistance is both a resistance to change and a reluctance to work on integrating new roles into the family dynamics.

The worker supports the child and the family to move forward independently by being consistent with the message. The play therapy is over, and the family can reconnect in six months (or 12) to share their new narrative of hope and progress.

Interpreting Play

In November 2008, the Canadian Council on Learning released an 18-part video series called 'Gorilla Parenting'; the subtitle was that Art Linkletter cliché, 'Kids say the darndest things'.[1] The series offered parents expert advice on 18 topics from bullying to tantrums to sex. The videos depicted children at play with other children, followed by parent and expert interpretation of the meaning of this play. The theme throughout was on positive parenting. Advice on tantrums, for example, included giving 'institutional hugs' and 'distract, disorient, and disengage'.

This 'survival series' assumed that relationships with children are hurtful, exhausting, and frustrating, assumptions that reflect a current understanding of play. The child does not reflect on or interpret play. Interpretation, manipulation, and control of play is an adult prerogative. Play therapy offers a different understanding of play. The adult steps back from the play, participating only when invited. The adult does not manipulate or contain the play, and there is no attempt to 'distract, disorient, and disengage'. The child has the strength and the competency to reflect on and learn from the process of play.

In the second stage of play therapy, for example, the child may act out, draw, scream, or bring out remembered feelings and events, or the current family dynamics. The worker listens and observes attentively (see Chapter 7), reflects, and interprets the chaos and struggle of the child's life. This latter act of translation or interpretation helps to uncover the meaning of play, and helps the worker to cogently scaffold the child's play episodes in order to uncover more and deeper meanings.

Interpreting play is complex and multi-layered. It requires knowledge of the child's family context and history, as well as knowledge of the child's current cognitive and socio-emotional health, culture, and temperament. Each of these factors feeds into the interpretation. Each is equally important to the worker who is trying to discover and support the child's meaning within the play. Interpreting play also requires a thorough understanding of the theoretical underpinnings of play therapy, as the worker uncovers the meaning of play from each theoretical framework.

The second stage of chaos and struggle can also be chaotic for the worker who tries to both interpret play and to consider all of the other personal, cultural, familial, and developmental information about the child. The worker may feel overwhelmed by the menu of possible interpretations. Sometimes a template can help in this interpretation; in this case, mapping or webbing is ideal. The play episode can be put into the middle of the web, with all of the possible interpretations of this episode. Through reflection and discussion with a supervisor, the worker can sift through all of these interpretations, uncovering those that match more closely to the child as understood now by the worker. An example of this webbing is in Figure 8.1.

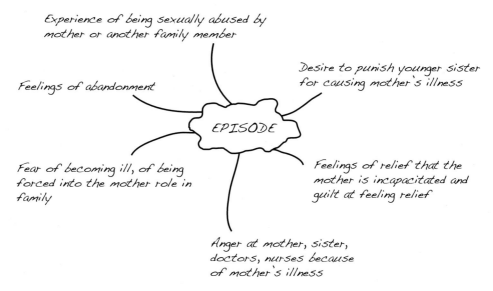

Figure 8.1   Webbing a Play Episode

This figure depicts the play episode of a girl who has been brought to the worker for play therapy by her mother. Her mother has cancer and is worried about the effect of her illness on her daughter. The particular play episode that is webbed lasts about 30 seconds and involves the girl giving the rag doll an injection in her upper leg. During this play episode the girl appears to be intently scowling and tense. The worker observes this play episode and, after the play session is over, uses webbing to try to unravel the many possible meanings of this play episode.

Webbing a play episode is one way to chart all possible interpretations. One might be correct, several may be correct, or none may be correct. Although the worker follows the child's lead and observes closely, the worker may still not fully understand either the play or the child. The child remains the keeper of the truth. Webbing is done as a visual summary of potential interpretations, and as a basis for discussion with the therapeutic team or the supervisor. During this discussion, one, or possibly several, interpretations may be selected as most likely.

After this discussion the worker checks out the potential interpretations with the child. This checking out is not done in a leading or suggestive way, but rather in a curious, honest, and open way because the worker honestly wants to know. The child may be asked how it feels to give the needle or to get a needle. Alternatively, the worker may simply state what is happening: you are giving dolly a needle. In either case, the child does the correction, while the worker listens carefully to the body and verbal language of the child. The child may cover up the doll, scowl at the doll, push the doll's legs apart, or stand on the doll. The child may give the injection a new name: 'poison', 'needles to help people to get better', or 'just what she deserves'. These verbal and non-verbal clues help the worker to focus on one or a couple of interpretations only.

Effectiveness

Children express ideas, opinions, stories, and feelings more easily and naturally through play than through written or verbal communication. Some adults, too, who are recalling early childhood trauma, abuse, or attachment injuries express their pain more easily through play therapy. Sometimes there are no words for their pain because it is so deep and all-encompassing, a part of their body history (Miller, 2005). That is when the adult can use paint, figurines in a sand tray, or other play materials to safely act out and express these emotions. Adult interventions are beyond the scope of this text, but the adults in the child's life may benefit as much as the child from the opportunity to engage in play therapy (Schaefer, 2003).

Play therapy is more commonly used with children because play itself is so familiar to them and so much part of their everyday lives. Children are used to seeing paint, markers, crayons, and paper in their schools and homes. Children are used to having puppets and toys in their playrooms. Children are encouraged, told, and urged to play. The familiarity of the medium makes it more accessible to children, more comfortable for them, and more conducive to their free expression.

Children learn best by doing, and play is the 'doing'. Play is the ideal context for children to learn about expressing their emotions and coping with situations that are frightening or sad. Play is also an ideal way to remember events and people from the past and to imagine how these events, emotions, and people can change. Play can be used to prompt communication, to develop ideas, or to discover and test new ways of behaving.

When we are in stressful situations we act in ways that we would not ordinarily act. We tantrum; we yell; we hit. When play is monitored, assessed, and contained, the child may feel stress and behave accordingly. The lack of stress, safety, and security of play therapy prompts the child to play out thoughts, feelings, and memories and, in this playing out, to cognitively restructure these same thoughts, feelings, and memories. The child becomes an expert on her or his own thoughts, feelings, and memories and draws connections between them. The advantage of this approach is that the child is an active and equal participant in the intervention process.

Provided the worker is open to following the child's lead in play, play therapy can elicit powerful communication from the child, particularly when the child's injuries are deep. Elizabeth Newson (1992: 105) reflects on the effectiveness and power of play therapy with a 12-year-old boy. This angry young boy actually ties her to the play structure, then leaves the room. She does not reprimand him or scold him. She accepts the action. 'Her ability to leave her feelings behind in the playroom, and so earn his trust, was rewarded a week later when Jack asked for "a talk" and proceeded to discuss his history and anxieties in a way that she had never achieved with him in two years of social work'.

Does play therapy qualify as an intervention? Perhaps play is just play—recreation, a chance to explore, a spontaneous activity. Play behaviour may mean only that a child explores in a particular way. Interpreting the meaning of a child's play may be a subjective response from a worker who is totally mistaken. The child hammering the doll may simply be testing an idea (I wonder if the material in that silly-looking head breaks easily?) in play rather than acting out an inner hostility or a memory of child abuse.

On the other hand, play therapy may reflect the narrative therapy work of Michael White (see Chapter 7). Narrative therapy helps the child to externalize problems of bullying, violence in the home, illness, death, and so on, and to deal with the externalized problem. The child tells the story through the figurines in the sand tray, putting the problem into one figurine or one play episode. The child can then control both the characters and the story. Grandma does not have to go away. Grandma can stay, or be magically brought back in a big tractor. In this way the child can test out solutions. What would happen if Grandma came back? What would happen if we buried Grandma?

A young boy, for instance, may choose a dog as a metaphor for himself. This dog may fall into a big ditch that the farmer has made or into a deep hole dug in the sand table. The dog may try to get out of the hole without success. The other animals may come around the hole and laugh at the dog. Then the child may decide that the dog can fly out of the hole. What makes the dog fly? The dog decides not to listen to the other animals but only to himself, and so he discovers wings and jumps over them all. This is the child's narrative and the child's solution to bullying. The child creates a particular story from his experiences and he also creates the solution to his story. Play is an alternative way for the boy to re-author himself from being a victim of bullies to being a controller of the situation.

Play therapy differs from role-playing in that the figurines or the puppets act out the story and do the talking. The child directs the action and supplies the dialogue but does not have to play roles from the story in front of the worker. The child manipulates figurines, buries them, resurrects them, and discards them, then adds trees, cars, and houses at will. The child is in control and decides what each character in the story will say and what each will do. By deciding where to place the figurines and what to make them do, the child maintains control of the play, beginning it and ending it.

The largest and most current analysis of play therapy outcome research (Ray, 2006) shows that play therapy is equally effective across age and sex, and has a moderate to large beneficial effect for internalizing, externalizing, and combined problem types. Empirical validation of play therapy and comprehensive research reviews of outcomes are emerging, pointing to the effectiveness of play therapy for children of all ages. Play therapy has been demonstrated to improve the self-concepts of children, decrease anxious behaviours, lessen problem behaviours, and increase social adjustment. By challenging fixed and pessimistic versions of events, play therapy opens up a space for the child's new and more optimistic life narrative.

Summary

In this chapter we learned how children tell their stories, their feelings, and their experiences through play, and how we can listen to and interpret this play using the theoretical foundations of psychoanalysis, family systems theory, cognitive-behavioural theory, and object relations. Our interpretation of play is not simple and straightforward but evolves through the three stages of relationship-building in the playroom. In the second stage, chaos and struggle, we struggle to interpret play, using webbing to plot possible interpretations, then checking out these interpretations with the child. The interpretation of play and behaviour is the subject of our next chapter. We will see how the adult and the child sometimes interpret behaviour quite differently, and how these different interpretations can prompt adults to exert power over the child. These control interventions can make behaviours change for a short time, but long-term change only occurs when the child takes charge of and responsibility for the change.

Review Questions

1. What is the difference between watching and supervising children at play, and play therapy?
2. Name and describe four theories that are fundamental to play therapy.
3. What is the difference between directive and non-directive play therapy? When would you choose to use directive play therapy?
4. Why is it important for the child to direct and control the play in play therapy?
5. What are the three elements of play therapy, and which one is the most important? Why?
6. How are play materials chosen? Give five examples of play materials in each of the three categories and the reasons for choosing them.
7. Name the three stages of play therapy and describe what is happening for the child at each stage.
8. What are three techniques workers use to support the child's change and re-integration with the family?
9. Why is play therapy so effective with children? Do you think it could be used with adults too?
10. How would you counter criticisms of play therapy from people who say that children's play is random and should not be interpreted?

Discussion Questions

1. Reflect upon your favourite kind of play as a child. Who supervised the play? Was it solitary play, parallel play, or group play? What did you learn from this play?
2. Design your own playroom for play therapy. What elements do you think are most important? Would the room have a window? Include lighting, wall colour, and

floor cover in your design, then make a list of the materials you would include in your ideal playroom. Research has shown that play therapy is equally effective for children of all ages.

3. Play therapy has been used with high school students and older children who are experiencing difficulties in their lives. How could you use play therapy with a 15-year-old boy who was engaging in self-injurious behaviour? Describe the play materials you might use, as well as your theoretical approach.

Chapter 9

Understanding Behaviours

Huckleberry was cordially hated and dreaded by all the mothers of the town, because he was idle and lawless and vulgar and bad—and because all their children admired him so, and delighted in his forbidden society, and wished they dared to be like him.

—Mark Twain, *The Adventures of Tom Sawyer*

An onlooker may see a behavioural crisis that seems to arise from nowhere: a screaming, kicking child lashing out at an adult; a shy, quiet child who suddenly rages; an ordinarily compliant youth who turns on his teacher and swears. These crises look and feel scary for everyone, particularly for the child who is lashing out, raging, or swearing. However, not one of these crises simply erupts. Each crisis is a symptom of a previously untended behaviour or feeling or an untended structural antecedent. Each one is an early warning system, a call from the child to the surrounding adults to pay attention. This scary behavioural crisis, if managed properly, can be a learning opportunity for everyone who is involved and can result in substantial structural and behavioural change.

In this chapter we will explore both internal and external causes of behaviour, and we will look at traditional ways of managing children's behaviour in Canada from spanking, to restraints and incarceration, to chemical restraints (medication). Each of these methods locates the child as the cause of the behaviour, and each method demands that the child change. Each method can prompt short-term behavioural change, while possibly causing further long-term damage and a spiral of escalating unwanted behaviours.

We will consider a more time-consuming behaviour management method, that of understanding the role and meaning of behaviour in the life of the child. This structural and strengths-based method draws on traditional Native child and youth socialization practices that have worked well for centuries. These practices position the child as a person with rights and responsibilities to the community in the present and to all those who have gone before, too. While the Elders in the community provide guidance, the child is responsible for personal behaviour management within the community. This premise radically changes the adult–child power dynamic, equalizing power, with the child assuming more power and responsibility for behaviour. This method assumes that the child is a competent person and citizen who is capable of contributing to the community.

Behaviour is the child's way to communicate, feel powerful, and learn, and when behaviour changes so does the child's method of communication, feeling of empowerment, and level of learning. What appears to be negative behaviour may be a sign of resiliency or of positive adaptation to a negative environment. There is no blame involved, only an understanding of both structural issues and antecedents that frame the behaviour. Sometimes structural change in the community is needed more than changing, containing, or eliminating the child's behaviour. Structural change is not as cheap or as quick as some methods, but it often results in the child's choosing to learn and to adopt new behaviours or to adapt to old ones.

Objectives

By the end of this chapter, you will:

- Understand how behaviour is socially constructed and what role behaviour plays in the life of the child, the family, and the child within that family.
- Identify the strengths of both traditional and structural interventions.
- Demonstrate an understanding of how you can intervene when there is a behavioural crisis.

The Social Construction of Behaviour

Behaviour is socially constructed to be either positive (assets) or negative (deficits). It acquires this meaning or value through the social location of the person who reports on the behaviour and categorizes it as either positive or negative. If this person has power, the label carries tremendous weight, both for the child labelled and for those interacting with her or him. If the person who reports on and categorizes the behaviour has little or no power, the label will be questioned, ignored, or rejected. The child may be the reporting agent: 'Wei-lee hit me!' In this report the child's tone indicates a negative categorization: the child labels the hitting as a negative behaviour. However, the child has little or no power. The child's report, categorization, and label are not greatly trusted or perhaps even believed to be true. The adult may dismiss the report and respond, 'Stop whining.'

The reality is that adults have the social location of authority and are the primary reporting agents and punishers of behaviour. They categorize and label behaviour, sometimes constructing it only to fit adults' needs. An adult observer of a child who is studying, attending school, and being polite constructs these behaviours as positive behaviours or social strengths because these activities usually please adults. The child who is engaged in the behaviour of studying, attending school, and being polite may construct these same behaviours as negative: boring, meaningless, and self-defeating.

The social location of adults who hold **coercive power** is quite different from the social location of children who hold little power, and the value or meaning of a particular behaviour depends on the social location of the person who categorizes it. One child may value the behaviour as positive, while another child

Photo 9.1 Is this boy's labour child abuse or meaningful community work?

values that same behaviour as negative. Some children may socially construct tantrums, whining, and hitting as powerful and effective communication skills, whereas most adults construct these same actions as negative behaviours. Some children (and some adults) construct their outdoor play as fun and positive, whereas other adults see the same play as aggressive, dangerous, and negative. The value of particular behaviours, and their negative or positive attributes, is socially constructed.

Children learn compliance to behavioural norms at an early age. If they appear cheerful and compliant to adults, adults reward them. Even if they only pretend to be interested in the lesson, the teacher rewards them. This system of rewards is **classical conditioning** of behaviour. On the other hand, if children express their negative feelings honestly, adults sometimes silence or belittle them. Many children learn early to hide their feelings, particularly the very raw feelings they have, and they inevitably are both impressed and oppressed by adults and adult behaviour.

This social construction is both cultural and co-relational. In an affluent society in which education is free (Canada), reading is socially constructed as a positive behaviour for children. In a less affluent society in which children are part of a family struggling to get enough to eat, paid work is socially constructed as a positive behaviour for children, and reading is considered an independent and selfish behaviour that does not help the family. This social construction of behaviour is cultural, changing over time and across social groups and societies to reflect gender, race, class, ethnicity, and socio-economic status. Behaviour takes place in this cultural context, against a backdrop of family norms, parenting practices, and attitudes to children.

Is it negative behaviour for a child to interrupt adults? In the past in Canada this typically was considered negative behaviour, and the child was punished for inter-rupting. Currently, this behaviour is construed by many in mainstream society to be positive behaviour: a sign of the child's confidence, high self-esteem, and communica-tion skills, particularly when the child interrupts with a clever statement. At the same time, many ethnic, cultural, and racial groups in Canada consider interrupting to be negative behaviour on the grounds that interrupting elders is disrespectful and rude. A child in one school in Canada may be praised for interrupting adults; in another school, the child may be punished.

Note From the Field   9.1

Zero Tolerance

Studies have shown that students with special needs tend to be punished for a disproportionately large number of school offences. These students form less than one-tenth of the student body, but they serve one-quarter of the suspensions (Rose, 1998). This punishing affects Alfred, a Grade 10 student at Wilmot High. Because of the Safe Schools Act (enacted in Ontario in 2000), his school has a policy of Zero Tolerance. By November, Alfred has been suspended for 22 days because he cannot sit in his desk for periods longer than about 15 minutes. Alfred gets up and wanders, and this is not allowed in Grade 10. Alfred also finds change very stressful, so that when he returns to school after being suspended, he takes several days to get used to his classroom again. Alfred will probably not pass his courses this year because of his frequent absences. It is likely that Alfred will eventually drop out of high school and join the other 25 per cent of Canadian boys who fail to complete their secondary school education by age 18. How would you engage Alfred in a change plan? How would you engage his teachers?

Is one child teasing another child of about the same age negative behaviour? In the past in Canada teasing was viewed as behaviour typical of children. If the teasing created an uproar, punishment was meted out to both the teaser and the teased (or sometimes only to the child who was teased because his/her reaction constituted the uproar). The teaser was told to stop being bossy, and the teased was told to stop whining. Sometimes both children were sent to their rooms or given a job to do together. Currently, teasing is considered to be negative behaviour in mainstream society. The teaser is scolded or redirected. If the teasing is considered by adults to amount to bullying, the bully may be suspended from school.

Social construction is also co-relational or contextual. Much depends on where behaviour happens and whom it affects. Some kinds of behaviour considered positive in the home may be considered negative at school, and vice versa. Shouting, for example, may be seen as aggressive behaviour in school, and may even lead to the child's suspension from school. However, in that same child's home, shouting may be the norm, as family members typically speak loudly, laugh loudly, and touch one another frequently (hugging, jostling, and wrestling). The person who succeeds in categorizing and labelling behaviour is the person who holds the social power and who is the acknowledged 'expert'. The adult in authority usually is considered to be the expert who socially constructs and labels the behaviour.

Parents and caregivers easily describe the 'negative' behaviour of their children: tantrums, whining, destruction of property, alcohol and drug abuse, self-harm, aggression, swearing, truancy, non-compliance. An overwhelmed, dispirited, and frustrated parent may describe the child's crying, whining, and tantrums as evidence of a developmental delay, of the other parent's lack of parenting skills, or of the child's intractable temperament. Brothers and sisters may describe this behaviour differently. They may describe the tantrums as attention-seeking or 'spoiled' behaviour. They may see the whining as childish and as a sign of 'how really dumb my brother is'. However, the whining child may see the whining as a necessary means of getting adult attention in a chaotic home.

An older child may seem aggressive and hostile, and may act out her emotions through the theft, destruction, or vandalizing of property. The worker may label the child's behaviour as **conduct disorder** or persistent, anti-social activities that violate the rights of others. The parent may describe this behaviour as threatening, criminal, and violent. The parent may describe the child's group of school friends as a 'gang'. The child may describe this behaviour as innovative and strong, a valid response to a problem-saturated world, and a rite of passage at the school the child attends. The child may see the vandalism as 'no big deal': to attain status or membership in the group, property must be vandalized, sacrificed, or stolen (see Chapter 11).

Some criticize such an understanding of the social construction of behaviour as a rationalization—as an excuse or justification of the deviant or bad behaviour of the child. This presupposes that behaviour has an absolute value by adults' standards and that this behavioural value does not change. However, social values do change. Asking a young child to sit still in school on a hot, sunny afternoon also can be constructed as deviant behaviour. Should the adult be punished for this deviancy? The child who refuses to sit still for some length of time can be seen as demonstrating positive behaviour, or simple survival skills. Should the child be rewarded for his refusal? As we have seen in the above examples, the value and meaning of behaviour change for each person and each situation according to that person's point of view.

Consider the behaviour of truancy or skipping school. This can be considered from the child's point of view or from the adult's point of view. One boy may skip school to avoid a situation in which he is unsuccessful, or to avoid being bullied. When he is not in school he is not mocked, bullied, or made to feel stupid. Truancy works for this boy. A girl may skip school to draw the attention of her feuding parents away from their feud and towards herself. Feuding parents unite and stop fighting when they both focus on a daughter's truancy. This works for her. Another child may skip school as a way to keep engaged in learning when schools and teachers fail to engage or teach relevant subjects. Truancy works for this child who feels he is learning more on the streets than in a boring and frustrating high school class.

In each of the above cases different social constructions of the behaviour come to bear on the child's behaviour. Truancy plays a positive role in the life of each child, but truancy also means that each child misses potentially valuable learning offered in the classroom. The worker who rigidly constructs truancy as bad or deviant social behaviour may regard alternate explanations simply as rationalizations. However, a worker who understands those differently constructed meanings as co-relational and culturally sensitive sees each child's explanation as just that: his or her social construction of behaviour.

Causes of Behaviour

Behaviour usually is attributed to the child's internal characteristics or temperament. When the child misbehaves, the adult infers that the child is spoiled, aggressive, or destructive. If the child steals, the adult suggests that the child is immoral, deceitful, or dishonest. This attribution of behaviour to the child's personality or temperament or inadequate morality equates the behaviour with the child. Vandergoot (2006: 150) notes: 'The assumption that young people don't understand the difference between right and wrong and must be taught is behind many punitive reactions to a child's delinquency.'

Behaviour sometimes is attributed to the physical condition of the child: fatigue, hunger, sickness, or boredom. Feed the child and the behaviour changes. Let the child nap, and the behaviour after the nap is different. Get the child out of hospital, and the child will become gentle and compliant. Changing physical conditions is typically easier than changing internal characteristics. Such attribution of causes is, at best, guess-work. There may be multiple guesses from several adults: teachers, parents, relatives, and others. Sometimes the child is asked to guess, 'What made you steal the money?' The child may attribute physical conditions such as boredom, hunger, or fatigue, or feelings such as anger or depression. The child may frame this response to suit the questioner, to elicit sympathy, or to evade consequences. The child may also be engaging in guess-work.

Causes of behaviour are complex and include the child's inner characteristics, the conditions in the meso-system, relationships, and structural determinants. Each has a part to play in prompting behaviour. The child may be aware of some of these causes, or may behave spontaneously without being aware of what motivates her/his behaviour. Adults who work with the child explore with the child the causes of behaviour not to stigmatize or label the child, but rather to uncover those causes as the child sees and feels them. As the child and worker identify causes, the child may choose to modify, stop, or increase a particular behaviour, and may come to understand how to do this by modifying, stopping, or increasing the cause.

Structural Determinants

Standard behavioural interventions focus on antecedents or triggers to behaviours. These environmental antecedents are said to cause the behaviour or, at the very least, to contribute to its meaning. Applied Behavioural Analysis (ABA) considers precipitating events, or precedents to behaviour, when analysing why the child behaves in certain ways. Change the precipitating event in order to change the behaviour. Antecedent, Behaviour, Consequence (ABC) is another method of behavioural analysis that suggests changing antecedents or triggers in order to change the behaviour.

One winter afternoon when I was on the bus going home, a man got on the bus with his three small children. The bus was crowded so he sat beside me with his youngest child on his lap. The two other children sat behind me. They started kicking the back of my seat, first slowly, then harder. I turned around and glared but my stern glare had little effect on them. The little girl on his lap started whining and thrashing, her winter boots knocking slush against my sleeve. At the end of a long work day I found myself becoming more and more irritated. Finally, I turned to the father and said, 'Excuse me, but could you ask your children to stop kicking my seat?' He didn't respond at first, so I nudged him again. Then he turned to me and apologized, 'I am so sorry. I will. We're on our way home from the hospital and my wife—their mother—died. I just don't know what to do.'

This was a moment I will never forget. It was the start of a relationship. I listened while he talked all the way to his bus stop. I thanked him again for sharing with me and for teaching me such an important lesson. His story seemed at first to be one of antecedents: mother dies, father cries, and children misbehave. However, this was a story about the importance of structure. While the trigger was traumatic and life-changing—the loss of a wife and mother—the structure that framed this loss needed to be understood in order to clearly see both the behaviour and the possibilities for behavioural change.

The man told me about his family's arrival in Canada three years ago and how hard it had been to face the first winter. He told me that he had been a doctor in Ghana and was now a cleaner in the hospital in which he had hoped to practise medicine. Then he told me about the remedies for his wife that he had not been able to get in Ottawa, the ones that he felt certain would have saved her life. These structural impacts were crushing him. His innate resiliency and that of his children were flagging. Over the past six months his usual self-contained and purposeful behaviour had changed. Even before his wife died he had started drinking, a behaviour he feared would get worse. He felt powerless to help anyone, least of all his own children. Now his wife was dead, too, and he as a doctor had been unable to save her. The structural impact on this man and his family was immense.

Changing the antecedents would have been easy. His children were tired and needed sleep. His children were hungry and bored after 10 hours in the hospital and many months of visiting their mother. His children were sad and angry. Change the antecedents by offering sleep, food, and change in stimulation, and the irritating behaviour (kicking the seats) stops.

Most behavioural interventions, such as ABA or ABC, suggest changing, eliminating, or applying antecedents or consequences in order to change or end the behaviour. Behavioural antecedents come from the microsystem, mesosystem, and macrosystem. All three systems interact with one another and impact the child's life and behaviour. Micro-system behavioural antecedents can include any or all of the following:

- lack of sleep, food, drink
- discomfort caused by dirty or constrictive clothing, diapers, or bedding
- discomfort caused by too much heat or cold
- shouting, whining, screaming, or violence from caregivers
- physical abuse
- neglect
- sexual abuse
- over-stimulation from loud noises, bright lights, rapid movement
- relocation or frequent changes in activities, and lack of transitional time between changes in location or activity.

However, all of these behavioural antecedents reflect larger structural determinants. Bereavement counselling might address the family's immediate loss (antecedent) but this counselling would not change the behaviours in the family or address those structural factors of poverty, under-employment, and racism that put this family at risk of falling apart. The father, devastated by the loss of his wife, would need tremendous support and caring for him to be able to summon enough strength to tackle these issues.

Addressing the structural issues is far more difficult; structural issues are seen to be 'political' and 'beyond our scope'. As deMontigny (1995: 42) notes: 'If I outlined that a client's problems were the effects of social factors, such as unemployment, poor housing, exploitative landlords, racial harassment, or unsupportive social workers, I was understood as rationalizing the client's failure to cope.' The structural approach demands worker advocacy and real change in the structure. It also demands understanding behaviour rather than penalizing and blaming.

Behaviour as Learning

How do children learn to behave? Or do they behave in order to learn? Vygotsky (1997) theorized that all learning is experiential. Like many others before him, he considered the infant a blank slate or 'tabula rasa' on which learning happens through the experiences of life. The infant associates cause with effect by pulling a string attached to a

Note From the Field   9.2

Kwiky-Mart Parents

Fourteen-year-old Tran was brought to counselling by his parents, a couple who ran a Kwiky-Mart convenience store while caring for their four children. Tran was responsible for caring for his younger brothers and sisters after school and for helping at the Kwiky-Mart on weekends. Recently, however, he had been disrespectful to customers and had even started skipping school. When he talked to his parents, he used street slang that they barely understood.

The school counsellor had called Tran's parents and suggested they go for family counselling. She also reminded Tran's parents that they had missed the last two parents' nights at the school and had not been regularly signing Tran's homework. This was very shaming for them and they used the word 'ashamed' several times when explaining Tran's behaviour. They said that they had come to Canada for their children's education, and they valued teachers highly. Tran barely spoke during the first meeting and, when he did, he used short phrases and expletives. His parents wondered if he was in a gang or doing drugs; both suggestions had been made by the school counsellor.

My next meeting was with Tran alone. After a few moments of awkward silence I asked him about his ball cap logo. That started him talking about his favourite show, *Trailer Park Boys*. He was also a big fan of *The Simpsons* and *South Park*. He seemed to be a veteran of television-watching after school and on weekends.

Since coming to Winnipeg at age eight, Tran had been exposed to thousands of hours of watching irresponsible and irrational parents on television, probably more hours than he had already spent watching and listening to his own parents. Tran had started to see his own parents as weak and stupid and his behaviour echoed those of his television heroes who always outwitted their parents. By exploring these media images together, we eventually came to a clearer understanding of how different his hard-working parents were from the parental prototypes on television. Tran started to talk about how much he respected his parents' struggles, and we both looked for ways for him to show them that respect.

mobile, kicking a blanket, cooing at caregivers, or mouthing a toy. When this movement produces a reaction, the infant begins to feel a sense of personal power with movement and continues to explore. When the environment reinforces this sense of power through repeated experiences, the infant feels empowered to continue learning or acting on the environment. To rephrase Vygotsky's theory, behaviour is learned from interacting with the environment.

Newborns begin to learn cause and effect when they root for milk, find a breast, and suck. This learning continues as children try new experiences and take risks. Rooting for milk can be classified as risk-taking behaviour. The milk may or may not be there, and the newborn risks dehydration in the search. But this risk-taking behaviour is necessary for the newborn to learn to seek nourishment.

Toddlers engage in risk-taking behaviour as they learn to roll, sit, crawl, then toddle. Their caregivers minimize the risks by their close supervision. This supervision becomes less as children join social groups and take part in activities in school and recreational groups. Caregivers try to minimize the risks by imposing curfews, setting limits, and curtailing the use of vehicles. However, there are risks to learning and the child learns through meeting and overcoming these risks. Michael Ungar (2005: xxi) cautions, 'To categorically say that risk-taking socially deviant behaviours are all bad, or all good, overlooks the variability in children's pathways to health.' Risk-taking behaviour is cheered on a sports team or in a sports competition, but punished in the schoolyard. The adults who categorically define a child's behaviour as bad or risky may themselves be averse to risk, unlike sport coaches who recognize that winning implies taking risks. Even this categorizing of behaviour is a risky act (see Chapter 10). The chances of being wrong (falling, taking a dive) are at least 50 per cent!

Behaviour as Communication

Children learn about their own cognitive, socio-emotional, and physical competence through their risky behaviours, and they also learn to communicate through their behaviour. Body language is 90 per cent of any message, so body language or behaviour is the child's best and most effective method of communication.

Body language is carefully learned and practised over many years. The child makes behaviours bigger and smaller to test response, limits, and results. Over two years a preschooler may learn how to communicate through whining, for example, by observing that others (adults as well as children) are rewarded for this form of communication. There may be specific mesosystem triggers or antecedents that precede the whining: an adult's yell, a smell of chocolate, or a chaotic evening. With each trigger the child may practise whining with increasing skill, testing which whine is rewarded most. This response is a behaviour that is conditioned by rewards or reinforcers: treats, hugs, or attention.

Whining communication may be practised for only two years, but in the four-year-life of a preschooler this counts as half of that child's life. Imagine learning a means of communication for half of your life then being asked to change. That change, or unlearning process, similarly requires positive reinforcement and takes considerable time, certainly not the few moments that caregivers often demand when they ask a preschooler to 'stop whining'.

Behaviour can communicate needs, wants, anger, joy, hurt, or loneliness to others. When cultures in the family clash, communication breaks down. A child may be trying to communicate love; the caregiver seeing and listening to the behaviour may see and hear only roughhousing and interpret this behaviour as hate. Others watching the behaviour see a variety of emotions: anger, loneliness, or grief. The parent imposing a curfew or insisting that the child finish the homework may be trying to communicate love, but the child hears the restrictions only as the parent's lack of faith, disapproval, and mistrust.

Children sometimes try to communicate their need for homeostasis by destabilizing the family. They engage in behaviour designed to capture the parents' attention and pull the family together. Rivka Yahav (2000: 353–64) describes a boy who routinely breaks the rules at school the morning after his parents argue with each other. The boy describes his behaviour as a way to get his parents together at the principal's office, to get them talking to each other again. Yahav also describes a young girl brought for help because of her frequent headaches. The young girl describes how her headaches help to draw her parents together to focus on something besides their very fragile relationship.

A girl may start to use alcohol as a way to feel closer to family members, to gain acceptance or to gain status in the family. As a young child, she may have started emptying the beer bottles left lying around in her parents' home. The beer in the fridge, the logos on the wall, the bottle marks on the furniture: all of these are environmental indicators of family culture. Her drinking may be a point of pride, a talent, that she can drink more than any of her friends, or that she can 'hold her liquor'. She may be drinking because everyone she knows does that. On the other hand, she may drink to escape the anger and misery in the home, or as a way of avoiding criticism and failure in social interactions.

She may be described by her worker as being 'in denial' about the drinking. This denial itself may be a positive behaviour, a way of expressing her acknowledgement that her behaviour is harmful, but also the only option she knows for coping in a harmful world. Or she may be terrified that she already cannot stop and has no idea how to get off the track. Seen this way, denial is a protective factor, the drinking itself a sort of skill that the girl has developed. She may not conceive of it in terms of failure or of risk. In the short term (and she still is young) the behaviour has provided an answer to particular stresses she has experienced. This is not to validate alcoholism or to say that drinking is developmentally appropriate or to rationalize the girl's behaviour of drinking alcohol. But her behaviour also needs to be understood in terms of *her* meaning of drinking. Her behaviour is a form of communication to be taken into account.

Behaviour as Power

Children start to assert personal power and competence with those first words of, 'Me do'. The toddler tests the limits of personal power and competence, pushes and pulls, toddles, then runs and explores. Erik Erikson describes this as 'industry' versus 'inferiority'; Maslow, as 'the need for self-esteem and achievement'. Children want to feel some power over their lives and, when they feel powerless in everyday life because of their social location, they look for opportunities to show their ability and competence and to prove their power.

Disempowerment usually begins early and continues through a series of humiliations and put-downs, curfews, and restraints on a child's independence and learning. The child learns that only children are hit and humiliated; adults do not easily put up with this cruelty. Children in homes in which adults do put up with being hit and humiliated learn that this behaviour is part of daily life, and that adults cannot protect them or even protect themselves. Anglin (2002: 108) describes the reaction of workers to children's expressions of pain and turmoil: 'Seldom did caseworkers acknowledge or respond sensitively to the inner world of the child. Often, a staff member would react to such behaviour by making verbal demands of a controlling nature . . . or give a warning of possible consequences in terms of lost points, time-out, or withdrawal of privileges.'

When they are categorized and treated as inferior, children react in various ways. Some consider their category to be unchangeable and deserved. They learn to hide their own emotions, and to put on other emotions that please the adults who are in control; in other words, they learn to meet the emotional needs of adults. Others socially withdraw and adopt self-destructive behaviours that confirm their categorization of vulnerable and inferior. They try to break themselves, venting their emotional pain on their own bodies over which they do have a degree of power. Such neural stimulation, however negative, can become addictive, each hurt reinforcing the last one.

Other children protest their disempowerment. They perceive adults as the immediate cause of their inferior position, and become aggressive towards adults, protesting, 'Stop treating me like a child!' They may externalize their frustration by finding someone smaller to bully, or an object to steal or to break. They may hurt another child. They may tear down an old shed that does not belong to them. They may steal a bicycle. Michael Ungar (2006a: 7) notes, 'Bullying and other problem behaviours as diverse as drug use, sexual promiscuity, and truancy all are attractive to adolescents because they satisfy the youth's need for power, recreation, acceptance, or a sense of meaningful participation in his or her community.' This meaningful participation may be non-participation, or escape from a community in which the child has no place or power.

Prepubescent girls, for example, are routinely disempowered by gender constructions of bodily beauty. No matter how hard they try, the impossible beauty of the models eludes them. Add to that a school system in which girls begin to slide academically, and consumer messages around clothing and makeup, and many girls begin to feel very powerless. The girl is neither a little girl nor a woman; she is somewhere in between and feeling insecure and lonely. However, sexual pleasure may feel like love and may bring both pleasure and prestige. Motherhood may seem like adulthood, and the power to have a baby is a power that brings attention and status. So a girl may engage in risk-taking behaviours that give her that sense of power (motherhood) in her life when she becomes a young mother.

In Ungar's International Resilience Project (Liebenberg and Ungar, 2008) the researchers interview children who have engaged in various kinds of risky behaviour. These children include:

- boys in a Palestinian refugee camp who pledge to protect their camp;
- seven-year-olds in Pakistan working in lightbulb factories;
- prepubescent girls in Turkey hooking silk rugs all day and every day;
- 11-year-old First Nations children in Canada who live on the land rather than attend school;
- child soldiers in Sierra Leone.

Their behaviours, generally held to be irrational and risky, are described by the children themselves as rational and responsible. Each child wants to contribute to family and country, rather than being a burden. Each child assumes personal responsibility for getting basic needs met both for self and for family. Ungar (2007: 131) asks, 'After all, what do we have to offer these children that they don't already have on their own terms? Power? Control? A sense of belonging? A meaningful role in their communities?'

Photo 9.2 Motherhood is a powerful place to be when you are young and marginalized.

This question speaks to the understanding of behaviour as power. Only when children feel empowered in their lives can they take charge of themselves and choose to modify their behaviour.

The children in the Resilience Project may choose to modify their behaviour when structural options are empowering. Structural options such as a school for which already struggling parents have to pay is not empowering, nor is a curriculum that is imposed rather than culturally appropriate. Empowering structural options might include school in which the child is paid to attend; a political peace movement to which children can make a real contribution; or a curriculum that offers skill acquisition appropriate to the local environment. These structural options could release children from the stifling oppression of hard labour and combat, oppression that offers moments of power in exchange for childhoods of misery.

Spanking

Adults in Canada assume that they have the right to personal security. Should someone threaten them, or threaten to harm them, they have legal recourse to take that person to court. The assault of adults is against the law. The *de minimus* rule of common law prevents prosecutions for minor breaches of the law: if one adult taps another or nudges an adult's shoulder, the *de minimus* rule prevents prosecutions. However, if someone uses excessive force against an adult without that adult's consent, this is considered assault and is a chargeable offence.

That charges are not always laid in cases of assault speaks to both personal choice and structural determinants such as tolerance of violence and aggression and social constructions of family and children. Elder abuse and spousal abuse are still under-reported, for example. Teacher assaults by children are often handled within the school, rather than having criminal charges laid against the child. Similarly, parents are loath to call in police when their own children assault them: 'Many parents do not call the police because they do not want their children to be charged with assault. Other parents are afraid that they will be charged with assault because they have physically attempted to restrain their abusive teenager' (Cottrell, 2001: 5).

Children in Canada do not have these choices when they are spanked. Section 43 of the Criminal Code of Canada allows parents and other adults in a position of authority to physically discipline children between the ages of 2 and 12 in order to 'teach' or 'correct' them: 'Every schoolteacher, parent or person standing in the place of a parent is justified in using force by way of correction toward a pupil or child, as the case may be, who is under his care, if the force does not exceed what is reasonable under the circumstances' (Criminal Code of Canada, Section 43).

This physical discipline or correction is constrained by age limits (2–12) and rejoinders such as 'reasonable' and 'by way of correction'. Instruments such as wood planks and belts are not allowed, nor is slapping the child's face allowed. Discipline must be reasonably applied in order to restrain, control, or express disapproval of certain behaviours. It cannot be applied randomly (for no reason) and cannot be excessive. This Section exempts adults from prosecution provided their attempts to discipline their children follow these guidelines. This defence of reasonable correction has been in the Criminal Code of Canada since 1892, so the social and legal underpinnings of this Section are solid.

However, language is as variable and ever-changing as the people who use it. While the majority of discipline probably does not result in physical injury of the child, there is a clear connection between spanking and physical abuse; in other words, 'reasonable force' has a wide variety of meanings. Trocme (2003: 1431) notes that 75 per cent of physical abuse incidents in Canada are described by parents as 'discipline'. The more often a parent spanks, the more severe the spanking tends to be. When parents injure their children, these parents are not charged with assault or arrested; usually their children are brought into care until the parents learn to be more 'reasonable in their correction'.

In addition, there is substantial Canadian research showing a clear connection between spanking and emotional harm (Durrant, 2004). When a person whom the child trusts (parent, teacher, caregiver) physically disciplines the child, that trust is eroded and the child suffers an emotional injury. Health Canada warns on its website:

'It's never okay to spank a child. It's a bad idea and it doesn't work.' The Health Canada warning is based on statistics from the NLSCY, which indicate that parents who spank are more likely to have children who exhibit behavioural and emotional damage. Such children tend to be aggressive, particularly against children smaller than themselves, and they exhibit anti-social behaviour such as gang fighting, hitting parents, sexual assault, and hitting teachers. These are the bullies who also exhibit depression, low self-esteem, poor self-concept, and feelings of inadequacy and helplessness. Adults who spank children typically describe spanking as 'punishment' or 'discipline' rather than as 'retaliation', but a child may perceive this differently. The child learns to retaliate for behaviour; when the child's friend does not give up the toy he wants, the child more likely hits his friend to make him co-operate and hand over the toy. This emotional damage is long-term, and there is a clear connection between having been spanked as a child and anxiety disorder, spousal abuse, and substance abuse in later life (Covell and Howe, 2001; Gershoff, 2002).

While Section 43 clearly allows physical discipline, this Section clearly contravenes Articles 19, 28, 37, and 38 of the Convention on the Rights of the Child. This contravention was cited in the 2004 legal challenge by Alisha Watkinson of the University of Regina and the Canadian Foundation of Children, Youth and the Law.[1] This challenge failed, with three judges (Bitensky, Arbour, Deschamps) dissenting from the decision. Bitensky (2006: 301), comments: 'Section 43 impairs the equal right of children, already a vulnerable group, to bodily integrity and security . . . there is no feature of section 43 that redeems the devastation it wreaks.'

The 'devastation' of emotional harm and coercion is not caused by a single slap on the wrist that is 'reasonable discipline' but by the regular (at least once a week) use of spanking as discipline.

My experience with the students I teach demonstrates that children who were regularly spanked become adults with high emotional needs. This conviction is based on students' reactions to the debate around Section 43. Students who were spanked occasionally (two or three times a year) usually comprise 30–40 per cent of the group. These students tend to remember the behaviours for which they were spanked, and tend to be ambivalent about the effects of the spanking on their behaviour; sometimes it helped, and sometimes not. Then there are the 10 per cent who admit to being spanked regularly. Some of this group defend spanking vociferously, citing its beneficial effects on their behaviour and morality. After much class discussion and reading, this 10 per cent typically waver and some even change their position and become highly emotional and reactive, often disclosing horrendous histories of their own childhood abuse. The following is an excerpt from a letter sent to me several years ago from a student who was regularly spanked as a child:

Last night's class actually brought up quite a few emotions for me and I left feeling sad and quite victimized. I guess I never realized how much I have been abused in my life. As you know I have a disability and this is severe anxiety problems. The class sheds some light for me on my childhood years. I was 'accidentally' slapped hard at two years old that sent me flying down a staircase. I broke my right leg femur in half and it was protruding through the skin. I do not remember this incident at all, but remember being in hospital for what seemed a long time . . . .

This boy was returned home after the 'accident', only to be spanked again and again and again. This contributed to his addiction problems in adolescence, and a subsequently troubled adult life. As Miller (2005) reminds us, recovery from childhood assault is long and hard, and not always successful.

Physical and Chemical Restraints

Spanking has an immediate effect on a child. Spanking captures a child's attention as the child tenses with fear. Spanking can bring about short-term behavioural change. Restraints and social isolation (a 'time-out' sitting on a chair or 20 minutes alone in the bedroom) have a similar impact. Restraints are a means of holding back or containing the child, and social isolation holds the child in a place away from other persons. Through restraints and/or social isolation the child stops the behaviour, at least for a short period of time.

By containing the child, restraints can keep a child safe. A parent restrains a child who is about to run in front of a speeding car. A teacher restrains a student who is about to turn on a propane burner without taking safety precautions. When children's behaviour escalates and the child is at risk of hurting self or others, restraints contain the child and keep the child safe. The child's arms may be restrained so that the child cannot hit another child. The child's whole body may be restrained so that the child cannot hurl herself off a ledge and into danger.

Caregivers of children in state care, educational assistants in classrooms, and workers in residential settings are taught restraint methods such as Therapeutic Crisis Intervention and Crisis Prevention Intervention so that they can safely administer restraints when the child is at risk of hurting self or others. Safe arm and leg restraints; correct methods of pulling out of a bite, hair pull, or choke hold; de-escalation techniques to prevent the spiral of behavioural aggression; and life space interviews to debrief and learn from the behavioural crisis: these techniques and understandings are taught in certified restraint programs. This training is both reactive and proactive: it prepares workers to react to behavioural outbursts, and to proactively de-escalate behaviours. Adults who are trained and certified in these methods rarely use physical restraint holds because their training provides them with an array of de-escalation techniques (Baker and Bissmire, 2000).

Untrained workers, caregivers, teachers, residential staff, and parents, on the other hand, have used physical restraints that have resulted in the injury and even death of children. In 1998 in Brampton, Ontario, Stephanie Jobin, a 13-year-old girl, was restrained under a bean bag chair by untrained staff who simply sat on the chair until

Stephanie stopped breathing. A year later (1999) William Edgar, also 13 years old, died after being restrained in a Peterborough, Ontario, group home. Both were restrained by untrained workers using unauthorized restraints. Workers might have been charged with child abuse had the children in their care not been in state care designed to protect them from child abuse. Physical restraint may be a spontaneous reaction to a child's behavioural outburst, a self-defence impulse of an adult confronted by a child who is acting in a violent and bizarre way. Unfortunately, however, physical restraint can be deadly when the person performing the restraint is untrained and unaware of other less physically intrusive de-escalation techniques.

More costly and less obvious than physical restraints are the chemical restraints used on children. Chemical restraints are psychotropic and other medications that produce a chemical effect on the children who take them. This effect is usually compliance to adults, but side effects may include drowsiness, heightened ability to focus, lethargy, slurred speech, and irritability. Chemical restraints are a quick fix and, like spanking and restraints, have an immediate, short-term effect on behaviour.

Psychotropic medications range in type from over-the-counter tranquillizing medication to prescription drugs such as anti-depressants, stimulants, anti-psychotics (neuroleptic medications), benzodiazepines, and other anxiolytics. Such medications are a primary intervention in the biomedical model or downstream approach (Chapter 1). The DSM-IV purports to identify an organic cause or chemical imbalance that produces the behaviour. This 'organic cause', which is not yet fully understood medically, can be treated with medication designed to restore the child's 'chemical balance'. As the popularity of the medication increases, so do the diagnoses of the sicknesses. This cause-and-effect cycle merits further discussion.

In 1980 the American Psychiatric Association defined a new category of illness called Attention Deficit Disorder (ADD). Seven years later, the Association added the category called Attention Deficit Hyperactivity Disorder (ADHD). Both categories were based solely on observable behaviours of children so, like autistic spectrum disorders and postpartum depression, they were included in the DSM-IV. The difficulty of diagnosing both ADD and ADHD is well documented. Diagnoses vary from doctor to doctor, and only the province of Quebec has province-wide guidelines for diagnoses (Steffenhagen, 2008).

Do the categories create the medication, or vice versa? The answer is elusive because the history, testing, and marketing of pharmaceuticals are hard to trace globally. However, there is no doubt as to the high financial stakes in their marketing. Diller (2006: 9) remarks: 'Clinical depression before Prozac's release was a rather infrequent psychiatric diagnosis in America. . . . By the mid-1990s, depression had replaced anxiety as the most frequently diagnosed adult disorder.' Certainly, the medication sales increase with the diagnosis and, as more children are medicated, more diagnoses of the category are made.

Prozac (Fluoxetine) is one of many selective serotonin reuptake inhibitors (SSRIs) that affect the levels of serotonin present in the brain. Serotonin is a neurotransmitter—it facilitates the conveyance of electrical connections between neurons. Another frequently prescribed drug is Ritalin (methylphenidate). First recommended by Dr Harold Levinson (1980), Ritalin was released in 1993 for the treatment of dyslexia (it was in use for other conditions prior to that) and was hailed as a drug to help children to focus.[2] It is also a powerfully addictive agent that has been described as a gateway drug to more stimulating and less legal mind-altering substances (Breggin, 2002). Similar in molecular structure to amphetamines, its short-term side effects include psychosis, nervousness, irritability, mood changes, high blood pressure, heart palpitations, and diarrhea. The long-term effects are unknown because of the age of the drug. However, the recent shift in neurological thinking regarding the plasticity of the brain (Doidge, 2007), leaves no doubt that the ingestion of this chemical has far-reaching effects on the brain of a child, a brain which in any case is vulnerable because it is still developing. Psychotropic drugs used to be administered mainly to adults, but the administration of these drugs to children in Canada increased dramatically in the last decade. In the first five years of its release (1993–8) the use of Ritalin to treat attention-deficit hyperactivity disorder, or ADHD, in Canadian children increased by 300 per cent (Eberstadt, 1999: 39). During this same five-year period, the use of this drug by very young children was banned in England, Sweden, Norway, and Finland. Increased drug use can be attributed partly to our cultural expectation of a painless life and cultural dispositions towards emotional self-control, and partly to our belief in the biomedical model and the treatment of symptoms.

Many pharmaceuticals for children are positioned as being necessary. Ritalin, for example, is now so commonly prescribed for PDD, ADD, ADHD, and Conduct Disorder that it is often referred to as 'Vitamin R', implying erroneously that it is a necessary nutrient for all children. Singer (2008: 163) remarks, 'Overprescription of drugs by physicians . . . has been traced to advertising efforts of the pharmaceuticals. Increasingly the advertising campaigns of the pharmaceutical industry are targeted via the mass media directly to consumers, creating a demand for pharmaceutical psychotropics and other drugs' by the parents and teachers who are looking for chemical controls of these children.

Pushing legal drugs for children is a much bigger business in Canada than pushing illegal drugs. Children as young as three and four years of age are prescribed drugs such as Ritalin and Risperdal with alarming, and sometimes fatal, results (Diller, 2006; Eberstadt, 1999; Lambe, 2006; Weir and Wallington, 2001). Ontario data from 2006 show that over half of the children in long-term foster care (Crown Wards) are given psychotropic drugs on a daily basis (Philip, 2007). Even more alarming is a 2009 research study (Lambe, 2009) which revealed that 70 per cent of Canadian youth in foster care had been prescribed psychotropic medication during their time in foster care. Medication may be costly, but if the parents have a drug plan or if the child is in state care, these costs are ignored.

Do these drugs work? Short term, certain medications can alter a child's mood, slow down the heart rate, and make the child feel more relaxed and able to focus—although with reduced mental acuity. In combination with variables such as a therapeutic relationship with a caring adult, this medication controls symptoms and definitely alters behaviour. However, it also is taking a toll on the body that may be extremely harmful and possibly permanent (Tallman, 2010). Health Canada continues to issue warnings, and some family doctors do refuse to prescribe psychotropic drugs to very young children. However, parents, workers, and teachers pressure doctors to continue prescribing, sometimes even in the absence of a child[3] whom they have not met. As a result, the number of over-medicated children is growing. Many of these develop drug dependencies and experience the drugs' side effects, most of which last much longer than any behavioural change induced by the drugs.

Incarceration

Incarceration is a way to protect society by keeping a child who misbehaves out of the general population and in a controlled environment in which rehabilitation and behaviour modification can occur. This controlled environment allows for the planned manipulation of antecedents and consequences or reinforcers. If the emotional tone of the environment is empowering and strengths-based, then positive **social learning**, as described by Albert Bandura (1997), can occur.

When behavioural plans are not implemented and the emotional tone of the restrictive environment is not positive, incarceration often has the opposite effect on the child. Doob and Cesaroni's (2004) research into the experiences of incarcerated children in Canada provides a grim picture of poorly managed and under-funded programs. Recidivism increases with custody: children who are incarcerated, perhaps because of the negative social learning in detention centres, tend to return to negative behaviour patterns and re-offend once their term of incarceration is over (Vandergoot, 2007: 175).

In recognition of the potentially negative social learning attached to incarceration, Article 37 of the Convention on the Rights of the Child requires incarceration to be used 'only as a measure of last resort and for the shortest appropriate period of time'. Instead, non-punitive correction is preferred. Section 42(2) of the Youth Criminal Justice Act outlines non-custodial sentences, ranging from a (1) reprimand to (2) intensive support to (3) deferred custody and supervision. One means of intensive support is the Community Restorative Justice Program in which the focus is on accountability and healing rather than on punishment. The young offender is required to acknowledge and describe the offence, using the principles of **behavioural contracting**. Section 38(1) of the Youth Criminal Justice Act describes its restrictions as: 'just sanctions that have meaningful consequences for the young person and that promote his or her rehabilitation and reintegration into society.'

Non-punitive correction has the potential to be highly effective in changing behaviour and in re-integrating children back into their communities at one-tenth the cost of incarceration (Moore, 2007). However, as may be said of many community programs, lack of structural support plays a significant part in how effective such a program can be. Russell Smandych (2006: 29) notes: 'under-resourced and over-burdened communities, such as many of Canada's remote Aboriginal communities, will eventually be seen to have failed at developing adequate community-based restorative measures for dealing with "their" youth.'

Eighty-one per cent of young offenders are incarcerated for non-violent, victimless, and minor offences (Mallea, 1999: 3). Most are sent to a boot camp, group home, or detention centre. In rural or northern areas, others are incarcerated in prison with adult offenders, even while awaiting trial for the alleged crime, because of the lack of adequate facilities. Prison can be a very damaging place for youth who are exposed to long-serving adult criminals, rape and other forms of sexual abuse, and the opportunities for

Photo 9.3 Incarceration may be a lesson, but what is being taught?

learning about much more serious crimes. Canada continues to incarcerate young offenders at twice the rate of most American states (Mallea, 1999: 3), and has one of the highest rates of child incarceration of all industrialized nations (Covell and Howe, 2001: 93). On a brighter note, this rate has been declining steadily since the passing of the Youth Criminal Justice Act. In 2005–6, on average 1,100 children aged 12 to 17 were in sentenced custody on any given day. This was a 12 per cent decrease from the previous year, and a 58 per cent drop from 2002–3 (Statistics Canada, 2007).

The majority (over half) of the children who are incarcerated already are familiar with state care because they are former wards of the state. One-quarter of the children who are incarcerated are identified First Nations children. The Youth Criminal Justice Act (YCJA) removes children 12 years of age and over from the category of children and calls them 'young offenders' rather than 'children who misbehave'. Incarceration removes these children from public view.

Behavioural Change

Spanking, physical and chemical restraints, isolation (time-out), and incarceration can bring about short-term behavioural change. All of these measures focus on the characteristics of the child. A threatened or drugged child can be made to be quiet, sit still, and pay attention. A bully can be made to apologize, refrain from a specific action, stay out of the schoolyard, and do chores in the classroom. A young thief can be sent to a residential facility. A young drug dealer can be isolated in a detention centre.

However, long-term behavioural change involves structural change. Rather than locating the cause in the characteristics of the child, then managing and controlling that child, structural interventions locate the cause in structural determinants that influence risk behaviour. Sinclair (2009) describes First Nations youth specifically in their struggles against social barriers: 'The literature thus states that adolescents "no longer fit" rather than that "a radicalized society does to allow them to fit" (p. 104).' Structural interventions locate the cause and the solution, adapting the structure so that it can support the child as a responsible person with strengths and abilities. The structure provides guidance, modelling, and affirmation for the child during this time of behavioural change, and requires the child to take responsibility for change.

Gilgun (2002: 69) describes structural support available in the context of First Nations traditions as a Medicine Wheel in which the major responsibility for the child's change belongs to the adults in the community. 'Questions about what are adults doing or not doing to promote belonging, mastery, independence, and generosity are as important as asking how young people are responding and what blocks their responses to positive interventions.' Gilgun asserts that the responsibility for initial behavioural change belongs with the community and the structure around the child. The adults in the community remind the child of past successes, skills, attributes, and abilities. They believe in the child as a person and a responsible member of the community, and their strengths-based questions reflect this:

- What does success look like to you?
- How would you know that you are successful?
- How does your behaviour help you to succeed?
- Who notices this behaviour? Do they approve or disapprove? Does this approval or disapproval matter to you?
- What are the barriers in your daily life that prevent you from being successful?

The child who hears these questions gradually develops the confidence to self-explore, understanding the unwanted behaviour and the role that it plays. The behaviour may be a way of communication, a way to have power, or an exciting experience in an otherwise monotonous daily life. The behaviour may unite the child's family or tear it apart. It may pull family attention away from a parent or another troubled sibling. It may distract a parent from abusing a younger brother or a mother. Behavioural change may mean modifying the behaviour, even eliminating it, but the change will impact every member of the family.

The boy who smokes marijuana every night as a means of coping with problems and falling asleep can modify his behaviour and use half the amount of marijuana when there are structural supports for this change: a positive education system, less

Group Exercises   9.1

Match and Mirror

This pairing exercise is an extension of the importance of the worker's listening to the client, which is discussed in Chapter 7. In this exercise the focus is behaviour. A talker decides in the first minute whether or not to engage with a listener. This unconscious decision is rooted deeply in the nervous system and is triggered by the listener's attentiveness. If the worker's listening response matches and mirrors the talker, the talker automatically engages.

This exercise begins with group members forming pairs. One person in each pair leaves the room, while the other person prepares a three-minute story on any subject. The leader then coaches the group outside the room. They are told to listen to their partners' stories without interrupting. In the first minute they are to match and mirror their partners' body language, breathing, and facial expression. In the next minute they mismatch their responses, and in the last minute they return to matching. The leader cues each change with music, playing soft music for the first minute, slightly louder music for the second, then softer music again for the last minute.

The pairs reunite in the room and, at a signal from the leader, the talker begins to tell a story while the listener attends to the story without interrupting. At the end of the three minutes the leader stops the exercise, then asks the talkers when they felt best-attended-to, and when they felt less heard. This exercise prompts discussion of the importance of building rapport and trust through matching and mirroring (the empathic response). The leader then asks what this matching reflects, and how body language can prompt a response.

violence in the neighbourhood, employment. The boy's reduced intake can be further reduced when he has access to more interesting social alternatives that do not involve the drug. The boy who smokes marijuana may decide to experiment with a different method of winding down (music, exercise, a video) every second night, then compare the two methods of relaxation. Similarly, the girl who self-harms as a consequence of sexual abuse may decide to write a letter to her abuser, join a group for children who have been sexually abused, or lay criminal charges against the abuser. These are healthier, strengths-based and structural ways of making behavioural changes of using less marijuana or of coping with memories of abuse.

Contemplating a behavioural change is often frightening and stressful. Once change has begun, it can be difficult for everyone: the child and each member of the family. It may mean pulling away from a peer group or leaving a neighbourhood school. It may mean taking on new responsibilities at home or at school. Sometimes family members sabotage change, covertly or inadvertently pulling the child back to the familiar old

Point to Consider   9.1

Thom Garfat

Dr Thomas Garfat is a Canadian behaviourist who has worked with children and youth, developing a compassionate and respectful practice that has inspired many workers in the field. He began as a child and youth care worker in an emergency placement program for youth, then became a director of a community-based family counselling program. He won the Governor General's Medal in 1996 for his dissertation on 'Effective Child and Youth Care Intervention: a Phenomenological Approach'. In his acceptance speech, Garfat spoke of his motivation: 'I wondered what makes things meaningful for kids and when it works, what's going on between the child and the worker.' His work in the field of children and youth has been prompted by this curiosity, and is characterized by his passion for understanding children and youth. Today, in his work in Canada and beyond, he carries that respectful inquiry forward, always searching for understanding rather than prescribing solutions.

ways, the old roles, even when these old ways are a source of pain and trouble in the family. This can be compounded when there is more than one behavioural change happening, or when more than one member of the family is directly involved in a program of change. The new and unfamiliar behaviour has to be tried out many times in order to fit into the changed family life. Adaptations have to be made by every member of the family, and each member needs encouragement and support to change. When the behaviour changes, so do the roles of each family member as each person responds to the behavioural change.

Ungar (2007: 121) cautions: 'Parents need to seek ways to offer children alternatives to dangerous, delinquent, deviant, and disordered behaviour. Alternatives must, however, offer the same quality of experience that the child achieved through his or her problem behaviour.' Attending a youth group, going to counselling, or going on a trip may not be adequate substitutes for activities that are risky, exciting, and powerful. Behaviours such as drug use, bullying, sexual promiscuity, and stealing are attractive to children because they satisfy a need for power and control that can lead to social acceptance. Most of these activities also involve physical changes in the neurology (stimulation of the amygdala) that become quickly attached to the impulses of the brain stem: i.e., they become addictive. Intervention needs to be early, emphatic, and, if possible, communal. Healthy alternate behaviours need to be just as powerful and exciting. To be just as powerful (to bond with life-source impulses) they are going to have to be physical: sport, music, construction (from building with wood and concrete to painting the walls of buildings), working with younger children, or other highly engaging community activity. The peer bonds for young people are strong and redefine those with family, so change needs to be planned with that awareness in mind.

These healthy, alternate behaviours can happen when structural interventions provide conditions conducive to such behaviour. One such intervention is the Bullying Bylaw enacted in Rocky Mountain House, Alberta, in 2004. Rather than imposing punishment on bullies, this bylaw is focused on the bystanders who allow bullying to happen. These bystanders provide a structure for bullying, a social climate in which bullying is tolerated or promoted. By changing the structure (bystanders), the negative behaviour is impacted. That structural interventions do work is evidenced by the lowered rates of bullying since the enactment of the bylaw.[4]

Summary

This chapter presented the child's perspective on behaviour as a way to learn, to communicate, and to feel power. Risky behaviours were seen to be growth experiences rather than simply 'bad behaviour'. Seen in this way, the child's behaviour takes on a new meaning as we better understand what role the behaviour plays in the child's life and the life of the child's family, too. Traditional interventions such as spanking, physical and chemical restraints, and incarceration have only short-term effects; sometimes they actually exacerbate the negative effects of the behaviour and have very damaging long-term effects on the child. Such interventions rarely prompt the child to make positive and substantive behavioural changes. When the child is the manager of behavioural change, deciding when and where to make these changes, the effects last longer. But what happens when a child is at risk, and there is no time to wait for the child to want to change? In these high-risk situations the worker brings a different understanding to the intervention. The next chapter challenges you to go beyond risk assessment and to find a new meaning for the risky behaviours and the risky situations in which children sometimes live.

Review Questions

1. Describe how the social construction of behaviour is both cultural and co-relational.
2. State one behaviour that can be seen as both negative and positive, and explain how social location affects this evaluation of behaviour.
3. What is the difference between an antecedent and a structural determinant? Give one example that illustrates this difference.
4. What was Vygotsky's behavioural theory? Do you agree with his theory? Why or why not?

5. How is cause and effect learned differently by an infant, toddler, and an older child?
6. When toddlers scream, what might they be communicating? When adults do not respond to the scream, how might toddlers perceive this?
7. How can 'denial' be seen as a positive behaviour?
8. What does Section 43 of the Criminal Code of Canada allow? What is the rationale for this law?
9. Why has the use of medication by children in Canada increased? Can this increase be described as both positive and negative? Explain.
10. What effect does incarceration have on the behaviour of children?

Discussion Questions

1. Suggest a child's behaviour that can be seen only as a negative behaviour. What makes this behaviour negative?
2. Reflect on your learning during childhood. Which behaviours helped you to learn? Were there any behaviours that prevented your learning? How might the adults around you have helped?
3. A child's behavioural change can happen quickly or slowly, and can be controlled by the adult or the child. Explain this statement, giving examples of behavioural changes you have made in your life and how these changes have happened.

Chapter 10

High-Risk Interventions

'Would you tell me, please, which way I ought to go from here?'
'That depends a good deal on where you want to get to', said the Cat.
'I don't much care where—' said Alice.
'Then it doesn't matter which way you go', said the Cat.
'—so long as I get somewhere', Alice added as an explanation.
'Oh, you're sure to do that', said the Cat, 'if you only walk long enough.'

—Lewis Carroll, *Alice's Adventures in Wonderland*

Reports are not written and interventions are not attempted with children and families who are content. It is discontent that brings in the worker. A behavioural crisis has occurred, and the worker is called. The worker meets the child and the family when the crisis is peaking. The worker has not known either the child or the family beforehand, so has no baseline for understanding the situation. The meaning of the crisis is different for the worker and for each member of the family who is affected by it. The parents may engage in self-blame or blame their partners. They may try to avoid the crisis by staying away from the family, or by using drugs and alcohol to forget about the behavioural crisis. The parents usually want the worker either to stop or to change the child's behaviour; they turn to the worker as a last resort, after this behaviour has been escalating and after they have tried every possible strategy in their parental toolbox from ignoring, to time-out, to punishment.

These are high-risk situations in which children do need the intervention of workers, and workers need to be prepared to protect the child. Infants have urgent basic needs and they cannot leave the home to get the help that they need. Toddlers who try to find help by themselves are sometimes found frozen or dehydrated miles from their bedroom walls. Immediate worker intervention can be crucial in saving a young child's life.

High-risk interventions typically happen quickly with little time to prepare. A home support worker arrives for a scheduled visit with the family in the evening, assesses an immediate risk to the child, and calls for assistance in removing the child from the home. The counsellor at the drop-in centre observes the child at play and recognizes that the child's play indicates abuse. The teacher sees injuries on the child's legs or arms. In each situation the worker, counsellor, or teacher intervenes because the child has been injured or is at high risk of being injured. Then other workers become involved: police officers, hospital staff, foster care providers, child protection workers, and more.

Because this is a critical time, equally critical decisions need to be made: to hospitalize, to place the child in a new home, or to access a residential program for the child. These decisions are made by workers at child welfare agencies sometimes, but not always, in consultation with the family. When these decisions are delayed or are inadequate, children suffer and the worker feels responsible. Worker turnover or re-assignment is frequent, often compounding the children's attachment issues as yet another caring adult leaves them. When workers intervene in high-risk situations they may also be placing themselves at high risk, as the article from an Ottawa newspaper describes (see Point to Consider, below). Although workers rarely are killed or injured, some workers are emotionally injured and, like the children, carry these emotional scars with them.

 Point to Consider   10.1

Social Worker Killed, 10-Month-Old Missing
A social worker who had taken a 10-month-old boy to his mother's house for a visit was found beaten and stabbed to death, and the baby was apparently abducted, authorities in Kentucky said. Police found the body of Boni Frederick, 67, at the house on Monday after she failed to return to work. Yesterday, police searched for the missing boy, who was believed to be with his mother, Renee Terrell, 33, and her boyfriend.
    Source: *Ottawa Citizen*, 18 Oct. 2006, A14.

In situations deemed to be high-risk, child welfare interventions have swung between family support, child support, and back again. Frontline protection work has changed to risk assessment and now has moved back to a mid-point between support and policing. This mid-point has been termed 'differential response', a policy and practice in Ontario from 2007 and in Manitoba from 2008. Differential response, like risk assessment, does not focus on either structural determinants of risk or advocacy for structural change. Both differential response and risk assessment do not account for or explain the resiliency of the child or the family, except as a notation under 'protective factors'. Because of these gaps, high-risk interventions sometimes are as wayward and unfocused as Alice's wanderings in Wonderland.

Objectives

By the end of this chapter, you will:

- Understand how to evaluate and manage a high-risk situation, and the difference between risk factors and protective factors.
- Identify specific risks in self-injurious behaviour and suicide.
- Identify the risks involved in placement, both no-home and foster home placements.
- Demonstrate your understanding of resiliency and how to foster this resiliency in a child through structural and strengths-based interventions.

The Meaning of Risk

Any action can be considered risky. Baking cookies is risky: the stove may be too hot, the ingredients wrong, or the recipe faulty. Learning to walk is risky: there are stairs to negotiate, uneven surfaces to manage, and toys that get in the way. Whitewater rafting, hockey, and skiing all are risky sports that have resulted in injury, and even death.

Is it risky to pierce a newborn's ears? Some adults would call this a risky practice, considering the possibility of infection and irritation and considering the pain inflicted on a child who cannot choose or defend her/himself. Is it risky for a child to sell lemonade on the street? Some adults would say that it is an open invitation to stranger danger. Is it risky for young children to travel on aircraft alone? These three questions can be answered reasonably in many different ways, depending on the social setting, the adult's culture, and personal definition of risk.

Adults typically see risky situations as problematic for children, and they intervene to protect or remove children from high-risk situations. Children who are assessed to be at high risk are positioned as being in a negative location, and these children are seen as both vulnerable and unable to manage risk. Adults intervene to 'save' or 'help' the child, and without this adult intervention some children could be injured or worse. Adult care and compassion are needed when a child's safety is at risk.

However, some risky situations are not easy to quantify, and adults may disagree as to whether to intervene or not. A father might intervene, while a community worker advises the father to let the child manage the risky experience alone. On the other hand, the community worker may intervene while family members refuse to do so, feeling the child needs to experience loss or failure during the experience in order to learn from it.

Haig-Brown (2004: 217) reminds us that the terminology of risk is imbued with personal bias and personal experience with risk. 'When we use the term "at risk" youth, we mean that a young person is at risk for not being middle class, not being white, not holding down a job or going to university.' These high-risk children fall outside the broad category of children and are socially constructed as less-than or deficits; these children are seen as being unable to manage risk and are seen to be in need of protection.

Parenting is risky. There are no guarantees, and at any time the adults involved in parenting can withdraw, become angry, or just give up in despair. The National Longitudinal Survey of Children and Youth (see Chapter 1) identified the five most important risk factors for parenting in Canada: low family income, low maternal education, single parenthood, teenage motherhood, and low paternal occupational status, with the most important and overriding risk factor being poverty. Each of these is a risk factor, and a constellation of these factors can make parenting even more risky.

A **risk factor** is a predictor of an undesired outcome; a risk factor signals that this undesired outcome has higher than average potential for happening. Low maternal education may cause a mother to minimize the risks to a child riding a tricycle without wearing a helmet, for example. Low maternal education is a risk factor or predictor of an undesired outcome, the injury of a child. However, many mothers with little or no education do an exemplary parenting job, and their children benefit from their warm and nurturing parenting.

Risk factors can be described as **proximal** or **distal**, and can be quantified as low, medium, or high. Proximal risk factors are immediate triggers or precipitants such as a loaded weapon in the kitchen or an inebriated parent supervising a very young child. Distal risk factors are potentiating influences, such as isolation, lack of support, or illness. A distal risk factor can change to a proximal one, increasing the volume of risk. These situations all come down to a matter of degree of risk. A parent's illness, for example, can change from a distal risk factor to a proximal one when the parent suddenly requires hospitalization, and there is no one in the family to care for the child and no money to pay for a childcare provider. Suddenly the child is at high risk, and an out-of-home placement through child welfare may have to be arranged.

Risk factors can be identified at every system level (micro, meso, and macro). The microsystem risks involve only the child and caregiver and include low birth weight, premature birth, low Apgar score at birth, physical or cognitive delay, loss of hearing or sight, unhealthy attachment, emotional or behavioural disorders, mental health issues, and difficult temperament. These immediate microsystem risk factors put the child at some potential risk for difficulty.

The mesosystem risk factors involve the child's interaction with the immediate environment of family and community. Mesosystem risk factors include the family's mental health issues, history of abuse, level of violence, family structure, family communication skills, and personal boundaries. Mesosystem risk factors also include

Group Exercises   10.1

Assessing Risk

This risk assessment exercise demonstrates Haig-Brown's reminder that personal bias and personal experience with risk affect the identification and assessment of risk. Each group member brings this bias and experience to this exercise, making this a powerful group experience.

This exercise begins with the large group being divided into five small groups of three to five members. Each small group is then given a card on which five activities are written that correspond to a particular age of a child. (The activities on the card can be modified to include local street names, restaurants, and sports.)

1. Ten-month-old child crawling on a rug at home; being pulled in a baby carrier behind a bicycle; sitting alone on a dearskin ottoman; being cared for by two grandparents who are over 70 years old; being cared for by a lone mother addicted to alcohol.

2. Four-year-old child being pushed in a stroller; using a cell phone; eating a hamburger and fries in a fast food outlet; living with a lone father addicted to cocaine; playing hockey.

3. Eight-year-old child skating on the rink without a helmet; walking two kilometres to school; selling Girl Guide cookies on a street corner with a friend; canoeing on the river with a friend; staying overnight with a school friend.

4. Twelve-year-old child babysitting a younger (six-year-old) brother after school; snowmobiling alone; shopping for clothes at a mall with friends; going on a week-end camping trip with an older brother; living with a lone mother (26 years of age) and her 20-year-old boyfriend.

5. Fifteen-year-old child staying in Pakistan for a month with a family friend; travelling to Las Vegas with a school trip; bussing tables on Sundays at a local restaurant; volunteering at a drop-in centre three nights a week; babysitting a newborn Saturday mornings.

The leader gives one card to each group, asking the group members to put the activities in order from the least risky to the most risky. When all of the small groups have completed this task, each group presents the activities in order from least risky to most risky. The group then accepts and answers questions from the large group. When all of the small groups have presented, the leader asks the participants why this exercise proved to be so difficult and what lessons can be learned from the exercise.

protective factors necessary if the child is to spend the three or more hours per week in lessons or practice. Probably the most important structural determinant is the finances to pay for the lesson and to allow the parent time to encourage the practice.

In addition to Sesma and Bronfenbrenner, some Canadians with strong spiritual or religious beliefs describe the most important structural protective factor to be a sense of community and spirituality. Aboriginal Canadians, for example, value community as a protective factor and a co-parent of the child. The child is connected with the earth and with those who have gone before the child. The child may take in the spirit of a recently deceased relative. Stout and Kipling (2003: 25) note: 'They are thus named after the dead family member who, in turn, gives the child certain physical characteristics, skills or personality traits.' This naming tangibly connects the newborn to the past and to the community. Actions such as preserving the child's umbilical cord in amulets, or telling traditional sayings and holding traditional ceremonies engender the child's feelings of being wanted and loved and valued as a person in the community. The child is a gift or a loan from the Creator to the community, and is connected forever with that community and with the circle of life. Most active church, mosque, and synagogue communities also prioritize the child, include naming ceremonies and other birth ceremonies, and honour the memory of community members who have died. Naming a child after a close relative or an honoured friend is often seen as a spiritual tie to that person, a protective factor.

Marsiglia and Kulis (2009: 90) describe other cultural factors that protect or promote the development of the child, and summarize these factors in a table of psychosocial protective factors for children. The following summary (Table 10.1) combines Marsiglia and Kulis's table with structural factors identified in the National Longitudinal Survey of Children and Youth.

This table also illustrates the interplay of structural and microsystem factors that promote the optimal growth and development of the child. This interplay happens when every person who is involved in the child's life values and respects that life.

Resiliency

Sometimes all of the child's actions suggest that the child is at high risk. The cumulative risk factors indicate a serious threat that is not counter-balanced by adequate protective factors. However, the child continues to succeed and to meet developmental milestones and maintain emotional stability. The reason for this success is said to be the child's resiliency.

Since the early 1970s a growing body of research has indicated that resiliency differentiates children who manage to succeed from those who fail. This research includes an ongoing debate on the exact nature of resiliency, a debate that echoes the nature versus nurture debate in child development (see Chapter 3). Researchers debate whether a child is born resilient or is made resilient by life experiences. Those who believe that

Table 10.1 Psychosocial Promotive Factors

Child Attributes	Caregiving Characteristics	Structural Factors
Optimal health	Ability to provide nurturance and to meet needs of child	Adequate health care system and social security
Sense of autonomy	Ability to provide consistency, stability, and an authoritative style of caregiving	Caring community with adequate social supports and quality, accessible, and affordable childcare
Optimism and hope for the future	Connection to community and community supports	Engaged citizenry with a respect for children and their valuable role in the community
Healthy attachment	Emotional health and commitment to consistent, nurturing caregiving	Stability and peace in the community
Social competence	Sense of connection to the immediate community and spirituality	Respect for spirituality and community
Cultural pride	Cultural pride	Respect for diversity of culture, ethnicity, race, ability, sexual orientation

resiliency can be nurtured also wonder how to nurture this resiliency. Those who believe that resiliency is innate or genetic feel that resiliency interventions are a waste of both time and funding.

Some parents describe their children as having been resilient from birth. Their resilient children tend to be firstborns: active, healthy, and good-natured infants who recover more quickly from childhood illness than other children do. As these infants grow, their parents describe them as independent, attractive, popular, and generally optimistic. In a 25-item resiliency questionnaire used with school-aged children, Rak and Patterson (1996) identify these characteristics of resilient children:

- active approach to problem-solving;
- positive view that life has meaning;
- ability to gain positive attention from others;
- tendency towards seeking out new experiences;
- proactive behaviour;
- optimistic view of life;
- ability to be independent and to engage in independent activities.

Resilient children engage with the environment to get what they need; they have problem-solving skills, and a sense of purpose and future. They rebound in situations of risk and adversity; they meet challenges and endure in situations when other children withdraw or fail to thrive. These resilient children are not always the class presidents or team captains. Such apparently successful children may or may not be resilient, depending on how they achieve their success or popularity.

Resiliency involves overcoming risks and challenges. These risks and challenges are an opportunity for the child to develop skills and to feel competent and successful. Ungar (2005) demonstrates how children develop skills and talents in his international resiliency project. The children overcome the adversity of war, discrimination, displacement, and hard labour. Ungar maintains that there is some value to incremental and age-appropriate risk, and that the elimination of risk may, in fact, discourage resiliency: 'Improving children's well-being is never as simple as removing risk from their lives' (p. xxiv).

HeavyRunner and Morris (1997) identify 10 factors for nurturing resiliency in First Nations communities. These factors include respect for nature; respect for age, wisdom, and tradition; generosity and sharing; co-operation and group harmony; autonomy and respect for others; composure and patience; relativity of time; non-verbal communication; spirituality; valuing extended family; and child-rearing. Some of these factors correspond to Sesma's protective factors: community involvement and caring neighbourhoods, for instance. Other factors, however, reflect the cultural roots of resiliency. The value of non-verbal communication, composure, and patience, for example, reflects a learning tradition in which children observe rather than verbally interact. This is a reminder of how important it is to understand and respect the child's culture when planning interventions designed to nurture resiliency.

Risk Assessment

'Risk' is a term borrowed from the world of business and finance, and risk discourse is a product of institutions and agencies. **Risk assessment** is the systematic classification or measurement of risk, a measurement used by insurance agents, health inspectors, and human resources staff in an attempt to assess or evaluate factors (lifespan, danger, working abilities) that are not easily quantified. Risk assessment is an *inexact* science often described as an attempt to measure the immeasurable. Like any kind of gambling, risk assessment is an attempt to predict the future. It is not a 'safety assessment', which relates to current dangers in the child's life with a view to prevention. A risk assessment is an estimate or prediction that a particular negative event will occur in the future.

All child welfare jurisdictions in Canada require the use of risk assessment tools by workers in child welfare, child health, youth justice, and education to predict the child's potential risk of harm, injury, illness, or failure. These tools contain checklists of factors, primarily from the child's microsystem, which are believed to determine the level of risk to the child. These factors vary from province to territory and from municipality to jurisdiction. Risk assessment is quick, cheap, and seemingly efficient, reducing the need for both worker–child relationships and interdisciplinary worker partnerships. The emphasis is on quantifiable inputs and outputs.

Risk assessment quantifies the constellation of risk or cumulative risk factors; for example, the family's domestic violence (mesosystem) coupled with the child's developmental level (microsystem) and the isolation of the family (macrosystem) may appear to be a deadly combination. Then, the protective factors are quantified: an acceptable level of income, a peaceful neighbourhood, and a well-organized community structure. Cumulative risk outweighs protective factors and the child is deemed to be at risk of getting caught up in the domestic violence of the home.

However, risk is both cultural and co-relational. Child welfare regulations for assessing potential foster families demonstrate these factors. In an urban area, an applicant who has a wood stove at home typically is not allowed to foster a child unless the wood stove meets additional agency safety requirements (special flooring, metal covering affixed to the floor, and so on). Even with the additional safety features, the stove in the home is considered to be a risk factor that suggests some level of irresponsibility. In a rural area, however, the wood stove in the home is rarely ever considered a risk factor for fostering, unless the stove is leaky or in poor repair. An applicant with a wood stove is assessed as being very responsible, considering winter weather and the potential for hydro outages.

Risk assessments of the hygiene and safety of a child's home and the parenting style of the caregivers are estimations based on constantly changing cultural and co-relational factors. Consider, for example, the behaviour of truancy and two different children who skip school regularly. Their behaviour may be the same, but one child is resilient and one child is at high risk. The adult (teacher, parent, worker) sees the same behaviour (truancy) and often assesses both children as being at risk without regard to other factors. The resilient child may be bored by school and truant in order to read in the public library, buy and sell shares on the computer, or engage in personal travel and learning opportunities. For this child, school is a risk factor, and truancy is a protective factor. The opposite is true for the at-risk child whose poor communication skills, fear of failure, illness, poor hygiene, malnutrition, or cognitive delays prompt truancy. This child sleeps at home rather than attending school and may soon begin to engage in risky and dangerous activities to escape boredom. School could prevent this downward spiral. School could be a protective factor, helping the child to develop socio-emotionally and cognitively.

Risk assessment in Canada often assumes that its Eurocentric wisdom is universal and applies to all children and families. Henry Parada (2002: 104) observes: 'The choice of risk reflects the society's beliefs about values, social institutions, nature and moral behaviour. Risks are exaggerated or minimized according to the social, cultural, and moral acceptability of the underlying activities.' Vandergoot (2006) describes risk assessment in the field of youth justice. In a Department of Justice study of how risk assessment was being used under the YCJA, there were serious flaws in both the understanding and assessment of risk. Vandergoot (2006: 140) notes: 'Researchers also found that the way in which the risk–need measures were used, modified, or interpreted resulted in a potential for gender, racial, or cultural disparity in how they were applied, leading them to question whether the measures were promoting discriminatory practices.'

A worker brings personal culture, race, gender, ethnicity, and socio-economic status to this assessment of risk. If the worker is white, Eurocentric, and middle-class, the risk may be assessed very differently from the risk assessed by a worker who is black, Jamaican, and working class. The white worker may see an eight-year-old child helping in his parents' store as being **parentified** and at risk of missing important schooling, whereas the black worker may see this as a competency-enhancing activity. These are stereotypes, of course. The opposite may also be true.

Two workers assessing the same situation rarely concur on the level of risk, despite the scales and checklists that they use. Risky situations for children in urban areas can include walking down a busy street to school, staying alone in the home after school, and bicycling without a helmet. These same activities are not deemed risky for children in northern and rural communities. Many risks are situational, despite workers who claim expertise in risk assessment because of their 'universal wisdom' and their long years of service within their particular agency.

Risk management is an attempt to manage the recorded risk factors and protective factors, or to quantify the child's or family's situation with a number or grade that the agency and the worker can understand. Risk management is litigation-based and is an attempt to 'manage' the agency funders (taxpayers) who want some assurance that the workers are managing the assessed risks. This is supposed to benefit the children. However, risk management seems primarily to benefit workers by protecting them from potential litigation. Kim Strom-Gottfried (2008: 14) notes: 'This strategy is most likely to disadvantage those who are already powerless and most in need of the social worker's help. Risk-driven decisions, by definition, put the professional's needs before the client's.'

Risk management not only is an inexact tool, but also can be a tool for punishment. Squarely rooted in the biomedical model and the deficit approach (see Chapter 1), risk management focuses on the assessed risks (deficits) within the child and family, rather than on structural risks. There are no race, gender, socio-economic, or class issues in the risk assessment. Kufeldt (2003: 424) observes, 'Child welfare agencies now known by titles such as *Ministries of Family and Child Welfare and Children's Aid Societies* would be more appropriately labelled as *Agencies for the Investigation of Parental Failure*.' Each deficit that is ticked off in the assessment is tied to funding; the more boxes checked, the more funding the child and family merit. Strengths do not merit funding; only risks or deficits bring in the money.

Risk management is filtered through the cultural expectations of the worker, the agency, and society at large, and often results in decisions that are very inappropriate for the child. 'Risk management' resulted in Inuit children being placed with southern families, First Nations children being placed with white adoptive families, children who were blind being institutionalized, and poor children in England being transported to

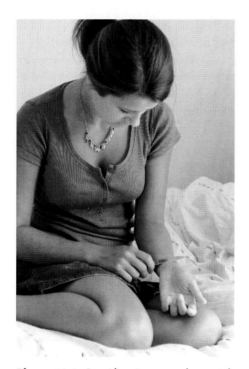

Photo 10.2 Scarification may be a risk factor and self-injurious behaviour, or a protective factor and coping mechanism.

Canada. Risk management does not have a proud history in child services.

Self-Harm and Suicide

Self-harm or **self-injurious behaviour** is behaviour that involves the deliberate destruction of body tissue without suicidal intent. This behaviour includes activities such as skin burning, pinching, scratching, cutting, and hair pulling. Self-injurious behaviour also includes self-embedding. This behaviour includes planting paper clips, wood slivers, staples, needles, pencil lead, stones, and other objects underneath the skin. When workers describe self-harm or self-injurious behaviour they do so in terms of severity and regularity. Severity refers to how harmful the behaviour is to the child, with the most harmful being the amputation of a body part and the least harmful being the faint pinching of skin. Regularity refers to how often the behaviour occurs, from daily to occasionally.

Self-injurious behaviour traditionally has been categorized in the biomedical model as a 'bad' behaviour and a symptom of the child's deficits: mental illness, depression, anxiety, poor communication skills, inability to cope, lack of social skills, or low self-esteem. The child who is depressed and has low self-esteem may become self-injurious, turning psychic distress inward. The child with mental health issues may begin to self-mutilate. The child with poor social skills and limited communication skills may become depressed and suicidal. The underlying assumption is that self-harm is morally wrong and a risk factor for the child. Self-harm or self-injurious behaviour is also seen as a gateway or precursor to suicide, with suicide being the extreme form of self-injurious behaviour.

This biomedical categorization of self-injurious behaviour as a symptom of the child's deficits, with the underlying assumption that this behaviour is a risk factor, suggests interventions that focus on the child's deficits or weaknesses. The child is positioned as a helpless (sick) person who is unable to cope with difficulties. The interventions for the child's behaviour might include out-of-home placements, support groups, crisis hotlines, intensive therapy, group work, or chemical restraints (psychotropic medication).

The structural and strengths-based approach changes this categorization of self-harm from a risk factor to a protective factor. The child is seen as a resilient person who copes with structural determinants (poverty, violence, abuse, racism, sexism, and homophobia) through self-injurious behaviour. This covert and maladaptive behaviour is in fact a protective factor that keeps the child from engaging in even riskier activities. The child manages personal pain without resorting to medication: cutting and burning can produce fast-acting endorphins that numb or anaesthetize emotional distress. The child not only manages personal pain but also covers up the scars and wounds in order to carry on with daily life.

Is this a positive behaviour, one that leads to success in the child's life? No, this leads to neither joy nor success, nor does it build the child's self-esteem. However, it does allow the child to manage structural pain over which the child feels no control. The girl who self-mutilates as a way to escape the hurt of homophobia and the boy who seeks relief from memories of childhood sexual abuse both gain temporary relief through feeling power over their bodies by cutting, burning, or starving. Self-injurious behaviour becomes a way to regain control, a coping mechanism or stress-reliever rather than simply a pathology. When this dangerous behaviour becomes addictive and a 'necessary' part of everyday life, however, the child loses control. The addiction takes control away from the child, and the self-injurious behaviour is no longer a coping mechanism or stress reliever; instead, it becomes another risk factor in an already painful life.

Instead of assessing the child, the worker assesses the structure to identify risk factors and the structural changes needed to lessen, or even extinguish, self-injurious behaviour. The worker asks the child open-ended questions that affirm the child as a problem-solver, a controller and director of the activity rather than a sick person:

- Where did you learn how to cut/burn yourself?
- If you could put a voice to your cutting/burning, what would it sound like?
- When you decide not to cut/burn yourself, what do you tell yourself that works?
- When you feel like cutting/burning yourself, which one of your friends do you turn to first?
- What advice has he/she offered you in the past that was helpful?
- Is there anyone, other than your parents, that you typically turn to for support when the going gets rough?

The worker listens to each answer carefully, affirming the child's ability to cope in a problematic world that sends messages encouraging self-harm and suicide. The worker and the child together create a re-authored narrative through recalling times when the behaviour was not needed. At the same time each structural determinant for self-injurious behaviour is deconstructed. The child joins with the worker as an advocate for structural change, an active change agent rather than a passive recipient of care or 'a sick person'.

In 1986 Richard Cardinal wrote the words 'Help Me' in his own blood while he was committing suicide. He had spent 13 years moving in and out of 28 foster homes, group homes, and shelters in Alberta. Over 20 years later, not much has changed for children. According to Kutcher and Szumilas (2008), suicide is the second leading cause of death for children aged 15 to 19 years, with the suicide rate in this population being 1.02 per 10,000.

Suicide rates among Canadian children continue to increase, surpassing those in many developed countries, including the United States, Australia, and the United Kingdom (Weir, 2001). Child suicide is more common among the marginalized: First Nations children, gay and lesbian children, and Inuit children. The suicide rates among identified First Nations children are currently five to six times higher than the rate in the mainstream population (Kirmayer, 2007: 22). According to Health Canada (2008), 22 per cent of all deaths of First Nations children between the ages of 10 and 19 were suicides in 2000.

These statistics are alarming because of their context: both self-injurious behaviour and suicide tend to be greatly under-reported. Because of family shame, religious implications, and sometimes the financial considerations surrounding insurance, the numbers of Canadian children who die through suicide tend to be hidden and kept from public view.

However, suicide and self-injurious behaviour are not prevalent among children in all First Nations communities. Lalonde (2006) demonstrates that Aboriginal communities that have self-government, youth employment, cultural facilities, and community control over education have fewer child suicides. In 2005 the Aboriginal Community Youth Resilience Network built on this information and supported communities in developing conditions that are empowering for children. Since the development of this Network with its structural supports, the child suicide rates in these communities have dropped (Blackstock, 2008).

Disclosures of Risk

The child's disclosure of high risk is most often non-verbal and expressed during play:

- Crystal may show her art teacher a painting—a black square with a red dot. When the teacher asks her about the red dot, she may say that the red dot is blood on her dolly that her daddy put all over her.
- Tyler may run to his daycare provider, crying and saying that Angie keeps putting her tongue into his mouth.
- Freddy may appear listless and hungry and does not bring a lunch to day camp all week.
- Baby Noah may arrive at his home daycare wearing the same soaked diaper from the previous day and he may have a severe diaper rash.

- Samantha may stay after pottery class to help clean up and then refuse to go home, saying she is afraid.
- Omar may 'forget' his winter boots and his snow pants every day even though there has been snow for over a month now.

Sometimes non-verbal disclosure is observed by chance. A teacher in a classroom sees a child in her class wearing an over-large, woollen sweater on a hot day. The child is sweating profusely and is obviously uncomfortable. When the teacher suggests that the child remove the sweater, the child refuses. Later the teacher notices the child pushing up her sleeves and she sees untended burn marks on her forearms.

A parent at a neighbourhood wading pool notices concerning injuries on a young bather's upper thighs. A shopper in a parking lot sees a young child left unattended in a public place or in a locked car. A child care worker who is at home in her own neighbourhood may see the next-door neighbour's school-aged child engaged in dangerous and unsupervised play. In any of these situations, the child may also be at no risk at all, and there may be no abuse or neglect. The injuries on the child's body may be from skipping rope in the playground or the bruises may be a result of leukemia. The seemingly unattended young child may, in fact, be with a family member the shopper does not recognize. The dangerous play of the school-aged child may be skateboarding, a sport seen as risky by some adults and as healthy by others.

However, the law is clear in Canada: adults must report any concerns of abuse and neglect of a child. 'The need to protect children from the risk of harm justifies [the worker's] overriding obligations of confidentiality' (Vogl and Bala, 2001: 54). The only exception is solicitor-client privilege, but ethical constraints may even then override this privilege. Non-verbal and often unintentional disclosures of abuse and neglect could be revealing a very serious situation; when an adult observes or overhears such disclosures, the response needs to be immediate. The adult's responsibility is not to interrogate the child or to ask the child for details, but to inform the local child welfare agency of any suspicion of abuse or neglect.

The penalties for not reporting suspected child abuse and/or neglect vary across Canada, but they usually include fines or imprisonment or both. Professionals and paraprofessionals, staff and volunteers—all adults in the community who work with children—are bound to report suspected child abuse and neglect. In addition, professionals such as doctors, teachers, early childhood educators, and social workers may face disciplinary sanctions from their licensing bodies for failing to report suspected child abuse or neglect. If the suspected abuse is not reported and the abuse continues, there could be a civil suit for damages against the professional who fails to report.

Disclosures of abuse and neglect are usually made during play, and rarely through actual words spoken by the child. When such words are spoken, they are brief. The child may say simply, 'Mommy hurt me' or 'My pee-pee is sore.'

Sometimes the adult response to a disclosure is inappropriate. An angry guardian who hears the disclosure may respond, 'That's awful. I'm going to kill your brother!'

Note From the Field   10.1

Handling Infant Disclosures

Rania welcomes you warmly on your first home visit. She shows you her apartment, brews you wonderful coffee, and serves you delicious baklava. She tells you that the baby is sleeping and she asks you appropriate questions about immunizations, feeding, and what toys to buy. She also tells you how exhausted she is, especially as her husband is very rarely at home because he drives a taxi. At the end of your visit you insist on seeing her baby and you notice that the baby appears listless and pale. You ask Rania to show you how she changes her baby's diaper and, when she complies, you notice bruises on the front of her baby's legs. Rania says that the baby had a fall, but the marks are inconsistent with her explanation. You telephone your supervisor who advises you that the local child welfare agency will be informed. Your supervisor also tells you not to leave the home but to stay with Rania until the child welfare worker arrives. You wait with Rania for two hours. What do you say to her?

The shocked teacher may say, 'What? That's horrible!' The dismissive camp counsellor may minimize the abuse and say, 'That's nothing! My dad used to spank me, too, and I learned from it.' These responses, some verbal and some non-verbal, further humiliate, frighten, and silence the child. The child is re-victimized and re-traumatized by the anger, shock, disgust, or dismissal. The child typically reacts by retracting the disclosure: 'I didn't mean it. It never happened!'

However, when the adult response is appropriate, the child feels a moment of safety and relief. Finally there is a calm and dependable adult who listens without judgement, sarcasm, or scorn. While the adult listens, the child may add, 'Don't tell anyone', or 'Promise me you'll keep my secret'. Usually, the child has held the secret for a long time, and is fearful of letting go of the secret. The child may have been told that telling the secret will result in a family member being hurt or even killed. The child wants to know that this secret will continue to be kept. At this point the listening adult is honest with the child and clearly states the following four key messages. These can be re-worded so that they are developmentally and culturally appropriate for the child:

- Acknowledgement: 'That [disclosure] must be hard for you to say.'
- Respect: 'I believe what you are telling me.'
- Contextualization: 'You know, sometimes children are hurt or injured. You are not alone.'
- Promising action: 'I am going to call a worker who will talk to you about this.'

All four messages are equally important. The first is an acknowledgement of the child's expression of feelings at the moment of disclosure. The second is a statement of respect, a statement that the child's words are believed. This does not mean that the abuse has happened, or that all of the details of the abuse or neglect are accurately recalled by the child. This *does* mean that the listener believes the statement of the child, or the contextual message, and this belief will engender the child's trust. The third key message counters that of the abuser and reassures the child that (s)he is not alone. Finally, the adult promises action and solution-seeking.

The adult's next step is to call the local child welfare agency to report the disclosure. This is the point at which the child typically becomes very angry with the adult. The child may affirm that this disclosure is a secret, and that the adult is breaking an assumed confidentiality. The child may cry, 'You told me you wouldn't tell anyone.' The child may also begin to deny the disclosure or to minimize parts of the disclosure. The child may scream, cry, and yell at the adult, 'I hate you!'

Considering the abuse or neglect that the child has already experienced alone and without support, this is a rational and logical reaction. The child is now faced with an interview by a stranger, a third party whom the child neither knows nor trusts. The courage needed to make the initial disclosure is now going to be re-tested through the involvement of this new and unknown adult. The child may have been primed by the abuser to expect to be in trouble because of the disclosure. Now this third adult may bring the trouble, the punishment, or even more abuse.

In addition, disclosures do not always mean help or support for the child. Sometimes the disclosure is not listened to, and sometimes the child is left to cope with the anger of a parent who is interviewed by the worker and then excused. The child may remain in the home to be further and more cruelly re-victimized because of the disclosure.

Non-verbal and verbal disclosures are very frightening for the child. The silence and secrecy imposed by the abuser has been broken. The child may have been told repeatedly that the abuse or neglect is deserved because the child is bad, or that the abuse is protecting another member of the family from being harmed. The child's relief from making a verbal disclosure fades quickly when outside workers are called, and an investigation begins.

Out-of-Home Placement

Every high-risk situation does not automatically result in an emergency out-of-home placement for the child. In some cases, the risk assessment that is conducted by the investigating child welfare worker will suggest strengthening the safety factors in the home to help protect the child. Intensive in-home support may effectively reduce imminent risk while simultaneously strengthening the family. Protective day care, homemaker services, and other in-home support can sometimes ensure that the child is not left alone with an alleged perpetrator, while a more complete family assessment and a case plan is completed.

In situations of high risk when the child cannot be protected from an alleged perpetrator at home, the child is sometimes brought to a place of safety, a foster home, or a group home. In child protection terms, this is called **apprehension** of the child. Apprehension means removal of the child from the home and into state care. Apprehension can also happen when the parent is unable to care for the child because the parent is ill or incapacitated, or when family support services are not available to keep the home safe enough for the child. Bennett and Sadrehashemi (2008: 5) critique this latter lack of structural support for children in high risk situations: 'Apprehensions are generally the result of a parent's struggle with poverty, addiction, mental health issues or family violence.'

In the initial days of interim care and custody, the family is given deadlines, schedules, and service agreements in an attempt to make the home safer for the child and to minimize the risk. The family court judge then decides whether the child will remain in care. The judge recognizes that the removal of the child from family and home can cause long-term physical, cognitive, and emotional damage to the child. DiCiacco (2008: 28–30) describes some of this damage: social withdrawal, depression, maladaptive development, cardiovascular and neurohormonal problems, and increased predisposition to disease. The judge weighs this potential damage against the risk in the home, and then orders the child either to return home or to remain in the care of the state.

Despite the high risk situation, the child understandably resists being removed from familiar surroundings and going into state care. The home may mean danger, pain, and injury, but it also means friends in the neighbourhood, brothers and sisters, a family pet, a familiar bedroom, and a classroom that is familiar and supportive. The child resists the change to a new home, new friends, new school, and a new foster family. The change and the move feel more like a punishment, and only confirm the abuser's prediction of what a disclosure would bring. The child may become very angry and hostile and deny earlier disclosures, even if these disclosures were made only hours earlier. The child may insist, 'I'm all right now and do not need to move.'

During this intervention the child reacts as any person would when faced with sudden separation and loss. The child expresses shock and denial, refusing to go, or going under the assumption that tomorrow everything will be back to normal. Then the child may express anger—at the worker, the new foster parent, the new foster sister or brother, or the new surroundings. The child may scream, hit others, throw things, and become very aggressive.

At the third stage of out-of-home placement, the child may attempt to bargain with the worker or the foster parent, promising good behaviour on condition of being allowed to return home. The child may also telephone home, asking the parent or a sibling to come to the foster home. The child may beg over the telephone, 'Come and get me. This place sucks.' The child may tell a foster sister or brother that the foster parent is bad and stupid, and that the worker is mean.

The fourth stage of depression typically happens when the bargaining does not produce results. The child realizes that the stay in the foster home will be longer than overnight, and that the first visit with family may not happen for several weeks. Sometimes the child refuses to eat or attend school, and sits alone for hours, moaning and crying. This depression is a natural and logical reaction when the child realizes that going home is not an immediate, or even certain, option.

Sometimes the child reaches the final stage of acceptance. However, even after years in foster care many children do not accept the loss of their own home and family.

The worker listens closely to the child at each stage of grieving. In the first stage, the child grieves for several days, weeks, or months and is unable to understand or absorb much of the information offered by the new foster parent or the worker. The most helpful intervention at this time is to make the child as comfortable as possible and to keep expectations minimal. This allows the child the time and space to absorb this huge life change. The worker may need to explain what has happened and what is expected to happen several times so that the child can gradually acclimatize to the new surroundings and lifestyle. Puppets, pictorials, diagrams, and photographs help in this understanding as the child starts to process this huge separation and loss.

Foster care is designed as a temporary solution to a high-risk situation. It is not meant to be a substitute for the child's own family and home. Foster care is supposed to have some therapeutic value for the child who is experiencing both the loss of family and the effects of abuse, neglect, or both. However, many studies (Trocme, 2003; Blackstock, 2005) question this therapeutic value in consideration of the poor training of foster parents, inadequate resources, frequent moves, use of private for-profit agencies, and poor child-home matching. Anglin, in his study of residential care in Canada (2002: 127), observes, 'This type of care was derisively labelled by the youth as "babysitting" or "putting in time".'

We have no accurate picture of the foster care situation in Canada, although millions of dollars have been spent in the provinces and the territories for studies and reports and analyses. A 2003 study commissioned by the Child Welfare League of Canada (Farris-Manning, 2003) reveals more unknown statistics than known. The percentage of First Nations children in care is estimated at 30 to 40 per cent (2003: 2), an extremely high percentage for a minority group, especially as First Nations children without status, Métis children, and others who lack birth information are not included in this estimate. That so many First Nations children are not living with their birth families in their home communities is often referred to as a national disgrace (Blackstock, 2005).

In at least five provinces in Canada in 2008, children still were being fostered by staff in motel rooms because of the lack of foster homes (Waldock, 2008). A motel room is an unlikely place for the healing process to begin for these children. In addition, poor cultural matching continues. In British Columbia in 2006, for example, only 15 per cent of First Nations children in care were living in First Nations foster homes; the other 85 per cent were in culturally dissonant homes (Bennett and Sadrehashemi, 2008: 40).

Nor is state care always a safe place for the child. Canadians expect that their children in daycare are looked after by qualified early childhood educators, graduates of

Photo 10.3 His bedroom may be clean and bright but right now it feels like loneliness.

a community college program. Such training, in addition to basic first aid, is a minimum standard for daycare staff, many of whom have university degrees as well. However, there is no community college diploma for foster parenting, even though foster care is 24-hours-a-day, unlike the seven or eight hours of daycare, and even though the children in foster care have higher than average emotional needs due to their removal from their own homes.

The sexual abuse of children in foster care is well-documented, beginning with the care formerly provided in residential schools and church-run orphanages. Placement in care may be the beginning of a life characterized by trauma, rejection, sexual and physical violence, self-blame, and self-destructive behaviour. One of the respondents in a recent British Columbia study of foster care comments: 'I was sexually abused in the foster home and I reported it to the social worker. The social worker didn't do nothing about it. The foster parents told me that my mom would call me a liar, so I never mentioned it to my mother. The social worker knew about it' (Bennett and Sadrehashemi, 2008: 25).

Injuries and deaths of children in foster care are investigated by child welfare agencies and sometimes by the police, but there is no federal accounting of these deaths. Rarely are foster parents or staff in placement agencies prosecuted for the deaths of the children in their care. Some of the more recent child welfare deaths reported in the media include:

- Stephanie Jobin, 13 years old, suffocated by staff (Ontario, 1998).
- Brandon Stonechild, two years old, suffocated (Saskatchewan, 1998).
- Karen Quill, 20 months , beaten to death (Saskatchewan, 1998).
- William Edgar, 13 years old, suffocated by staff (Ontario, 1999).
- Savannah Hall, three years old, beaten to death (British Columbia, 2001). Savannah was tied to her crib with a leather harness on instructions from the child protection worker.
- Sherry Charlie, 19 months, beaten to death (British Columbia, 2002).
- Jeffrey Baldwin, five years old, starved to death (Ontario, 2002).

- Zachary Turner, 13 months, drowned (Newfoundland and Labrador, 2006).
- Toddler Doe, three years old, beaten to death (Alberta, 2007).

These are only the media-reported deaths; others are unreported due to the confidentiality that allows the stories of children in the care of the state, even stories of their deaths, to remain untold. If there is no inquest and no charges are laid against foster parents or group home staff, the deaths of these children go unnoticed, except by the birth family, who—like the mother of Toddler Doe—may even have been unaware that their child was in a new foster home. In a review of the mortality rates of children and youth in care from 1986 to 2005 in British Columbia, children in foster care were 4.2 times more likely to die of natural causes and 3.1 times more likely to die of external causes than children who were not in foster care. This leads to the question: Why is more expensive child care also more deadly?

Occasionally, coroners' reports are open to public scrutiny. When that happens, the public expresses outrage at the lack of scrutiny and assessment of foster parents. The answer from child protection agencies and government ministries is always the same: not enough workers, not enough money, and not enough time. The Chief Coroner of Ontario, Jim Cairns, said of the deaths of Stephanie Jobin and William Edgar, both suffocated by foster care staff within months of each other, 'To my knowledge there has been no follow-up to most of the recommendations that were made' (Frontline, 2005). Advocacy groups for foster children have been calling for public inquiries, ministerial interventions, or some government help for years. To date these calls remain unanswered.

In every province and territory, there are guidelines as to how long a child can remain in foster care. Despite these guidelines, children often remain in foster care longer than anticipated and move from foster home to foster home in what is called **foster care drift**. Provincial and territorial statistics on foster care drift are difficult to get, but estimates are that, on average, a child has seven moves during foster care.[2]

Some children have substantially more moves than this, even in one year, while others, because they are discharged from care, may have only two or three moves in all. Each move is the disruption of a relationship for which the child typically assumes blame. Children who move more than once often assume that there is something wrong with them and that they are unlovable. Negative self-worth and low self-esteem compound in the child, with each move making the wounds larger, and the feelings of belonging to a family or a community much more remote (see Chapter 4).

Children who 'age out' of foster care often end up on the streets, or form alliances with other persons without permanent attachments. Boys often graduate from foster care to the justice system, and girls to early motherhood (Kufeldt, 2003: 420). The numbers of former foster children who are in juvenile detention centres, prisons, and on the streets far outweigh the numbers of any other identified group. These outcomes, however, are not measured, nor are the risks of foster care assessed on a checklist. If the outcome of a very expensive state system is the child's lifelong dependency on the state, something is radically wrong.

Some out-of-home placement programs take into account the potential negative effect of intervention. These include (1) kinship adoption, which places children in culturally relevant foster care with connections to the child's birth family (Blackstock and Trocme, 2005); (2) the case review process of Looking After Children (Klein, 2006); and (3) Family Group Conferencing, which offers a collaborative response to the child's needs (Burford and Hudson, 2000). Each of these out-of-home placement programs begins with the child's needs in shaping a placement to meet the needs of that child. This is quite different from a placement system into which all children must fit, regardless of their personal culture and personal needs.

No-Home Placement

The title 'no-home placement' is intended to provoke a response from those who accept children living on our streets. 'No-home' means: no birth home, no adoptive home, no foster home, and no treatment home. Some children are placed on the streets without a home by a social structure that fails to recognize and honour the Convention rights of these children.

Homeless children usually do not choose their social location, nor are they placed on the streets by workers concerned for their welfare. Canadian adults do not think of themselves as having placed children on the streets. The current popular fiction is that these children are runaways who choose to live on the street because of lifestyle choices—including drugs and sex—that motivated them to leave home. This fiction may be comforting for adults eating dinner in a warm home on a frosty January night. However, it fails to explain the throwaways and the castaways who, like the runaways, are adrift and alone and unsupported in their no-home placements.

Children are excluded from homes, even group homes, and from birth, adoptive, and foster families for a variety of reasons. They may have special needs, behavioural issues, mental health issues, or addictions; they may seem to pose a risk to the other family members because of their violent behaviour; or they may simply be disliked and disowned by the adults living in the home. Some adults throw out their children (even infants), and others drop them off at the local child welfare agency. If the child is 16 years old or older, the child welfare agencies in most jurisdictions will not take these children, so the throwing away of these older children is less overt. Sometimes it involves the police removing the child because of behaviour; sometimes it involves changing the locks when the child is away for a week-end. In every case the result is the same: children trying to survive alone on the streets of Canadian cities and towns.

Children also run away from their birth, adoptive, and foster families for a variety of reasons: abuse, neglect, anger, or simply the lure of living on their own or with friends. Children may couch surf for a few nights; they may stay at shelters for periods of time; they may even live with family or friends on the streets. Street-involved children are a diverse group that Statistics Canada has yet to count, partly because of the transient nature of their lives, and partly because they live under the radar. They are described as throwaways, runaways, street youth, homeless youth, and youth at risk. They have varying cultures and backgrounds, dreams and talents. What they have in common is that they all have to quickly learn to live and survive on the streets without any of the fundamental rights guaranteed in the Charter and the Convention, rights that most Canadians take for granted.

Martin describes these 'no-home' children: 'Most of my research participants had never had a childhood and never would; they had always had to take care of themselves, in natal families, in foster families, group settings, and living on their own. Some had a perpetual childhood; they had never taken care of themselves and never would' (2003: 268). As a result of these different reactions to the early childhood experience, some no-home children survive on the streets for many years without support, whereas others seek the parenting and care they have not yet experienced, often by becoming victims to predatory adults.

No-home children share similar wellness issues. They tend to suffer from respiratory illnesses, skin problems, lice, foot problems, and depression. This suffering has been described as 'street sickness, which is a constant feeling of malaise related to exposure to the elements, sleep deprivation, and the inability to maintain personal hygiene' (Kelly and Caputo, 2007: 732). Some become addicted to drugs and/or alcohol. Whether the drugs and alcohol numb the pain or cause the pain, whether they are risk factors or protective factors, is open to debate.

There are emergency youth shelters in some cities; however, most of these shelters depend on annual municipal and provincial funding. The shelters have limited numbers of beds and even more limited supports. Child welfare provides housing for children under 16 years of age, provided they attend school and follow the rules of the home. Social assistance may provide limited income for children over that age, provided they have a social insurance number and a home address. Street children often have neither; many do not even have a birth certificate. As Grover (2007: 336) remarks: 'In a real sense, neither home nor street belong to the homeless child in Canada. Street-involved children are not welcome in public spaces, yet they have no decent place of their own to inhabit. They are forced to be constantly on the move within the community and between communities as their integration at even the most marginal level is blocked in a myriad of ways.'

Structural Interventions

High-risk interventions tend to be reactive and crisis-driven: foster care crisis, abuse crisis, children in critical condition. Adults react quickly to situations that are identified as high-risk and temporary. Children are housed on a short-term basis in emergency foster care placements, emergency shelters, or crisis units. Because these situations are considered to be temporary, long-term supports, if available, are usually not deployed. These placements are not seen as learning opportunities, nor are the voices of children part of the solutions. Adults take charge in these situations and often continue to dictate the rules once the 'crisis' is over.

The reactions to high-risk situations are often the same interventions of a century ago under new names. 'Orphanages' have become 'permanency planning', and 'workhouses' have become 'preparation for independence' programs. The focus on 'family support' changes to a focus on 'the best interests of the child', then back again. 'Clinical work' changes to 'risk management', then back to 'differential response', a combination of both. The child who suffers abuse and neglect is removed, moved, returned, and then removed again in a downward spiral of expensive and reactive casework, spurred on by bureaucratic risk-management tools from the biomedical model. Barter (2005: 317) calls this a 'reactive response to cope with symptoms'.

Targeted programs for at-risk children, such as Headstart Nursery Schools, Infant Stimulation Programs, and Social Skills Groups, are typical of this reactive, biomedical model with its deficit approach to children. The focus is on fixing the child's deficits rather than changing the structural determinants for the child. The child is positioned as the problem, categorized as at-risk, and becomes unlikely to move beyond that category. Strengths are not identified, except as they correspond to or counter risks.

These quick-fix interventions for at-risk children may be highly effective for the enrolled children while they are in the programs. However, there is little or no evidence that these short-term programs have long-term benefits, even for the children who participate; this diminution of effects has been well-researched (Lee et al, 1990). In addition, these targeted programs have little impact on community rates of childhood difficulties, or on siblings in the family who do not attend the program. As with the system of foster care, the child who is removed from the home and given a dose of middle-class medicine then is returned to the same set of home conditions in the hopes that the medicine cures all of the child's 'problems'.

The 2008 National Social Work Conference in Toronto featured many speakers from the field of child welfare in Canada. Almost every speaker suggested that the current child welfare system should be dismantled rather than revived and put on a system of life support. Analogies were drawn to the Canadian Red Cross, which, because of the tainted blood scandal, was dismantled. Researcher and practitioner alike concluded that the biomedical model with its deficit approach just has not worked. Indeed, Ted McNeill, Director of Social Work at Toronto Hospital for Sick Children, suggested that health dollars be put into poverty prevention rather than hospitalization in order to bring about real long-term change in children's health and wellness.[3] Each speaker affirmed the need for the structural and strengths-based approach to high risk. Some workers suggested the term 'at-promise' rather than 'at-risk' to redirect the focus to the child's potential and positive attributes. These speakers used the term 'at-risk' to describe instead the institutional structures that create and maintain the inequality and discrimination impacting the child and family.

The structural and strengths-based approach begins with the assumption that the child and family are competent and are partners in change. This approach positions children as persons with rights and persons who have promise, rather than persons with needs and persons at risk. This positioning is basic to the structural approach. Begin

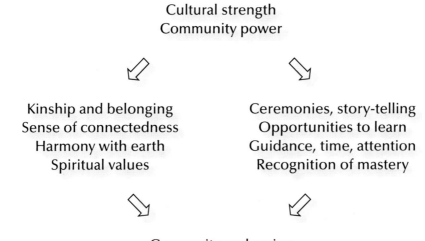

Cultural strength
Community power

Kinship and belonging   Ceremonies, story-telling
Sense of connectedness   Opportunities to learn
Harmony with earth   Guidance, time, attention
Spiritual values   Recognition of mastery

Generosity and caring
Responsibility for welfare of others

Figure 10.1 Structural Supports for Resiliency

with health and wellness, and the abuse and neglect of the child become structural issues that can be addressed. Social change is the methodology, rather than social control of children and families through service plans, time limits, apprehensions, and litigation.

Structural determinants can foster and support resiliency in children, while still responding to the safety of these children and preventing their abuse and neglect. Community capacity-building projects in Canada (Chapter 5) have done just that. Reported cases of child abuse and neglect lessen, and parental participation increases in well-baby clinics, in the child's classroom, and in family recreation programs. Children in these communities feel a sense of belonging. They demonstrate civic pride and participate more actively in school, sport, and volunteer work. They are valued participants within their communities. They have a placement and it is permanent.

Jane Gilgun (2002) describes this approach in her study of resilience in First Nations children in care. She applies the Medicine Wheel framework to identify which structural factors actually support resiliency in children as they journey through the foster care system. She indicates that a key structural factor is spirituality as it is offered through the guidance, modelling, and affirmations of the Elders in the Native community. Her framework assumes that there is trust, mutuality, and reciprocity in the relationship, and that children are willing and able to listen and to learn. A summary of her structural supports for resiliency is depicted in Figure 10.1.

The risk and protective factors that affect children are embedded within multiple levels of the child's world. Unless fundamental changes happen at all of these levels, any high-risk intervention will be inadequate for the child. Structural and strengths-based interventions can meet the challenges of high risk while valuing families and keeping children within their own families and communities.

Summary

This chapter outlined how risk and protective factors can be assessed and managed, how resiliency can be supported, and what steps can be taken to address structural determinants in high-risk situations. Protective factors are balanced against risk factors, with the child's resiliency being one of those protective factors. This system appears logical, yet the human factors involved in high-risk situations defy such quantitative measures. Resiliency, for example, may be genetic and may be a reaction to structural factors; certainly, it does not fit neatly into a risk assessment checklist.

High-risk situations demand a worker who is culturally competent in handling disclosures. In high-risk situations a child is often removed from the community and placed in another home and another community. Sometimes the child lives on the street, a placement that itself poses risks. If the child is alone, significant physical and socio-emotional risks are involved. If the child is in a group or gang, there are also risks as the child adjusts to working with peers. In this next chapter we will look at the child's working with peers, and whether groups or gangs can be helpful in high-risk situations. Risk assessment and risk management will be useful when considering the dynamics, leadership, and membership of both groups and gangs.

Review Questions

1. Describe a high-risk situation. Differentiate between the protective and risk factors in the situation. Describe the risk factors as either proximal or distal.
2. How do Sesma's developmental assets framework and Bronfenbrenner's ecological framework complement each other? Provide examples.
3. What is resiliency, and how does it develop?
4. Why is risk assessment such a difficult task?
5. How do children typically disclose abuse or neglect?
6. When a child discloses abuse, what four key messages should the adult offer to the child?
7. What steps are taken by child welfare workers when a child discloses abuse or neglect?
8. How can foster placement be both a protective factor and a risk factor for a child?
9. What is meant by 'no-home placement'? How many children in Canada are in this situation?
10. How can self-harm be seen as a protective factor? How can the child reduce the risks of this behaviour?

Discussion Questions

1. How do you apply risk management in your own life? Has your risk management ever proved to be faulty? Why has this happened?
2. Has a child ever made a disclosure of abuse or neglect to you? If so, what steps did you follow in supporting the child's disclosure? If not, how do you think you might react to such a disclosure?
3. Both self-harm and attempted suicide are high-risk situations. Suicide rates for Canadian children continue to be higher than suicide rates for American children. Discuss the reasons for this, as well as potential structural interventions that might reduce the risk of suicide.

Chapter 11

Groups and Gangs

You are never really alone in the city at night. There are always taxi drivers, coffee shop people, the 7-Eleven guy, people in their homes watching talk shows. It just feels lonely.

—Mariko Tamaki, *Skim*

Human beings are social and have an innate need to belong. In evolutionary terms, humans who separated from the group were at risk, and those who stayed with the group tended to survive. The Goth heroine in *Skim* samples many different groups, and attaches herself briefly to the English teacher, the preppy boys, Lisa, and random Wicca friends in her search for inclusion. When one of her classmates feels excluded because of his sexual orientation and commits suicide, Skim begins to understand and absorb the price of exclusion. On the outside looking in, she can only conclude, 'Being sixteen is officially the worst thing I've ever been' (p. 103).

The family is the first natural group that a young child experiences. This group can be supportive or threatening, comforting or abusive, or anywhere within this range. This group may also be larger, more extended through the generations, or constantly evolving. Skim's family is dual: herself and her mom in one home, and herself and her dad in another. Canadian writer Tamaki describes clearly the group skills that Skim learns from each family group model. Even a very young child who joins a group or a gang already has experienced group leadership and group dynamics, and has learned group skills that are shaped and sharpened by this family group experience.

The child may have already developed quite a different construct of turn-taking. For the child it may not be the regularity of maypole communication: the leader prompting each member to make a contribution in turn. Turn-taking in the family may mean pushing very hard to have your voice heard. It may mean shouting, screaming, or edging out other family members. Because the child has learned these turn-taking skills over many years in the family, these skills are entrenched and may take an equally long time to change.

The worker recognizes and builds on the diversity of group skills that children bring to groups, and tries to pull these skills together to form a cohesive, strengths-based group. The worker relies on the contributions of all the members, for they are the glue that holds the group together. The influence the members exert on one another and their interactions with one another are powerful agents for change. Members and leaders construct a power dynamic that can have a tremendous influence on the child within the group and on the group as a whole.

The same skills are used by gang leaders who engage children in activities that can be described both as deviant and as empowering. Power and control are used by leaders to engage members; when the power is shared, members benefit. In this chapter we will examine the social construction of gangs, as well as the structural interventions that can change gang membership into group membership.

We will start by defining a 'group' and then will discuss several models of gangs and of groups, each with a specific goal and a specific dynamic. We will review techniques for leadership, which include facilitation, mediation, and reinforcement. The worker can use this information in matching the child to the group so that group work can be a positive and helpful intervention. The worker can also use this information in understanding gang formation and dynamics and in working with gang members.

Objectives

By the end of this chapter, you will:

- Understand how groups and gangs form and evolve and maintain a dynamic equilibrium.
- Understand how structural determinants impact the development of gangs.
- Identify a leadership skill set that matches your own skill set.
- Demonstrate your understanding of how to initiate and facilitate a group for children that attracts their voluntary participation and meets their evolving needs.

Gang Models

When two or more children gather together with one focus, this gathering is sometimes called a **group** and sometimes called a **gang**. These labels are value-charged. 'Group' tends to be a neutral, benign, or positive label. 'Gang' has become a perjorative label that connotes drugs, violence, illegal activities, and possible incarceration.

The difference in labelling reflects the changing social construction of children and their relative (to adults) powerlessness in society. When several senior citizens walk through the neighbourhood at night, they are called a 'group' of walkers, women, or friends. When several children walk through the same neighbourhood on the same night, they may be called a 'gang'. The person making these assessments may be the same adult; the location (neighbourhood) is the same; and the activity (walking) is the same. Only the age of the members differs. Therein lies the power differential, and the reason for the label of 'gang' being applied to the children's group.

Gangs that are labelled today are quite different from 'Our Gang' or 'The Little Rascals', groups of small-town neighbourhood children who played pranks and had dangerous and comedic adventures in the 1930s Hal Roach comedies. The Little Rascals were a 'play-tough' gang with wild schemes. Neighbours scolded them, shouted at them, and threatened them; and the police occasionally chased them. But the Little Rascals always outwitted the police and escaped to enjoy another day of freedom. These comedies reflected the prevailing social construction of the child as mischievous and vulnerable. Childhood was seen as a time of innocence and waywardness, and children were seen to be susceptible to corruption (see Chapter 2).

The climate today and the social construction of children as social capital have put a quite different spin on the word 'gang'. Youth 'gang' behaviour is seen as anti-social and unproductive at best, criminal at worst. Much of the research on gangs is American, and much of what we think about gangs tends to be influenced by the American law-and-order urban context or 'get tough on crime' approach (Wortley and Tanner, 2004). Canadian statistics on gangs are compiled by Public Safety Canada, the RCMP, and provincial, territorial, and municipal police forces. Gangs are studied by criminologists rather than by sociologists, and many view the first solution to gangs to be the arrest and incarceration of youth who are gang members.

Adults have been taught to fear the congregating of both children and youth when adult leadership is absent. Media reports about gang warfare and raves fuel this fear, and change the meaning of the word 'gang'. The Little Rascals are now the fourth-graders of South Park who get together to trick their teachers, their parents, and other adults who seem to be uninformed and rather silly. The children, on the other hand, are smart. They talk tough and strong in this mountain town. Kenny is eaten by rats, a boy toasts marshmallows over a burning Vietnam vet, and another calls his school bus driver a 'fat ugly bitch'. These little rascals—the South Park Gang—prompt fear in the world of adults.

Gangs are associated with criminal activity rather than with waywardness. Youth gangs have been made synonymous with youth criminal gangs. There is no leeway for informal congregation of youth as a positive entity or activity, and a child or youth's membership in a gang can be cause for detention (Chatterjee, 2006; Wortley, 2006). The Montreal Police Service defines a youth gang as 'an organized group of adolescents and/or young adults who rely on group intimidation and violence, and commit criminal acts in order to gain power and recognition and/or control certain areas of unlawful activity' (Public Safety Canada, 2008). This definition clearly identifies a youth gang with criminal activity and reflects the biomedical model and the deficit approach to children and youth.

This working definition means that when the focus is illegal (vandalism, theft, assault, selling illegal drugs, reckless driving), a group automatically is labelled as a 'gang'. However, children experience this label even when the focus of their group is legal, such as attending a rock concert, walking at night, skateboarding, or playing music. The child to whom the label of 'gang member' has been attributed is immediately suspected of violence and of involvement with weapons and criminal activity. This child may also be subjected to random police checks and unprovoked searches.

The age of the children and youth involved in violent gangs is open to question and debate. Almost all of the violent gang members who have been found guilty of criminal activity in Canada are adults over the age of 21 years. However, newspaper headlines generate fear that this age is becoming lower by regularly associating 'violence' with 'youth'. How old are these youth? The Canadian Police Survey on Youth Gangs (2002) refers to 'youth' as persons between 14 and 18, adding a year to the Youth Criminal Justice Act (YCJA) legislative definition of 'youth' as persons between the ages of 12 and 17. The Wortley study of Canadian gangs (Wortley, 2006) refers to 'youth' as persons aged 16 to 24, thus drawing into a range that legally includes 'children' an older cohort of young people more likely to be engaged in criminal activity. Police reports on gangs never refer to 'children'; their term of choice is 'youth', and this term is regularly associated with violence and crime.

Youth gangs that have been researched tend to be both ethnically diverse and neighbourhood-specific, a reflection of the multicultural composition of most Canadian cities. A 2008 Ottawa report (Seymour, 2008) on the two major gangs—West Side Bloods and the Ledbury Banff Crips—found that their memberships reflected 57 different nationalities. A minority of gangs are comprised of one ethnic or racial group; however, on the Public Safety Canada website, gangs are described as Asian, Latino, Filipino, Haitian, Hispanic, and Black. Certain groups of youth may form a gang based on their ethnicity or race when prompted by events in their country of origin or affiliation, or when prompted by discrimination and racism. However, the Public Safety Canada website and headlines such as 'Asian gangs roam the streets' and 'Hispanic gangs on the rise' associate violence and crime with a specific race or ethnicity, an association that fuels pockets of anti-immigration and racist sentiment in the general population.

Wortley and Tanner (2004) challenge this racial profiling of gangs, noting that most youth who belong to gangs were born in Canada and are not new to the country. In addition, their study shows that, as with the general Canadian population, 'white youths reported more membership of gangs than racial minority youths' (p. 79). This may reflect actual gang membership, or it may reflect a reticence by non-white youth to claim gang membership. However, it seems likely that youth gang membership is largely multi-ethnic and multi-racial and is neighbourhood-based. More research is needed to confirm these findings, however.

One of the few non-police studies of Canadian gangs (Mellor, 2005) describes five gang models: Group of Friends, Spontaneous Criminal Activity Gang, Purposive Gang,

Youth Street Gang, and Structured Criminal Organization. Each model has a specific focus and goal-directed activity, and all five models fit into the classic group types identified by French and Raven (1959): task, mutual aid or peer support, and treatment. Understanding each gang model is essential to understanding the child's role within the gang.

The first gang model is the Group of Friends. This gang tends to be interest-based and usually does not involve criminal activity even though the gang may be subject to police scrutiny. A girl may describe her friends as 'my gang' because they share a common social interest: shopping, going to movies or clubs, skateboarding. A boy may hang out with his 'gang' because they all live in the same neighbourhood. This 'gang' can also be described as a 'growth' group or a 'mutual aid' group, using classic group typologies, because the girl and the boy derive support from their friends in the gang and develop peer skills through their interactions with the gang members. Their membership in their respective gangs persists as long as they share the same social interests or neighbourhoods as other gang members.

The second model is the Spontaneous Criminal Activity Gang. This gang is social in nature and usually is located in a neighbourhood. Membership in this gang is transitory and tied to the fun that the gang offers at that moment. This 'gang' can also be described as a 'task' group, the task primarily being to socialize through roaming streets, attending concerts, and other activities, with gratuitous violence and bullying being spontaneous and occasional acts rather than regular events. Criminal activity when it occurs is situationally motivated, impromptu, and peripheral to the main task of having fun.

The third model is the Purposive Gang which comes together for a specific purpose such as stealing cars, engaging in vigilante-type violence, or mob activity. This model can be described as both a task and a growth group. The task is specific and typically illegal. Accomplishing this task develops or grows the members' feelings of competence, power, and self-esteem. These gang members tend to be disenfranchised children and youth who use their gang membership and the risky gang tasks as a way to ameliorate feelings of depression, alienation, and low self-esteem. These members gradually build their social skills and feelings of competence through empowering gang activities.

The fourth model is the Youth Street Gang. These highly visible and cohesive gangs come together primarily for illegal activities. Like the Spontaneous Criminal Activity Gang, members tend to live in the same neighbourhood. They usually have a gang name, a uniform (tattoos, brand name clothing), and meeting place or turf. The Youth Street Gang can also be described as a task group because membership cohesion revolves around the task, or as a mutual aid group because of the peer support offered within this gang.

The fifth model is the Structured Criminal Organization in which children play only peripheral roles, for example, as drug mules or runners. The gang leader uses these children only for specific jobs, and the children tend to have low or no status within the gang. This type of task group may function as a treatment group for the children and youth on its margins who seek an escape from their own marginalized lives and an entry to social acceptance by adults.

Each gang model is a discrete category. There is no current research evidence that children move from one gang model to another. Some children may find that they enjoy the risky behaviour, and their engagement increases as the risks increase; they may move from stealing a bicycle to stealing a car, for example. Other children may belong to the gang as long as they live in the neighbourhood; when their family moves, their membership in the gang ceases.

Many adults tend to assume that children in gangs all belong to the fifth model, the highly structured criminal network. This description may or may not be true. A 2002 Canadian Police Survey in the provinces of Alberta, Saskatchewan, and Manitoba reported that a large proportion of youth gang members were involved in drug trafficking (74 per cent), assault (68 per cent), and theft of automobiles (55 per cent). However, we do not know what percentage of the larger population of youth these young persons represented. Wortley's 2006 study of youth gangs in Canada reported that 6 per cent of Toronto high school students were gang members and, of this percentage, an even smaller group engaged regularly in criminal activity. Whether or not the majority of youth gang members engage in criminal activity is unknown. Much depends on who is doing the survey, how 'children' and 'youth' are defined, and what data are being used in the research. What seems clear, however, is that gang membership, like group membership, is usually a transitory experience. The majority of children who belong to gangs do so for one year or less (Chatterjee, 2006: 5).

Group Models

Group work is goal-directed activity by individual members and the group as a whole. Groups are categorized according to this group work: task, treatment, and growth groups. Sometimes a group is a combination of two types: 'treatment and growth', for example. The group work may be focused on treatment for a particular difficulty, and through this work the child grows both cognitively, in terms of understanding, and socio-emotionally, in terms of a change in attitude and feeling towards that difficulty. Sometimes a group begins as a task group and the task is forgotten or put aside as the group evolves into a growth group.

Task groups have a specific goal to accomplish: building a garden, writing a report, making a video. The focus is the task, and there are time frames within which to achieve the task. When the task is complete, the group disperses. A task group may also be organized according to knowledge needs; children learn about specific topics such as eating disorders, anger management, pre-natal health, or healthy sexuality each time the group meets. The group has a leader and often a manual or a colouring book to guide the group sessions. The group considers a particular topic each week, considers pre-set discussion questions, and perhaps has a video to watch. Sometimes the structured, time-limited, and educational group is run in tandem with another related group, such as when a group for the parents' children is run at the same location and the same time as the group for parents. In this way, both groups follow the same curriculum. The children learn about healthy eating, for instance, while the parents learn about healthy meal preparation.

Task groups can also be growth groups for some members who benefit from the interpersonal dynamics of the group. They feel empowered by the group dynamics and the accomplishment of the group task, and they develop new skills through completing a set task with other group members.

Treatment groups include both psychodynamic treatment and self-help or mutual aid groups. The psychodynamic treatment group is a structured and time-limited group organized to address behavioural or mental health needs. Members of this group may have been diagnosed as aggressive, addictive, violent, anorexic, or lacking in social skills, and typically have been directed to attend this group. Others—victims of bullies, children of alcoholics, or victims of abuse—attend a group voluntarily, with some initial encouragement from significant adults in their lives. The leader pre-selects and pre-screens members for the group and usually follows a set program and booklet, adapting the materials to meet the specific behavioural needs of the members.

The self-help, mutual aid, or growth group is more open-ended and flexible. A child may choose to attend for a month, a year, or longer, and membership is determined by felt social needs. The focus of the group is personal growth in each or all of the domains as children learn from the experiences of other children in similar situations. The theory is that children enjoy being with their peers, and that children learn best by actively engaging and participating with others. The most common technique is role-play. Children reflect on and act out situations and emotions, sometimes alone and sometimes with other members of the group. In family support growth groups, family members sometimes change roles and engage in dialogue in an attempt to gain insight into the roles of other family members.

Adults are often asked to lead a group, form a group, talk to a group, or engage a child or parent in a group. When the adult looks for more information about the group, the answer is often thematic. The group is described according to its content or theme as a 'self-esteem group', or 'for kids on drugs'. There is little information about the factors that influence a successful match between the child and the group, factors such as the following:

- purpose of the group;
- current leadership style;
- composition of the group;
- applicability of the group model to the temperament and the perceived needs of the child;
- length of the meetings;
- timing of the meetings (day of the week, time of day);
- and accessibility of the group (cost, space, location, transportation issues).

The right match between the child and the group is essential for the group to function and for the child to function in the group. Because the child is often placed in a
group by an adult who does not understand the factors that determine a successful
match, it is up to the leader in the group to gently place the child out of the group
before the child is in any way damaged by the group experience.

Power and Control

Power is understood as authority or influence that may be assertive, strong, or forceful.
Power imposed on others is called **control** or 'power from without'. Power can also
come from within: **self-control** or 'power from within' is a feeling of competence and
self-confidence that develops through activities that are empowering. Children who
participate in these empowering activities begin to feel more strength within themselves. On the other hand, activities that diminish or disrespect the child engender feelings of low self-worth and **dependency**. These activities are disempowering.

The following comments from two gang members from the Toronto area describe
the empowerment they experience through their membership and participation in
their individual gangs (Wortley, 2006: 16).

'It's like people in my neighbourhood give you respect when you is in the gang.
They know who you are and they don't mess. Nobody knew me before I got
involved. Now I'm famous in my area. People know me now.'
'I like the respect. I like the power. You walk into a place with your boys and
people notice you, ladies notice you. Ya got status, you can swagger. People know
you ain't no punk.'

Their comments echo those of many other youth who belong to Toronto-area gangs.
Throughout these comments there is a theme of empowerment or power from within.
The youth in the gangs express:

- feeling respected through membership in the gang and by the gang itself;
- being able to make a difference or make a contribution;
- being able to make an impact on the community or make their presence known in
  the community;
- feeling appreciated for being an individual or being different;
- being acknowledged as a unique person and at the same time, as a member of the
  gang and not alone;
- feeling influential and valued because of a specific skill, style, knowledge, or way of
  life.

The second quotation refers to the child in the gang being disrespected in the
past and called a 'punk'. Pejorative terms such as 'punk', 'loser', and 'nobody' are often

ascribed to children living in poverty in neighbourhoods lacking resources, and in situations in which school success and even part-time employment is limited. The gang, on the other hand, promises power and a chance to do something. The gang offers the child the opportunity to be respected and, in some cases, to earn money.

Group members also describe feeling empowered by group membership and the common purpose of a task group. In mutual aid groups and growth groups the child feels a similar affiliation and acceptance, necessary components to feeling empowered. The shared values or the shared triumph of accomplishing a task are empowering for children who are group members.

Power in gangs or in groups can be seen as a positive force, a productive, assertive, and helpful element in interaction. While absolutely shared or balanced power is unlikely, a sharing of power is empowering for the members. In both gangs and groups, empowerment is engendered when members are encouraged to take on leadership roles such as organizing, selling, or telling. When every member is seen to have some leadership potential and is given the chance to take a leadership role in evolving leadership, then the interpersonal dynamic is democratized and the power dynamic is equalized.

The member feels necessary to the success of the gang or group, and feels that leadership is possible, even for one activity. The activity or task prompts the member to try out different roles as the work evolves. The child or youth may begin as a passive member, silent and rarely contributing. Because a certain issue arises or a certain skill is needed, the child may temporarily take on an indigenous leadership role. Others may vie for this leadership, and the child may step down, assuming instead a mentoring role with another child. The child or youth may also hold on to the leadership role and compete with other members for that role.

When indigenous leadership is a possibility, then the power of the group or gang has positive potential for that member. On the other hand, when power is centred on a stagnant, controlling leader who wields power in a coercive way over the members, then the power becomes a negative force for that member. The members begin to mould themselves to fit the personal style of the leader, rather than to develop their own skills.

Foucault (1977) reminds us that power comes from everywhere. Both leaders and members exert power in complex and often covert ways. A leader may claim to be democratic and invite members to participate and suggest rules for the gang or group. As each member contributes, however, the leader may mock and undermine the contribution. This both diminishes the contributor and discourages other members from wanting to contribute or lead. Similarly, a member may undermine the leader, forming sub-groups or sabotaging any activity suggested by the leader. These power differentials and struggles evolve continually as members take on indigenous leadership roles, then move back to membership roles. Foucault's description of power differentials suggests that these differentials can be changed to power sharing in order to create an empowering and positive experience for all of the members.

Leaders exert power and influence over members in many ways. French and Raven's (1959) original typology of leadership power is useful in understanding this. Five sources of leadership power are described: rewards, coercion, legitimacy, reference, and expertise. Each of these sources of power can be used to influence members and to build a cohesive gang or group as indicated in Table 11.1, an adaptation of the French and Raven typology. Leaders use these sources of power in their many roles with members. In both groups and gangs the leader assumes a role of organizer, teller, seller, tester, consultant, and joiner both simultaneously and at different times, depending on the activity and the membership. Each role is multi-faceted and each one requires both energy and charisma, so the sharing of roles with members becomes a mark of effective leadership. Evolving leaders tend to encourage members to

Photo 11.1 Taking on an indigenous leadership role in a group can be an empowering experience.

share in all of these roles and to take on indigenous leadership from time to time. They do this both to achieve membership cohesion or 'buy-in', and to get the members to become proactive.

Organizing is a leader's primary role. The leader decides on and creates the space, design, and membership. The leader finds a space that fits the needs of the members, or adapts the available space for the first meeting. The leader recruits and pre-selects (assesses, screens) members. The leader provides refreshments for the first meeting, plus all of the materials that the members may need: markers, paper, orientation game materials, and so on. A gang leader may provide cash, drugs, or alcohol at the first meeting, tangible signs of power within a particular neighbourhood. The leader may design and control the first meeting, deciding who speaks, when, and on what subject. This organizing role continues as new situations arise: need for new members, change of dates, new location, need for resources, and so on.

The most autocratic and coercive role in leadership is 'telling'. The leader may say, 'If you want to stay with us, you'll have to behave.' In this role the leader is the gate-keeper and the decision-maker, deciding who will be a member and who will not. This method of coercion is often used with young children, children who are developmentally delayed, or children with disabilities in the belief that they cannot participate without strict controls and leadership. This method also is used by staff in group

Table 11.1 Gang Leaders and Group Leaders

Gang Leader	Group Leader
Rewards such as money, cars, drugs, status in neighbourhood	Rewards such as praise, certificates, field trips
Coercion such as threats, violence, shaming	Coercion such as threats to notify parents, shame, marks
Legitimacy through intelligence, knowledge, experience, age, personal status, physical characteristics, family, money	Legitimacy through intelligence, organizational status, knowledge, experience, age, personal status, physical characteristics
Reference through personal attractiveness, ethnicity	Reference through power attribution from others
Expertise such as experience, social skills, street knowledge, physical skills, and information	Expertise such as experience, social skills, knowledge and information

homes, residential treatment, or detention centres on the grounds that these children have low impulse control and need constant direction and supervision from a leader who tells them what to do. Stagnant leaders tend to focus on organizing and telling; the other roles do not suit their purposes.

A more charismatic role is required to sell the task to the members, trying to convince members to participate and attend and develop cohesion. This role is essential when members may not accept the activity or structure if they come to realize how little control of this activity or structure they actually have. This role is also essential when members are passive and have little sense of direction, and need to be motivated and inspired to do the task. As a result, the leader sells a focus group by convincing the children that their participation and written comments will make a difference to the decision-makers. The leader sells a fight proposal by convincing the children that their honour is at stake because the person being fought has brought the honour of the gang into question. Most groups and gangs need a leader who takes on the selling role, if only to keep the members motivated and task-oriented.

The leader also takes on a testing role when members lose interest, argue with the leader, or fail to accomplish their tasks. The members may not know one another; they may be reticent or withdrawn, or have emotional difficulties. They may need encouragement and coaching in their social interactions. This role also is taken by leaders of children who have been in foster care, abusive homes, or institutions, on the grounds that their passivity needs to change in order to accomplish the task of the group or gang.

The leader tests involvement through a set written or physical test, by asking for input, by coaxing and urging the children to participate and act. The leader of a group may use thoughtful questions, scenarios, videos, or role plays to provoke and confront members. The leader then responds and encourages the other members to respond as well. A gang leader may test a member by getting the member to shoplift a particular item, fight a particular person, or engage in a dangerous activity. When the member does it, this successful test result is broadcast to the other members and thus universalized. In other words, the underlying message is 'What one member can do, all members can do.' In this way, the leader makes the implicit explicit for all of the members.

The role of consulting is played when the group or gang is well-established. When the leader consults a particular member, that member feels special and important. The other members may vie for the role of being consulted by the leader. The leader may choose to publicly consult either a less active or a more troublesome member in order to convert that member or win that member's attention and allegiance. Consulting also can be used to break up troublesome sub-groups, or to de-stabilize dissent among the membership.

The final role of joining is played by an experienced leader with a membership that is stable, energized, and cohesive. The power is vested in the members who take indigenous leadership roles. The leader steps back, joining with the members and providing assistance only when asked. The gang may move as a unit to vandalise a property, and the gang leader may not even be present for the activity. The group may facilitate a dance or a fundraiser, and the group leader may not be present for the event. Leaders play this role of joining as a way to further empower members to invest in the activity or task and to co-operate with one another in the absence of direction from without. This empowers the group or gang as a whole and allows it to become even stronger.

Structural Determinants

Group work preceded individual worker-client work. It was the first kind of recorded social work in Canada, and was often political or religious in nature. Groups of people gathered in settlement houses to discuss labour and citizenship issues, went to progressive education centres to learn, and participated in recreational groups and church groups. This early group work was intrinsically strengths-based; the underlying principle of the group was that people have much to share both intellectually and materially and much to learn from one another. There was always a struggle for internal cohesiveness and integration as members argued, exchanged ideas, joined and left the group.

Structural determinants were focal issues as groups, particularly political and labour groups, interacted with society, sometimes with tension and sometimes with harmony. Today, every gang or group both affects and is affected by structural determinants, although these may not be immediately apparent either to the observer or to the members. A six-week support group operating in a residential facility appears to have an internal dynamic that keeps it cushioned from the outside environment or structure. A group of girls who regularly sing together seems affected only by continually changing music and venues, not by major structural issues. However, in both cases structural determinants affect membership, leader-member dynamic, timing and continuity, and the range of activities in which the members participate.

Consider membership in both groups and gangs. The dominant Canadian culture overtly discourages children from gang membership, while at the same time covertly encouraging this participation, especially by children who are marginalized through gender construction, poverty, systemic racism, inadequate schooling, violence in neighbourhoods, and the lack of recreational facilities (Wortley, 2006). Most gangs of children and youth function in lower-income neighbourhoods, although middle and upper-income neighbourhoods do have a small number of gangs. These children get together for security: the gang provides a feeling of safety, a secure base from which these children can operate. Ungar (2008: 27) describes children who join gangs in order to resolve the stress and tension of being marginalized: 'Gang behaviour is not always emblematic of a desire to be bad, but is more often a response to threats from others.'

Chatterjee (2006: 4) describes the effects of structural determinants. In his study of Canadian youth gangs he demonstrates that youth join these gangs because of socio-economic factors (poverty and unemployment), family-related difficulties, lack of school success and low attachment to school, and community violence and disorganization. The boredom that results from the lack of educational and employment opportunities, lack of recreational activities, and mainstream exclusion combines with access to weapons, alcohol, and drugs to form a violent combination These factors marginalize children and youth, who then seek a sense of belonging, safety, and power from the neighbourhood gang.

Totten (2000: 159) describes three children in a gang that becomes violent: 'Brad, Brian, and Phil spent a significant portion of their waking hours with their gangs, where activities were characterized by substance abuse, crime, violence, and boredom. . . . With few resources, they found excitement and adventure in violent crime, simultaneously finding an outlet to express their anger and rage.' These children lived in communities that discounted their needs for self-worth, power, and importance. The social, educational, spiritual, and financial resources were not in these communities now or previously when these children were much younger, experiencing abuse and neglect at home. All of the boys in Totten's study had witnessed domestic violence, and most had abusive fathers who glorified violence against others. 'The participants were robbed of their childhood, which was characterized by terror and trauma' (Totten, 2000: 195).

The past and present lack of community resources does not in any way justify the violence in youth gangs, but it does provide a context for understanding why youth turn to gangs and violence and suggests what sort of structural interventions could be developed to counter the violence. Totten (2000: 198) concludes, 'One of the primary reasons youth join gangs and engage in criminal behaviour lies in the context of poverty and ethno-racial minority segregation in which many of them live.'

Vancouver media regularly report on Indo-Canadian youth gangs. One Filipino-Canadian, Makilan, describes how these media reports, and the systemic racism and bullying in his school, drove him to join a gang that engaged in criminal activity but that gave him that sense of security he needed in a seemingly hostile and racist world. Then, a less violent political gang called UKPC/FCYA offered him the opportunity to speak out about the racism in his high school and to take anti-racist political action (Makilan, 2007). At the same time the school system opened up to him and accepted him as a student again. He remained a gang member, but this time his gang (UKPC/FCYA) was political, legal, and responsible. His gang activities became focused on socio-political change rather than crime, and his membership prompted him to return to school to complete his educational program.

When structural issues change—alternate educational facilities open, community houses develop, or part-time employment becomes available—gang membership tends to evolve into something more positive. Interventions such as Chicago's Little Village Program and Boston's Operation Ceasefire, for example, have been highly successful in decreasing gang membership. Both are structural approaches that do not focus on the elimination of gangs. Instead, both interventions follow the Irving Spiegel Comprehensive Gang Model and its strategies: community mobilization; social intervention; provision of academic, economic, and social opportunities; and organizational change and development. Gang structure is not dismantled but is used to transmit messages about viable and safe opportunities for gang members. Gangs become a source for safe and secure employment and housing opportunities, reducing the members' need to carry handguns for self-protection. In this way the structural changes obviate the felt need for violence.

Culture and Interaction

Internal integration or cohesion of a group or gang involves both cultural issues and interaction patterns. Culture affects interaction and vice versa in an interwoven pattern that may be uniform and cohesive or torn and disjointed. The worker who understands how this dynamic happens is able to work with the members to support a positive internal integration of the group or gang.

The culture of the leader plays off the culture of each member and the culture of the group or gang as a whole. The leader's culture, for example, may be authoritarian and power-centric. When the members' culture is submissive, the leader is able to take control and become more and more authoritarian. When the members' culture is also authoritarian, the members may quarrel with the leader and with one another over leadership. If the leader does not adjust his or her own authoritarian culture, the task may never be accomplished, and members may gradually drift away from the continuous cycle of arguments and power struggles.

Through these leader–member dynamics the cultures of the individual leaders and members begin to change to match the culture of the gang or group. This shift does not happen at the first meeting, but evolves over time as the child's membership becomes stronger through consistent attendance and participation. If the child decides after the first meeting not to continue membership, then the child's culture is barely touched by the culture of the group or gang. A group or gang culture refers to values, beliefs,

Photo 11.2 Wearing hoodies in the 'hood, hanging together and feeling the power.

customs, and traditions held in common by the members. At the surface, this culture is displayed in symbols and rituals such as special handshakes, opening statements or prayers, tattoos, bandanas, or check-ins. On a deeper level, this culture is displayed in the way members interact with one another either verbally or non-verbally. At the deepest level, this culture involves the norms and beliefs of the members who may share some belief in such things as religion, anti-racism, money, police corruption, or social action. It is at this deepest level that members integrate into the group or gang and develop their cohesion as a group or gang.

This culture evolves gradually from the first meeting when the members begin to articulate their rules or norms. When an authoritarian leader dictates the rules, members listen and respond either by tacitly agreeing or by questioning, arguing, or withdrawing. The evolving leader solicits membership input and supports indigenous leadership. Each member contributes to the rules or norms as the leader tries to achieve initial consensus. This process of identifying norms weaves the members together into a cohesive and confident unit. The unit develops confidence through the members, and the members develop confidence through the unit. Members gradually develop a sense of safety and predictability and a sense of acceptance and belonging. This reciprocal relationship creates internal integration or cohesion.

Interaction involves established communication patterns. Interaction may follow the maypole pattern of communication, with the leader asking or prompting each member to speak in turn. This prompt may be phrased as a challenge, 'What're you doin' here?' This prompt may be phrased as a question, 'What are your hopes for this group?' Alternatively, this prompt may be a look or a nudge. Either verbally or with body language, the leader asks each member for input, and the member replies. The leader then asks the next member the same question, and so on. The regularity of the maypole pattern is comforting and safe in an initial meeting in which the members do not know one another and do not trust the leader or the process.

 Point to Consider   11.1

What Kind of Group Do You Want?

I want to be a member, not a client, not a patient, not a kid with a problem.

I want to be me, not holding back, not pretending.

I want you to be real, too, and I want to know why you care.

I want the group to be real, not some phony, 'turn to page 3' thing.

I want to be the leader sometimes but not every time.

I want to talk about my stuff and my life, not some stuff from a book.

I want to feel connected, not just with the group, but with the whole world, too.

I want to be valued and needed by the group.

I want to have fun and laugh, and do fun stuff, not just talk all the time.

Sometimes members take turns talking in a **round robin** pattern, and the leader steps back from the questioner role. The leader actively observes as each member makes a statement or introduction and each speaks in turn. This again has a comforting regularity; however, for those who dread speaking in front of others, this can be intimidating unless they are given the option of passing or skipping a turn. Sometimes a visual cue such as a talking stone or feather is passed around to signal each member's opportunity to talk while other members listen.

The round robin pattern can be used to end meetings, also. In traditional treatment groups the members may sit or stand in a circle, holding a length of ribbon or rope. Each member mentions one positive thought about the group meeting. When all of the meetings of the treatment group finally end, the ribbon is cut, and a piece given to each member.

Sometimes a member is more animated or defensive or aggressive than others. This member may block any action suggested by the leader, asking endless questions, or

Note From the Field   11.1

Fitting In with the Group

Chantal, a 12-year-old girl, is referred to your social skills group by the court after her second charge of shoplifting. She arrives late for the pre-group interview and appears to be very unwilling to talk. Her denim jacket smells strongly of smoke. In the ensuing half hour you create a genogram together and she describes her position as the eldest daughter in a blended family. Her father's partner has three younger children, aged six, four, and 18 months, whom Chantal occasionally babysits in the evening. Although she is not paid to babysit, she says she enjoys her younger step-sisters and thinks they are 'cute'. She especially loves the baby and expresses the wish to some day have a baby of her own. Chantal denies the shoplifting charge and says that the clerks were hassling her, and that she only wanted to show the clothes to her friends. It appears that Chantal has very few friends because most of her evenings and week-ends are spent either babysitting or helping out at home. She says that her step-mom sometimes gets on her case about chores, and that her parents are 'really mad' about the shoplifting. Chantal says she doesn't really have time to go to the group but will join 'if she really has to'. How would you assess this group's suitability for Chantal?

telling unrelated personal stories that stop the action. This member may joke about the task or action or about other members, scoffing and making snide remarks that stop the gang or group from developing cohesion. The leader may engage this member in one-to-one dialogue called the **hot-seat** pattern of communication. Other members observe the tone and mood of this intensive interchange, and may learn to keep quiet and withhold their own opinions, or to challenge one another. Soon the members start to hot-seat one another.

Beyond maypole, round robin, and hot-seat modes of group interaction, is a democratic communication pattern called **floating communication** in which members are free to contribute at any time. They learn to take turns, to listen empathically, to advise their peers, to share their stories and opinions, and to deal with other members' anger, lateness, silence, or sadness. This interaction encourages members to take responsibility for one another and for the whole unit; for example, challenging members who interrupt, tease, intimidate, or laugh at others.

The culture of the whole group or gang affects the contribution of each member and the pattern of interaction. In the dynamic of communication the child or youth tests certain words and certain ideas; in a sense, this is a skill-practising session. This is a chance to re-phrase, to explain, maybe to back off and to express other thoughts. The member develops these social skills and communication skills within the safety of the gang or group until the skills are razor-sharp and ready for the street.

Effectiveness

In groups and gangs, children and youth play and work with a common focus, problem-solve and collect ideas from others, and discuss and argue. The learning opportunities are immense and multi-faceted. Sugata Mitra noted this when he began his hole-in-the-wall experiments in New Delhi in 1999. His research team embedded a computer (PC) in a wall in front of a public lot used as a toilet by local street children. The team also installed a camera to record the interaction between computer and passers-by. Over a six-month period the camera captured peer learning and social interaction as the children learned computer skills, taught one another English, argued about software programs, and acquired functional numeracy and literacy skills through play. Over 300 children interacted with the computer, and typically this interaction was in groups of three to 20 children aged six to 12 years old.

The researchers evaluated the effectiveness of this group learning and replicated the hole-in-the-wall experiment in other Indian cities. Their evaluation results prompted the experiments to be replicated elsewhere, in Asia and in South America. The street children and youth there learned more skills in groups than would ever be possible in the far more expensive traditional school setting. 'They were driven purely by their own interests. Conventional pedagogy, on the other hand, focuses on the teacher's ability to disseminate information in a classroom setting' (Mitra, 2009).

It seems that the absence of adults and the resulting reliance on peers was a key ingredient in the effectiveness of these groups. Sometimes the six-year-olds gave directions, and sometimes an older child did. The leader (director) was the one with skills, not necessarily the eldest. None of the children spoke English at the outset, and most spoke some rudimentary English words by the end of the six months. The children learned a new language and skill set, and developed problem-solving and group skills out of necessity; they had to work together in order to play on the computer.

Children also have to work together in peer support groups in which shared experiences and stories of survival can be empowering for a child who feels isolated and alone in a personal narrative. The members have solutions, each one different and each one unique to that child. Each child can provide an example of resiliency, as well as potential stability and social support for other group members. A child who hears another child talk about a treatment centre or a foster home as being a positive place, for example, is more likely to be open to going there. Victims of sexual abuse, victims of war, children of divorced parents, children whose parents are incarcerated, and children with addictions: these members know the value of support from their group.

Despite this evidence for the effectiveness of peer learning and peer support, most groups for children continue to be adult-led. Children may be assigned to do small group work without an adult, but their small group reports are written or spoken in front of the large group and the adult leader. Similarly, provincial, territorial, and national youth groups bring their reports and their discussion papers forward to adults who then decide on continued funding and support for these groups. This is to be

Photo 11.3 Trust is a balancing act for children who walk the line.

expected in our socio-political structure. Children do have much to learn from adults, and adult leadership is helpful when children are learning a skill (skiing, karate, woodworking), developing socio-emotionally (social skills groups, co-operative playgroups), or recovering from traumatic life events (bereavement groups).

Children do choose to be in groups: Girl Guides, choirs, hockey teams. Children also are placed in groups: social skills groups, anger-management groups, sexual abuse victims' groups. Sometimes this placement is a response to the child's expression of anger, anxiety, or fear; and sometimes this placement is a response to a caregiver's observation of the child's behaviour. Sometimes, also, this placement is a response to limited worker resources: one worker can treat 10 children in an hour-long group, rather than meeting with each child individually for an hour during the week. Because placement in groups is both voluntary and involuntary, the effectiveness of groups is difficult to measure. Paula Allen-Meares (2004: 525) cautions: 'Although open-ended supportive or interpersonally focussed groups appear to be widely used treatment modalities for adolescents, we found no research investigating their efficacy, either in reducing symptoms or in improving overall functioning.'

The measurement of the effectiveness of groups tends to be qualitative rather than quantitative, and baselines rarely are taken prior to group membership. An evaluation form at the end of the group experience is more typical, with evaluation results affecting the next group (perhaps) rather than the current one. There is little evidence of a feedback loop or circular causality with feedback affecting group leadership, which then affects participation and feedback, and so on. This lack of ongoing evaluation and adjustment in response to evaluation supports the previous cautionary note from Allen-Meares.

Children are not placed in gangs; they choose gangs, although sometimes this choice may be coerced or influenced by peers. This element of choice changes the child's participation to 'voluntary', and makes the length and the quality of membership the child's prerogative until, of course, adult or peer sanctions may end or change gang membership. It is this element of choice that differentiates gang membership from group membership. This choice may be based on factors such as the child's situation or the gang activities. Both may preclude the child's participation in groups, and may actually prompt the child's participation in gangs.

The child's situation may make joining and belonging to a group difficult. The child may be anxious, depressed, withdrawn, or shy and may not want to join a group of children in which there is social interaction, role play, and close contact with other children. The child may be developmentally delayed and may fear the ridicule of other members of the group. The child may have a syndrome or disorder (Asperger's syndrome, autistic spectrum disorder) that makes communication with other children and following directions in a group problematic. The child may have behaviours that frighten or threaten other children. The child may have different norms and values from those of the group and may find the group threatens these personal norms and values. Alternatively, the child may not have the transportation and time to get to the group and may not have the financial resources to buy the equipment to join the group.

Point to Consider   11.2

Forum Theatre

As a co-leader and as an observer of mutual aid groups for over a decade, I have often witnessed children's unease and discomfort and frequent misery at being asked to act out their emotions. Regardless of the skill and enthusiasm of the group leader, not all children feel comfortable in a performance role and not all children benefit from public performance. The additional stress of role-playing in front of peers can compound a child's problems, and cause the child to withdraw further or become hostile and aggressive. In the gang situation role-play also is demanded, albeit in a less structured and more spontaneous way. The shy child may try to engage and act out situations but the role play may prove too stressful and the shy child may find recourse in side-lining, encouraging other members to take the lead parts.

An exception to the discomfort of role play is forum theatre, developed by Augusto Boal and used with children in many countries. Forum theatre involves both players and audience in finding solutions to local structural oppression. There are three set roles in forum theatre: oppressor, oppressed, and joker. The first two children act out the local problem—one child playing the oppressor and the other child playing the oppressed. The third child, the joker, describes what is happening. The joker asks the audience for ideas, new dialogue, new actions. Everyone (audience and players) is part of the play and everyone is responsible for finding a solution to the oppression. Boal shows how effective this is in positioning problems within the structure and in collectivizing both problems and solutions. Workers who take the structural approach use forum theatre to build the group dynamic and to help children and youth to identify structural determinants relevant to them (Spratt, 2005).

In any of the above situations, forced or coerced group membership may prove to be a negative experience; in deShazer's (1984) terminology, these children are visitors. They do not want to be there (in the group). The child assigned to the group may struggle to function in the group and may repeatedly fail, an experience that compounds the child's difficulties and makes the child feel more inadequate and socially inept. 'Groups are contraindicated for people whose behaviour is so alien to others that it results in negative rather than positive interactions or when it leads to the failure of others to continue with the group' (Dufour and Chamberland, 2003: 7). Some would argue that children with 'alien' behaviours who tend to have such personal attributes as social alienation, low intelligence, and poor communication skills are in gangs, and that is where these children belong. However, no research supports this argument. While gang members may not communicate effectively with authority figures, they appear to communicate well with one another through a variety of traditional and non-traditional means.

A child's choice to join a gang also is affected by the activities of the gang. These activities tend to be play-based and risky, and children tend to seek and enjoy both play and risks; in fact, the risks in the activities may be an attraction rather than a deterrent. Children living in poverty who do not have access to exciting adventures such as rock climbing, scuba diving, surfing, and fast cars may find excitement and stimulation in risky adventures within the safe confines of a neighbourhood gang. Converting these children to groups is difficult because 'very few programs offer healthy substitutes for unhealthy expressions of sensation seeking' (Zuckerman, 2007: 235).

While adults tend to discourage and punish gang membership, they also subsidize and sanction memberships in mainstream groups such as Girl Guides, choirs, and organized athletics, provided these groups are approved and led by adults. This dichotomy in support is evidenced in the legislative, organizational, and financial controls of groups and gangs. Municipal legislation in many Canadian cities imposes curfews and sanctions on gangs. Provincial child welfare funding supports remedial groups for children in care, and restricts all-children groups from meeting without adult supervision. When children choose a group they change from visitors to (voluntary) customers. Similarly, when they choose to convert illegal and lethal activities to legal and exciting but less risky ones their gang activity can be an equally positive and competency-building experience. The effectiveness of either group or gang experience is determined by the power of choice the child has in joining, participating, leading, and affiliating, and it is this same power that prompts a child to develop skills and competency within the gang or group.

Summary

In this chapter we explored the similarities between groups and gangs: how they are formed, their styles of leadership, communication, and group dynamics. We also saw the differences and the dangers offered by the third gang model. This understanding will help you to design and develop groups that appeal to children while supporting their strengths and encouraging indigenous leadership. Recognizing strengths has been an ongoing theme, and both gangs and groups offer children an opportunity to support the strengths of other children and to have their own strengths validated, too.

Review Questions

1. What is the first natural group to which a child belongs? Explain why this is a 'group' rather than a 'gang'.

2. How has the word 'gang' evolved? What factors have helped to create the negative connotations of this word?
3. List the five gang models, correlating each model with a type of group.
4. Compare and contrast treatment groups, task groups, and mutual aid groups.
5. What factors make gang membership empowering? Can these same factors be applied to group membership? Why or why not?
6. Compare group leaders and gang leaders according to their rewards, coercion, legitimacy, reference, and expertise.
7. What is dynamic equilibrium and how is it achieved?
8. State the four styles of communication in a group or gang and how each one evolves as members begin to feel empowered.
9. Which style of leadership is most empowering for the members? Why?
10. What factors could influence a gang member to join a group instead?

Discussion Questions

1. Have you ever belonged to a gang or known someone who has belonged to a gang? If so, how does this experience compare with the information presented in this chapter? What information about gangs do you feel is missing?
2. Imagine that your task is to facilitate a group for 10-year-olds boys who have been excluded from the classroom because of their aggressive behaviour. What kind of group would you choose? How would you design this group, and how would you encourage the boys to become customers rather than visitors in this group?
3. One of the groups described in this chapter is forum theatre. Why do you think this kind of group works so well with children? Suggest other kinds of groups that you have found children voluntarily join and enjoy.

Afterword

Setting Structural and Strengths-Based Targets

I shot an arrow into the air,
It fell to earth, I knew not where.

—Henry Wadsworth Longfellow

Interventions with children are often random shots in the air, and where they land is anyone's guess. We try one intervention and, when it does not work, we try another. We review a child's file with its history of failed interventions, and sadly note that the original behavioural difficulty is much worse now, and that the child is even more troubled and unhappy.

Interventions often are ineffective, although the case file or the agency mythology may suggest the opposite. The child goes back to class; the letter of apology is written; the child promises not to drink. Two weeks later, the behaviour recurs. Another intervention is tried, sometimes at the same agency and sometimes at another one. The first intervention is reapplied over and over again with a continuing lack of success. The worker is now invested in the intervention and believes it to be right; the child is simply being 'unco-operative'. The child may be described as being 'damaged' or having a 'mental health issue', umbrella phrases that hold off the rain.

When we look at a child's case file, why do we see these years of repeated interventions and a spiral of escalating behaviours? The answer to this question lies in a systemic lack of ongoing qualitative and quantitative evaluation of intervention effectiveness. Science is replaced by ideology. Interventions are used because we believe in them, whether or not they have been proven to be effective. This lack of intervention evaluation in Canadian child welfare agencies is described by Sarah Dufour and Claire Chamberland (2003). They cite many examples of interventions that continue to be applied because they are 'what the agency does' or because 'everyone knows they work'. The agency may specialize in specific interventions such as residential treatment for addictions. A child being served by that agency is sent to residential treatment, whether or not this intervention is appropriate or what the child would choose. Without the child's commitment to the treatment, this intervention is likely to fail.

Furthermore, the intervention offered by the agency may no longer be relevant. It is offered simply because that funding silo, that executive director, or that board of directors believes in its efficacy. One example is the CAPC-funded drop-in programs for lone mothers in Ontario. Since Ontario Works was approved in April 1996, most lone mothers on social assistance have either enrolled in school or training programs or have started paid work outside the home, so they are unlikely to participate in day-time drop-in programs. Despite this low attendance, agencies lobby for continued funding for drop-ins for lone mothers, and the funding and the drop-ins are still in operation.

The outcome measurement of effectiveness may be largely anecdotal and come from random children who praise the staff and claim to be 'saved'. These children are the success stories who are routinely selected as guest speakers at award dinners and annual general meetings. They are the bursary winners, the college graduates, the ones who 'made it'. Those who are critical of the agency or of their workers; those who are homeless and addicted; and those who are 'unco-operative' and are not 'saved' by the interventions are never the keynote speakers and they never get the rose bouquets. They are the 'failures' or 'kids with issues'.

But whose failure? Is the child a failure, or are we the failures for using the same, tired interventions that fail to meet the needs of children? Learning about interventions is learning about self. The questions we ask and the questions we are asked begin to balance out. In each child we meet our own limitations of service and of self. In each one of our child-specific interventions, we learn about the effectiveness of that intervention for that child at that time and we learn to question the intervention itself. The next time we use that intervention with a different child, we learn more. Carl Rogers (1980: 66), who never ascribed to the universal wisdom claimed by many workers, comments, 'I have confidence in the young, from whom I have continuously learned.'

Lifelong learning includes training and experience. Training is valuable and we need it to work effectively. Yet, to identify only with know-how is to turn the child-worker relationship into one of control. We say—and the child does. We teach—and the child is taught. We order—and the family complies. This power imbalance is contingent on a social construction in which the child is a dependent and helpless person, unable to change without adult intervention. Training sometimes leads us to see children and youth in categories, as subjects for intervention, as labelled case files: 'deadbeat dads'; 'abuse victims'; and 'exceptional children'. Analysis of behaviour is important, but it is equally important to see and develop a relationship with the whole person.

The structural and strengths-based approach challenges this traditional biomedical and deficit approach by providing defined structural targets and clear concepts of what achievement means in altering systems for the child: those concentric micro, meso, and macrosystems. Such a shift may feel new and strange. However, it is clear that the traditional methods of assessing and intervening do not meet the needs of children today. In *Bowling Alone* David Putnam (2000) laments the current tendency towards isolation and away from community because this tendency discounts the strength of structural intervention: 'Where civic engagement in community affairs in general is high, teachers report higher levels of parental support and lower levels of student misbehaviour, such as bringing weapons to school, engaging in physical violence, playing hooky, and being generally apathetic about education' (p. 301). Fix the structure first and the child is empowered to become positively involved in community and in life.

Children teach us to pause and observe play, watching each episode closely to uncover hidden meanings within the play. They teach us to listen affirmatively and in the here and now and to unravel the subtexts of behaviour. In solitary play or in play within groups or gangs children reveal their strengths and their understandings of their personhood. By refocusing on the child as person, and by taking the structural and strengths-based approach we can change that weary and ultimately costly habit of shooting arrows into the sky. We can hear the lessons, shoot straight, and finally find the target.

Glossary

Absolute poverty A condition characterized by severe deprivation of basic human needs; also referred to as dire or severe poverty.

Action The stage of change during which the person actually participates in the change process and learns change skills through this participation.

Affidavit A legal and sworn document attesting to facts of relevance to a court case.

Affirmation The validation of the importance and worth of the child's feelings, condition, or personhood.

Apprehension The removal of a child from the family for reasons of a perceived risk of physical, sexual, and/or emotional abuse or neglect.

At risk A situation in which the cumulative risk factors in the child's life do not outweigh the child's protective factors.

Attachment A strong, lifelong commitment that develops, usually from infancy, between a person and that person's significant caregiver or community of caregivers.

Attachment injuries Socio-emotional and spiritual wounds caused by the sudden and inexplicable loss of the attachment figure or by abuse or neglect being perpetrated on the child by this same attachment figure.

Attunement An internal working model of a positive relationship between two persons in which each responds to the other's inner emotional messages. When applied to the caregiver–baby dyad, this is described as the caregiver following the baby's cues.

Authoritarian parenting A parenting style that uses punitive, forceful methods to ensure children obey parental commands and comply with parental wishes.

Authoritative parenting A parenting style that provides nurturance and structure for children while still respecting their input and negotiation.

Autobiographical reasoning A lifelong reflective process in which a person tries to make sense of both past and current events as they fit into that person's dominant narrative.

Behavioural contracting Verbal or written agreement on the rewards contingent to behaving in certain ways.

Bisexual A person whose sexual orientation is towards both males and females.

Blamestorming Reciprocal and self-sustaining process of assigning blame that continues without resolution.

Bonding A process in which a socio-emotional or affective bond develops between the infant and the primary caregiver.

Case note A simple, honest, accurate, and objective recording of an event.

Categorization of persons The division of persons into discrete categories or subsets in order to manage or control these persons effectively.

Cephalocaudal Neurological development that proceeds downward from the head.

Chemical restraints Psychotropic medication that is administered in order to restrain, modify, or curb behaviour.

Child custody The guardianship of a child and the authority to make decisions about the child's daily care.

Child support Privately arranged or court-ordered financial support for the child that is paid by the non-custodial parent.

Classical conditioning Behavioural learning that associates a neutral stimulus with a significant stimulus for behaviour; for example, keys may be associated with the fun of a drive so that when a child hears keys rattle, the child may smile in anticipation.

Circular causality An ongoing series of actions and reactions, one affecting the next.

Coercive power The control over others by influencing them to do things against their preferences.

Cognitive development The gradual change or evolution of the organizing and thinking systems of the brain.

Cognitive behavioural theory A theory that behaviour is prompted by cognition or thinking.

Collaborative practice A respectful sharing of viewpoints among persons of any age rather than a struggle to control and dominate. Collaborative practice reflects a belief in ongoing, shared learning and in power-sharing.

Community capacity-building A process of building on individual and community assets that begins *inside* the community and continues due to the will of the community.

Conduct disorder A behaviour labelled as a syndrome and characterized by persistent, repetitive anti-social activities that violate the rights of others. Symptoms of this disorder include physical or verbal aggression directed towards others, repeated violation of age-appropriate social rules and norms, stealing, and lying.

Congruence A quality of being direct and honest in sharing information, provided this information does not harm the client.

Conscientization Reflection on and understanding of collective oppression through learning about structural impacts.

Contact comfort The socio-emotional reassurance produced by close physical contact with a trusted person.

Contemplation The stage of change during which the person considers the possibility of change, its advantages and disadvantages.

Contextualizing The process of placing an individual's narrative within the ecological environment that impacts the narrative.

Control Power from without; authority or influence.

Co-relational Interconnected or allied in an equal relationship in which one entity affects the other.

Countertransference An interactive process in which the child's narrative stimulates the worker's unconscious thoughts, emotions, and memories, and the worker responds by projecting these thoughts, emotions, and memories onto the child's narrative.

Critical learning periods Specific times in the life cycle at which a person most readily absorbs crucial information or skills needed to transition from one stage to the next. Before or after the critical learning period, the same learning is more difficult and sometimes impossible.

Cultural competency One's understanding of personal culture and of its inherent bias in relating to the culture of others.

Customer deShazer's term for a person who comes voluntarily and willingly to participate in counselling.

Deculturation A systematic devaluing and stripping away of the cultural identity of others.

Dependency The degree to which we rely on others to meet our physical, social, spiritual, and emotional needs.

Determinants of health Structural and personal factors that have a major impact on health or wellness.

Development Sequential change or unfolding that is brought about by increasing age and accumulating life experiences. Development can be stopped or slowed down in response to both genetic and environmental factors.

Developmentalists Those who advocate that development occurs in a linear progression through set stages.

Developmentally appropriate practice The provision of structural supports that meet both the individual and developmental needs of the child. This practice is based on close observation of a child or youth's interests, social location, culture, and overall development.

Developmental perspective A theory that children evolve or develop in a natural, orderly progression through cognitive, physical, and socio-emotional stages, and that particular milestones must be reached before the child can move on to the next stage.

Developmental tasks Specific tasks that must be completed during a critical learning period.

Distal Descriptor for a risk factor that is a potentiating influence rather than an immediate and close risk.

Domains Interrelated areas of human development: physical, cognitive, spiritual, and socio-emotional.

Dominant family narrative A family's narrative that permeates and overshadows the individual narratives of each member of the family.

DSM-IV The fourth edition of the Diagnostic and Statistical Manual of Mental Disorders of the American Psychiatric Association, the standard psychiatric diagnostic text in use in Canada and the United States.

Emotionally focused therapy (EFT) A therapeutic approach rooted in attachment theory that focuses on intrapsychic and interpersonal processes.

Empathy The ability to understand the feelings and thoughts of another person and to communicate this understanding to that person. Empathy, which implies sharing, can be contrasted with sympathy or pity, which is part of the power construct of helper–helped. 'Pity' implies that the person being pitied has little to teach and much to learn.

Empowerment The process in which a person gains self-assurance through successfully overcoming obstacles or solving problems. Empowerment is experienced and cannot be imposed on or given to an individual.

Eurocentric A perspective of privilege reflecting the belief that the cluture of the so-called developed world is superior to that of the so-called third world.

Express consent Oral or written expression of consent. Express consent from a child is valid if the child has the mental capacity to understand consent, is fully informed, and freely gives such consent.

Externalizing Describing a problem by identifying both its role and its antecedents in order to place the problem outside of or external to the person.

Family systems theory A theory premised on a concept of the family as a mutually supportive unit rather than as a mere collection of individual members. The members act to keep the unit intact and healthy rather than solely to pursue individual goals.

Floating communication A pattern of group or gang communication in which members dialogue with one another rather than through or to the leader.

Fontanel The space between the bones in the skull of a newborn that allows the newborn's head to be compressed during its passage through the birth canal without this compression causing injury to the brain.

Foster care Temporary, short-term placement for a child whose safety is at risk in the home.

Foster care drift The placement practice of moving the child among different foster homes over a period of several years without considering either permanency planning or an ultimate destination for the child.

Gender construction The learning process by which children assume the cultural norms, expectations, and behaviours that have been socially constructed for males and females.

Gender roles Arbitrary rules assigned by society that define what clothing, behaviour, feelings, and relationships are considered appropriate and inappropriate for members of each sex.

Gender stereotype A biased and oversimplified conception of maleness or femaleness.

Genogram A pictorial case note of family relationships that is simple to read and that evolves as the family relationships change.

Group or gang Three or more persons interacting with a particular focus.

Group work Goal-directed activity by individual members in a group and by the group as a whole. Group work may be centred on a task, personal growth, mutual aid, or treatment.

Growth-faltering The non-organic failure of an infant to thrive.

Heterosexism An ideology that considers heterosexuality as natural and any other forms of sexuality as unnatural.

Heterosexual orientation An erotic attraction to and preference for developing a sexual relationship with members of the opposite sex. Heterosexual children may be called 'straight'.

Homeostasis A state of stability or equilibrium. Persons tend to seek or crave homeostasis.

Homophobia The irrational fear, hatred, and intolerance of gay men and lesbian women that is based on myths and stereotypes.

Homosexual orientation An erotic attraction to and preference for developing sexual relationships with members of one's own sex. Homosexual boys may be called 'gay' or 'queer'; and homosexual girls may be called 'lesbians' or 'dykes'.

Hot-seat A pattern of group or gang communication in which the leader engages only one member in dialogue.

Implied consent A form of consent that the child signals to a worker simply by coming to the worker (school guidance counsellor, club counsellor) with a problem or by staying with the counsellor until help arrives.

Imprinting A pattern of spontaneous attachment to a figure who supplies nutritional needs.

In loco parentis A Latin phrase meaning 'in the place of the parent', which refers to an individual's or a state organization's acceptance of the legal and functional responsibility of a parent.

Intersex A person who is born both male and female; historically, a hermaphrodite.

Intimacy Contact comfort or feelings of closeness and connection with another person.

Low-income cut-off (LICO) The after-tax income threshold below which a family will likely devote a larger share of family income to necessities than the average family would.

Lone-parent family A household comprised of one parent living with her or his never-married children.

Macrosystem The overarching socio-political and cultural context that affects every aspect of a child's life.

Maintenance The stage of change in which the child consolidates the change into the daily routine, becoming more comfortable with this change on a daily basis.

Marginalized The situation of persons who have been excluded from mainstream society through bias and discrimination.

Market basket A fixed list of consumable items or a commodity bundle that is used to measure the rate of poverty in a society.

Maternal deprivation theory The theory that a healthy relationship with a mother is crucial to a child's healthy development. This theory was critiqued by Michael Rutter and others, and later disproved by research on healthy children raised only by fathers.

Mature minor A child who is chronologically under the age of majority but who demonstrates the competence and maturity of that age.

Maypole communication A pattern of group or gang communication in which members communicate only with the leader and not with one another. The leader becomes the pivot (maypole) around which communication revolves.

Mesosystem The interrelationships among systems that affect a person; for example, a meso-system may include home, daycare, and school.

Metaphor A comparison of two like things; an object or symbol that is used to represent a problem or difficulty.

Microsystem The part of the social system that constitutes the immediate daily environment of a person.

Milestone A marker of a critical learning achievement in the child's development.

Monocultural bias Ethnocentrism, or the tendency to judge or value all cultures from the perspective of one's own culture, which is tacitly assumed to be superior.

National Longitudinal Survey of Children and Youth (NLSCY) Launched in 1994, the NLSCY is the first truly national assessment of the wellness of Canadian children. It tracks how well children are meeting their milestones of development. The survey also shows which structural determinants most influence this development.

Object relations Relationships with the important people in our lives, and the continuing impact of these relationships on our lives.

Object relations theory A theory based on the premise that relationships are built on expectations formed by earlier relationships.

Open-ended questions Questions with no definitive answer, which allow the respondent to give detailed answers. Open-ended questions can begin with such words as 'why', 'how', 'explain', and 'describe'.

Paraphrasing Rewording the speaker's words so that both the speaker and the listener have the same understanding of the meaning of those words.

Parentified A parentified child is one who takes on the duties and tasks normally expected of a parent, such as daily housework and childcare.

Persistent poverty Chronic poverty that is both long-lasting and severe.

Pervasive developmental disorder (PDD) refers to the autistic spectrum of childhood disorders.

Physical discipline A contradictory term; 'discipline' means 'teaching or guiding', and should not include physical force.

Physical punishment Includes the entire range of painful and injurious acts inflicted by the powerful upon the powerless.

Play Activity that is usually pleasant and voluntary.

Play episodes Specific, time-limited units of play that have a beginning and an end.

Play therapy An approach to working with children through their play towards their self-realization.

Power Authority or influence that may be assertive, strong, or forceful.

Praxis Practice based upon reflection; reflection being a process of dialogue, analysis, and consciousness-raising. Praxis challenges assumptions and traditional mores, and is a pause to consider non-traditional approaches to practice.

Pre-contemplation The first stage of change, said to occur when the child is not even thinking about change and has no intention of changing in the foreseeable future.

Preparation The stage at which the child begins to plan actual change.

Presenting problem The overt and expressed problem that is the focus for the child, or for the child and the family. The presenting problem is rarely the primary problem.

Protective factors Positive influences that are obvious only when measured against risk factors, or factors that have the potential to harm a person.

Promotive factors The developmental assets that promote the healthy development of the child.

Proximal Descriptor of a risk factor that is immediate or precipitating.

Proximo-distal Physical growth and development that proceeds from the trunk outwards.

Psychoanalytic theory A theory based on the premise that intrapsychic processes—repressed memories, dreams, and the unconscious—determine the behaviour of the individual.

Re-authoring The development of an alternative and more hopeful personal narrative based on a new understanding of past events.

Relative poverty Poverty measured relative to the wealth of the society around it.

Resiliency The positive adaptation to adverse circumstances by an individual, or the ability to rebound when faced with severe hardships or obstacles.

Respect Complete acceptance or unconditional positive regard for the child as a unique person.

Risk assessment Systematic classification or measurement of risk in order to predict outcomes.

Risk factor An element considered to be a predictor or signal of an undesired outcome.

Risk management An attempt to manage and minimize risk by balancing or weighing risk factors against protective factors.

Rogerian model Client-centred social work practice based on mutual respect and shared power and control.

Role model A person whose behaviour is patterned by another person.

Round robin The pattern of group or gang communication in which each member speaks in turn when prompted by the leader.

Routine Regularity and rhythm in activities and tasks.

Self-concept The learned and conscious sense of being separate and distinct because of one's intrinsic qualities, relationships, and culture.

Self-control Power from within, or a feeling of self-confidence and competence that is evidenced in outward emotional control.

Self-injurious behaviour The deliberate destruction of body tissue without suicidal intent.

Sexual orientation The erotic attraction towards, and interest in developing a sexual relationship with, members of one's own or the opposite sex or both.

Silo approach A person-centred or agency-centred approach to solving social problems. The contrasting approach (interdisciplinary) involves collective problem-solving through the sharing of information, opinions, and expertise.

Social construction A socio-political act that attributes social meaning to information, persons, or events through culturally shared assumptions; a view that may be expressed as 'context is everything'.

Social learning Observational learning that takes place in a social context. Learning happens through observation rather than through direct instruction or classical conditioning.

Social location A person's position of relative power that includes that person's race, class, socioeconomic status, sexuality, gender, and ethnicity.

Social referencing The child's action of looking first to the caregiver to read social clues regarding a new event or a new person in the room.

Social structure The macrosystem that affects the individual and that includes the political, legal, economic, health, social, and educational systems as well as the culture, mores, and traditions of the larger society in which the individual lives.

Stereotype An association of a word or image with an activity, emotion, group, or class of persons. This association is an over-simplification because no one word or image can capture individual differences.

Strengths-based approach An approach to working with people that focuses on their assets and strengths rather than deficits. This approach is fundamental to the empowerment model.

Structural approach An approach to working with people that focuses on how societal structures, such as legal, educational, or political systems, influence and determine people's lives.

Social structure A constellation of interrelated social elements that affects a child's achievement of his or her potential.

Synapses Multiple connections between individual nerve cells in the human brain.

Synchrony Natural and ongoing attunement that develops over time between two persons, enabling one person to instantaneously sense the unspoken needs of the other. Synchrony is marked by the split-second timing of responsiveness between the two persons.

Termination The stage of change when the change is so much a part of the child's routine that it is no longer perceived as change.

Transitory poverty Short-term or short-lived poverty that is not expected to last.

Transtheoretical Integrating or encompassing many theories into one.

Two-spirited English word used by First Nations and other Canadians to refer to those who are gay, lesbian, intersex, transgendered, transexual, or who have multiple gender identities.

Upstream approach A version of the structural approach that regards 'upstream' structural determinants as toxins or pollutants that must be changed first so that the 'downstream' area, or microsystem, will be healthier.

Visitor deShazer's term for a person who does not participate in counselling voluntarily.

Notes

CHAPTER 1

1. The legal age at which children can be employed varies across Canada and is affected by the existing provincial and territorial legislation that requires attendance in school. In Ontario and New Brunswick, for example, the minimum age at which children can legally be employed is 14; in Alberta, the minimum age is 12. In some cases, parental consent is required, and in others it is not. Over the years, there have been injuries and deaths of child workers in Quebec, some of whom were as young as 8 years old (Arsenault, 2008). Although the employment age is variable across Canada, social assistance typically is available only to children aged 16 years and over. Under that age, children have access only to child welfare services.

2. 'Criminals-in-waiting' refers to the situation in youth detention centres where a preponderance of the children come from families living in poverty. Heather O'Neill's *Lullabies for Little Criminals* (2006) graphically describes the street poverty and homelessness that can lead to crime and, possibly, incarceration.

3. The Fraser Institute is an independent international research and educational organization that reports on economic issues. The Fraser Institute often is described as a right-wing think-tank, and its forecasts and reports tend to be used by Conservative politicians and economists to support their recommendations and policies.

4. OECD is an acronym for the Organization for Economic Co-operation and Development. In 2008, the organization consisted of 30 market economies. The OECD regularly compares these countries and publishes reports on these comparisons.

5. Gross domestic product (GDP) refers to the total market value of all goods and services produced within a country within a fixed time period, usually a calendar year.

6. This film is part of a package of educational resources available at low or no cost from the Children's Hospital of Eastern Ontario, Ottawa. Some of the resources from the package are available on their website.

7. Smith (1998) describes the 'third trick' that workers play on clients as reflecting back to these clients the information in their file so that the clients perceive the worker's echo to be their reality. Clients who hear the word 'bipolar' repeated and read to them from their files, for example, come to identify themselves predominantly as bipolar.

8. For the sake of brevity, the Convention on the Rights of the Child is referred to simply as the Convention.

CHAPTER 2

1. The Famous Five are five Canadian women (all from Alberta) who advocated in support of the *Persons* case of 1927: Emily Murphy, Irene Marryat Parlby, Nellie Mooney McClung, Louise Crummy McKinney, and Henrietta Muir Edwards. The Supreme Court of Canada upheld the ruling, supported by the British North America Act, that women were not persons and, therefore, could not sit in the Canadian Senate. With the help of Canadian Prime Minister Mackenzie King, the Famous Five appealed the Supreme Court of Canada's decision to the Judicial Committee of the Privy Council in England, at the time the highest court of appeal for Canada. They won in 1929, and in 1930 the first Canadian female senator took her place in the Canadian Senate.

2. Bjorklund (2007: 172–6) describes systems such as *BabyPlus* and *The Classwomb* that aim to educate the fetus, as well as instruments such as the 'pregaphone', a device that

purports to enable a mother to talk to her fetus. Even without such devices, the fetus can hear from about the fourth prenatal month and as a result distinguishes the sound of the mother's voice from others, at birth.

3. National youth groups often call for fewer restrictions rather than more. The controversy over the age of consent to sexual activity illustrates this conflict between the perspectives of adults and youth regarding the rights of the young. For a complete list of debates, visit the websites of the Commission des droits de la personne et des droits de la jeunesse du Québec (www.cdpdj.qc.ca/en/home. asp) and the Canadian Council of Provincial Child and Youth Advocates (provincialadvo-cate.on.ca/main/en/ccpcya).

CHAPTER 3

1. Although boys engage in aggressive play more than girls, the incidents of physical aggression by girls against other girls or against family members is increasing. This is described by Artz (1998).

2. Groups such as Pink Triangle Services estimate that 10 per cent of Canadians are homosexual, and their advocacy, funding requests, and educational programs are based on this statistic. In the National Film Board film *Out*, cited in this section, the 10 per cent statistic is also referenced.

CHAPTER 4

1. In this chapter, the caregiver is assumed to be female, even though many caregivers, parents, and guardians of children are male. This sex-specific attribution is made because the references are largely to infants and, in infancy, caregivers are predominately female.

2. The word 'purchase' may seem offensive to some who adopt. These adults tend to position adoption as caring and in the best interests of the child. However, there can be no doubt that money is involved, most of it going to agencies, and some occasionally taking the form of a stipend to the birth family willing to part with their child. This purchase of children and its ramifications for children and their birth families are described online by adoptee groups such as Transracial Abductees (www.transracialabductees.org) and Bastard Nation (www.bastards.org). The members of these adoptee groups describe their losses as children when they were taken from their homelands and brought to Canada to be raised by Canadian adults.

3. In 2002, in his acceptance speech for the Booker Prize, Martel referred to Canada as the best hotel in the world. This was captured on all the national television networks and was typically accompanied by comments on Martel's early childhood spent in Alaska, British Columbia, Costa Rica, France, Ontario, and Mexico. Brian Bethune (*Maclean's*, 6 Sept. 2006) comments on this description of Canada as a hotel in his article, 'Noah Richler: In Search of Nowhere'.

CHAPTER 5

1. Katherine Kelly and Mark Totten (2002) illustrate how unique a child's reaction to family culture can be in *When Children Kill: A Social-Psychological Study of Youth Homicide*. One child in a family commits murder, while the child's siblings are gentle and law-abiding citizens. On the other hand, a family culture of violence does not necessarily mean that the child in that family will become a killer.

2. 'Minor' and 'major' are terms that relate to the legal age of majority, or of adult responsibility. The age of majority is 18 in the provinces of Ontario, Quebec, Manitoba, Saskatchewan, Alberta, and Prince Edward Island. In all other provinces and in the territories, the age of majority is 19.

3. This happens when one parent has custody of one child in the family and another parent has custody of a second child or of more children. One parent may live in one part of the city, while the other parent lives in another area, or just outside the city borders. Child welfare agencies are not permitted to disclose client information to other agencies without express consents. In addition, parents who are being investigated for suspected child abuse can sometimes move only a kilometre or two to cross provincial borders. When they do this, the possibility of sharing information is even more remote.

4. This process is called community mapping. Benson (2006) presents a 156-item survey that can be modified to suit individual community cultures. Implementing this survey is one way to map community assets or strengths.

CHAPTER 7

1. Parenting books advise parents to listen to their children, then offer advice, direction,

or parables. Although listening is stressed in the following books, the adults do most of the talking: Adele Faber and Elaine Mazlish, *How to Talk So Kids Will Listen and Listen So Kids Will Talk* (2002); Lynn Kleiner, *Kids Can Listen, Kids Can Move!* (2003); and Ann Douglas, *The Mother of All Parenting Books* (2003).

CHAPTER 8

1. This 18-part series was produced by the Canadian Council on Learning and features parenting experts such as Barbara Coloroso. Each part is supported by a video of children. The series can be viewed on-line at: <www.ccl-cca.ca/CCL/Newsroom/MultimediaCentre/AudioVideoArchive/GorillaParenting.htm?>.

CHAPTER 9

1. The Canadian Foundation for Children, Youth and the Law, also called Justice for Children and Youth, is a non-profit charitable organization with a mandate to promote the rights of children and their families through education, research, and advocacy. This organization, based in Toronto, received funding by the Court Challenges Program to challenge Section 43. The court challenge was opposed by the Attorney General, the Canadian Teachers' Federation, and the Coalition for Family Autonomy. Although the court challenge failed, this organization continues to advocate for the repeal of Section 43.

2. Alan Edmunds, an educational psychology professor at the University of Western Ontario, estimates that about 15–20 per cent of children who take Ritalin are actually

helped in some way by this drug. He regularly speaks and writes about the overuse of this drug in Canada (Steffenhagen, 2008).

3. This author participated in many case reviews in which the consulting psychiatrist wrote and renewed prescriptions for children in care. These prescriptions were prompted solely by the worker's descriptions and case notes. The child did not attend these case reviews and was never actually seen by the psychiatrist.

4. This bylaw became a model for other cities in Alberta. The positive effects of this bylaw on the community are described in detail at: <www.menet.ab.ca/bins/view_practice.asp?pid=896>.

CHAPTER 10

1. Kübler-Ross (1972) identified five stages of grieving that have now become a foundation for much of our work around separation and loss. These five stages of the grief or mourning process are shock or denial, anger, bargaining, depression, and acceptance. Kübler-Ross also noted that these five stages are a guideline only. Some people only experience the first few stages, while others go through all five stages in a short period of time.

2. This estimate comes from Andrée Cazabon's film, *Wards of the Crown*. Andrée herself was in foster care and is well aware of foster care drift. She is currently involved with the National Youth in Care Network.

3. Conference proceedings can be read at: <www.caswacts.ca/celebrating/nationalconf_e.html>. (10 Jan. 2009)

References

Ainsworth, M.D.S., et al. 1978. *Patterns of Attachment: A Psychological Study of the Strange Situation.* Hillsdale, NJ: Erlbaum.

Allen-Meares, Paula, and Mark W. Fraser. 2004. *Intervention with Children and Adolescents: An Interdisciplinary Perspective.* Boston: Pearson.

Ambert, Anne-Marie. 2007. *The Rise in the Number of Children and Adolescents Who Exhibit Problematic Behaviours: Multiple Causes.* Ottawa: Vanier Institute of the Family.

Ames, E. 1997. *The Development of Romanian Orphanage Children Adopted to Canada.* Final Report to National Welfare Grants Program, Human Resources Development Canada. Burnaby, BC: Simon Fraser University.

Anglin, James P. 2002. *Pain, Normality, and the Struggle for Congruence: Reinterpreting Residential Care for Children and Youth.* New York: Haworth Press.

Archard, David. 1993. *Children: Rights and Childhood.* London: Routledge.

Armstrong, Jeanette C. 2005. 'Blue against white', in Daniel David Moses and Terry Goldie, eds, *An Anthology of Native Literature.* Toronto: Oxford University Press, 240–2.

Arsenault, Michael. 2008. 'Child's play', *The Walrus* (Oct.–Nov.): 26–8.

Artz, Sibylle. 1998. *Sex, Power and the Violent School Girl.* Toronto: Trifolium Books.

Axline, Virginia M. 1964. *Dibs: In Search of Self.* Boston: Houghton Mifflin.

Baker, Amy, et al. 1999. 'The home instruction program for preschool youngsters', *The Future of Children* 9: 116–33.

Baker, Maureen. 2005. *Families: Changing Trends in Canada*, 5th edn. Toronto: McGraw-Hill Ryerson.

———. 2007. *Choices and Constraints in Family Life.* Toronto: Oxford University Press.

Baker, Peter A., and Dianne Bissmire. 2000. 'A pilot study of the use of physical intervention in the crisis management of people with intellectual disabilities who present challenging behaviours', *Journal of Applied Research in Intellectual Disabilities* 13: 38–45.

Bala, Nicholas, et al., eds. 2004. *Canadian Child Welfare Law: Children, Families and the State.* Toronto: Thompson Educational.

Bandura, Albert. 1997. *Self-Efficacy: The Exercise of Control.* New York: W.H. Freeman.

Barbara, A., et al. 2004. Asking the right questions 2: *Talking about sexual orientation and gender identity in mental health and addiction settings.* Toronto: Centre for Addiction and Mental Health.

Barber, J.G., and P.H. Delfabbro. 2004. 'Placement stability and the psychosocial well-being of children in foster care', *Research in Social Work Practice* 13: 415–31.

Baril, R., P. Lefebvre, and P. Merrigna. 2000. 'Quebec family policy: Impact and options', *Choices* 6, 1: 1–52.

Barrie, T., and Z. Luria. 2004. 'Sexuality and gender in children's daily worlds', in M.S. Kimmel and R.F. Plante, eds, *Sexualities: Identities, Behaviors, and Society.* New York: Oxford University Press, 74–85.

Barron, Christie L. 2000. *Giving Youth a Voice: A Basis for Rethinking Adolescent Violence.* Halifax: Fernwood.

Barter, Ken. 2005. 'Alternative approaches to promoting the health and well-being of children: Accessing community resources to support resilience', in M. Ungar, ed., *Handbook for Working with Children and Youth: Pathways to Resilience across Cultures and Contexts.* Thousand Oaks, Calif.: Sage, 343–55.

———. 2009. 'Community capacity building: A re-conceptualization of services for the protection of children', in Joanne C. Turner and J. Francis, eds, *Canadian Social Welfare.* Toronto: Pearson, 270–88.

Beauvais, Caroline, and Jane Jenson. 2001. *Two Policy Paradigms: Family Responsibility and Investing in Children*. Ottawa: Canadian Policy Research Networks.

Bennett, Darcie, and Lobat Sadrehashemi. 2008. *Broken Promises: Parents Speak about B.C.'s Child Welfare System*. Vancouver: PIVOT.

Benoit, Diane, et al. 2004. 'Infant–parent attachment: Definition, types, antecedents, measurement and outcome', *Pediatrics and Child Health* 9, 8: 541–5.

———. 2005. *Efficacy of Attachment-based Interventions*. Toronto: Centre of Excellence for Early Childhood Development. At: <www.excellence-earlychildhood.ca>. (7 Sept 2009)

Benson, P.L. 2006. *All Kids Are Our Kids: What Communities Must Do to Raise Caring and Responsible Children and Adolescents*. San Francisco: Jossey-Bass.

Bitensky, Susan H. 2006. *Corporal Punishment of Children: A Human Rights Violation*. Ardsley, NY: Transnational.

Bjorklund, David F. 2007. *Why Youth Is Not Wasted on the Young: Immaturity in Human Development*. Malden, Mass.: Blackwell.

Blackstock, Cindy. 2003. 'First Nations child and family services: Restoring peace and harmony in First Nations communities', in K. Kufeldt and B. McKenzie, eds, *Child Welfare: Connecting Research, Policy, and Practice*. Waterloo, Ont.: Wilfrid Laurier University Press, 331–42.

———. 2008. Keynote Address, National Conference of CASW, Toronto, May.

——— and Nico Trocme. 2005. 'Community-based child welfare for Aboriginal children', in Michael Ungar, ed., *Handbook for Working with Children and Youth: Pathways to Resilience across Cultures and Contexts*. Thousand Oaks, Calif.: Sage, 105–20.

——— et al., eds. 2006. *Reconciliation in Child Welfare: Touchstones of Hope for Indigenous Children, Youth, and Families*. Ottawa: First Nations Child and Family Caring Society of Canada.

Bowlby, John. 1969. *Attachment and Loss (Volume 1): Attachment*. London: Hogarth Press.

———. 1988. *A Secure Base: Parent–Child Attachment and Healthy Human Development*. London: Routledge.

Brant, Beth. 2005. 'A long story', in Daniel David Moses and Terry Goldie, *An Anthology of Native Literature*. Toronto: Oxford University Press, 145–50.

Breggin, Peter. 2002. *The Ritalin Fact Book: What Your Doctor Won't Tell You About ADHD and Stimulant Drugs*. Cambridge, Mass.: Da Capo Press.

Brodzinsky, David M., et al. 1998. *Children's Adjustment to Adoption: Developmental and Clinical Issues*. Thousand Oaks, Calif.: Sage.

Bronfenbrenner, U. 1979. *The Ecology of Human Development: Experiments by Nature and Design*. Cambridge, Mass.: Harvard University Press.

Brownell, Marni, et al. 2006. 'Is the class half empty? A population-based perspective on socioeconomic status and educational outcomes', *Choices* 12, 5: 3–29.

Brownstone, Harvey. 2009. *Tug of War: A Judge's Verdict on Separation, Custody Battles, and the Bitter Realities of Family Court*. Toronto: ECW Press.

Bruner, Jerome. 1986. *Actual Minds, Possible Worlds*. Cambridge, Mass.: Harvard University Press.

Brunnée, J., and S. Toope. 2002. 'A hesitant embrace: *Baker* and the application of international law by Canadian courts', *Canadian Yearbook of International Law* 40: 3–60.

Burford, Gail, and J. Hudson, eds. 2000. *Family Group Conferencing: New Directions in Community-centered Child and Family Practice*. New York: Aldine de Gruyter.

——— and Joan Pennell. 1995. 'Family group decision-making: An innovation in child and family welfare', in Joe Hudson and B. Galaway, eds, *Child Welfare in Canada: Research and Policy Implications*. Toronto: Thompson Educational Publishing, 140–54.

Callahan, M., and C. Lumb. 1995. 'My cheque and my children: The long road to empowerment in child welfare', *Child Welfare* 74, 3: 795–819.

Calverley, Donna. 2007. 'Youth custody and community services in Canada, 2004–2005', *Juristat* 27, 2. Statistics Canada Catalogue no. 85-002-XIE.

Cameron, Gary, et al., eds. 2007. *Moving toward Positive Systems of Child and Family Welfare: Current Issues and Future Directions*. Waterloo, Ont.: Wilfrid Laurier University Press.

Campaign 2000. *2008 National Report Card on Child and Family Poverty in Canada*. At: <www.campaign2000.ca/rd/C2000%20Report%20Card%20FINAL%20Nov%2010th08.pdf>. (7 Sept 2009)

Campbell, A. 2006. 'Proceeding with "care": Lessons to be learned from the Canadian parental leave and Quebec daycare initiatives in developing a national childcare policy', *Canadian Journal of Family Law* 22: 171–222.

Canada. 2003. *The Well-being of Canada's Young Children: Government of Canada Report 2003.* At: <www.socialunion.ca/ecd/2003/RH64-20-2003E.pdf>. (7 Sept 2009)

Canadian Association of Social Workers (CASW). 2005. *Code of Ethics for the Canadian Association of Social Workers.*

Canadian Council on Social Development. 2006. 'The Progress of Canada's Children & Youth'. At: <www.ccsd.ca/pccy/2006/index.htm>. (7 Sept. 2009).

Canadian Institute, ed. 1994. *Children and the Law.* Toronto: Canadian Institute Publications.

Canadian Institute for Health Information. 2004. *Improving the Health of Canadians.* Ottawa: CIHI.

Canadian Police Survey on Youth Gangs. 2002. At: <www2.ps-sp.gc.ca/publications/policing/pdf/gangs>. (10 Jan. 2009)

Cartwright, D., ed. 1959. *Studies in Social Power.* Ann Arbor: University of Michigan Press.

Cech, Maureen. 1991. *Globalchild: Multicultural Resources for Young Children.* Menlo Park, Calif.: Addison-Wesley.

———. 2000. *Adoption: An Annotated Bibliography.* Ottawa: PFNCR.

Cederborg, Ann-Christin. 1997. 'Young children's participation in family therapy talk', *American Journal of Family Therapy* 25, 1: 23–38.

Center for Disease Control and Prevention. 2000. *Childhood Injury Fact Sheet.* At: <www.cdc.gov/ncipc/factssheets/childh.htm>. (15 May 2008)

Chamberlain, David B. 1995. 'What babies are teaching us about violence', *Pre- and Perinatal Psychology Journal* 10, 2: 57–74.

Chamberlain, Mark, and Liz Weaver. 2008. 'Feds must join child poverty fight', *Hamilton Spectator*, 12 Dec.

Chang, Jeff. 1998. 'Children's stories, children's solutions: Social constructionist therapy for children and their families', in Michael F. Hoyt, ed., *The Handbook of Constructive Therapies.* San Francisco: Jossey-Bass, 251–76.

Chansonneuve, Deborah. 2005. *Reclaiming Connections: Understanding Residential School Trauma among Aboriginal People.* Ottawa: Aboriginal Healing Foundation.

Chatterjee, Jharna. 2006. *Gang Prevention and Intervention Strategies.* Ottawa: Royal Canadian Mounted Police.

Chunn, Dorothy E. 2003. 'Boys will be men, girls will be mothers: The legal regulation of childhood in Toronto and Vancouver', in Janovicek and Parr (2003: 188–207).

Collin, Chantal. 2007. *Poverty Reduction in Canada—the Federal Role.* At: <www.parl.gc.ca/information/library/PRBpubs/prb0722-e.htm>. (23 Aug. 2009)

Conway, J.F. 2001. *The Canadian Family in Crisis.* Toronto: James Lorimer.

Cottrell, Barbara. 2003. *Parent Abuse: The Abuse of Parents by Their Teenage Children.* Ottawa: National Clearinghouse on Family Violence.

Couture, M.D. 1940. *The Canadian Mother and Child.* Ottawa: King's Printer.

Covell, Katherine, and R. Brian Howe. 2001. *The Challenge of Children's Rights for Canada.* Waterloo, Ont.: Wilfrid Laurier University Press.

Darwin, Charles. 1877. 'A biographical sketch of an infant', *Mind* 2: 285–94.

Dass, Ram, and Paul Gorman. 1997. *How Can I Help? Stories and Reflections on Service.* New York: Knopf.

Davey, Ian E. 2003. 'The rhythm of work and the rhythm of school', in Janovicek and Parr (2003: 108–22).

Davis, Wade. 2009. *The Wayfinders: Why Ancient Wisdom Matters in the Modern World.* Toronto: Anansi.

deMontigny, Gerald A.J. 1995. *Social Working: An Ethnography of Front-line Practice.* Toronto: University of Toronto Press.

deShazer, S. 1984. 'The death of resistance', *Family Process* 23: 79–93.

Deslandes, Rollande. 2006. 'Designing and implementing school, family, and community collaboration programs in Quebec, Canada', *The School Community Journal* 16, 1: 81–105.

DiCiacco, Janis A. 2008. *The Colors of Grief: Understanding a Child's Journey through Loss from Birth to Adulthood.* London: Jessica Kingsley.

Dickerson, James L., and Mardi Allen. 2006. *The Basics of Adoption: A Guide for Building Families in the U.S. and Canada.* Westport, Conn.: Praeger.

Diller, Lawrence H. 2006. *The Last Normal Child: Essays on the Intersection of Kids, Culture, and Psychiatric Drugs.* Westport, Conn.: Praeger.

Dishion, Thomas J., and Elizabeth A. Stormshak. 2007. *Intervening in Children's Lives: An Ecological, Family-centred Approach to Mental Health Care.* Washington: American Psychological Association.

Doidge, Norman. 2007. *The Brain that Changes Itself: Stories of Personal Triumph from the Frontiers of Brain Science*. New York: Viking Penguin.

Donaldson, Margaret. 1978. *Children's Minds*. London: Fontana.

Doob, A.N., and C. Cesaroni. 2004. *Responding to Youth Crime in Canada*. Toronto: University of Toronto.

Dorais, Michel, with Simon L. Lajeunesse. 2004. *Dead Boys Can't Dance: Sexual Orientation, Masculinity, and Suicide*. Montreal and Kingston: McGill-Queen's University Press.

Doucet, Andrea. 2006. *Do Men Mother?* Toronto: University of Toronto Press.

Driedger, Leo. 2003. *Race and Racism: Canada's Challenge*. Montreal and Kingston: McGill-Queen's University Press.

Drolet, Bonita, and Melissa Sauve-Kobylecki. 2006. 'The needs of children in care and the Looking After Children approach: Steps towards promoting children's best interests', in Flynn et al. (2006: 297–316).

Dufour, Sarah, and Claire Chamberland. 2003. *The Effectiveness of Child Welfare Interventions: A Systematic Review*. Montreal: Centre of Excellence for Child Welfare.

Dumbrill, Gary, and Sarah Maiter. 2004. 'Moving from clients evaluating services to clients designing services', *OACAS Journal* 48, 4: 17–21.

Durrant, J.F., R. Enson, and Coalition on Physical Punishment of Children and Youth. 2004. *Joint Statement on Physical Punishment of Children and Youth*. Ottawa: Coalition on Physical Punishment of Children and Youth.

Eberstadt, Mary. 1999. 'Why ritalin rules', *Policy Review* 94 (Apr.): 24–46.

Edmunds, Alan. 2008. 'Children with ADHD routinely misdiagnosed: Study', *Ottawa Citizen*, 2 June, A5.

Erikson, Erik. 2000. *The Erik Erikson Reader*. New York: Norton.

Esbenson, S. 1985. *Good Day Care Makes a Difference: A Review of the Research Findings on the Effects of Day Care on Children, Families and Communities*. Report submitted to the Task Force on Child Care. Ottawa: Status of Women.

Fahlberg, Vera. 1988. *Fitting the Pieces Together*. London: BAAF.

Fallis, Kirk, and Susan Opotow. 2003. 'Are students failing school or are schools failing students? Class cutting in high school', *Journal of Social Issues* 59, 1: 103–19.

Farris-Manning, Cheryl, and Marietta Zandstra. 2003. *Children in Care in Canada: A Summary of Current Issues and Trends with Recommendations for Future Research*. Ottawa: Child Welfare League of Canada.

Feeney, Judith A. 2005. 'Attachment and perceived rejection: Findings from studies of hurt feelings and the adoption experience', *E-Journal of Applied Psychology* 1, 1: 41–9.

Ferguson, I. 2008. *Reclaiming Social Work: Challenging Neo-liberalism and Promoting Social Justice*. London: Sage.

Fewster, Gerry. 2002. 'The hardest advice: Listen to your kids', *Journal of Child and Youth Care* 15, 4: 17–19.

————. 2005. 'I don't like kids', *Relational Child and Youth in Care* 18, 3: 3–5.

Field, Tiffany. 2007. *The Amazing Infant*. Malden, Mass.: Blackwell.

Flynn, Robert J., Peter M. Dudding, and James G. Barber, eds. 2006. *Promoting Resilience in Child Welfare*. Ottawa: University of Ottawa Press.

Foot, Richard. 2008. 'How about an Inuit child? Infertile East Coast couples are heading to Nunavut', *National Post*, 2 Jan. 2008, A7.

Foucault, M. 1977. *Discipline and Punish*. London: Allen Lane.

Fox, Bonnie J. 2001. *Family Patterns, Gender Relations*. Toronto: Oxford University Press.

Frankish, C.J., et al. 1996. *Health Impact Assessment as a Tool for Population Health Promotion and Public Policy*. Vancouver: Institute of Health Promotion Research, University of British Columbia.

Freire, Paulo. 2000. *Pedagogy of the Oppressed*. New York: Continuum.

French, J.R.P., Jr, and B. Raven. 1959. 'The bases of social power', in D. Cartwright, ed., *Studies in Social Power*. Ann Arbor: University of Michigan, 259–68.

Freud, Anna. 1935. *Psycho-analysis for Teachers and Parents: Introductory Lectures*. New York: Emerson Books.

Garfat, Thom. 2003. *A Child and Youth Care Approach to Working with Families*. New York: Haworth Press.

Garrett, Paul Michael. 2003. *Remaking Social Work with Children and Families: A Critical Discussion on the 'Modernisation' of Social Care*. London: Routledge.

Gershoff, E.T. 2002. 'Parental corporal punishment and associated child behaviors and experiences: A meta-analytic and theoretical review', *Psychological Bulletin* 128: 539–79.

Gilgun, Jane. 2002. 'Completing the circle: American Indian medicine wheels and the promotion of resilience of children and youth in care', *Journal of Human Behaviour in the Social Environment* 6, 2: 65–84.

Gilligan, Robbie. 2006. 'Promoting resilience and permanence in child welfare', in Flynn et al. (2006: 18–34).

Goldstein, Sam, and Robert B. Brooks. 2005. *Handbook of Resilience in Children*. New York: Kluwer Academic/Plenum.

Gorilla Parenting. At: <www.ccl-cca.ca/CCL/Newsroom/MultimediaCentre/AudioVideoArchive/GorillaParenting.htm?>. (1 Dec. 2008)

Gottman, John. 1997. *Raising an Emotionally Intelligent Child*. New York: Simon & Schuster.

Green, R.G., and K.F. Healy. 2003. *Tough on Kids: Rethinking Approaches to Youth Justice*. Saskatoon: Purich Publishing.

Greene, Sheila, and Diane Hogan, eds. 2005. *Researching Children's Experience: Methods and Approaches*. Thousand Oaks, Calif.: Sage.

Griffin, Sandra. 2007. *Why the Investment in Children? Costs and Benefits of Investing in Children*. Ottawa: Centre of Excellence for Early Childhood Development.

Grover, Sonja. 2007. 'Homeless children and street-involved children in Canada', in R. Brian Howe et al., eds, *A Question of Commitment: Children's Rights in Canada*. Waterloo, Ont.: Wilfrid Laurier University Press, 343–73.

Habermas, T., and S. Bluck. 2000. 'Getting a life: The emergence of the life story in adolescence', *Psychological Bulletin* 126: 748–69.

Haig-Brown, Celia, with Carl James. 2004. 'Supporting respectful relations: Community-school interface and youth "at risk"', in Kidd and Phillips (2004: 216–35).

Hamilton, Claire E. 2000. 'Continuity and discontinuity of attachment from infancy through adolescence', *Child Development* 71, 3: 690–4.

Harlow, H., and M. Harlow. 1962. 'Social deprivation in monkeys', *Scientific American* 207: 136–46.

———— and S. Suomi. 1972. 'Social rehabilitation of isolate-reared monkeys', *Developmental Psychology* 6: 487–96.

Harris, Barbara. 2006. 'What can we learn from traditional Aboriginal education? Transforming social work education delivered in First Nations communities', *Canadian Journal of Native Education* 29, 1: 117–46.

Health Canada. 1999. *Population Health*. At: <www.phac-aspc.gc.ca/ph-sp/index-eng.php>. (7 Sept. 2009)

Health Canada. 2008. *Aboriginal Health: Suicides*. At: <www.hc-sc.gc.ca/fniah-spnia/pubs/aborig-autoch>. (30 July 2008)

HeavyRunner, I., and J. Morris. 1997. *Traditional Native Culture and Resilience*. At: <www.education.umn.edu/carei/Reports/Rpractice/Spring97/traditional.html>. (17 July 2008)

Heckman, James J., and Dimitry V. Masterov. 2007. *The Productivity Argument for Investing in Young Children*. Cambridge, Mass.: National Bureau of Economic Research, Working Paper 13016.

Hick, Steven, et al. 2005. *Social Work: A Critical Turn*. Toronto: Thompson Educational Publishing.

Hollander, J. 2002. 'Resisting vulnerability: The social reconstruction of gender in interaction', *Social Problems* 49, 4: 474–96.

hooks, bell. 1994. *Teaching to Transgress: Education as the Practice of Freedom*. New York: Routledge.

Howe, R. Brian, and Katherine Covell. 2005. *Empowering Children: Children's Rights Education as a Pathway to Citizenship*. Toronto: University of Toronto Press.

———— et al., eds. 2007. *A Question of Commitment: Children's Rights in Canada*. Waterloo, Ont.: Wilfrid Laurier University Press.

Hoyt, Michael F., ed. 1998. *The Handbook of Constructive Therapies*. San Francisco: Jossey-Bass.

Hudson, J., and B. Galaway, eds. 1995. *Child Welfare in Canada: Research and Policy Implications*. Toronto: Thompson Educational Publishing.

Huether, John. 2003. 'Lessons learned: The inquest into the death of Stephanie Jobin', *OACAS Journal* 47, 1 (June): 4–13.

Hulbert, Ann. 2003. *Raising America: Experts, Parents, and a Century of Advice about Children*. New York: Knopf.

Human Resources and Skills Development Canada (HRSDC). 2004. *A Canada Fit for Children*. At: <www.hrdsc.gc.ca/en/cs/sp/sdc/socpol/publications/2002-002483>. (18 June 2008)

James, Allison, and Chris Jenks. 1996. 'Public perceptions of childhood criminality', *British Journal of Sociology* 47, 2: 315–30.

James, S., and F. Mennen. 2001. 'Treatment outcome research: How effective are treatments for abused children?', *Child and Adolescent Social Work Journal* 18, 2: 73–95.

Janovicek, Nancy, and Joy Parr, eds. 2003. *Histories of Canadian Children and Youth*. Toronto: Oxford University Press.

Jenks, Chris. 2005. *Childhood*. New York: Routledge.

Jenson, J. 2002. *Social Inclusion as Solidarity: Rethinking the Child's Rights Agenda*. Toronto: Laidlaw Foundation.

Jodoin, Nadine, and Madeleine Dion Stout. 2006. *MCH Screening Tool Project: Final Report*. At: <www.afn.ca/cmslib/general/MCH-ST.pdf>. (28 Apr. 2009)

Johnson, Candace. 2008. 'Entitlement beyond the family: Global rights commitments and children's health policy in Canada', in Tom O'Neill and Dawn Zinga, eds, *Children's Rights: Multidisciplinary Approaches to Participation and Protection*. Toronto: University of Toronto Press, 115–37.

Johnson, Sue. 2004. *The Practice of Emotionally Focused Marital Therapy: Creating Connection*. New York: Bruner/Routledge.

———. 2008. *Hold Me Tight: Seven Conversations for a Lifetime of Love*. New York: Little, Brown.

Jones, Laura, and Edward Krak. 2005. 'Life in government care: The connection of youth and family', *Child and Youth Care Forum* 34, 6: 405–21.

Jordan, Judith V. 2005. 'Relational resilience in girls', in Sam Goldstein and Robert B. Brooks, eds, *Handbook of Resilience in Children*. New York: Kluwer Academic/Plenum, 79–91.

Joyal, Renee, et al., eds. 2005. *Making Children's Rights Work: National and International Perspectives*. Cowansville, Que.: Editions Yvonne Blais.

Kail, Robert V., and Theresa Zolner. 2005. *Children*, Canadian edn. Toronto: Pearson.

Kaufman, J., and C. Heinrich. 2000. 'Exposure to violence and early childhood trauma', in C. Zeanah Jr, ed., *Handbook of Infant Mental Health*. New York: Guilford Press, 195–207.

Kazura, K. 2000. 'Fathers' qualitative and quantitative involvement: An investigation of attachment, play and social interactions', *Journal of Men's Studies* 9, 1: 41–57.

Kelly, Katharine, and Tullio Caputo. 2007. 'Health and street/homeless youth', *Journal of Health Psychology* 12, 5: 726–36.

——— and Mark Totten. 2002. *When Children Kill: A Social-Psychological Study of Youth Homicide*. Peterborough, Ont.: Broadview Press.

Kelly, Yvonne, et al. 2006. 'Ethnic differences in achievement of developmental milestones by 9 months of age: The Millenium Cohort Study', *Developmental Medicine & Child Neurology* 48: 825–30.

Kendrick, Martyn. 1990. *Nobody's Children: The Foster Care Crisis in Canada*. Toronto: Macmillan.

Kidd, Bruce, and Jim Phillips, eds. 2004. *From Enforcement and Prevention to Civic Engagement: Research on Community Safety*. Toronto: Centre of Criminology, University of Toronto.

Kimelman, E.C. 1985. *No Quiet Place: Review Committee on Indian and Metis Adoptions and Placements*. Winnipeg: Manitoba Department of Community Services.

Kimmel, M.S., and R.F. Plante, eds. 2004. *Sexualities: Identities, Behaviors, and Society*. New York: Oxford University Press.

Kingsley, J., and Levitz, M. 2007. *Count Us In: Growing up with Down Syndrome*. New York: Harcourt & Brace.

Kirmayer, Laurence J., et al. 2007. *Suicide among Aboriginal People in Canada*. Ottawa: Aboriginal Healing Foundation.

Klebanov, P.K., J. Brooks-Gunn, and M.C. McCormick. 2001. 'Maternal coping strategies and emotional distress: Results of an early intervention program for low birth weight young children', *Developmental Psychology* 37, 5: 654–67.

Klein, Melanie. 1965. *Contributions to Psychoanalysis, 1921–1945*. London: Hogarth Press.

Klein, R.A., et al. 2006. 'Resilience theory and its relevance for child welfare practice', in Flynn et al. (2006: 34–51).

Knapp, Vincent J. 1998. 'Major medical explanations for high infant mortality in nineteenth-century Europe', *Canadian Bulletin of Medical History* 15: 317–36.

Knoke, Della, and Nico Trocme. 2004. *Risk Assessment in Child Welfare: CECW Information Sheet 18E*. Toronto: Faculty of Social Work, University of Toronto.

Kraemer, Gary. 1997. 'Psychobiology of early social attachment in rhesus monkeys: Clinical implications', *Annals, New York Academy of Sciences* 807, 1: 401–18.

Kübler-Ross, Elisabeth. 1972. *On Death and Dying*. New York: Macmillan.

Kufeldt, Kathleen, et al. 2003. 'Critical issues in child welfare', in Kufeldt and Mackenzie (2003: 395–429).

——— and Brad McKenzie, eds. 2003. *Child Welfare: Connecting Research, Policy, and Practice*. Waterloo, Ont.: Wilfrid Laurier University Press.

Kutcher, Stanley P., and Magdalena Szumilas. 2008. *Youth Suicide Prevention*. At: <www.cmaj.ca/cgi/content/full/178/3/282>. (23 Aug. 2008)

Lalonde, C.E. 2006. 'Identity formation and cultural resilience in Aboriginal communities', in Flynn et al. (2006: 52–71).

Lambe, Yolanda. 2006. *The Chemical Management of Canadian Systems Youth*. Ottawa: National Youth in Care Network.

———. 2009. *Drugs in Our System: An Exploratory Study on the Chemical Management of Canadian Systems Youth*. Ottawa: National Youth in Care Network.

Lane, David A., and Andrew Milner, eds. 1992. *Child and Adolescent Therapy: A Handbook*. Buckingham, UK: Open University Press.

Langhout, Regina, et al. 2004. 'An exploratory study of youth mentoring in an urban context: Adolescents' perceptions of relationship styles', *Journal of Youth and Adolescence* 33: 293–306.

Latimer, J., et al. 2001. *The Effectiveness of Restorative Justice Practices: A Meta-analysis*. Ottawa: Department of Justice.

Leadbeater, Bonnie J., et al., eds. 2004. *Investing in Children, Youth, Families, and Communities: Strengths-based Research and Policy*. Washington: American Psychological Association.

Lee, Valerie E., J. Brooks-Gunn, Elizabeth Schnur, and Fong-Ruey Liaw. 1990. 'Are Head Start effects sustained? A longitudinal follow-up comparison of disadvantaged children attending Head Start, no preschool, and other preschool programs', *Child Development* 61: 495–507.

Le Mare, L., Karen Kurytnik, and Karyn Audet. 2006. 'The implications of early institutional caregiving for the socio-emotional development of internationally adopted children', *Child and Family Journal* 9: 16–26.

Levine, H. 2000. 'Book review of children's rights education curriculum resource', *International Journal of Children's Rights* 8: 391–4.

LeVine, Robert A., and Rebecca S. New, eds. 2008. *Anthropology and Child Development: A Cross-cultural Reader*. Malden, Mass.: Blackwell.

Levinson, Harold. 1980. *Smart but Feeling Dumb: A Solution to the Riddle—Dyslexia*. New York: Springer-Verlag.

Liebenberg, Linda, and Michael Ungar. 2008. *Resilience in Action: Working with Youth across Cultures and Contexts*. Toronto: University of Toronto Press.

Lightman, Ernie. 2003. *Social Policy in Canada*. Toronto: Oxford University Press.

Lindsey, Duncan. 2004. *The Welfare of Children*. New York: Oxford University Press.

Lodermeier, J., et al. 2002. 'Factors affecting timely permanency planning for children in care', *Canadian Social Work* 4: 136–53.

Lorenz, Konrad. 1970–1. *Studies in Animal and Human Behaviour*, 2 vols. London: Methuen.

Louv, Richard. 2005. *Last Child in the Woods: Saving Our Children from Nature-Deficit Disorder*. Chapel Hill, NC: Algonquin Books of Chapel Hill.

McCain, Margaret N., and Fraser J. Mustard. 1999. *Reversing the Real Brain Drain: The Early Years Study Final Report*. At: <www.childsec.gov.on.ca>. (2 Apr. 2008)

McCarthy, Shawn. 2000. 'National poverty rate dips but number of poor children up 42% since 1989 despite booming economy', *Globe and Mail*, 16 Dec. 2000.

McKinlay, Linda, and Heather Ross. 2008. *You and Others: Reflective Practice for Group Effectiveness in Human Services*. Toronto: Pearson.

Makilan, Aubrey. 2007. 'Filipino youth in Canada driven to gangs, drug tailing', *Philippine Reporter*, 1 Feb. At: < migrante-europe.net/index.php?option=com_content&task>. (10 Jan. 2009)

Malekoff, Andrew. 2004. *Group Work with Adolescents: Principles and Practice*. New York: Guilford Press.

Mallea, Paula. 1999. *Getting Tough on Kids: Young Offenders and the 'Law and Order' Agenda*. Winnipeg: Canadian Centre for Policy Alternatives.

Mandleco, B., and G. Perry. 2000. 'An organizational framework for conceptualizing resilience in children', *Journal of Child and Adolescent Psychiatric Nursing* 13, 3: 99–111.

Marsiglia, Flavio Francisco, and Stephen Kulis. 2009. *Diversity, Oppression, and Change*. Chicago: Lyceum Books.

Martel, Yann. 2002. *Life of Pi*. Toronto: Vintage Canada.

Martin, Fay. 2003. 'Knowing and naming "care" in child welfare', in Kufeldt and Mackenzie (2003: 261–73).

Maslow, Abraham. 1943. 'A theory of human motivation', *Psychological Review* 50: 370–96.

Masten, Ann S. 2006. 'Promoting resilience in development: A general framework for systems in care', in Flynn et al. (2006: 3–18).

Meichenbaum, Donald. 2006. 'Comparison of aggression in boys and girls: A case for gender-specific interventions'. At: <www.melissainstitute.org/documents>. (16 June 2008)

Mellor, Brian, et al. 2005. *Youth Gangs in Canada: A Preliminary Review of Programs and Services*. Calgary: CRILF.

Miller, Alice. 2005. *The Body Never Lies: The Lingering Effects of Cruel Parenting*. New York: Norton.

Mitra, Sugata. 2007. 'Hole-in-the-wall experiments in India'. At: <www.hole-in-the-wall.com>. (7 Sept. 2009)

Mondschein, E., et al. 2000. 'Gender bias in mothers' expectations about infant crawling', *Journal of Experimental Child Psychology* 77, 4: 304–16.

Montgomery, Lucy Maud. 1972 [1917]. *Anne's House of Dreams*. Toronto: McClelland & Stewart.

Moore, Shannon. 2007. 'Restorative justice: Toward a rights-based approach', in Howe et al. (2007: 179–209).

Morrisseau, Calvin. 1998. *Into the Daylight: A Wholistic Approach to Healing*. Toronto: University of Toronto Press.

Moses, Daniel David, and Terry Goldie, eds. 2005. *An Anthology of Native Literature*. Toronto: Oxford University Press.

Muncie, John, and Barry Goldson, eds. 2006. *Comparative Youth Justice: Critical Issues*. Thousand Oaks, Calif.: Sage.

National Film Board of Canada. 1993. *Out: Stories of Lesbian and Gay Youth*.

———. 2005. *Wards of the Crown*.

National Social Work Conference. 2008. *Conference Proceedings*.

Newson, Elizabeth. 1992. 'The barefoot play therapist: Adapting skills for a time of need', in Lane and Milner (1992: 89–108).

Novick, Marvyn. 2007. *Summoned to Stewardship: Make Poverty Reduction a Collective Legacy. Campaign 2000 Policy Perspectives*. Toronto: Campaign 2000.

O'Brien, Michael. 2006. 'The child and adolescent functional assessment scale', *OACAS Journal* 50, 1: 2–5.

O'Callaghan, Clare. 2008. 'Lullament: Lullaby and lament therapeutic qualities actualized through music therapy', *American Journal of Hospice and Palliative Medicine* 25, 2: 93–9.

O'Donnell, Susan. 2009. 'Learning, not labels, for special-needs students', *Edmonton Journal*, 9 June.

O'Neill, Heather. 2006. *Lullabies for Little Criminals*. New York: Harper Perennial.

O'Neill, Tom, and Dawn Zinga, eds. 2008. *Children's Rights: Multidisciplinary Approaches to Participation and Protection*. Toronto: University of Toronto Press.

Owen, Frances, et al. 2008. 'Human rights for children and youth with developmental disabilities', in O'Neill and Zinga (2008: 163–94).

Parada, Henry Ubaldo. 2002. *The Restructuring of the Child Welfare System in Ontario: A Study in the Social Organization of Knowledge*. Toronto: Ontario Institute for Studies in Education.

Pearson, Landon. 2008. 'Foreword', in O'Neill and Zinga (2008: vii–ix).

Perrin, Benjamin. 2008. '146 Canadians charged overseas with child sex crimes; only one convicted', *Ottawa Citizen*, 3 Apr., A3.

Peters, Ray DeV. 2005. 'A community-based approach to promoting resilience in young children, their families, and their neighbourhoods', in Ray DeV. Peters et al., eds, *Resilience in Children, Families, and Communities: Linking Context to Practice and Policy*. New York: Kluwer Academic/Plenum, 157–77.

Peterson, C., and M.E.P. Seligman. 2004. *Character Strengths and Virtues: A Handbook and Classification*. New York: Oxford University Press.

Philip, Margaret. 2007. 'Nearly half of children in crown care are medicated', *Globe and Mail*, 9 June.

Piaget, Jean. 1929. *The Child's Conception of the World*. New York: Harcourt, Brace.

Pless, Barry, and Wayne Millar. 2000. *Unintentional Injuries in Childhood: Results from Canadian Health Surveys*. Ottawa: Health Canada.

Pollard, Juliet. 2003. 'A most remarkable phenomenon: Growing up Metis: Fur traders' children in the Pacific Northwest', in Janovicek and Parr (2003: 57–71).

Potter, Cathryn C. 2004. 'Gender differences in

childhood and adolescence', in Paula Allen-Meares and Mark W. Fraser, eds, *Interventions with Children and Adolescents*. Needham Heights, Mass.: Allyn & Bacon, 54–80.

Prochaska, James O., and John C. Norcross. 2007. *Systems of Psychotherapy: A Transtheoretical Analysis*. Belmont, Calif.: Thomson Brooks/Cole.

Public Safety Canada. 2008. *Youth Gangs in Canada: What Do We Know?* At: <www.publicsafety.gc.ca/prg/cp/bldngevd/2007-yg-l-en.asp>. (1 June 2008)

Putnam, Robert D. 2000. *Bowling Alone: The Collapse and Revival of American Community*. New York: Simon & Schuster.

Rak, C.F., and L.E. Patterson. 1996. 'Promoting resilience in at-risk children', *Journal of Counseling and Development* 74, 4: 368–73.

Raphael, Dennis. 2007. *Poverty and Policy in Canada: Implications for Health and Quality of Life*. Toronto: Canadian Scholars' Press.

Ray, Dee C. 2006. 'Evidence-based play therapy', in Schaefer and Kaduson (2006: 136–61).

Regehr, Cheryl, and Karima Kanani. 2006. *Essential Law for Social Work Practice in Canada*. Toronto: Oxford University Press.

Risk Assessment Model for Child Protection in Ontario. 2000. Toronto: Queen's Printer.

Ritzer, G., ed. 2004. *Handbook of Social Theory*. Thousand Oaks, Calif.: Sage.

Rogers, Carl. 1951. *Client-centered Therapy*. Boston: Houghton Mifflin.

———. 1980. *A Way of Being*. Boston: Houghton Mifflin.

Rose, T.L. 1998. 'Current disciplinary practices with handicapped students: Suspensions and expulsions', *Exceptional Child* 55: 230–9.

Rosenhan, David. 1973. 'On being sane in insane places', *Science* 179: 250–8.

Royal Commission on Aboriginal Peoples. 1996. *Report*, 6 vols. Ottawa: Canada Commission Group.

Rozovsky, L. 2003. *The Canadian Law of Consent to Treatment*. Toronto: Butterworths.

Ruane, Janet M., and Karen A. Cerulo. 2004. *Second Thoughts: Seeing Conventional Wisdom through the Sociological Eye*. Thousand Oaks, Calif.: Pine Forge Press.

Ruch, G. 2005. 'Relationship-based practice and reflective practice: Holistic approaches to contemporary child care social work', *Child and Family Social Work* 10: 111–23.

Russ, S. 2004. *Play in Child Development and Psychotherapy: Toward Empirically Supported Practice*. Mahwah, NJ: Erlbaum.

Rutman, Deborah, et al. 2000. *Substance Use and Pregnancy: Conceiving Women in the Policymaking Process*. At: <www.swc-cfc.gc.ca/pubs/pubspr/factsheets/200211_020510_37_e.pdf>. (4 Apr. 2008)

Rycus, Judith S., and Ronald C. Hughes. 1998. *Field Guide to Child Welfare*, vol. 1. Washington: CWLA Press.

Saleebey, D. 2002. *The Strengths Perspective in Social Work Practice*. Boston: Allyn & Bacon.

Sameroff, Arnold J., et al., eds. 2005. *Treating Parent–Infant Relationship Problems: Strategies for Intervention*. New York: Guilford Press.

Scales, P.C., and N. Leffert. 2004. *Developmental Assets: A Synthesis of the Scientific Research on Adolescent Development*. Minneapolis: Search Institute.

———, A. Sesma Jr, and B. Bolstrom. 2004. *Coming into Their Own: How Developmental Assets Promote Positive Growth in Middle Childhood*. Minneapolis: Search Institute.

Schaefer, Charles E., ed. 2003. *Play Therapy with Adults*. Hoboken, NJ: John Wiley & Sons.

——— and H.G. Kaduson. 2006. *Contemporary Play Therapy: Theory, Research, and Practice*. New York: Guilford Press.

Schissel, Bernard. 2006. *Still Blaming Children: Youth Conduct and the Politics of Child Hating*. Halifax: Fernwood.

——— and Terry Wotherspoon. 2003. *The Legacy of School for Aboriginal People: Education, Oppression, and Emancipation*. Toronto: Oxford University Press.

Selekman, Matthew D. 2002. *Living on the Razor's Edge: Solution-oriented Brief Family Therapy with Self-harming Adolescents*. New York: Norton.

Sesma, Arturo, et al. 2005. 'Positive adaptation, resilience, and the developmental asset framework', in Goldstein and Brooks (2005: 281–97).

Seymour, Andrew. 2008. 'City street gangs contain multitude of ethnicities', *Ottawa Citizen*, 31 July, A1.

Shebib, Bob. 2007. *Choices: Interviewing and Counselling Skills for Canadians*. Toronto: Pearson.

Sinclair, Raven, Michael Anthony Hart, and Gord Bruyere. 2009. *Wichihitowin: Aboriginal Social Work in Canada*. Halifax: Fernwood.

Singer, Merrill. 2008. *Drugging the Poor: Legal*

and Illegal Drugs and Social Inequality. Long Grove, Ill.: Waveland Press.

Smandych, Russell. 2006. 'Canada: Repenalization and young offenders' rights', in Muncie and Goldson (2006: 19-34).

Smidt, Sandra. 2006. *The Developing Child in the 21st Century: A Global Perspective on Child Development*. New York: Routledge.

Smith, Dorothy E. 1998. *Writing the Social: Critique, Theory and Investigations*. Toronto: University of Toronto Press.

———. 2001. 'Texts and the ontology of organizations and institutions', *Studies in Cultures, Organizations, and Societies* 7, 2: 159–98.

———. 2005. *Institutional Ethnography: A Sociology for People*. Oxford: AltaMira Press.

Smith, Mark. 2009. *Rethinking Residential Child Care: Positive Perspectives*. Bristol, UK: Policy Press.

Spratt, Trevor. 2005. 'Radical drama with children: Working with children using critical social work methods', in Hick et al. (2005: 105–21).

Standing Senate Committee on Human Rights. 2007. *Children: The Silenced Citizens. Effective Implementation of Canada's International Obligations with Respect to the Rights of Children*. Final report, Apr. At: <www.parl.gc.ca/39/1/parlbus/combus/senate/com-e/huma-e/rep-e/rep10apr07-e.htm> (22 Nov. 2009).

Stanley, Timothy J. 2003. 'White supremacy, Chinese schooling, and school segregation in Victoria: The case of the Chinese students' strike, 1922–1923', in Janovicek and Parr (2003: 126–43).

Statistics Canada. 2004. 'The gap in achievement between boys and girls', *Education Matters* 4 (Oct.). At: <www.statcan.gc.ca/pub/81-004-x/200410/7423-eng.htm>. (14 May 2009)

———. 2007. *The Daily*, 21 Nov.

———. 2009. 'Population of working age and either gainfully occupied or labour force, in non-agricultural and agricultural pursuits' (table). At: <www.statcan.gc.ca/pub/11-516-x/sectiond/D1_7-eng.csv>. (10 May 2009)

——— and Human Resources and Social Development Canada. 1994–present. National Longitudinal Survey Children and of Youth (NLSCY).

Stearns, Peter N. 2006. *Childhood in World History*. New York: Routledge.

Steffenhagen, Janet. 2008. 'Children with ADHD routinely misdiagnosed: Study', *Ottawa Citizen*, 2 June, A5.

Steingraber, Sandra. 2007. *Falling Age of Puberty in U.S. Girls: What We Know, What We Need to Know*. San Francisco: Breast Cancer Fund.

Steinhauer, Paul D. 1996. *Methods for Developing Resiliency in Children from Disadvantaged Populations*. Toronto: Sparrow Lake Alliance.

Stout, Madeleine Dion, and Gregory Kipling. 2003. *Aboriginal People, Resilience and the Residential School Legacy*. Ottawa: Aboriginal Healing Foundation.

Strom-Gottfried, Kim. 2008. *The Ethics of Practice with Minors: High Stakes, Hard Choices*. Chicago: Lyceum Books.

Sutherland, Neil. 2003. 'When you listen to the winds of childhood, how much can you believe?', in Janovicek and Parr (2003: 19–34).

SWOVA. 2007. 'Respectful relationships'. At: <swova.org/awards.php>. (2 Aug. 2008)

Tallman, Laurna. 2010. *Listening for the Light: A New Perspective on Integration Disorder in Dyslexic Syndrome, Schizophrenia, Bipolarity, Chronic Fatigue Syndrome, and Substance Abuse*. Marmora, Ont.: Northern Light Books.

Tamaki, Mariko. 2008. *Skim*. Toronto: Groundwood Books.

Toseland, Ronald W., and Robert F. Rivas. 2005. *An Introduction to Group Work Practice*. Boston: Pearson.

Totten, Mark D. 2000. *Guys, Gangs, and Girlfriend Abuse*. Peterborough, Ont.: Broadview Press.

Tramo, Mark. 'How your brain listens to music'. At: <www.wildmusicorg/research/tramo>. (10 Jan. 2008)

Transracial Abductees. 2009. At: <www.transracialabductees.org> (13 Nov. 2009).

Tremblay, R.E., et al. 2004. 'Physical aggression during early childhood: Trajectories and predictors', *Pediatrics* 114, 1: 43–50.

Trocme, Nico, et al. 2002. *The Changing Face of Child Welfare Investigations in Ontario: Ontario Incidence of Reported Child Abuse and Neglect 1993/1998*. Toronto: Centre of Excellence for Child Welfare, Faculty of Social Work, University of Toronto.

——— et al. 2003. 'Major findings from the Canadian incidence study of reported child abuse and neglect', *Child Abuse and Neglect* 27: 1427–39.

Turner, Joanne C., and J. Francis, eds. 2009. *Canadian Social Welfare*. Toronto: Pearson.

Tutty, M. Leslie, and Cathryn Bradshaw. 2002. *School-based Violence Prevention Programs: Prevention Programs Addressing Youth Dating Violence.* At: <www.ucalgarya/resolve/violenceprevention/English/reviewprog/youth-progs.htm#prog1>. (1 Aug. 2008)

Ungar, Michael. 2005. *Handbook for Working with Children and Youth: Pathways to Resilience across Cultures and Contexts.* Thousand Oaks, Calif.: Sage.

——. 2006a. *Strengths-based Counseling with At-risk Youth.* Thousand Oaks, Calif.: Corwin Press.

——. 2006b. *Nurturing Hidden Resilience in Troubled Youth.* Toronto: University of Toronto Press.

——. 2007. *Too Safe for Their Own Good: How Risk and Responsibility Help Teens Thrive.* Toronto: McClelland & Stewart.

——. 2008. 'Putting resilience theory into action', in Liebenberg and Ungar (2008: 17–39).

UNICEF. 1989. UN Convention on the Rights of the Child.

——. 2007. *UNICEF Report Card 7: Child Poverty in Perspective.* Florence, Italy: Innocenti Research Centre.

Vandergoot, Mary E. 2006. *Justice for Young Offenders: Their Needs, Our Responses.* Saskatoon: Purich.

van Daalen-Smith, Cheryl. 2007. 'A right to health: Children's health and health care through a child rights lens', in Howe et al. (2007: 73–99).

Vetere, Arlene, and Emilia Dowling, eds. 2005. *Narrative Therapies with Children and Their Families: A Practitioner's Guide to Concepts and Approaches.* New York: Routledge.

Vogl, Ann, and Nick Bala. 2001. *Testifying on Behalf of Children: A Handbook for Canadian Professionals.* Toronto: Thompson Educational Publishing.

Vygotsky, L.S. 1997. *Educational Psychology.* Boca Raton, Fla: St Lucie Press.

Waldock, Thomas. 2008. *Taking Children's Rights Seriously: Implications and Possibilities for Child Welfare.* At: <www.casw-acts.ca/celebrating/nationalconf_e.html>. (10 Jan. 2009)

Warry, Wayne. 2007. *Ending Denial: Understanding Aboriginal Issues.* Peterborough, Ont.: Broadview Press.

Webber, Marlene. 1998. *As If Kids Mattered.* Toronto: Key Porter.

Weir, Erica, and T. Wallington. 2001. 'Suicide: The hidden epidemic', *Canadian Medical Association Journal* 165, 5: 634–6.

Westcott, Helen L., and Karen S. Littleton. 2005. 'Exploring meaning in interviews with children', in Greene and Hogan (2005: 141–58).

Wharf, Brian, ed. 2002. *Community Work Approaches to Child Welfare.* Peterborough, Ont.: Broadview Press.

—— and Brad McKenzie. 2004. *Connecting Policy to Practice in the Human Services.* Toronto: Oxford University Press.

White, Michael. 1989. *Selected Papers.* Adelaide, Australia: Dulwich Center Publications.

——. 2007. *Maps of Narrative Practice.* New York: Norton.

Willms, J.D., ed. 2002. *Vulnerable Children: Findings from Canada's National Longitudinal Survey of Children and Youth.* Edmonton: University of Alberta Press.

Wilson, Jeffery. 1994. *Wilson on Children and the Law.* Toronto: Butterworths.

Wilson, Jim. 2005. 'Engaging children and young people', in Vetere and Dowling (2005: 90–107).

Winnicott, D.W. 1953. 'Transitional objects and transitional phenomena', *International Journal of Psychoanalysis* 34: 89–97.

Wortley, Scott. 2006. *Urban Youth Gangs in Canada: Results from Two Toronto-Area Research Projects.* At: <www.policyresearch.gc.ca/doclib/Wortley_Dec06_e.pdf>. (18 June 2008)

—— and Julian Tanner. 2004. 'Social groups or criminal organizations? The extent and nature of youth gang activity in Toronto', in Kidd and Phillips (2004: 59–80).

Wotherspoon, Terry, and Bernard Schissel. 2001. 'The business of placing Canadian children and youth "at risk"', *Canadian Journal of Education* 26, 3: 321–39.

Yahav, Rivka, and Shlomo A. Sharlin. 2000. 'The symptom-carrying child as a preserver of the family unit', *Child and Family Social Work* 5, 4: 353–64.

Youth Criminal Justice Act. At: <www.laws.justice.gc.ca/en/Y-1.5/index.html>. (10 Jan. 2009)

YTV Tween Report 2008. At: <www.corusmedia.com/ytv/docs/2008>. (20 May 2008)

Zeanah, C., Jr, ed. 2000. *Handbook of Infant Mental Health.* New York: Guilford Press.

Zuckerman, Marvin. 2007. *Sensation Seeking and Risky Behaviour.* Washington: American Psychological Association.

Credits

Children's Books
The following children's books are sources of the citations that begin each chapter.

Carroll, Lewis. 2000 [1865]. *Alice's Adventures in Wonderland*. New York: Norton.

Cleary, Beverly. 2006. *Ramona and Her Father*. New York: Harper Trophy.

Giovanni, Nikki. 1971. 'drum', from *Spin a Soft Black Song*, rev. edn, by Nikki Giovanni, illustrated by George Martins. Copyright © 1971, 1985 by Nikki Giovanni. Reprinted by permission of Hill and Wang, a division of Farrar, Straus and Giroux, LLC.

Keller, Helen. 1993 [1903]. *The Story of My Life*. Mahwah, NJ: Watermill Press.

Lee, Laurie. 1959. *Cider with Rosie*. London: Hogarth Press.

Saint-Exupery, Antoine de. 1971 [1943]. *The Little Prince*. New York: Harcourt, Brace.

Spalding, Andrea. 2002. *Solomon's Tree*. Victoria, BC: Orca Books.

Tamaki, Mariko. 2008. *Skim*. Toronto: Groundwood Books.

Twain, Mark. 1938 [1876]. *The Adventures of Tom Sawyer*. New York: Harper.

Index